16.9
.U7
1971

PHILOSOPHIES
OF HISTORY

Philosophies Of History

*Meeting of East and West in Cycle—
Pattern Theories of History*

GRACE E. CAIRNS

GREENWOOD PRESS, PUBLISHERS
WESTPORT, CONNECTICUT

Copyright 1962 by Philosophical Library, Inc.

Reprinted with the permission
of Philosophical Library, Inc., New York

First Greenwood Reprinting 1971

Library of Congress Catalogue Card Number 71-139126

SBN 8371-5742-0

Printed in the United States of America

FOREWORD

This scholarly volume fills a big gap in the Western philosophies of history and theories of social and cultural change. Until recent times the Western philosophers of history and social scientists expounded mainly linear conceptions of historical evolution and progress while the Western historians adhered to what Oswald Spengler calls "an incredibly jejune and meaningless scheme of history," divided into linear "Ancient-Mediaeval-Modern" periods viewed exclusively from the standpoint of Western culture. In their adherence to the linear ideologies of evolution and progress the Western historians and social scientists greatly neglected almost all the non-linear particularly "cyclical" interpretations of cosmic, biological, and sociocultural processes and especially the magnificent cyclical theories conceived and developed by the eminent thinkers of the great Eastern civilizations of the past. In most of our texts dealing with sociocultural change, evolution and progress, these theories are hardly mentioned at all and, if mentioned, are disposed of within a few paragraphs as something unimportant and insignificant.

Among the tremendous changes that occurred in the twentieth century in the human universe—in human social life and institutions, in all compartments of culture beginning with science and ending with religion, in system of values—notable change has also taken place in the field of Western historical, philosophical, and sociological theories of cosmic and sociocultural change. The hitherto monopolistic domination of the linear theories of historical development has been broken by emergence and growth of the "cyclical," "rhythmical," and "trendlessly fluctuating" theories of historical change and sociocultural dynamics.

These theories are exemplified by the works of O. Spengler, A. J. Toynbee, J. Ortega y Gasset, N. Berdyaev, F. S. C. Northrop, A. K. Kroeber, and many others. In connection with this change there appeared a growing interest in and increasing study of the previous cyclical and non-linear conceptions of cosmic, biological and sociocultural processes. As a result of this, the Western literature dealing with these conceptions as well as with an investigation of cosmic, biological, economic, political, aesthetic, religious, philosophical and other sociocultural cycles, rhythms, fluctuations and periodicities has been rapidly growing during the last few decades.

In this already vast literature however there hardly has been published as yet a single work which would give in one volume a concise history of all the important cyclical theories developed by the eminent thinkers of the great cultures of the East and the West. This volume of Dr. Cairns fills this gap to a great extent. The volume gives a concise account of most of the important cyclical conceptions of cosmic and historical processes beginning with the ancient and ending with the contemporary ones, together with the metaphysical and philosophical background of such theories. In this sense it is a unique contribution to the historical and social sciences. Scholars and intelligent lay-readers will find it helpful and rewarding. Among its many uses it can serve also as a supplementary text in courses dealing with historical and sociocultural change, evolution and progress.

Pitirim A. Sorokin

CONTENTS

Foreword v
Preface xiii
Introduction: Outline xv

PART I: RECURRENT COSMIC CYCLES

Chapter I
Early Ideas of Time-Cycles: Serpent, Sun and Mythopoeic Thought 1

Chapter II
Dawn of Cyclical Concepts of Time in Mesopotamia ... 10
The annual cycle and its cosmic significance. The Tablets of Destiny: theocratic determination of history for a one-year period as the significance of New Year's Day. Development of the idea of the Macrocosmic Year, the Great Year of the universe. Summary.

Chapter III
Development of the Idea of Recurrent Cosmic Cycles in Indian Thought 35
Cyclical symbolism of the cosmic Dance of Shiva. Cyclical Great Years of the cosmos: the Kalpa and its four Yugas. The space-time cyclical symbolism in architecture (continued in chapter VI). The cyclical symbolism of the Fire-altar ritual. The Great Horse Sacrifice and the cyclical year. Summary: significance of the cyclical symbolisms studied in this chapter, but see chapter VII for higher interpretations in the light of the great yogic philosophies.

Chapter IV
Development of the Cyclical Pattern of History in India: Buddhism 62
The Buddhist pattern of recurrent cosmic cycles and its symbolic significance. Chapters VI and VII continue Buddhist cyclical philosophies of the yogic Mahayana schools of thought.

Chapter V
Development of the Cyclical Pattern in India: Jainism 69
The pattern of cosmic cycles. The significance of cosmic cycles in relation to human goals.

Chapter VI

Cyclical Time and the Philosophy of the Mandala   76

(This theme is continued in Chapter VIII). The Tibetan *mandala* in relation to the cyclical return or reintegration of man with the macrocosmic reality. *Borobudur,* monumental *mandala* in stone: its space-time symbolism of the cyclical return. Summary of the philosophical significance of *mandala* symbolism in relation to the meaning of human history (this theme is continued—with comments upon Jung's approach to the psychological and philosophical meaning of mandala symbolism—in the following chapter).

Chapter VII

Maya, Yoga, and Cyclical Patterns of Time in Eastern yogic philosophies: Sankhya-yoga, Vedanta, Later Taoism and Zen Buddhism. 111

Sankhya-yoga and the cycle of the return. Advaita Vedanta, *maya,* cosmic cycles and the yogic cyclical return *mandala.* Cyclical return to the Center (the Tao) in a Taoist form of Chinese yoga: *The Secret of the Golden Flower.* Zen Buddhism: cyclical return and the identity of *samsara* and *nirvana.* Jung's comments on the significance of *mandala* symbolism, its philosophy and psychology. Summary: yogic experience, *maya* and cyclical time-symbolism.

Chapter VIII

Organismic Cyclical Patterns of History in Chinese Thought 159

Yin-yang, the Five Elements and the Son of Heaven. Tung Chung-shu's organic cyclical views of history: background in the ideology of Tsou Yen and the *Yin* and *Yang* and Five Elements School. Tung's organic cycles: the Five Elements, the Cycle of the Seasons, Government and Virtue: the Three Sequences and other minor cyclical sequences. Shao Yung's theory of the Great Year of the Cosmos. Chinese thought and the West.

Chapter IX

Mythical Cyclical Time Patterns in Greek and Roman Thought 196

Hesiod's Five Ages. Ovid's *Metamorphoses* and the Ages. Virgil's *Messianic Eclogue* and world cycles.

Chapter X

Greek Naturalism Applied to Cosmic Cycles 204

Early naturalistic thought. The Pythagoreans and the

cyclic Great Year of the cosmos. Empedocles. Cosmic and culture cycles in Plato's thought. Cycles in Aristotle's philosophy of nature and culture. Stoic cycles: the *ecpyrosis*. Epicurean cyclic views. Firmicus: the Sothic cycle, the Five Planets and Five Ages. Ancient and modern naturalism and cosmic cycles.

PART II: ONE-GRAND-CYCLE PATTERNS OF COSMIC AND HUMAN HISTORY

Chapter I
Background of one-grand-cycle patterns: From Eden to Eden: Idea of the Golden Age 233
Idea of the Golden Age in ancient Egypt. The Golden Age and the Wonder Child in Hebrew thought. Zoroastrian beliefs about the cycle of world history and its goal: a "new heaven and a new earth."

Chapter II
Hebrew-Christian One-Cycle Views: Cycle of the Return to Paradise: the Coming Kingdom of God 244
The four-epoch periodization of history in *Daniel*. Apocalyptic eschatology of *Daniel* and its significance. Apocalyptic literature and the supernatural Messiah. New Testament apocalyptic thought.

Chapter III
St. Augustine's One-Grand-Cycle: The Great Week of the World: The Mandala of Man's Journey from God to God or from the Earthly to the Heavenly Paradise 251
The Fall and the Seven Epochs of History: the Great Week of the World. The Eighth Eternal Epoch in Paradise. Augustine and Toynbee.

Chapter IV
The One-Grand-Cycle in Moslem Thought 256
The apocalyptic historical cycle described in the *Koran*. Avicenna and al-Ghazzali in relation to Koranic apocalyptic thought. The historical cycle and the Neoplatonism of the Sufis' mandala-of-the-return cycle. The Isma'ili theory of the cycle of cosmic and human history. Transition to "secular" one-cycle patterns: influence of Augustine's apocalyptic one-cycle pattern upon subsequent Western thought.

Chapter V

The Sacred-Secular Synthesis in Hegel's Cyclical Pattern of History and its Marxian Materialistic Version 277

Influence of the apocalyptic-providential cyclical views upon modern secular historical thought. Condorcet and the influence of the Idea of Progress upon modern ideas of history. The dialectical cycle of history in Hegel's thought: alienation and return. The Marxian materialistic version of the dialectical cycle. Reconciliation of spiritual and materialistic interpretations of the cycle and its goal: Freedom.

Chapter VI

Contemporary Indian One-Cycle Patterns of History: Sri Aurobindo 299

The cycle of the Involution and the Evolution of the Infinite. The goal of history: the advent of the Gnostic Being. Aurobindo's "spiritual socialism" and Marxism.

Chapter VII

Contemporary Indian One-Cycle Patterns: Professor Radhakrishnan's Philosophy of History 306

The involution-evolution cycle. The goal of history: transmutation of Intellect into Spirit. Necessity for an end of this world cycle. Refutation of charges of escapism directed against Indian thought. Similarities between Radhakrishnan's and the Christian and Hegelian theories of history.

PART III: CULTURE CYCLES: TWENTIETH CENTURY VIEWS

Chapter I

Great Forerunners of Twentieth Century Culture-Cycle Theories: Ibn Khaldun and Vico.

Section I: Ibn Khaldun 322

Ibn Khaldun. Group feeling and culture integration. Religion as the foundation for a large civilization. The stages in the rise and fall cycle-pattern of dynasties and civilizations. The ruin of states: the evils of sedentary culture.

Section 2: Vico. 337

History as a sociological science. Similarity with Ibn Khaldun's sociological approach to history. The pattern of the culture cycle: the major epochs. Recurrence of the pattern in Western culture. Providence and history.

Chapter II
Oswald Spengler's Theory of Culture Cycles: The Cycle of the Macrocosmic Organism 353
The Prime Symbol of the culture-organism. Time and culture-forms. Space and culture-forms. Art as the expression of the Grand Style of a culture. Cycle of the Grand Style in art. Society and the cycle: nobility, priesthood, bourgeoisie and the "mass." Science, mathematics, logic in relation to the culture style.

Chapter III
The Cyclical Pattern of Sorokin's Cultural Dynamics 379
The cyclic culture-pattern: Ideational-idealistic-sensate. The cyclic pattern in the fine arts; in the system of truth; in ethics and law; in social relationships. Dawn of a new culture-epoch: era of Creative Altruism and the Supraconscious level of human life. Meeting of East and West in Sorokin's prognosis of the dawning era of history. Summary of Sorokin's culture-cycle pattern of history.

Chapter IV
Cyclical Form of the Culture-Pattern in Toynbee's Philosophy of History: the Pattern of the Rise and Fall of the Great Civilizations 403
The cycle-pattern of every great culture: First stage of the Cycle, Challenge and Response; Second stage of the cycle, the Growth of civilizations and the significance of growth in the physiognomy of a culture; Third Stage, the Breakdown of civilizations; Fourth Stage, the Disintegration of civilizations. The significance of religion in Toynbee's philosophy of history: the churches "a higher species of society." Progress in human history lies in the sphere of religion with spiritual self-realization as the goal. Summary: the goal and meaning of total human history and similarities with Oriental thought.

CONCLUSION: SIGNIFICANCE OF THIS STUDY 456
Is the cyclic patterning of history defensible? Eastern and Western cyclical patterns compared: similarity in goals and meanings of history. Cosmic cycles and contemporary science. Prognostications: the next epoch in history.

Bibliography 478

Acknowledgments 484

Index 489

PREFACE

The purpose of this essay is to give the interested reader an introduction to some of the important approaches to the cyclical patterning of history in Eastern and Western thought. The thematic subject of this book, if treated thoroughly and comprehensively would require a work of many volumes by many scholars. The purpose of this brief study is to draw together for the mature student or reader of wide interests some of the outstanding approaches to a cyclical patterning of historical thought. The author has divided cyclical patterns of historical thinking into three main types: (1) theories of cosmic cycles everlastingly repeated; (2) one-grand-cycle theories of cosmic or of merely human history; and (3) theories of culture cycles repeated or repeatable in pattern. An attempt has been made to give a brief introduction to some of the more famous examples of each of these types of historical thinking.

The author is not a professional historian, but history as it is approached today is no longer a chronology of merely political events, nor the traditional pattern of ancient-medieval-modern. The emphasis today is centered far more upon man's spiritual odyssey, upon the development of man's creations in the Humanities, his discoveries in scientific knowledge and his technological innovations. Scholars in the Humanities areas, therefore, especially in the broadest fields—philosophy and religion—have an appropriate background for the examination of man's historical journey in the universe. For this reason the author, whose special fields are philosophy and religion and the Humanities area of culture in general, believes that no apology is needed for attempting an essay in the field of philosophies of history. Furthermore, as will be apparent in this study, many of the attempts to comprehend history through cyclical patterning are deeply grounded in philosophico-religious *Weltanschauungs*. Although this is true especially of Oriental historical thought, the reader of this book will find that Western cyclical philosophies of history, also, show such philosophico-religious influences.

Perhaps, in these troubled times, the most important *raison d'etre* for such a study as this is the bringing together side by side some of the significant Eastern and Western cyclical philosophies of history. It will be seen that East and West have much in common in their views of the meaning, the value and the goal of human history. Intelligent minds are keenly aware of the need for a rapprochement in spiritual goals and meanings between East and West. This book is an endeavor to show such spiritual unity between East and West as applied to ideas of the meaning and goals of cosmic and human history.

The author realizes keenly the inadequacy of the treatment of so broad a subject matter; but it is hoped that this essay will stimulate some thinking on the themes presented and provide the reader with materials (not easily found between the covers of one volume) for the study of some of the outstanding philosophies of history of the Eastern and Western worlds.

INTRODUCTION

In our contemporary global culture East and West and the Marxian world are becoming much more directly acquainted with each other's basic and great ideas. Extremely important among these ideas are the Eastern, Western and Marxian concepts of the meaning and goal of human history. A major purpose of this book, which it is hoped will be an aid in world understanding and cooperation, is to show that Eastern, Western and Marxian theories of the meaning and goal of human history have much in common. This will be shown more directly in the Conclusion of the book after some of the famous types of cyclical philosophies of history have been presented.

Cyclical philosophies of history are one of the three main approaches to the problem of the meaning of history, human and/or cosmic. The other two approaches are (1) the Idea of Progress, by which is meant the continuous linear progress of the human race into the indefinite future; and (2) the skeptical view of history which asserts that history as such has no ascertainable meaning or pattern. The concepts of history enumerated as Cyclical and the Progress idea may be combined into a spiral pattern as we shall see in Part III below, or into a one-cycle pattern-with-progress as in the Hegelian and Marxian views discussed in Part II. The meaningful concepts of history, it will be apparent, are related to one or another of the cyclical forms described below.

For greater clarity our book will organize the cyclical concepts of history, the only *pattern* concepts, into three main types: (1) theories of cosmic cycles; (2) one-cycle views and (3) culture-cycle approaches to the understanding of human history.

In Part I which treats of cosmic cycles we shall begin with origins of the view in the dim past in the cultures of Mesopotamia and Egypt. These origins are related to observations of the birth-death cycle of life, the cyclic shedding of the skin by the serpent, and the cycles of the sun and moon. Man the thinker and inventor of hypotheses soon developed philosophical ideas of cosmic cycles which became the typical view of history in the great civilizations especially of India and Greece; also in China this notion is found in a unique and indigenous form.

Our chapters dealing with the development of the idea of cosmic cycles in Indian thought begin with the more mythological symbolic forms (often given a profound philosophical interpretation) which express the idea of cosmic cycles—for example, the cosmic Dance of Shiva, the Doctrine of the Yugas, architectural forms, and the Fire-altar ritual. Similar symbolic approaches are found in Buddhist and Jaina thought. In all cases great minds have given a deep philosophical interpretation to the symbols. This is dramatically evident in interpretation of the symbolism of the Tibetan *mandala,* a cosmic diagram used as a basic aid in the reintegration of the devotee with absolute reality. Extraordinary and similar in significance is the Buddhist architectural mandala-in-stone, *Borobudur,* monumental witness to, and revelation of one of the most profound philosophies of the meaning of human and cosmic history.

Other mature spiritual and philosophical views of the meaning and purpose of cosmic cycles and human history which are variations on the ground-theme of the *mandala* are described in the chapter "*Maya, Yoga,* and the Cyclical Patterns of Time in Eastern Yogic Philosophies." The point of this chapter is the emphasis in these yogic philosophies upon (1) solution of the problem of man's deep psychological need for reintegration of himself with man and cosmic reality and (2) the philosophy of the meaning of time and history which harmonizes and integrates man with the basic metaphysical reality. Such "socialization" or reintegration of man in a more limited way is a goal also of Western Christianity and of Marxism and is spiritual freedom similar to the freedom of the yogi. Altogether we shall find that in Oriental thought as in Western, man's view of the meaning and goal of history is much the same, *viz.*, spiritual self-realization or, in other words, spiritual freedom which involves also freedom from bondage to the material world, the Marxian emphasis. This, it will appear, shows that the Eastern, Western, and Marxian worlds have much more in common than is suspected by the uninitiated.

Chinese thought, also, in its indigenous form lays great emphasis upon spiritual freedom. This idea is approached from an organismic point of view; man is held to be part of the total organism, the macrocosm of Nature itself; as an organic part of this total organism he must play his harmonious part or the balance of nature may be upset. The actions of men, especially those of the Ruler, must harmonize with the seasonal cycle of the year which in its turn is related to the *Yang-Yin* cycle and numerous other phenomena in a perfectly organic universe. Freedom lies in harmonious integration of the individual with human society and with nature. Tung Chung-shu's thought is an example of the organismic idea applied to history. In Taoism the mystical yogic type of philosophy is central and therefore has been included in the Yoga chapter mentioned above. Although in this chapter a yoga form of Later Taoism is emphasized, early Taoism too is included because both are mystical and have very much the characteristic Chinese slant—mystical unity with Nature in the experience of self-realization or spiritual freedom; it is this which is a major emphasis in Chinese yogic systems unlike Indian philosophies. This unique emphasis is the inspiration of Ch'an Buddhism (called Zen in Japan). Finally, a clear-cut theory of cosmic cycles, inspired no doubt by Buddhist theories but amalgamated with *yang-yin* concepts, appears in the writings of Shao Yung, though the foregoing ideas of cosmic and human history are far more typical of the Chinese version of cyclical thought.

Then we travel to the Western world where the cosmic cycle, eternally recurrent (perhaps an idea borrowed from the Orient), was a familiar approach to an understanding of history. The mythical-symbolic and the philosophico-naturalistic expositions of the view, already familiar to most Western readers—and therefore treated very briefly—are mentioned because of their twofold significance, one religious and the other scientific. In religion the Golden-Age-and-the-Wonder-Child idea is significant because it is related to similar idea-patterns among the Zoroastrians and Hebrews and is an important aspect of the one-cycle views of history of the latter two groups which in turn influenced later very important theories of history. In science the Greek views are fathers of modern scientific approaches in all areas including history; therefore fathers of modern scientific cyclical ideas of cosmic and human history (see also the Conclusion chapter).

In Part II we present some of the outstanding one-cycle patterns of cosmic and human history. The early more mythological views, particularly the Zoroastrian are treated because of their influence upon later developments. The Zoroastrian notion of the Golden Age, the Wonder Child, the Return to Paradise at the end of the Great Year of the World has many elements of the Hebrew-Christian Great Cycle idea which begins with Eden and ends with the Return to the Golden Era, the Kingdom of God (or City of God). Both the Hebrew drama of the cycle from Eden to the Kingdom and the Christian cycle as conceived in St. Augustine's thought (still the orthodox view for most Christians) which is patterned by him as a Great Week of the World are described. All these views of the coming new Golden Age, Kingdom of God, or Return to Paradise—the era when man becomes truly free both materially and spiritually — are very significant because they have inspired mankind with hope for the future despite the misery and confusion of the present. Such Golden Age hopes for the human race have fired, also, materialistic thinkers such as Condorcet and Karl Marx. This influence is brought out in the sections dealing with their philosophies of history.

Similar in pattern to the Hebrew-Christian one-cycle view of history is that of orthodox Islamic thought; but we add a description of such sectarian views as those of the famous Isma'ili group of whom the Aga Khan (recently a student at Harvard) is leader. The Isma'ilis hold to an involutionary-evolutionary cyclic theory of cosmic history similar to the Indian yogic views already described. The Sufis, another important group with a similar yogic philosophy are also included.

In dialectical style our book swings from cyclic philosophies with a religious orientation to those with an opposite orientation, a secular one. This occurs with the influence of the Idea of Progress through Reason and Science, so important in the eighteenth century in the Western world; Condorcet represents this Progress approach. Then Hegel in accordance with his famous dialectical logic develops a one-cycle-with-progress idea of history. The cycle of the development of Spirit in History reaches its climax in the German World. Here the Spirit attains the idea of self-realization or Freedom, secular and spiritual, and this is the goal of history (*cf.* yogic views of the goal).

Marx applies the Hegelian dialectical development of history seen as Spirit to history seen as materialistic. At the same time Marx adds powerful prophetic drama borrowed from Hebrew-Christian apocalyptic thought already described. And Marx too, like Hegel and the Oriental thinkers, sees Freedom as the goal of man's journey in history; but the Marxian emphasis falls upon freedom from human bondage to material needs. Marx declares this must first be accomplished. Only then will man be able to develop freely his higher powers of cooperative, constructive creativity in all areas.

There are one-cycle theories of history, also, in Oriental thought; examples are the philosophies of history of the two greatest Indian philosophers of the twentieth century, Aurobindo and Radhakrishnan. Aurobindo sees cosmic history as the Involution-Evolution cycle of the Infinite. The purpose of this cycle is the evolution of the Gnostic Being. This is the kind of being which is the yogin's goal except that the Gnostic Being lives everlastingly on two levels. He is one with the Infinite Being at the highest level, thereby achieving absolute and complete Freedom, but at the same time he remains on this earth as a center-of-consciousness of this Infinite Being in a society of similar Gnostic Beings, all living on these two planes of consciousness. This resembles the Kingdom of God or Return-to-Paradise of Zoroastrian, Hebrew, Christian and Moslem thought. The difference is that the angelic or Gnostic Being lives and acts in this world rather than in Heaven. In the world of Gnostic Beings each is all in the Infinite and the All is in each; it is permissible, therefore, to call this society a spiritual socialism, for the maxim of Marxian socialism is similiar: "All for each, and each for all."

Radhakrishnan's one-cycle philosophy of history has a goal similar to Aurobindo's. Radhakrishnan thinks that the next and final epoch of history will see the present plane of Intellect superceded by the plane of Spirit, the plane of Freedom. The meaning and goal of the one cycle of history is to "establish a kingdom of free spirits." Only a few saints have reached this level thus far, but eventually all men will achieve this high plane of Freedom. Then death will be conquered, Time overcome and the Kingdom of God (Brahmaloka) will have arrived on earth; but when this occurs cosmic existence will be reabsorbed into the Infinite Being. The cosmic cycle is (*cf.* Aurobindo's, St. Augustine's and the similar one-cycle views) one of alienation-from and return-to the Divine Source represented graphically in *mandala* symbolism. There is similarity, also, with Hegel's dialectical pattern in the major triad of Abstract Infinite with its alienation from Itself in its opposite the Material World of finite particulars, and the Return-to-Self as the Concrete Infinite or Absolute Whole-Idea, the Individual. The difference from Hegel's thought lies in Radhakrishnan's typical Indian view that the Absolute or Infinite does not need to manifest Itself since such manifestation is a merely accidental quality of its nature.

We now pass on to the Culture-Cycle approaches to human history. The culture-cycle idea in the patterning of history is more characteristic of the twentieth century Western world since it is closest to the more scientific and sociological methods of handling historical materials. First we acknowledge two of the greatest forerunners of twentieth century culture-cycle theories of history, Vico of the Western world and the great Islamic philosopher of history, Ibn Khaldun. These earlier thinkers, it will be evident, anticipate many of the ideas of such contemporary culture-cycle theorists as Spengler, Sorokin and Toynbee. Ibn Khaldun and Vico both delineate a definite cyclical pattern for the rise and fall of civilizations and both see religious faith in some form as the foundation stone for the integration of a civilization. Both agree, also, that luxurious living with its vices, neglect of religion and moral values, is a basic cause for the decline and fall of a civilization.

Among twentieth century culture-cycle theorists the first great philosopher of history is Oswald Spengler whose *Decline of the West* was popular reading after World War I. Spengler's thesis is that every culture is a unique macrocosmic organism which follows a birth, growth, and decline pattern similar to that of a microcosmic organism. Each great culture-organism develops a characteristic personality or Style integrated around a "religious" idea. This Style is revealed in the arts, the sciences, and the social and political organizations of the culture. Decay and decline begin when skepticism about the major integrating idea sets in. History has no purpose other than the development of such great culture-organisms.

Sorokin, the well-known Harvard sociologist, also defends the culture-cycle view. Each culture goes through a characteristic Ideational-Idealistic-Sensate cycle. Yet subsequent cultures may build upon their predecessors so that an overall progress of the human race is possible. This makes Sorokin's theory of history a spiral one. The core-idea around which a culture may begin to develop may be Ideational (a religious idea) or Idealistic (also called Integral). The Idealistic or Integral is preferable since it emphasizes both the religious (intuitive-mystical) and the rational-scientific. But when the integrating idea of the culture begins to lose its creative spirituality, the culture declines and disintegrates.

Finally Toynbee's culture-cycle view is described. His cycle-pattern, too, is definite. His overall view is a spiral one since he argues that religion as a basic aspect of human civilization shows a general progress. The rise and fall pattern of all great civilizations of the past has been for the Divine purpose of alienating men from a this-worldly, materialistic ultimate goal to a spiritual ultimate goal. This means the general progress of religion understood in its highest sense. Toynbee patterns a definite rise and fall cycle for secular cultures but holds that the fall of every secular culture is a vital aid in educating man for a religious goal. The fall of a culture causes disillusionment with secular goals and an advance in the progress of religion — the birth of a higher religion which directs man to a goal in a spiritual plane. It is only in this eternal world of Spirit that man becomes truly free; in the fleshly world self-love holds most men in varying degrees of bondage. Here Toynbee is in agreement not only with St. Augustine and orthodox Christianity but with Indian and Buddhist ideas of the goal and meaning of history. Nevertheless, Toynbee is much interested as are most of the contemporary Eastern philosophers in establishing a peaceful, brotherly society in this world, one in which all persons will have as much freedom as is possible, both material and spiritual. Only in the light of a transcendent spiritual ideal can man build the great international society in this world. St. Francis is the bodhisattva, Toynbee says, who can be our guide in this necessary task.

Our Conclusion presents first a defense of cyclical patterning of history as an approach to human and cosmic history; then Eastern and Western (and Marxian) cyclical patterns are compared to point out the large degree of similarity in the general concepts of the goal and meaning of history. Finally there is an attempt to predict the nature of the next great epoch in human history.

Chapter I

Introduction: Serpent, Sun, and Mythopoeic Thought

The real nature of time has been a riddle for human thought from the time of the earliest civilizations. The pathos of man's ancient preoccupation with this riddle in relation to his own life cycle is brought out in early tales such as the Babylonian *Epic of Gilgamesh* of about 2000 B.C., the oldest epic in Western literature. The climax and ending of this story have as the major part of the theme the valiant but unsuccessful attempt of the hero, Gilgamesh, to win immortality for himself and mankind. The climax comes with the death of the hero's bosom friend, Enkidu, and the subsequent search for everlasting life. In the words of the Epic:

> For Enkidu, his friend, Gilgamesh
> Weeps bitterly, as he ranges over the steppe.
> "When I die, shall I not be like Enkidu?
> Fearing death, I roam over the steppe.
> To Utnapishtim, Ubar-Tuttu's son
> I have taken the road to proceed in all haste." [1]

To learn the secret of immortality Gilgamesh searches for his ancestor, the Babylonian Noah, Utnapishtim, who survived the universal flood and was then made immortal by the gods.

After a perilous and wearying journey, Gilgamesh comes upon the wise Utnapishtim who tells him how he may obtain everlasting life. The secret lies in a rare plant grow-

---
[1] Isaac Mendelsohn, editor, *Religions of the Ancient Near East* (New York: The Liberal Arts Press, 1955), "The Epic of Gilgamesh," Tablet IX, p. 88.

ing on the bottom of the sea which, if eaten by man, will confer immortality. Gilgamesh bravely dives to the sea bottom, finds the plant and plucks it. Unfortunately he has become so hot and weary by this time that instead of eating the plant he bathes in the cool waters of a stream he has chanced to come upon. While he is bathing, a serpent carries off the plant, eats it and then sloughs off its skin. This sloughing off of the skin signifies that the serpent has become immortal, since the serpent has only to shed its skin to renew its life everlastingly. Such is the manner in which the wily serpent gains immortality and man loses it.

The notion that the serpent renews its life everlastingly by shedding its skin is found among primitive tribes of the twentieth century [1] as well as among early ancient peoples. It was probably as a result of this line of thought that the serpent became the symbol (or associated with the symbols) of everlasting time in various ancient cultures. For example, the Zervanitic Magi of the fourth century B.C. symbolized Infinite Time, the primary principle of the Universe, as an impersonal nude lion-faced male figure with an enormous serpent entwined six times about its body.[2] As used symbolically in later Graeco-Roman times in the mystery religion of Mithraism the serpent was said to symbolize the tortuous path of the sun on the ecliptic.[3] This meaning is in keeping with ideas of much earlier civilizations such as the Egyptian where the serpent was definitely associated with cycles of the sun. In Egypt it was believed that the sun was swallowed nightly by a serpent from which it issued victoriously at dawn.[4] In Babylonia

---

[1] Sir James George Frazer, *Folklore in the Old Testament*, abridged ed. (New York and London: The Macmillan Company, 1923), Chap. II, section 2, "The Story of the Cast Skin," pp. 26-31.

[2] Franz Cumont, *The Mysteries of Mithra*, sec. rev. ed. trans. Thomas J. McCormack (Dover Publications, 1956), pp. 105-111.

[3] *Ibid.*, p. 107.

[4] H. and H. A. Frankfort, John A. Wilson and Thorkild Jacobsen, *Before Philosophy*, Penguin Books ed. (Baltimore: Penguin Books, 1949), "Myth and Reality" by Frankfort, p. 34.

the dragon goddess, Tiamat (a serpentine deity), was conquered each New Year's Day by Marduk, champion of the powers of fertility and abundance and a sun god. This symbolism reflects the ancient war between the serpent and man aided by the benevolent deities for the gift of life eternally renewed.

In the Graeco-Roman world artists commonly represented the revolving year, the endless cycle of time, as a serpent in circular form swallowing its tail. This symbol is used in Hindu culture also and by contemporary Theosophists to symbolize the endlessly recurrent cycle of time. This serpent symbolism of the Afrasian culture of Mesopotamia, Egypt, and Crete was prevalent in ancient prehistoric India. Recent archaeological discoveries have shown that a culture similar to the Mesopotamian flourished in India around 2000 B.C. A Shiva prototype and mother-goddess prominent in this culture were bequeathed to the later Aryan invaders. The great god Shiva's special emblem is the cobra which represents the life principle and principle of cosmic evolution, while the deadly poison contained in its fangs (drunk by Shiva) represents the death principle and principle of cosmic involution. This symbolism originated in observation of the serpent's habit of shedding its skin at regular intervals and was a symbol also of the individual's reincarnation or rebirth.[1]

There is serpent symbolism attached to the other of the two most prominent Hindu gods, Vishnu, under the aspect of the Absolute called Ishvara who takes the form Narayana. The symbolism here is cosmic. E. B. Havell, an authority on the interpretation of Indian art, says:

> This philosophic concept of the evolution of the universe is often symbolized in Hindu art by the figure of Ishvara, under the name of Narayana, sleeping on the waters of chaos on the serpent Sesha, or Ananta,

[1] E. B. Havell, *The Ideals of Indian Art* (London: John Murray, 1920), p. 75.

'the Endless' — the symbol of eternity, which encircled the world in its vast coils — . . .[2]

Another ancient Indian religion, Jainism, which may have originated as early as the eighth century B. C., associated the serpent with endless time. The great Indologist, Heinrich Zimmer, describes this symbolism:

> The cycle of time continually revolves, according to the Jainas. The present "descending" *(avasarpini)* period was preceded and will be followed by an "ascending" *(utsarpini)*. *Sarpini* suggests the creeping movement of a *"serpent" (sarpin); ava* — means "down" and *ut*—means "up." The serpent-cycle of time (the world-bounding serpent, biting its own tail) will go on revolving through these alternating "ascending" and "descending" periods forever.[1]

The Mayan and Aztec cultures, too, associated the serpent with cycles of endless time. This is evident in the design of their circular calendar-stone.[2] The two outer rings are serpents as the symbols of Time. The endless time cycles were calculated exactly and were given a length of fifty-two years. The end of a cycle (or calendar-round) was considered "as the death of one life and the beginning of a new one . . . The New Fire Ceremony was symbolized by the extinction of the old altar fire, which had burned perpetually for fifty-two years, and the kindling of a fresh one in token of the new grant of life."[3] Of even great-

---

[2] *Ibid.*, p. 67.
[1] Heinrich Zimmer, *Philosophies of India*, ed. Joseph Campbell (New York: Meridian Books, 1957), n. 44, pp. 224-225.
[2] George C. Vaillant, *The Aztecs of Mexico*, Penguin ed. (Baltimore: Penguin Books, Inc., 1950), Plate 52. The Aztecs borrowed the Mayan calendar.
[3] *Ibid.*, p. 195.

er religious significance was the end of two cycles (104 years). At this time there was a coincidence of the beginning of a fifty-two year cycle, the beginning of a Venus year of 584 days, of a solar year, and of a month (20 days constituted a month).[4]

The widespread association of endless time with the serpent apparently began with primitive man's observation that the serpent renews its skin. From this fact the erroneous conclusion was drawn that endless renewal of life was thereby obtained. Since human beings lack this power of skin-shedding, they must die.

Mythopoeic thought such as this was man's first approach to the scientific-philosophical-religious problems that confronted him. Since the first cyclical views of time were mythopoeic a brief summary of the characteristics of this ancient method of thinking as given by H. and H.A. Frankfort will be given.[1] These characterisics are: (1) The universe is conceived basically in terms of an I — Thou world of personal relationships; (2) *Pars pro toto* thinking as the typical methodology. In this methodology, the part can stand for the whole, the microcosm for the macrocosm; it is closely related to the *topocosm* concept of T. H. Gaster described in the following chapter.

The first characteristic (number 1 above) means that primitive man and men of the earliest civilizations of the Near East, Far East and the Americas conceived their world as alive. Rivers, wells, odd stones, the sun, moon and stars, as well as vegetation and animals—the entire universe of things—all entities were things with wills to work good or ill for man. Man was involved in his world emotionally, subjectively in what is called by Lévy-Bruhl a *participation mystique*.[2] For example if the Nile river in

---

[4] *Ibid.*, p. 194 See also *Encyclopaedia Brittanica*, articles "Calendar" Vol. IV, pp. 581-583 and "Chronology" Vol. V, pp. 660-662.

[1] H. and H. A. Frankfort, *op. cit.*, Chap. I, pp. 11-36.

[2] In later mature philosophical and religious thought this *participation mystique* is superceded by self-conscious integration with the cosmic Reality.

Egypt did not rise so that man could have good crops it did not *want* to rise. To circumvent such possible negative conduct gifts were thrown into the river at the appropriate time each year; or, if a man injured his foot by stumbling over a stone, the stone *desired* to hurt him. Animals had extraordinary powers, friendly or fearful. The sun, the moon, the stars—especially the sun—were very powerful beings. Apparently early man had no notion of impersonal laws and causes, the scientific thinker's objective world, the world of the IT rather than the THOU. Perhaps early man's intuitive approach was justified, for in recent thought Whitehead, for example, defends the view that the universe can be comprehended most coherently as being made up of *experiencing* "actual occasions."

The second characteristic enumerated above, *pars pro toto* thinking (the part can stand for the whole) as a methodology is very important in relation to early ideas of cause, of space, and of time. Ancient man did not think abstractly and quantitatively, but very concretely and qualitatively. Frazer in the *Golden Bough* gives numerous examples of this kind of thinking, for it pervades imitative and sympathetic magic. As an example of imitative magic pouring water (rain on the microcosmic scale) will cause the rain (the macrocosmic counterpart of the water-pouring); thus imitative magic plainly exemplifies *pars pro toto thinking*. Sympathetic magic illustrates it just as clearly. A lock of hair, a finger-nail paring, an article of clothing, even the name can mean the entire person to whom these things belong. Anything done to these "parts" of the person can affect by contagion the person himself (the whole) in a corresponding way.

Important early religious rituals, *e.g.* the New Year's Day celebration in Babylonia show this kind of thinking. The ritual drama of the renewal of the annual cycle of nature enacted on the microcosmic scale was an essential part of the cause in bringing about the macrocosmic annual renewal of the cycle.

Pars pro toto thinking about space is brought out most clearly in the Egyptian notion of the "primeval hill" made by the creator of the world when first he emerged from the waters of chaos. This primeval hill was located in the sun temple at Heliopolis since the sun god was usually thought to have been the creator. Nevertheless the Holy of Holies of each temple was equally sacred and every divinity was a source of creative power. Therefore the primeval hill was recognized as present in each and given appropriate architectural symbolic expression. Royal tombs utilized the primeval hill. H. and H.A. Frankfort tell us that "In the cenotaph of Seti I at Abydos the coffin was placed upon an island with a double stair imitating the hieroglyph for the primeval hill . . . Thus the dead king was buried and thought to rise again in the locality of creation."[1] Similar in macro-microcosmic symbolism are Buddhist and Hindu religious architectural works (see especially chapter VI below).

Time in *pars pro toto* thinking is conceived as concretely and picturesquely as space. In Egypt, for example, the daily cycle of the sun, its rising and setting, is taken to be a death and rebirth; this brief cycle, the part, stands for, is essentially the same as, the annual cycle of the sun celebrated each New Year's Day. Each day as each year, the sun combats the demons of darkness and death and is reborn anew in full vigor even as on the primeval day of creation. There is no notion here of an objective, impersonal abstract time stream such as the world of science posits. Time means concrete events in a subjective order significant in the life stream of man and nature. It is a biological, emotionally colored sequence of rhythms in which the human life crises of birth, puberty, and death play the major roles. Human motives, human pathos are applied to the observed sequential order which is the other source of cyclical time ideas: the regular sequences of day

---

[1] *Ibid.*, p. 32.

Chapter II

Dawn of Cyclical Concepts of Time
in Mesopotamia and Egypt

The oldest written records that inform us about man's first notions of time cycles are those discovered in Mesopotamia where the first known historical culture appeared. Prior to the appearance of these historical records, our only clues to man's earlier, primitive notions of time are the kinds of time counting found among primitive tribes today. Professor Nilsson has made a careful study in his book *Primitive Time Reckoning* [1] which attempts to trace the evolution of time concepts through a study of data gathered from various primitive cultures around the world. He concludes that the first unit of time was the cycle of day and night, next were the cycles of phases of the moon as larger time units, then seasonal cycles of heat and cold, rainy and dry, periods of plenty and periods of famine. Last of all the regular cycle of the year became known—last, because "for the primitive intellect the year is a very long period, and it is only with difficulty and at a later stage that it can be conceived and surveyed as a whole." [2]

The annual cycle and its cosmic significance. By the time of the dawn of the earliest civilization in Mesopotamia the yearly cycle was known, celebrated and activated in myth and ritual.[3] The myth and ritual celebration was the New

---
[1] Martin P. Nilsson, *Primitive Time Reckoning* (Oxford: Oxford Press, 1920).
[2] *Ibid.*, p. 11.
[3] The Osiris-Isis annual cyclical festival was identical in meaning and function with the Babylonan New Year's festival; therefore we shall not find it necessary to describe it. Frazer in his *Golden Bough* and Gaster in his *Thespis* give very adequate accounts of this Egyptian fertility cult.

Year's festival the oldest account of which is written in Akkadian and dated about 1500 B.C. The myth is called *Enuma Elish* (*When Above*) by scholars from the first two words of the text and is the Babylonian Epic of Creation. Beyond doubt the New Year's festival and the ideas in the Epic of Creation go back to a much earlier time, the Epic itself in its original version to the Sumerian inventors of literature in the third millenium B.C.; and the main features of the New Year's *ritual* such as the humiliation of the king, the mock combat, and the ritual marriage to prehistoric times.[1]

The Creation Epic was recited, dramatically reenacted, reactivated, as it were, each New Year's Day to inaugurate a New Year, a new annual cycle of the seasons on which depended the well-being of the community; a new creation was in order but always conceived on the pattern of the first primeval creation, therefore the same Creation Epic was always recited on this occasion. The archetypal divine events, the archetypal divine heroes had set the general pattern once and for all, the present could do no more than approximate as closely as possible the divine pattern set by the gods in the beginning. In the beginning, the Epic declares, this is what happened. At first there were no gods and nothing existed except a watery chaos. This watery chaos contained two or perhaps three intermingled elements: (1) the sweet waters called "primordial Apsu," (2) the salt waters called Tiamat, and according to Thorkild Jacobsen perhaps (3) cloud banks and mist, called Mummu.[2] To quote from the beginning of the Epic itself:

> When on high the heaven had not been named,
> Firm ground below had not been called by name,
> Naught but primordial Apsu, their begetter,
> (And) Mummu Tiamat, she who bore them all,

---

[1] Frankfort, *op. cit.*, chap. VI by Thorkild Jacobsen, "The Function of the State," pp. 214-216.
[2] *Ibid.*, p. 189.

Their waters commingling as a single body;
No reed hut had been matted, no marsh land had appeared,
When no gods whatever had been brought into being,
Uncalled by name, their destinies undetermined—
Then it was that the gods were formed within them.[3]

The Epic relates that Apsu begot Lahmu and Lahamu the first gods with Tiamat as mother. Lahmu and Lahamu probably represent silt in the waters; from Lahmu and Lahamu are born Anshar and Kishar, two circles of the horizon. Jacobsen comments, "The mythmaker apparently viewed the horizon as both male and female, as a circle (male) which circumscribed the sky and as a circle (female) which circumscribed the earth."[1] Anshar and Kishar give birth to the sky god, Anu, who becomes one of the four great gods of the Babylonian pantheon. Then Enki "lord of earth" was born of Anu and fashioned in the round, disk-shaped image of his father (sky and earth were thought to be round by the Mesopotamians). The two enormous disks, sky and earth, were forced apart probably by the wind (the god Enlil) in the oldest versions, but by the god, Marduk of Babylon, in the myth as we have it.[2] Marduk as storm and wind god apparently blew the disks of heaven apart separating the firmament above from the firmament below, with wind (air) between. Marduk was son of Ea/Enki and early in the history of the process of creation was called upon to take a leading part. The events which led to his participation are humanly amusing. When the new young gods had been created, Apsu and Tiamat regretted having parented these children. The children were too noisy, hilarious, and overbearing.[3] Apsu complained to his wife Tiamat:

[3] Mendelsohn, *op. cit.*, Enuma Elish, p. 19.
[1] Frankfort, *op. cit.*, Jacobsen, p. 185.
[2] The Babylonians made their national god, Marduk, the hero of this ancient tale derived from the Sumerians whose storm-god was Enlil.
[3] Mendelsohn, *op. cit., Enuma Elish*, Tablet I, p. 19.

Their ways are verily loathsome unto me.
By day I find no relief, nor repose by night.
I will destroy, I will wreck their ways,
That quiet may be restored. Let us have rest![4]

Tiamat did not wish to have her offspring destroyed. Ea heard of Apsu's drastic plans to get peace and quiet and acted immediately. By means of his powers as magician, he put Apsu to sleep and then killed him. (*cf.* Kronos, the primeval father, killed by his son, Zeus, in Greek mythology.) Tiamat had to avenge her husband's death. Her first step was the elevation of the god, Kingu, as her second consort to help lead the battle to avenge the death of her first. The gods were fearful; none felt able to face Kingu and Tiamat, except Marduk, son of Ea and his wife, Damkina. Marduk is glowingly described in the Epic as the most glorious of the gods.

When Ea saw him, the father who begot him,
He exulted and glowed, his heart filled with gladness.
He rendered him perfect and endowed him with a double godhead.
Greatly exalted was he above them, exceeding throughout.
Perfect were his members beyond comprehension
....
Four were his eyes, four were his ears;
When he moved his lips, fire blazed forth.
Large were all four hearing organs,
And the eyes, in like number, scanned all things.
He was the loftiest of the gods, surpassing was his stature;
.... [1]

He is called "Sun of the Heavens," [2] and "clothed with the halo of ten gods," [3] "Son of the Sun, most radiant of gods." [4]

---
[4] *Ibid.*, p. 20.
[1] *Ibid.,*, p. 21.
[2] *Ibid.*, p. 22.
[3] *Ibid.*
[4] *Ibid.*, Tablet VI, p. 39.

The Tablets of Destiny. Marduk is given sovereign power by the Assembly of the gods signified by bequeathing upon him the power to utter the decrees of Fate.

> From this day unchangeable shall be thy pronouncement.
> To raise or bring low—these shall be (in) thy hand.
> Thy utterance shall come true, thy command shall not be doubted.
> No one among the gods shall transgress thy bounds![5]

Unfortunately, the official Tablets of Fate had been given to Kingu by Tiamat but apparently the Assembly had the power to invalidate them until Marduk was able to obtain them when he won the victory over Kingu and Tiamat. Possession of the Tablets made his power to determine the Destinies of all things legal. Before the victory, however, there must have been conflicting destiny patterns, those of Kingu versus those of Marduk, but this happened before the cosmic order was completed, when a return to the primeval chaos was threatened if Tiamat and Kingu conquered the other gods. Of course Marduk won in a single combat with Tiamat, monster dragon of chaos. Marduk then completed the work of creation. He split the body of Tiamat like a shellfish into two parts, "Half of her he set up and ceiled it as sky," the firmament to divide the waters above (in the heavens) from the waters below the earth (Ea's realm). He next "constructed stations for the great gods, fixing their astral likenesses as constellations."

> He determined the year by designating the zones:
> He set up three constellations for each of the twelve months.
> ....
> The Moon he caused to shine, the night (to him) entrusting.

---
[5] *Ibid.*, Tablet IV, p. 31.

He appointed him a creature of the night to signify
    the days:
"Monthly, without cease, form designs with a crown.
At the month's very start, rising over the land,
Thou shalt have luminous horns to signify six days.
On the seventh day be thou a [half] crown.
At full moon stand in opposition in mid-month.
When the sun [overtakes] thee at the base of heaven,
Diminish [thy crown] and retrogress in light.
[At the time of disappearance] approach thou the
    course of the sun.
And [on the twenty-ninth] thou shalt again stand in
    opposition to the sun.[1]

The next great event was the creation of man. Marduk says:

Blood I will mass and cause bones to be.
I will establish a savage, 'man' shall be his name.
Verily, savage-man I will create.
He shall be charged with service to the gods
That they might be at ease! . . .[2]

At the suggestion of Ea man was created from the blood of Kingu the rebel.

"It was Kingu who contrived the uprising,
And made Tiamat rebel, and joined battle."
They bound him, holding him before Ea.
They imposed on him his guilt and severed his blood
    (vessels).
Out of his blood they fashioned mankind.[3]

It is plain, as in the Genesis story, that man was from the beginning a rebel, a "savage" and bound to earn his living by the sweat of his brow. The difference lies in the

---
[1] *Ibid.*, Tablet V, pp. 35-36.
[2] *Ibid.*, Tablet VI, p. 36.
[3] *Ibid.*, p. 37.

concern for justice in the Genesis story: man because of the sin of pride and rebellion merits the punishment of having to work. The Babylonian story has no concern with the justice of man's being compelled to work, but is simply a rationalization of the cultural fact that the economic unit was the temple of a god and all labor done was in his name.

Finally the Epic tells us that Marduk divided the gods into two bands of three hundred each, three hundred in the heavens and three hundred on earth and below for the purpose of maintaining the established order in the universe that he decreed through possession of the powers of the Tablets of Destiny.

In this way the created order of the universe and of human lives was established, but it was necessary to recite, to re-enact ritually, to dramatize and thus reactivate this myth of creation each New Year's Day to maintain the order set up by Marduk in the beginning.[1]

The annual reactivation or New Year's festival survives only in late written editions which is true also, we noticed, of the Epic of Creation. In its oldest form it probably conformed to the following pattern delineated by Theodore H. Gaster: (1) The king who temporarily incarnates the deity is slain; (2) A temporary king is appointed; (3) The king is humiliated, made to shed tears; (4) The king engages in a mock combat; (5) The king participates in a sacred marriage ("this includes rites of sexual license to stimulate vegetation; relume the sun, promote human fecundity.") (6) With great ceremony the king is again reinstated in office or his successor.[2]

---

[1] Frankfort, *op. cit.*, p. 16. H. and H. A. Frankfort define myth as follows: "Myth is a form of poetry which transcends poetry in that it proclaims a truth; a form of reasoning which transcends reasoning in that it wants to bring about the truth it proclaims; a form of action, of ritual behavior, which does not find its fulfilment in the act but must proclaim and elaborate a poetic form of truth." (p. 16.)

[2] Theodore H. Gaster, *Thespis* (New York: Schumann, 1950), Chap. III, "The Seasonal Pattern in the Ancient Near East," pp. 34-48.

This is the ancient fertility cult pattern for which Frazer presents so much evidence in the *Golden Bough*. Gaster is interested in the civilized versions which gave rise to literature and drama. Gaster's "topocosm" idea belongs to the *pars pro toto* (mythopoeic) kind of thinking important not only in the rise of myth and the enactment of myth which is drama; but of the greatest significance also, in the rise of the cyclical view of history which is an integral part of the topocosmic or *pars pro toto* kind of thinking. The following passages from *Thespis* make clear the meaning of the "topocosm," and its relation to seasonal rituals:

> Drama evolves from seasonal rituals. Seasonal rituals are functional in character. Their purpose is periodically to revive the *topocosm,* that is, the entire complex of any given locality conceived as a living organism. But this topocosm possesses both a punctual and a durative aspect, representing, not only the actual and present community, but also that ideal and continuous entity of which it is but the current manifestation. [cf. Frankfort's notion of *pars pro toto* thinking—the part stands for the whole.] Accordingly, seasonal rituals are accompanied by myths which are designated to interpret their purely functional acts in terms of ideal and durative situations. The interpenetration of myth and ritual creates drama.[2]

A further passage relates the myth and ritual to the annual cycle:

> Seasonal rituals follow a uniform pattern. This is based on the conception that life is vouchsafed in a series of leases which have annually to be renewed. The renewal is achieved, however, not through divine providence, but through the concerted effort of men; and the rituals are designed to recruit and regiment that effort. They fall into the two clear divisions of Kenosis, or Emptying, and Plerosis, or Filling, the former representing the evacuation of life, the latter its replenishment. Rites of Kenosis include the ob-

---
[2] *Ibid.*, p. 3.

servance of fasts, lents, and similar austerities, all designed to indicate that the community is in a state of suspended animation. Rites of kenosis include mock combats against the forces of drought or evil, mass-mating, the performance of rain charms, and the like, all designed to promote the reinvigoration of the community.

The rites originally performed by the community as a whole tend in time to be centered in a single representative individual, *viz.* the king. It is the king who then undergoes the temporary eclipse, who fights against the noxious powers, and who becomes the bridegroom in a 'sacred marriage.'

What the king does on the punctual [*pars pro toto*] level, the god does on the durative. Accordingly, all the ceremonies performed by the king are transmuted, through the medium of myth, into deeds done by the god. This later gives rise to the idea that the king and the other performers of the seasonal rites are merely impersonating acts originally done by the gods. The ritual then becomes drama, that is, mimetic representation.[1]

Some or all of the elements of the pattern described by Gaster as given above and the topocosmic idea are found not only in the Babylonian New Year Festival and Near Eastern culture generally, but in India, China and even America (cf. the Mayas and Aztecs) either directly or in vestigial form. The notion of the Emperor as the organic link between the supernatural macrocosmic powers and the human world was retained in China and Japan until recent times, as we shall see below.[2]

In Babylonia, and in Mesopotamian culture generally, the New Year celebration was an affair of ten or eleven days. These were intercalary days, the interim period between the end of the old seasonal cycle and the rebirth of the new. This was a period fraught with great danger, no doubt because this eleven day intercalary period was not a

---

[1] *Ibid.*, p. 6.
[2] Chapter VIII below.

part of the year and therefore had no definite god-given order; it was necessary to restore order again immediately through the appropriate ritual-drama. The first half, the Kenosis, was probably marked in prehistoric times by the death of the god Marduk in the person of the king who at this time incarnated him. Later a temporary king was the victim, but in the accounts that survive (which most scholars think are very late records) the king was ritually deposed by taking from him his sceptre, circle and sword.[1] Then the priest of Marduk struck the king's cheek and dragged him by the ears making him bow down to the ground to make a confession before the statue of Marduk. The confession was the negative declaration: "I did not sin, lord of the countries. I was not neglectful (of the requirements) of your godship. I did not destroy Babylon; I did not command its overthrow. I did not rain blows on the cheek of a subordinate ... I did not humiliate them." [2] If the king shed tears it was a good omen; if he did not the coming year would be bad. The king was then reinstated.

Ritual purifications were also important in the first part of the New Year celebrations as part of the Kenosis rites. The climax of these rites was a three-day dramatic representation in which everyone participated.[3] The theme dramatized was the death and resurrection of the god, Marduk. Professor Hooke thinks this is what happened:

> People ran about asking 'Where is he?' There was confusion and fighting in the streets. The fighting would be pre-arranged, one party representing Marduk and the other his enemies. Finally the gods, represented by priests in masks and ritual dresses, broke into Marduk's prison tomb and set him free.[4]

---

[1] Mendelsohn, *op. cit.*, texts from the "Temple Program for the New Year's Festival at Babylon," p. 138.

[2] *Ibid.*

[3] Samuel H. Hooke, *New Year's Day* (London: Gerald Howe, Ltd., 1927), p. 11

[4] *Ibid.*, p. 12.

Next came the rites of plerosis. As described by Professor Hooke:

> The last part of the ceremony called the 'fixing of destinies,' featured a sacred procession of Marduk and his consort, the gods, the king (who probably took the place of Marduk) and all the people, to the festival house outside the city, and a sacred marriage of the god. Then all returned to Marduk's temple and the ritual was complete. The last two days were probably enlivened with games of all sorts, wrestling, leaping, shooting of burning arrows, and rolling fiery wheels about [to relume the sun?] with the usual accompaniments of plentiful feasting and drinking.[5]

Professor Hooke mentions all of the elements of the seasonal pattern [1] outlined by Gaster except "rites of sexual license to stimulate vegetation," but these rites are mentioned elsewhere by Hooke and are implied in the "sacred marriage" part of the festival, a rite which probably is prehistoric in origin.[2] It is well known that sacred prostitution was a vital part of Mesopotamian and Syrian religion.

Another fertility symbol probably involved in the New Year rites was a sacred tree, the "tree of life." (This parallels a similar tree symbolism in the cult of Osiris in Egypt.) This sacred tree is given the form of a pole or tree trunk in Babylonian friezes which have been discovered. It is shown in process of being anointed, so it is plain that it represents the god and the king who is identified with the

---

[5] *Ibid.*, p. 12.

[1] The New Year's festival was a spring festival, but Hooke tells us that "in very early times both spring and autumn were the New Year season in Mesopotamia." He explains the later choice between the two as the New Year depended upon the festival which became more important in a particular city-state. Babylon featured the vernal equinox as the New Year and celebrated the death and resurrection of Marduk after the death-era of winter. (Hooke, *ibid.*, p. 25.)

[2] Thorkild Jacobsen cites a text dated about the end of the third millennium B.C. describing the sacred-marriage rite. (Jacobsen, *op. cit.*, p. 214.)

god. The anointing symbolizes the giving of new life powers to the sacred tree, therefore to the king-god upon whom depends the prosperity of the community for the coming year; for the king-god is the key figure in harmonizing relations between heaven and earth.[3]

Significance of the Tablets of Destiny in relation to history. All of these plerosis rites solemnly signified a new creation. This is made evident by the recital of the Creation Epic described above (on the fourth day of the festival in late times [4]) at various times during the ceremonies. The grand climax of the Epic is concerned with the Tablets of Destinies recovered by Marduk from Kingu, since these are needed for the business of creation; therefore, in the New Year festival Professor Hooke thinks it is clear that "the central object was the 'fixing of destinies,' i.e., the magical determination of the course of the New Year"; and "It is this tablet of destiny, full of the magic virtue of the written word and of the secret knowledge which it contains, that points us back to the original meaning of *New Year,* to the magic instrument of destiny that was the primitive calendar."[1] Professor Irwin, another Near Eastern religions scholar mentions the importance of the "destiny" rites in this festival. He tells us that Marduk and Nabu went in "solemn pilgrimage to the Akitu house, there to settle the fates of the incoming year . . ."[2]

The new-creation idea attached to the beginning of a new cycle of nature is emphasized further in the postponement both in Babylonia and in Egypt of a new king's coronation until the beginning of the new cycle. In Egypt this might be the beginning of the rising of the Nile in early summer or in autumn when the Nile had receded and the fields were about to be seeded. In Babylonia the new king began his reign on New Year's Day as the most auspicious

---
[3] Hooke, *op. cit.*, pp. 13-14.
[4] Mendelsohn, *op. cit.*, p. 129.

time. In China, as we shall see below, a new king changed the beginning of the year to the inaugural day of his reign. It is significant, also, that the inauguration of a new temple could take place in Babylonia only on New Year's Day.[3]

These examples show that in early mythopoeic thought time meant certain concrete cyclically recurrent phases of waxing and waning symbolized by day and night, new moons; and finally by the annual cycle of the seasons, each a "new creation" or "new year" yet patterned after the original creation "in the beginning" as related in the Epic. The destinies in the famous "tablets of destinies" were apparently the same year by year as they were originally given to the seasons, the sun, moon, and the stars. Yet seasons could be "good" or "bad" and human fortunes likewise, both group (the city-state) and individual. There was nothing mechanical or automatic about these phenomena. Man observed quite early the irregularities involved in them. This made him believe all the more that their functioning was controlled by psychic entities, "wills" similar to his own. It has already been mentioned above that in Mesopotamia as elsewhere these "wills" were personalized as the gods who were responsible for all phenomena. When Marduk conquered the goddess-monster of chaos, Tiamat, and her consort, Kingu, he was enabled through possession of the powers of the Tablets of Destinies to create the ordered cosmos by giving each deity a definite post and function in the universe. This was the given "destiny" of the deity. Thus the cosmos was conceived as a state [1] modelled on the pattern of the Mesopo-

---

[1] Hooke, *op. cit.*, p. 15.

[2] Frankfort et al, *Intellectual Adventure of Ancient Man* (Chicago: University of Chicago, 1946), Chap. VIII, "God," by William A. Irwin, p. 236.

[3] H. and H. A. Frankfort, *Before Philosophy, op. cit.*, Chap. I, "Myth and Reality," by H. and H. A. Frankfort, p. 35.

[1] H. and H. A. Frankfort, *op. cit., Jacobsen*, Chap. V, "The Cosmos as a State."

tamian city-state; not the state of historic times, but that of the early formative period, the Heroic Age of "primitive democracy."[2] There was a king, Marduk, whose functions corresponded to those of the earthly king in times of crisis. His powers were not absolute but subject to the approval of the division of government called the Assembly of the gods. This corresponded on the human level to the Assembly in the early democracy of all adult males. This Assembly in the early city-state was the ultimate controlling power except in times of crisis such as war when absolute power was conferred upon a king for the duration of the peril. In time of peace a Council of Elders ordered the community's everyday affairs. However, in the macrocosmic state permanent kingship was conferred by the Assembly of the gods upon Marduk to prevent chaos (personified in Tiamat and Kingu) from regaining power. This is made plain in the Creation Epic, Tablet IV:

> They erected for him a princely throne.
> ....
> "Thou, Marduk, art the most honored of the great gods,
> Thy decree is unrivaled, thy command is Anu.
> From this day unchangeable shall be thy pronouncement.
> To raise or bring low—these shall be (in) thy hand.
> Thy utterance shall come true, thy command shall not be doubted.
> No one among the gods shall transgress thy bounds!
> ....
> We have granted thee kingship over the universe entire.
> When in Assembly thou sittest, thy word shall be supreme.
> ....
> O lord, spare the life of him who trusts thee,

---
[2] Ibid., pp. 141 f.

But pour out the life of the god who seized evil.
....
Lord, truly thy decree is first among gods.
Say but to wreck or create; it shall be."[1]

After Marduk vanquished Tiamat and her consort he created an ordered universe by posting the gods at definite "stations" and giving them orders designed to stabilize a definite pattern in "nature." For example:

> He constructed stations for the great gods,
> Fixing their astral likenesses as constellations.
> He determined the year by designating the zones:
> He set up three constellations for each of the twelve months.
> After defining the days of the year [by means] of (heavenly) figures,
> He founded the station of Nebiru[2] to determine their (heavenly) bands,
> That none might transgress or fall short.
> ....
> The moon he caused to shine, the night (to him) entrusting.
> He appointed him a creature of the night to signify the days:[3]

In similar fashion he contrived the rest of an ordered cosmos-state. But since personal wills were involved there was no *mechanical* order. Moreover, Marduk was not an omnipotent being. His power could be affected not only by the Assembly, but by such "accidents" as the theft of the Tablets of Destiny. In addition, it seems that ritual performances on the part of man such as the New Year's ritual just described were also necessary for the functioning of the cosmic order. Cosmic disorders such as floods or droughts as well as other misfortunes such as the downfall

---
[1] Mendelsohn, *op. cit.*, *Epic of Creation*, p. 31.
[2] *Ibid.*, Translator's (E. A. Speiser's) note, p. 35.
[3] *Ibid.*, *Epic of Creation*, p. 35.

of a dynasty or city-state could result from some such "accident" as that mentioned above; or such disasters could be caused by an offense given Marduk or some other powerful deity by the King or others in high official positions.

Thus history, cosmic and human, was controlled by the gods directly, but indirectly to some extent by human behaviour insofar as this caused positive or negative reactions on the part of the gods. History thus becomes essentially theocratic history; the gods control the cycles of nature and of human history year by year.

The beginnings of human history, described in myths is eulogized in a "before the Fall" poem, the Uttu poem of the third[1] millennium B.C.:

> In Tilmun the raven did not cry,
> The *dar* (bird) did not utter the *dar's* cry,
> The lion did not slay,
> The wolf did not carry off the lambs,
> The dog did not (attack) the resting kids,
> ....
> The doves did not lay (eggs),
> A sick eye did not say, 'I am a sick eye,'
> A sick head did not say, 'I am a sick head,'
> An old man did not say, 'An old man am I.'
> An old woman did not say, 'An old woman am I.'
> 'A man has dug a canal,' one did not say,
> An overseer did not go around in his arrogance (?),
> 'A liar has lied (?)' one did not say.

Professor Albright, who quotes this poem in his essay "Primitivism in Ancient Western Asia," [1] comments as follows on its significance: "The picture illustrated by the above lines is that of a state of life where wild beasts were

---

[1] Professor Albright [who quotes this poem in his essay, "Primitivism in Ancient Western Asia," in the book edited by Lovejoy and Boas, *Primitivism and Related Ideas in Antiquity* (Baltimore: Johns Hopkins Press, 1935)], gives this date. Mendelsohn (*op. cit.*) in his introduction to this poem (which he entitles "Enki and Ninhursag: A Paradise Myth") says the translation was made from tablets of the first half of the second millennium B.C. but "the date when the myth was composed is unknown." (Mendelsohn, p. 3.)

peaceful and did not prey on one another, where there was no disease or old age, where there was no sexual intercourse and no offspring ... where there was no agriculture (no irrigation), and no organized society—in other words, a primeval paradise." [2] But then there was a "sacred marriage" between the god, Enki, and his consort which brought fertility into existence. The rest of the poem is too difficult to interpret, Albright says, but evidently fertility was the beginning of the many ills which subsequently beset the animal and human world. This myth is the original prototype, probably, of many similar myths of a Golden Age of paradisiacal bliss at the dawn of creation with all subsequent history a progressive deterioration from happiness to misery. Such myths are typical of Indian, Chinese, Zoroastrian, Hebrew, Greek, and Roman thought.

The Age of the Moon God and the Great Year of the Cosmos

In Babylonian literature the paradise myth is one of several conflicting accounts of the origins of things. Albright thinks the variant stories "almost inevitably led to the development of a theory of successive world-ages," [3] or series of partial destructions of the world, and developed thereafter into a definite theory of recurrent world cycles. In Babylonia a mention of cycles of partial destructions of the world are found most clearly in the Atrakhasis Epic, probably put into written form before the nineteenth century.[4] This Epic relates that three times man aroused the anger of the gods to such a degree that they decided to exterminate the human race, at one time by drought and

---

[1] William F. Albright, "Primitivism in Ancient Western Asia," *Primitivism and Related Ideas in Antiquity*, ed. by Arthur O. Lovejoy and George Boas (Baltimore: Johns Hopkins University Press, 1935), p. 424.
[2] *Ibid.*, p. 425.
[3] *Ibid.*
[4] *Ibid.*, p. 425 f.

famine, at another time by pestilence, and finally by a great deluge. Each time a wise man, Atrakhasis (whose name means "the very wise one") saved the human race from total extinction. The third disaster, the Great Deluge, is the same one mentioned in the Gilgamesh Epic and in the Bible. No doubt it refers to an actual enormous flood in the Mesopotamian-Syrian area. It is only after this Deluge that plausible history begins. History before the Flood and for some time thereafter comes to us in a cuneiform document of about 2000 B.C. known as the Sumerian King List. The List may not be too reliable, however, since the length of rule of the kings before the Flood is fabulous. The name of the ruler, the city-state over which he was king and his length of rule as given in the List is as follows:[1]

Ruler	City	Length of reign
Alulim	Eridu	28,800 years
Alalgar		36,000 "
Enmenlu-Anna	Badtibira	43,200 "
Enmengal-Anna		28,800 "
divine Dumuzi, a shepherd		36,000 "
Ensipazi-Anna	Larak	28,800 "
Enmendur-Anna	Sippar	21,000 "
Ubar-Tutu	Shuruppak	18,600 "

The List is prefaced with the phrase, "When kingship was lowered from heaven . . ." This and the length of the reigns make it appear that these primeval rulers were demigods. A well known but much later form of this List is that given us by Berossus, a priest of Marduk at Babylon under Antiochus I (281-261 B.C.). Berossus' list is a late and textually corrupted version of the early one [2] and

---

[1] Jack Finnegan, *Light from the Ancient Past* (Princeton, 1946), p. 25.

[2] George A. Barton, *Archaeology and the Bible* (Philadelphia: American Sunday-School Union, seventh rev. ed., 1937), p. 320.

has the lengths of the reigns of the kings greatly exaggerated. In the original list (as given above) the reigns total 241,200 years whereas in the version of Berossus the reigns total 432,000 years. This latter number is very significant in relation to the idea of a grand cosmic cycle or Great Year of the Universe. Hindu mythological speculation about the Great Year of the cosmos gives this figure as the length of the last quarter of the world-cycle (the Kali-yuga). Professor Albright believes that India borrowed the world-cycle idea from Mesopotamia; for although "nothing like a cycle of world years has yet been discovered in Mesopotamia," there is much evidence that a world year of 36,000 years was known to the Babylonians "before the end of the third millennium."[1] The reasons he gives are mainly two: (1) An "age of the moon-god" is mentioned in the inscriptions of Sargon II. This period is 3,000 years or thirty days of a century each. Thus in a luni-solar world-year of twelve months each of thirty hundred (3000) years there would be 36,000 years, an "age of the sun-god" or world-year, although there seems to be no record of its being called by this name. (2) The second reason given by Professor Albright is based on the numbers given in all recensions of the King Lists. He comments that the number 36,000 and its multiple 72,000 appear so frequently in the King Lists that a luni-solar world-year of 36,000 years was very likely known in Mesopotamia before 2000 B.C. However, these numbers need not have this significance, because the Babylonian system was duodecimal and all numbers would therefore be multiples of six or twelve. The enormous totals of the numbers may simply be another instance of the tremendous exaggeration of the lengths of reigns of early mythical gods, demi-gods or heroes found in the "histories" of other peoples, *e.g.*, the Egyptians. It is significant that the renowned authority on ancient astronomy, Otto Neugebauer, is very skeptical of this view that the early Mesopotamians had a notion

---

[1] Albright, *op. cit.*, p. 427.

of a Great Year of the world. Neugebauer tells us that the Babylonian word for the number 3600, *sar*, "has among others, the meaning 'universe' or the like. As a number word it represents 3600, thus being an example of the transformation from a general concept of plurality to a concrete high numeral . . . In the special meaning of 3600 years it was used by Berossos (about 290 B.C.)"[1] He adds that an astronomical significance was not given this period of years until 1000 A.D. in the encyclopedia of Suidas.[2]

If Neugebauer's views are correct it appears that the 36,000 year or Great Year might not have been known until the time of Berossos at the earliest, and perhaps not even then. However, the total of 432,000 years given by Berossus as the length of the era before the flood seems to be too significant a number to be merely accidental. It is exactly a year of divine luni-solar years (12 times 36,000). In any case the number 36,000 and its multiples are applied, in India, to cosmic cycles, the Great Years of the universe. In India the tradition of cosmic cycles seems very old; the Jaina and Buddhist philosophies both of which must be early (no later than the sixth century B.C.) posit world cycles of immense periods. Orthodox Hinduism posits a divine year of 360 human years; 12,000 divine years constitute a full *Mahayuga* or world cycle (Great Year). P.E. Dumont thinks that the Great Year idea is as old as the ninth century B.C. in India.[1] The early Indus valley culture recently discovered appears related to the Mesopotamian; this makes it interesting to speculate about the dissemination of world-cycle ideas.

Whatever the truth may turn out to be with reference to the idea of a Great Year in ancient Mesopotamia, there remains, at least, the notion of an "age of the moon-god" of 3000 years mentioned above. In the ancient King List of around 2000 B.C. the 241,200 years would represent 80.4

---

[1] Otto Neugebauer, *The Exact Sciences in Antiquity* (Princeton: Princeton University Press, 1952), p. 135.
[2] *Ibid.*

ages of the moon-god whereas Berossus' list would represent the more satisfying number of 144 moon-god ages.

The idea that a month-cycle of 30 days, a microcosmic time-span, is represented at the divine macrocosmic level by the "age of the moon-god" of 3000 years is an important step in the mythopoeic development of the cyclical view of history. The *pars pro toto* method of thinking, the part, the small month, standing for the whole, the great month, and probably the great month in its turn becoming a part of a Great Cosmic Divine Year is illustrated here. Such a view of the relation between part and whole is typical of the organismic philosophy of nature so much a part of mythopoeic thought.

The significance of such macrocosmic cycles for human history is not clear. Professor Speiser in his essay on the idea of history in ancient Mesopotamia [2] does not mention the moon-cycle or luni-solar cycle of 36,000 years.[3] He holds the view that Mesopotamians of later ages viewed history as a series of dynasties that rose to power and then declined. (This sounds strikingly modern.) The age of Sargon of Akkad at the end of the third millenium B.C. was looked upon as the "period of unprecedented achievement,"[1] yet even this glorious dynasty fell at last.

> Sargon, as the founder of Akkad's might, was obviously fortune's favorite. By the same token, Naram-Sin must have been marked for ill fortune, since the waning years of his reign were disastrous for Akkad. Similarly, the end of any dynasty was the direct result of the gods' displeasure.[2]

---

[1] P.-E. Dumont, "Primitivism in Indian Literature," *Primitivism and Related Ideas in Antiquity*, op. cit., p. 433.

[2] E. A. Speiser, "Ancient Mesopotamia," *The Idea of History in the Ancient Near East*, ed. Robert Claude Dentan (New Haven: Yale University Press, 1955).

[3] Toynbee accepts the view that between the eighth and sixth centuries B.C. the Babylonians "apparently" discovered a periodic recurrence covering all planets as well as the sun, moon and earth. The length of this cycle "dwarfed the solar year into insignificance." See Arnold J. Toynbee, *A Study of History*, abridged by D. C. Somervell (Oxford University Press, 1947), p. 251.

It appears, therefore, that there was no idea of progress in Mesopotamian historical thought. The age of Sargon had not been surpassed. The idea of history was cyclical but the cycle-idea was applied to the rise and fall of dynasties and peoples. Speiser says:

> ... the social philosopher of the Old Babylonian period had every reason to see the past in terms of recurring cycles. But did he apply such finding to the future? Was Marduk certain to do to Babylon as Nidaba had done to Lagash or Enlil to the Guti? ... The question is of considerable interest, but the available data do not add up to a conclusive answer.[3]

The only certain outstanding idea, it appears, which dominated all Mesopotamian thought about historical events was the idea of the control of history by the gods,[4] the theocratic philosophy of history which is an integral part of the mythopoeic philosophy of the universe.

Summary of the Developments towards a Cyclical View of History in Mesopotamia

(1) *Methodology and epistemology of ancient man.* Man's approach to the universe was mythopoeic, that is, the relations between himself and natural phenomena were emotive, subjective, aesthetic, and personal. I ... Thou relationships rather than modern I ... It were characteristic. Man felt the "powers" in natural phenomena as friendly or hostile insofar as they helped or hindered his pursuits.

---

[1] Speiser, *op. cit.*, "Ancient Mesopotamia," p. 55.
[2] *Ibid.*, p. 56.
[3] *Ibid.*
[4] Neugebauer says that in the Old Babylonian period in the reign of Ammisaduqa the appearances and disappearances of Venus were recorded because celestial phenomena were correlated with important events in the state. This kind of thinking represents the beginnings of the development which centuries later led to a definite judicial astrology and finally the horoscopic astrology of the Hellenistic age developed by the Greeks. Neugebauer, *op. cit.*, p. 95.

These "powers" were later personalized and hierarchically organized into a "state" similar to man's early type of government ("primitive democracy") in Mesopotamia.

(2) Probably the first notion of a recurrent cycle came from observation of the daily sun cycle conceived mythopoeically as the daily death and rebirth of the sun-god.

(3) A much longer recurrent cycle celebrated later, no doubt, but still as early as prehistoric times was the cycle of the seasons so important when agriculture became known. This, too, was mythopoeically conceived as the death and rebirth of fertility powers personified first in the king (perhaps a mere chieftain in earliest times) with his actual death. His "spirit," which meant essentially his fertility powers, resurrected in his successor who then celebrated the "sacred marriage" amidst general festivities in which sexual promiscuity helped fertility by means of imitative magic.

(4) Myth and drama (dramatization of the myth) developed around these rites of death (kenosis) and resurrection and sacred marriage (plerosis).[1] The myth universalized on the macrocosmic plane the particular concrete microcosmic seasonal situation. The myth-drama, the Epic of Creation, represented an "eternal" or universal or durative once-and-for-all divine creative act of the god (Marduk in Babylonia). At the human level the microcosm with the king as the organic link in the harmony between heaven and earth reactivated what the god had done on the durative level. This ritual reactivation was necessary; man and the gods had to work together to secure a good New Year.

(5) The gods ultimately controlled "destinies." This is dramatized at the end of the New Year festival when Marduk and Nabu went in pilgrimage to the Akitu house to settle all things for the coming year. Thus events in each annual cycle, good or ill, were controlled by the gods. This is the usual pattern of mythopoeic history—history year by year is theocratic history.

---

[1] The rites of kenosis and plerosis were parents of our tragedy and comedy. See Gaster's *Thespis, op. cit.*

(6) From the annual cycle controlled by the gods, the Mesopotamians seem to have gone on to a much larger cycle, the cycle of 3,000 years, each 3,000 being an "age of the moon-god." They may have conceived the notion which would follow from this, that of a recurrent Great Year of the cosmos, of twelve divine months (36,000 years) which parallels the twelve lunar months in the luni-solar microcosmic or human year.

(7) This idea of a Divine Year cycle is found in many other civilizations and may have originated in Babylonia. We have already mentioned India where borrowing seems to have been direct if Professor Albright's views are correct. In Zoroastrian religion the Bundahish quotes a world cycle of 12,000 years[1] probably borrowed from Mesopotamia. In China there seems to have been borrowing of some ideas related to a world cycle. In Egypt, however, there does not seem to be a world-year idea. The Sothic cycle about which more will be said below [2] seems to have been merely an astronomical calendrical period without significance for human history. The civilization of the Mayas curiously shows a pronounced emphasis on the cyclical idea and a temple architecture very similar to the Babylonian ziggurat.[3]

The chapters immediately following will review the cyclical ideas of the Indians, the Chinese, and the Zoroastrians.[4]

---

[1] Jack Finegan, *The Archaeology of World Religions* (Princeton: Princeton University Press, 1952), pp. 26-27.

[2] See chap. X.

[3] Henri Frankfort attaches great religious significance to the Ziggurat. He tells us that the ziggurat of the god Enlil at Nippur was called "House of the Mountain, Mountain of the Storm, Bond between Heaven and Earth." He claims that the "mountain" is "the place where the mysterious potency of the earth, and hence of all natural life is concentrated." See Henri Frankfort, *The Birth of Civilization in the Near East* (Garden City, New York: Doubleday Anchor Books, Doubleday & Company, Inc., 1956) p. 56. In note 5 on this same page he comments further on the significance of the mountain-symbolism of the ziggurat: "It is sometimes said that the Sumerians, descending from a mountainous region, desired to con-

tinue the worship of their gods on 'High Places' and therefore proceeded to construct them in the plain. The point is why they considered 'High Places' appropriate, especially since the gods worshipped there were not sky gods only but also, and predominantly, chthonic gods. Our interpretation takes its starting-point from 'the mountain,' not as a geographical feature, but as a phenomenon charged with religious meaning. Several current theories have taken one or more aspects of 'the mountain' as a religious symbol into account and we do not exclude them, but consider them, on the whole, subsidiary to the primary notion that 'the mountain' was seen as the normal setting of divine activity." On p. 57 Frankfort adds that the myths say that the god "dies" or is kept captive in the "mountain" from whence he comes forth during the New Year festival. The rain also comes from the mountain. "The Sumerians created the conditions under which communication with the gods became possible when they erected the artificial mountains for their temples."

[4] The Zoroastrians held to a one-cycle theory and are important especially because they provide a link between Divine-Year Indian cycles and Western One-Grand-Cycle-Apocalyptic philosophies of history.

CHAPTER III

DEVELOPMENT OF THE CYCLICAL VIEW IN INDIA: HINDUISM

Section 1. Cyclical symbolism of the cosmic dance of Shiva.
In India mythopoeic thought about the nature of history begins naively and then becomes profound poetry and philosophy. This fascinating development begins with a myth of primitive type about the daily cycle of the sun, the microcosmic phenomenon, which becomes the analogue of the everlastingly recurrent macrocosmic cycles of the universe poetized in the cosmic dance of Shiva.

The daily cycle of the sun was symbolized by the cosmic cross throughout the Aryan world.[1] Each arm of the cross represented the position of the sun at midnight, sunrise, **noon, and sunset respectively.** In Hindu mythology Narayana in his sleeping or yogic state is the sun from its disappearance at sunset through midnight until sunrise (the midnight arm of the cosmic cross); Brahma, the creator-god, is the sunrise (the east arm of the cross); Vishnu, the principle of equilibrium, the Preserver-god is the sun at noon; and Shiva, the Destroyer-god, with the moon for his symbol is the sun at sunset beyond the high Himalayas.[2] The movement of the sun from east to west was suggested also diagramatically by the swastika which adds four short lines of direction to the cosmic cross.[3] Havell says that

> The ascending movement of the sun naturally represented the whole principle of order and well-being in the

---
[1] Ernest B. Havell, *The Ideals of Indian Art* (London: John Murray, Albemarle Street, W., 1920), p. 68.
[2] *Ibid.*
[3] *Ibid.*, p. 69.

universe, and thus the swastika became the symbol of life and of man's material prosperity. The reverse movement, indicated by the sauwastika, was the descending principle, connoting disorder and dissolution.[4]

It is interesting to notice that circumambulation of a shrine, one of the most ancient Hindu religious rites which continues to the present day, begins at the east and follows the auspicious ascending movement of the sun. Sun worship is the ancient origin also of the prayer of the Brahmins to the Supreme Being at sunrise, noon and sunset.

The sacred recurrent daily cycle of the birth and death of the sun as a microcosmic time phenomenon was applied early (at least as early as the beginning of the Christian era) in Hindu belief to the macrocosm, the everlastingly recurrent birth and death of the total cosmos. The deities Brahma, Vishnu, and Shiva performed the functions on the macrocosmic scale which they had performed on the microcosmic i.e., Brahma is Creator of the cosmos (the rising sun); Vishnu, the principle of equilibrium (the sun at noon), the Preserver of the cosmos; and Shiva the Destroyer (but destroys to regenerate) is the setting sun. The impersonal Brahman, the impassive Absolute, corresponds with Narayana Sleeping (the midnight position of the swastika) and signifies the long period between a creation and destruction of the universe.

In this analogical thinking in which the part, the daily sun cycle stands for the whole, the cosmic cycle, we have another example of *pars pro toto* thinking so typical of the mythopoeic approach to an understanding of time and of nature in general. The qualitative, concrete, picturesque characteristics of such thinking about time are brought out further in the emotive personification of important aspects of time: sunrise: Brahma; sunset: Shiva; night: Narayana; creation: Brahma: equilibrium: Vishnu; destruction: Shiva; and non-being: the Impersonal Brahman. But this intuitive organismic approach to an understanding of the cosmos can be defended today and is

---
[4] *Ibid.*

thought by many to be truer than the mechanistic, materialistic metaphysics of much recent Western philosophy.

In more mature Indian thought one god, usually either Vishnu or Shiva receives the attention of the worshipper. For our study of cyclical time the Shaivites (devotees of Shiva) are the more important since for this large segment of Hinduism all phases of cosmic change, from creation to destruction in a cycle, are poetically conceived to be the cosmic dance of Shiva-Nataraja. (Nataraja means Lord of Dancers, or King of Actors.[1])

To appreciate the full significance of Shiva's cosmic dance we need to know something of his outstanding characteristics. Shiva is a very old god, historically speaking. Statuettes of this deity have been recovered from excavations at Harappa, one of the major sites of the ancient Indus Valley culture which was contemporary with the ancient Mesopotamian civilization of the third millenium B. C. The Indus valley culture was at as high a level as the Mesopotamian to judge by the archaeological remains, which demonstrate also a cultural interchange between these civilizations. The Indus valley culture, however, was itself creative and no mere borrower of Mesopotamian ideas. The script used by the people of the Indus valley culture has not yet been deciphered, however, so the full extent of their creativity is as yet unknown. The god, Shiva, worshipped by these people was represented, at least in a statuette recovered from Harappa, as a dancing male figure, four-armed and three-headed. This means that Shiva was an indigenous god taken over into the Aryan pantheon along with other religious borrowings such as the idea of reincarnation. In another representation of the Indus valley Shiva takes the form of a motive on a seal recently discovered. Shiva is portrayed here seated, in yogic posture. He has horns, three heads and a trident above his heads. The trident (which has cosmic significance) becomes important later in the Buddhist symbol called the

---

[1] Ananda Coomaraswamy, *The Dance of Shiva* (Bombay, Calcutta: Asia Publishing House, 1948), p. 83.

trisula. The horns may represent the bull, the fertility animal *par excellence,* as associated with Shiva as early as this time.

The prototype of Kali, the wife or female energy (Shakti) of Shiva in her destructive aspect in the later religion (Hinduism), is found also in the Indus civilization. Figurines recognized as the typical Afrasian mother goddess and goddess of fertility have been found in great numbers. The Great Mother appears with wild beasts, snakes, birds, fishes, and plants as the universal principle of fertility in all nature. In Hinduism sculptures showing the Dance of Shiva represent him with a male's earring on one ear and female's earring on the other ear. This symbolizes the male-female energies of the cosmic dance of creation, but in popular myth and art his female energy takes the form of "wives"—Uma, the noble and gentle one; Durga, the demonic mistress of demons and war; and Kali, the Great Mother who wears skulls and human hands and signifies death and the brutal side of nature. Yet all of these energies are philosophically understood in Hinduism as aspects of the one god, Shiva.

The association of the *lingam* with Shiva may have originated in the Indus culture, also, since many phallic emblems "suggesting the *lingam* of later Saivism" [1] have been discovered.

Later, [2] Hinduism developed a fascinating philosophical and most beautiful symbolism around this great god, Shiva, especially around his dance called the *Nadanta.* This dance is represented in many South Indian bronze images which vary in minor details, but agree in a fundamental iconography. The great authority on Indian art, Ananda Coomeraswamy, describes this iconography:

---

[1] Benjamin Rowland, *The Art and Architecture of India* (Baltimore: Penguin Books, 1953), p. 19, footnote number 14.

[2] By 1000 A. D. southern India had practically eliminated Buddhism. Hinduism remained, and Shiva worship was its most popular form. The Cola bronzes famous in Hindu art come from southern India around this period and set the style for great bronzes of the thirteenth and fourteenth centuries.

The images, then, represent Shiva dancing, having four hands, with braided and jeweled hair of which the lower locks are whirling in the dance. In His hair may be seen a wreathing cobra, a skull, and the mermaid figure of Ganga; upon it rests the crescent moon, and it is crowned with a wreath of Cassia leaves. In His right ear He wears a man's earring, a woman's in his left; He is adorned with necklaces and armlets, a jewelled belt, anklets, bracelets, finger and toerings. The chief part of his dress consists of tightly fitting breeches, and He wears also a fluttering scarf and a sacred thread. One right hand holds a drum, the other is uplifted in the sign of do not fear: one left hand holds fire, the other points down upon the demon Muyalaka, a dwarf holding a cobra; the left is raised. There is a lotus pedestal, from which springs an encircling glory *(tiravasi)*, fringed with flame, and touched within by the hands holding drum and fire. The images are of all sizes, rarely, if ever exceeding four feet in total height.[1]

This type of image represents the cosmic dance of Shiva in the process of which the universe is brought into being, evolves to a climax, and then is destroyed. The dance is performed significantly in Chidambaram (or Tillai), the center of the universe and represents Lord Shiva's five cosmic activities: "*Shrishti* (overlooking, creation, evolution), *Sthiti* (preservation, support), *Samhara* (destruction, evolution? [probably misprint for involution])[2] *Tirobhava* (veiling, embodiment, illusion, and also, giving rest), *Anugraha* (release, salvation, grace)."[3] All of these activities are symbolized in the images described above in the following manner: *Shrishti*, (creation and evolution) are represented by the *drum*, the rhythmic vibration of which signifies the creative dance of the energies of physi-

---

[1] Coomeraswamy, *op. cit.*, p. 86.
[2] Coomeraswamy's book reads "evolution" but this must be a misprint; involution would harmonize with destruction.
[3] *Ibid.*, p. 87.

cal and organic nature; *Sthiti,* (preservation, support), is symbolized by the lifted right hand in the sign 'do not fear' and by the right foot planted on the ground which "gives an abode to the tired soul struggling in the toils of causality." [4] One of the left hands holds fire, symbol of destruction, death and the "burning-ground," which means the end of the cosmic cycle. The other left hand points downward to the demon-dwarf Muyalaka, the personification of Evil, trampled underfoot by Mahadeva (Shiva). The left foot is raised which means the release of sanctified souls forever from involvement in the everlasting cosmic dance and their eternal nirvana of bliss in union with that aspect of Mahadeva which represents the eternal impersonal Absolute beyond the world of process and becoming. The crescent moon always associated with Shiva belongs perhaps originally to the sun worship mentioned above (Shiva as the sun at sunset with the moon rising); or it is related also to Shiva's significance as controller of mystic dark powers of night, since he is the great yogin or ascetic which is represented also in the images by the part of his hair which is braided. The moon may symbolize Shiva's endless life-giving powers as does the serpent; for the moon renews its life-cycle everlastingly from practical invisibility, to new moon to full moon just as the serpent and certain other creatures renew their life cycles endlessly. The goddess, Ganga, in Shiva's hair personifies the Ganges River and refers to the notion that this and other great rivers of the world have their source in the center of the universe, the Himalayas of which Mt. Kailasa,[1] abode of Shiva, forms the "axis of the universe" from which the world's great rivers flow. It is significant that Shiva's headdress in many of the images is in the shape of the sacred mountain, also of the *lingam;* the two symbolisms coalesce in representing the core or naval of the uni-

[4] *Ibid.,* p. 88. Coomaraswamy quotes this from *Chidambara Mummani Kovai.*
[1] Mt. Kailasa corresponds with the "Chidambaram" mentioned above.
[2] See below in the discussion of Indian architecture.

verse, the pivot of all life.[2] The male and female earrings symbolize Shiva as source of all the reproductive life forces, male and female. The horseshoe arch bordered with flames which forms an aureole around the entire figure represents the cosmos. The hands holding the flame (the flame symbolizes the energy of cosmic forces) and the drum which stands for the rhythmic vibrations of the forces (laws, patterns of evolution) apparently touch the arch of the cosmos while the hands and the feet signifying release are free from the arch.

Another attribute of Shiva when he is shown as the great ascetic, the Yogin of yogins, is his third eye placed vertically in the center of his forehead. This third eye is important in relation to Indian views of time; Shiva's three eyes symbolize knowledge of the past, present, and future—all knowledge of all time in all cycles of time.[1] Shiva's cosmic nature is manifested further in the notion that there are five faces of Shiva, each one equated with one of the five elements of the universe: earth, wind, ether, fire, water.[2] Finally, the cobra has cosmic significance as an attribute of Mahadeva. The interpretation of this emblem as given by one of the greatest authorities on Indian art, E.B. Havell is as follows:

> The cobra became Siva's especial emblem because, while its spiral coil represented the principle of cosmic evolution, or of life, the deadly poison contained in its fangs represented the principle of involution, or death; and its habit of shedding its skin periodically was a symbol of reincarnation, or rebirth.[3]

The serpent in general symbolizes endless life or eternity as early as Sumerian times in Mesopotamia as we pointed out in chapter two above. Finally, the bull, Nandi,

---

[1] E. B. Havell, *op. cit.*, p. 50.
[2] Jack Finnegan, *The Archaeology of World Religions, op. cit.*, p. 170. Other, more metaphysical interpretations, are also given.
[3] E. B. Havell, *op. cit.*, p. 75.

is always shown with Shiva as his "vehicle" and this like the *lingam* is a symbol of the god as the source of fertility, of creation, of all life.

Altogether, Shiva is the Cosmos, his dance the process of evolution and involution, the entire life-process span of each cosmic cycle from generation to annihilation. This is expressed in poetry in the ninth tantra of Tirumular's *Tirumantram:*

> His form is everywhere: all-pervading is His Shiva-Shakti:
> Chidambaram is everywhere, everywhere His dance:
> As Shiva is all and omnipresent,
> Everywhere is Shiva's gracious dance made manifest.
> His five-fold dances are temporal and timeless.
> His five-fold dances are His Five Activities.
> By His grace He performs the five acts,
> This is the sacred dance of Uma-Sahaya.
> He dances with Water, Fire, Wind, and Ether,
> Thus our Lord dances ever in the court.
> ....
> Our Lord dances His eternal dance.
> The form of the Shakti is all delight—
> This united delight is Uma's body:
> This form of Shakti arising in time
> And uniting the twain is the dance [1]
> ....
> The eight quarters are His eight arms [2]
> The three lights are His three eyes ... [3]

Dr. Coomeraswamy concisely summarizes the entire interpretation of Shiva's dance, including its purpose and its philosophico-religious meaning:

---

[1] Uma is the female energy (Shakti) of Shiva under its gentle aspect. The symbolism means that the devotee's soul and Uma are one.

[2] Shiva images may have eight arms and here the eight arms are taken to mean the eight quarters of the universe (N, E, S, W, and N.E., N.W., S.E., and S.W.) This means that Shiva rules the entire cosmos.

[3] Coomeraswamy, *op. cit.*, p. 88. Perhaps the "three lights" are Vayu (Wind), Agni (Fire but stands for Earth), and Sun.

> The essential significance of Shiva's Dance is threefold: First, it is the image of his Rhythmic Play as the Source of all Movement within the Cosmos, which is Represented by the Arch: Secondly, the Purpose of his Dance is to Release the Countless souls of men from the snare of Illusion: Thirdly the Place of the Dance, Chidambaram, the Centre of the Universe, is within the Heart.[4]

Dr. Coomeraswamy comments wisely, also, on the Dance as a philosophy of science:

> Every part of such an image as this is directly expressive, not of any mere superstition or dogma, but of evident facts. No artist of today, however great, could more exactly or more wisely create an image of that Energy which science must postulate behind all phenomena. If we would reconcile Time with Eternity, we can scarcely do so otherwise than by the conception of alternations of phase extending over vast regions of space and great tracts of time. Especially significant, then, is the phase alternation implied by the drum, and the fire which 'changes,' not destroys. These are but visual symbols of the theory of the day and night of Brahma.
> In the night of Brahma, Nature is inert, and cannot dance till Shiva wills it: He rises from His rapture, and dancing sends through inert matter pulsing waves of awakening sound, and lo! matter also dances appearing as a glory round about Him. Dancing, He sustains its manifold phenomena. In the fulness of time, still dancing, he destroys all forms and names by fire and gives new rest. This is poetry: but none the less, science.[1]

We shall return here and there in later chapters but mainly in the Conclusion to a scientific defense of the cycli-

---
[4] *Ibid.*, p. 93.
[1] *Ibid.*, pp. 94 f.

cal view which Dr. Coomeraswamy considers the only intelligible way of reconciling time with eternity, but at this point we shall continue with the exploration of mythopoeic cyclical views in Indian thought.

Section 2. Cyclical Great Years of the Cosmos: the Kalpa and the four yugas. Shiva's dance is a day of Brahma; his rest a night of Brahma (to Shaivites Brahma is equivalent to Shiva), and a precise length is given to the "day" and the "night." The day is 4,320,000,000 years in length and the night is exactly the same. The enormous "day" is called a **kalpa. A kalpa contains** one thousand mahayugas. The mahayuga equals 4,320,000 human years or 12,000 "divine" years (a divine year is equivalent to 36,000 human years). This notion of divine years called the "doctrine of the Yugas," is an old one in Indian thought, at least as old as the ninth century B.C.[2] Perhaps the idea was borrowed from Mesopotamia by inhabitants of the Indus valley civilization and passed on to the Aryan invaders in this way; we mentioned above in the preceding chapter Professor Albright's view that the notion of a divine year of 36,000 human years was probably known in Mesopotamia as early as the third millenium B.C.; but the borrowing may have proceeded in the opposite direction—the Indus culture may have given the idea in some form to the Mesopotamian. In any case we do not find the explicit idea of a cyclically recurrent divine year in Mesopotamia, but we do have a very clear cut divine year cyclic pattern in Indian thought in the doctrine of the yugas.

The Mahayuga of 12,000 divine years is divided into four yugas. Each of the four is named after a face of the Indian die. The names and characteristics of each are:

1. The *Krta* Yuga. This name means "the lucky one" and is the side of the die with four dots. This era is the longest of the four and is 4800 divine years in length. Its

---

[2] Dumont, "Primitivism in Indian Literature," *Primitivism and Related Ideas in Antiquity, op. cit.,* p. 433.

color is white. Vishnu,[1] the "soul of all beings" is white in this epoch. The *Mahabharata* [2] describes this period as one of paradisiacal bliss:

> In that age there were neither Gods, Danavas, Gandharvas, Yaksas, Raksasas, nor Pannagas; no buying or selling went on; the Vedas were not classed as Saman, Rig, and Yajus; man's life was effortless (there was no manual labor) ; the fruit of the earth was obtained by mere wish; no disease or decline of the organs of sense arose through the influence of age; there was no malice, weeping, pride or enmity; no contention, no lassitude, no hatred, cruelty, fear, affliction, jealousy or envy.[3]

2. The *Treta* Yuga. This name means the side of the die with three dots. It is three-fourths as long as the *Krta* Yuga, 3600 divine years. The *Mahabharata,* Vanaparvan, 149 ff. describes this era:

> In the Treta age, sacrifice commenced, righteousness decreased by a fourth, Visnu became red.
> In that age the men were devoted to truth and to righteousness dependent on ceremonies.
> In the Treta age men acted with an object in view, seeking after reward for their rites and their gifts; and no longer disposed to austerities and to liberality from a simple feeling of duty.
> In that age they were devoted to their own various duties and to religious ceremonies.[1]

3. The *Dvapara* Yuga. This means the side of the die with two dots. It is one-half the length of the Krta Yuga,

---

[1] Vishnu in popular Hinduism is commonly looked upon as the Preserver aspect of the threefold god, the Trimurti. The other two are Brahma the Creator and Shiva, the Destroyer or Dissolver of the Universe.

[2] Dumont, *op. cit., p.* 434. Quoted from the *Mahabharata* by Dumont.

[3] *Ibid.*

2400 divine years. Virtue, too, decreases by one-half. The *Mahabharata,* Vanaparvan, 149, 33 ff. says:

> In the Dvapara age righteousness was diminished by two quarters; Visnu . . . became yellow and the Veda fourfold . . . Owing to ignorance of the one Veda, Vedas were multiplied. And now from the decline of the quality of goodness few only adhered to truth. When men had fallen away from goodness, many diseases, desires and calamities, caused by destiny, assailed them, by which they were severely afflicted, and driven to practice austerities. Others desiring enjoyments and heavenly bliss, offered sacrifices. Thus, when the men had reached the Dvapara age, they declined through unrighteousness.[2]

4. The *Kali Yuga.* This means the side of the die with one dot, the losing one. It is only one-fourth the length of the Krta Yuga, i.e., 1200 divine years. Vishnu's color is black in this period. The *Mahabharata's* description paints an evil picture of this miserable age:

> In the Kali age righteousness remained to the extent of one-fourth only. In that age of darkness Visnu became black. Practices enjoined by the Vedas, works of righteousness and rites of sacrifice ceased. Calamities, diseases, fatigue, anger and other faults, distresses, anxiety, hunger, fear prevailed.[3]

---

[1] *Ibid.,* Quoted by Dumont from the *Mahabharata,* p. 434 f.

[2] *Ibid.,* Quoted by Dumont from the *Mahabharata,* p. 435.

[3] *Ibid.,* Quoted by Dumont from the *Mahabharata,* p. 435. The *Mahabharata* is one of the two great Indian epics. The collection of epic poetry which it represents was gathered together by devotees of Vishnu between 200 B. C. and 200 A. D. but much of the poetry is much earlier. Professor Dumont chose these passages (not given here in full) as examples of chronological primitivism in Indian thought. Chronological primitivism puts the Golden Age of man's history at the beginning with subsequent history a regression.

The present era is a Kali yuga, the most corrupt of the four ages. When this epoch ends, a Mahayuga of 12,000 divine years will be completed. Then the *Krta* yuga will return to be followed by the *Treta, Dvapara,* and Kali yugas again until another Mahayuga is completed. The cycle of Mahayugas repeats itself one thousand times. This equals one kalpa or 12,000,000 divine years (4,320,000,000 human years). Then Brahma dissolves the universe and rests from this kind of activity for a period of one kalpa in length. Then he creates another universe of the same time, space, and event pattern and the cycle is repeated again. This rhythmic activity of Brahma, like an inhalation and exhalation, continues forever. The Mahayuga and period of rest, however, are merely one day and night of the god, Brahma. This god lives for one hundred years of such days and nights. Then another soul in the samsara takes his place, but the cycle-pattern of human history remains exactly the same.

Because there are no changes in the cyclic yuga-pattern, the true yogin, like his divine exemplar, Shiva with the third eye, the eye of "supramental time vision," [1] can know past, present, and future. This is because all time is in Brahma (as described above) in the eternally recurrent cycle; the yogin achieves the state of *samadhi* in which he is one with Brahman and therefore has Brahman's knowledge. Brahman is the cosmic Absolute beyond all time and change while the god, Brahma, is a temporary phenomenal manifestation of Brahman's *shakti.* The yogin in samadhi becoming one with the absolute Brahman knows Brahman in his Shakti or energizing manifestation in the cosmic dance of Shiva (symbol of the day of Brahma) and Brahman in his infinite night of rest (night of Brahma). The yogin's knowledge is described by the great twentieth century Indian philosopher, Sri Aurobindo, who calls this knowledge the "supramental time vision":

---

[1] Sri Aurobindo, *The Synthesis of Yoga* (Pondicherry: Sri Aurobindo Ashram, 1955), chap. XXV, "The Supramental Time Vision."

The supramental consciousness on the other hand is founded upon the supreme consciousness of the timeless Infinite, but has too the secret of the deployment of the infinite Energy in time. It can either take its station in the time consciousness and keep the timeless infinite as its background of supreme and original being from which it receives all its organising knowledge, will and action, or it can, centered in its essential being, live in the timeless but live too in a manifestation in time which it feels and sees as infinite and as the same Infinite, and can bring out, sustain and develop in the one what it holds supernally in the other. Its time consciousness therefore will be different from that of the mental being, not swept helplessly on the stream of the moments and clutching at each moment as a stay and a swiftly disappearing standpoint, but founded first on its eternal identity beyond the changes of time, secondly on a simultaneous eternity of Time in which past, present and future exist together forever in the self-knowledge and self-power of the Eternal, thirdly, in a total view of the three times as one movement slightly and invisibly seen even in their succession of stages, periods, cycles, last—and that only in the instrumental consciousness—in the step by step evolution of the moments. It will therefore have the knowledge of the three times, *trikaladrsti*,—held of old to be a supreme sign of the seer and the Rishi,—not as an abnormal power, but as its normal way of time knowledge.[1]

The true yogin, then, loses his private space-time stream of consciousness and becomes one with Brahman's infinite Self, knower of past, present, and future. The self, the

---

[1] *Ibid.*, p. 1013. Aurobindo anticipates here the next stage in human evolution, from the mind-level to that of super-mind. He conceives the cycle of the history of the cosmos as evolution and involution of the Infinite. There is involution of the Infinite from the highest or Absolute Consciousness into the lowest level—inorganic nature; then evolution from this level back to the highest—Absolute Consciousness. The next stage of evolution is that of Superman or Supermind, the stage in which the "separate" selves will see their true nature as centers of consciousness of the Absolute Self. These selves will be able to see themselves as one with the Absolute and centers of its divine activity. See the chapter on Aurobindo, Part II below.

microcosm, has become the macrocosm, Brahman, who is knower and evolver of the time cycles.[2]

This is a mature philosophical understanding of the universe and its time-cycles, but earlier Indian views belong to a more mythopoeic approach. The earlier more mythopoeic microcosm-macrocosm idea of the space-time world is found early in the Vedic period (1500-800 B.C.) in architecture and in religious ritual such as the Fire-altar ceremony.

Section 3. The space-time cycle in architecture. The early Aryan village, according to E. B. Havell, had a plan derived from the fortified camps of the Aryans rather than from the indigenous culture.[1] This plan was a rectangle in shape with sides oriented to the four quarters of the universe and intersected by two avenues terminating in four gateways. It was a plan, Professor Rowland explains,

> intended as a kind of microcosm, with the five divisions of the village corresponding to the five elements of the universe, and each of the gateways dedicated to one of the four Vedic deities typifying the positions of the sun in its course through the heavens. These village plans also included a broad path girding the buildings within the outer walls which the householders circumambulated with recitations to ensure the favour of the gods. This feature, together with the metaphysical symbolism attached to the gateways, is perpetuated in the plan and ritual of the Buddhist stupa. It may be added that the regularity of these early plans, based on straight intersecting avenues, is possibly a survival of the systematic arrangements of the Indus cities adapted to the metaphysical and architectural needs of the new Aryan civilization.[2]

---

[2] The traditional powers of the yogin are stated in *The Yoga Sutras of Patañjali* under *Vibhutis* (Attainments). One of these *Vibhutis* is knowledge of the past and future. (See S. Radhakrishnan and C. A. Moore, *Source Book in Indian Philosophy,* "Yoga" p. 473.

[1] Rowland, *op. cit.,* p. 22. Professor Rowland quotes E. B. Havell as his authority for this information.

[2] *Ibid.,* p. 22.

Similar cosmical ideas are found in pre-Mauryan[3] times in tumuli that have the domical shape of later Buddhist stupas and probably
> mark the sites of royal burials. Consequently, there is every reason to recognize in them the prototype for the Buddhist relic mound. Wooden masts were found embedded in the centre of the solid earthen tumuli.[4]

These masts represent symbolically the "tree of life" or "axis of the universe," prominent in ziggurat symbolism (part of the potency of the sacred mountain symbolism prevalent in the ancient world—see chapter I above).

Later Buddhist and Hindu architecture reproduces a much more complex magic replica of the cosmos. To use the language of Professor Gaster the architecture represents the *topocosm,* or replica in miniature of the entire space-time universe. Professor Spiegelberg describes the general symbolic significance of this topocosm:

> The basic pattern of the Hindu temple, as well as of the similar Buddhist stupa or relic container, is explained from the bottom upwards. The lowest part, the base, a yellow cube, represents the element earth; next the assembly hall, a green ball, symbolizes the water element; the spire, cone-shaped, red, and pointing upwards, represents fire; the half-moon, bowl-like white top stands for the element of air; and the blue flame above stands for the Akasha, or "ether," above us, which in turn symbolizes liberation and emergence into the Brahman realm.[1]

There are elaborations on this basic pattern. The cone-shaped spire is frequently divided into a number of

---
[3] Prior to 322 B. C.
[4] Rowland, *op. cit.,* p. 22.
[1] Frederic Spiegelberg, *Living Religions of the World* (Englewood Cliffs, N. J.: Prentice-Hall, 1956), p. 186. Spiegelberg adds, "The analogies between this ancient pattern and Greek nature philosophy, Chinese pagodas, Muslim mosques, and much of European architecture are striking, and have not yet been historically investigated or explained (note, p. 186).

heavens, and terraces on the base may represent lower paradises.[2] The general theme is a hierarchical pattern of the space-time universe everlastingly the same in all cycles. The soul in the samsara of space-time is born now in one, now in another of the levels represented in the temple-replica, cycle after cycle in the round of mahayugas unless it escapes altogether from the bondage of the space-time cyclical world. The release, the *freedom* from Time and Space is symbolized by the blue flame at the top of the architectural symbol, as Spiegelberg explains above.

All of this outward concrete manifestation of philosophico-religious ideas stems from the esoteric symbolism centered around the sacrificial altar and the sacrifices offered thereon as interpreted and developed by priests in the literature known as the *Brahmanas* (ca. 800-500 B.C.)

Section 4. *The cyclical symbolism of the Fire-altar ritual.*
The altar and sacrifice were in idea like the ziggurat of Mesopotamia and the primeval hill of Egypt powerful bonds between heaven and earth.[3] The altar, built of bricks in the shape of a bird, represents the god, Agni, himself the messenger and priest-god, mediator between the gods and man. He is also god of the element, Fire. The altar is built up in layers, in spatial diagrams to represent the topocosm. Clearly symbolized are the three regions of the cosmos (earth, air, and the heavens as in the Hindu temple); the four quarters of the earth; all life forms; all gods; but most significant of all for this study, the days, the months and the seasons of the year are represented to symbolize a complete creation-cycle of the cosmos.

The altar-building process requires one year to perform; thus the completion signifies the end of one annual cycle and the beginning of another. This in the *pars pro toto* kind of thinking[1] symbolizes the end of one cosmic cycle

---

[2] See Evans-Wentz, *Tibet's Great Yogi Milarepa:* A Biography from the Tibetan, According to the Late Lama Kazi Dawa-Samdup's English Rendering, ed. by W. Y. Evans-Wentz, sec. ed. (London: Oxford University Press, 1951), facing p. 269.

[3] See chapter I.

[1] See chapter I.

and the beginning of the next. The building of the Fire-altar was thought necessary for the annual renewal of the cosmos and of the seasons upon which all life depends for existence. This notion is similar to the Mesopotamian idea of the necessity of the New Year's ritual as an essential aid to the gods in their renewal of the cosmos symbolized by a New Year of the seasonal cycle. In the Fire-altar rites there is the same symbolism and the same organic bond between microcosm and macrocosm; the Fire-altar is a topocosm, a replica in miniature of the space-time universe.

An important background idea in the Fire-altar symbolism is the identification of the god, Agni, in whose birdlike form the fire-altar is built, with the god Prajapati (lord of creatures). Agni is both father and son of Prajapati. As son he, along with the rest of the universe, is created by Prajapati, and as father he "subsequently restores Prajapati by giving up his own body (the fire-altar) to build anew the dismembered Lord of Creatures, and by entering into him with his own fiery spirit,—'whence, while being Prajapati they yet call him Agni.'"[1]

> By offering up his own self in sacrifice, Prajapati becomes dismembered; and all those separated limbs and faculties of his come to form the universe,—all that exists, from the gods and Asuras (the children of Father Prajapati) down to the worm, the blade of grass and the smallest particle of inert matter. It requires a new, and ever new, sacrifice to build the dismembered Lord of Creatures up again, and restore him so as to enable him to offer himself up again and again, and renew the universe, and thus keep up the uninterrupted revolution of time and matter.[2]

Thus, as in Mesopotamia, a New Year is a renewal of creation, symbolic repetition of the original event. This is described in precise detail in the *Brahmanas*. The sacrifi-

---

[1] The *Satapatha Brahmana*, trans. Julius Eggeling, *Sacred Books of the East* (Oxford: Clarendon Press, 1897), Vol. XLIII, Introduction by Julius Eggeling, p. xxi.
[2] *Ibid.*, p. xvii.

cer, himself, it is important to notice, becomes **Prajapati-Agni** by performing this rite and through its performance gains immortality.

Some of the significant steps in building this great fire-altar as set forth in that part of the *Brahmana* called the *Agnikayana* are the following:

1. Construction of the first of the five layers of the altar:

The altar (agni) is constructed in the form of a bird, the body (atman) of which consists of a square ... forty feet ... on each side. The ground of the 'body' having been ploughed, watered, and sown with seeds of all kinds of herbs, a square mound ... is thrown up in the middle of the 'body' and the whole of the latter then made level with it. In the centre of the 'body' thus raised, where the two 'spines'—connecting the middle of each of the four sides of the square with that of the opposite side—meet, the priest puts down a lotus-leaf, and thereon the gold plate (a symbol of the sun) which the Sacrificer wore round his neck during the time of initiation. On this plate he then lays a small gold figure of a man (representing Agni-Prajapati, as well as the Sacrificer himself), so as to lie on his back with the head towards the east; and beside him he places two offering-spoons, one on each side, filled with ghee and sour curds respectively. Upon the man he then places a brick with naturally-formed holes in it, *viz.*, in the centre of the first, third, and fifth layers, supposed to represent the earth, air and sky respectively, and by their holes to allow the Sacrificer (in effigy) to breathe, and ultimately to pass through on his way to the eternal abodes. On this stone he lays down a plant of durva grass ... meant to represent vegetation on earth, and food for the Sacrificer. [Various bricks are then laid in special positions. One of these represents the Sacrificer's consort and must be laid in the proper position to produce fertility. Then south and north of the "consort" brick a live tortoise is placed facing the gold man and also a wooden mortar and pestle.] On the wooden mortar he places the ukha, or the fire-pan, filled with sand and milk; and thereon the heads of the five victims, after chips of gold have been thrust into their mouths, nostrils, eyes, and ears ... He now proceeds to lay down the Pranabhritah, meant to represent the orifices of the vital airs, in five sets of ten bricks each. The first four sets are placed on the four diagonals connecting the centre with the four corners of the body of the altar, beginning from the corner (? or, according to some, optionally from the centre), in the order S.E., N.W., S.W., N.E.; the fifth set being then laid down round the central stone.[1]

Creation and fertility symbols abound here. The lotus leaf represents the matrix or womb from which Agni-Prajapati is born. The fire-pan formed in a shape which signifies the three regions of the cosmos, earth, air and sky (heaven) is the embryo in which Agni has been growing during the year. The gold plate is the sun, nourisher of life, and the gold man the man-in-the-sun (Agni-Prajapati and the Sacrificer are this Man-in-the-Sun) may probably reflect the New Year's human sacrifice of more ancient times practised by primitive peoples almost everywhere. This is indicated in the ancient Vedic literature (Rig-veda X, 90) in the Purusa hymn. In this hymn "the supreme spirit is conceived as *the* Person or Man (Purusa), born in the beginning, and consisting of 'whatsoever hath been and whatsoever shall be,' the creation of the visible and invisible universe is represented as originating from an all-offered sacrifice (yajna) in which the Purusa himself forms the offering-material (havis), or, as one might say, the victim."[2] In the *Brahmanas* Prajapati-Agni takes the place of the Purusa, the world-man whose "periodical sacrifice is nothing else than a microcosmic representation of the ever-proceeding destruction and renewal of all cosmic life and matter."[3] Another creation-symbol seems to be the tortoise and the mortar and pestle placed facing the gold man (sun); for in a favorite old creation myth (perhaps better called a vestigial creation myth), the "Churning of the Ocean of Milk" Vishnu changes into a tortoise to

[1] Ibid., p. 1, footnote.
[2] *Ibid.*, p. xiv.
[3] *Ibid.*, p. xv.

serve as a pivot while the gods and asuras use the holy mountain, Mandara, abode of the gods, as the churning pestle or stick, with the serpent, Ananta (symbolizing eternity), as the cord.[3] (Is this the origin of the sacred cord worn by the twice-born of Hinduism? The twice-born are those eligible to become eternal.) The milk means the waters of chaos which, when churned by the gods, produces the divine cow Surabhi, the celestial Parijata tree, symbol of all the flowers and fruits of earth, the moon (seized immediately by Shiva) and finally the nectar of immortality (*amrta*). Thus the tortoise, mortar and pestle and the firepan filled with sand and milk symbolize that initial creation of the cosmos as given in the myth of the Churning of the Ocean of Milk. This repeats again the notion which is the essence of the entire Fire altar ceremony, since it is the "microcosmic representation of the ever-proceeding destruction and renewal of all cosmic life and matter."[4]

2. Construction of the second layer. As the first layer symbolizes earth, the second layer represents the space, time and creatures characteristic of the earth's surface. Various kinds of bricks are arranged to represent the regions of space—north, south, east and west—and are "laid down at the same time, proceeding again in sunwise fashion (east, south, etc.)"[1] The sun, too, is given a place in this region. The seasons are symbolized by two seasonal bricks which signify the "two summer seasons."[2] The wind or breath is put into the altar in this layer by placing therein the Pranabhrit bricks, for the second layer is the region of the wind (air). Rain is symbolically put into the wind with a prayer "Make the waters swell! Quicken the plants! Bless thou the two-footed! Protect the four-footed! Draw thou rain from the sky!"[3] Finally the animals and man are put into the edifice.

---

[3] E. B. Havell, *op. cit.*, pp. 60-63.
[4] *Op. cit. SBE*, Vol. XLIII, p. xv.
[1] *Ibid.*, *Satapatha-Brahmana*, VIII Kanda, 2 Adhyaya, 1 Brahmana, note by Professor Eggeling, pp. 23-24.
[2] *Ibid.*, p. 29.
[3] *Ibid.*, VIII Kanda, 2 Adhyaya, 3 Brahmana, 6, p. 35.

Time is symbolized in this and all layers of the Fire-altar by the Lokamprina bricks placed in each as well as by the regional and seasonal bricks and the sun. The Lokamprina bricks, in one interpretation, stand for the *muhurtas* or hours of the day. In the entire Fire-altar there are a total of 10,800 of them, the number of hours in the Indian year.[4]

3. Construction of the third layer. This is the layer of air. Bricks are placed symbolizing the four quarters of space, the animals of the air (by which is meant "animals, that dwell on, not in, the earth"),[5] Vayu, the wind-god who is called the "light of the air-world," seasonal bricks —two for the rainy season and two for the autumnal season—which symbolize the year as a whole and generative power; other details are enumerated but are less relevant to our topic. The importance of the time symbolism just mentioned is brought out in the following passage:

> And as to why he places these (four bricks) in this (layer),—this fire-altar is the year, and the year is the same as these worlds, and the middlemost layer is the air (-world) thereof; and the rainy season and autumn are the air (-world) thereof: hence when he places them in this layer), he thereby restores to him (Agni) what (part) of his body these (formed),—this is why he places them in this (layer).
> And, again, as to why he places them in this (layer),—this Agni (the fire-altar) is Prajapati, and Prajapati is the year. Now the middlemost layer is the middle of this (altar), and the rainy season and the autumn are the middle of that (year): hence when he places them in this (layer), he thereby restores to him (Agni-Prajapati) what part of his body, these (formed),—this is why he places them in this (layer).[1]

---

[4] *Ibid.* X Kanda, 4 Adhyaya, 3 Brahmana, p. 360.
[5] *Ibid.*, footnote, p. 46.
[1] *Ibid.*, VIII Kanda, 3 Adhyaya, 2 Brahmana, pp. 49 f.

4. Construction of the fourth layer. The first and second layers symbolized the reconstitution of Agni-Prajapati from his feet to his waist; the third the reconstitution of his waist or "middle"; the fourth layer reconstitutes his body from the waist up to his head.[2] Macrocosmically it represents "what is above the air and below the heavens,"[3] and it is the layer that upholds heaven and earth. It is the Brahman. The priesthood is created in this layer as well as the inspired authors of the Vedas, the Rishis. All the rest of creation is brought forth symbolically again in this layer. The seasonal bricks in this layer represent the two winter months:

> And as to why he places these two (bricks) in this (layer),—this Agni (fire-altar) is the year, and the year is these worlds: what part thereof is above the air, and below the sky, that is this fourth layer, and that is the winter-season thereof; and when he places these two in this (layer), he thereby restores to him (Prajapati-Agni, the year and fire-altar) what part of his body these two constitute.[4]

5. Construction of the fifth layer. This layer is the "head" of Prajapati-Agni. It is the "heaven of peace" of the gods and completes the fire-altar. Symbolically, the sacrificer now, by ascending this structure to and through this fifth layer, enters heaven. Some of the significant features of the symbolism of this region in relation to our theme are apparent in these excerpts:

> The seasonal (bricks) are the same as these seasons: it is the seasons he thereby lays down. And, indeed, the seasonal ones are everything here, for the seasonal ones are the year, and the year is everything here: he thus lays down everything here. And generative power they also are,—for the seasonal ones

---

[2] The idea that the Universe or Macrocosm is in the form of a giant man may have originated with the Jainas, according to Heinrich Zimmer.

[3] *Ibid.*, VIII Kanda, 4 Adhyaya, 1 Brahmana, p. 59.

[4] *Ibid.*, VIII Kanda, 4 Adhyaya, 2 Brahmana, p. 70.

are the year, and the year means generative power: it is generative power he thus lays down (or bestows on Agni and the Sacrificer).[1]

And, again, as to why he lays down seasonal (bricks),—this fire-altar is the year, and it is joined together by means of the seasonal (bricks): he thus makes the year continuous, and joins it together, by means of the seasons.[2]

This fire-altar is the year, and the year is these worlds: the fifth layer of this (altar) is the sky, and the dewy season of this (year) is the sky ...[3]

Let him not derange these (seasonal bricks) lest he should derange the seasons ...[4]

But the seasonal (bricks), indeed, are also these (three) worlds: by the (different) layers he thus builds up these worlds one above the other. And the seasonal (bricks), indeed, are also the nobility: by the (different) layers he thus builds up the nobility above (the peasantry). And the seasonal ones, indeed, are also the year: by the (different) layers he thus builds up the year ...[5]

In these passages there is frequent repetition of the idea that the year of seasons is a complete whole; it is "these worlds" and includes even the class distinctions. The sun, filler of space, is set up as the "light" of heaven, and generator of life as is Agni the "sun" (fire) of the terrestrial layer.

At the end of this process of building the fire-altar Agni is bestrewn with chips of gold which signifies making him (and the Sacrificer) immortal:

With two hundred (chips he bestrews him) each time,—two-footed is the Sacrificer, and Agni is the

[1] *Ibid.*, VIII Kanda, 7 Adhyaya, 1 Brahmana, p. 125.
[2] *Ibid.*
[3] *Ibid.*, p. 127
[4] *Ibid.*, p. 128.
[5] *Ibid.*, p. 129.

> sacrificer: as great as Agni is, as great as is his measure, with so much he thus bestrews upon him immortality, that highest form. Five times (he strews)—five-layered is the altar, five seasons make a year, and Agni is the year: as great as Agni is, as great as is his measure, with so much he thus bestows upon him immortality, that highest form. With a thousand (chips he bestrews him),—a thousand means everything: with everything he thus confers upon him immortality, that highest form.[1]

He scatters the gold chips through all the four regions of space and in a sunwise direction—"this is from left to right (sunwise), for that is (the way) with the gods."[2] Thus the round of the sun, the year, is symbolized as completed with its concrete content, for "this Prajapati, the year, has created all existing things, both what breathes and the breathless, both gods and men."[3]

But the Year (or time-process) is Death as well as life:

> The Year, doubtless, is the same as Death, for he it is who, by means of day and night, destroys the life of mortal beings, and then they die: therefore the Year is the same as Death . . .[4]

Death can be overcome and immortal life obtained by building the fire-altar for this identifies the builder-sacrificer with Agni-Prajapati. Through the symbolic ascension through the three regions of the universe the sacrificer is ready to be deified at the end of "one-hundred years" (which means a complete human life-time) and ready to ascend to the *invisible* world, the world beyond the Year or cosmic time-process.[5] (*Cf.* the similar symbolism of the mandala, chapter VI, below.)

---
[1] *Ibid.*, VIII Kanda, 7 Adhyaya, 4 Brahmana, p. 146 f.
[2] *Ibid.*, p. 147.
[3] *Ibid.*
[4] *Ibid.*, 3 Brahmana, p. 356.
[5] *Ibid.*, Introduction, p. xxiii.

Apart from the Fire-altar symbolism, the significance of the Year is brought out elsewhere in the Satapatha-Brahmana. For example, in a section devoted to the Seasonal Sacrifices we read:

> Verily, imperishable is the righteousness of him that offers the Seasonal sacrifices; for such a one gains the year, and hence there is no cessation for him. He gains it (the year) in three divisions, he conquers it in three divisions. The year means the whole, and the whole is imperishable (without end) . . .[1]

Here again the Year stands for the entire space-time cosmos, the Whole.

The Great Horse Sacrifice and the Year. The Year is also represented by the sacrificial horse of the famous Ashvamedha sacrifice (Great Horse Sacrifice) equivalent in symbolism to the Agni-Prajapati sacrifice. We read in the Brahmana describing the Great Horse Sacrifice [2] that dawn is the head of the sacrificial horse, the sun the eye, wind the breath, Agni Vaisvanara (the fire belonging to all men) the open mouth, the Year is the body of the horse, the sky the back, the air the belly, the four quarters of the earth the flanks, the intermediate quarters the ribs, the seasons the limbs, the months and half-months the joints, the days and nights the feet, the stars the bones, the welkin the flesh, the sand the intestinal food of the horse, the rivers the bowels, the mountains the liver and lungs, the herbs and trees the hair, the rising sun the forepart, the setting sun the hindpart, the lightning the yawning, the thunder the whinnying, the rain the horse's voiding urine, and speech the voice of the horse. The horse carries all classes of important beings: "As Haya (steed) it carries the gods, as Vagin (racer) the Gandharvas, as Arvan (courser) the Asuras, as Ashva (horse) men."[2] Then we are told: "Therefore they

---
[1] *Ibid., SBE*, Vol. XII, *Satapatha Brahmana*, II Kanda, 6 Adhyaya, 3 Brahmana, 1, p. 444.
[2] *Ibid., SBE*, Vol. XLIII, X Kanda, 6 Adhyaya, 4 Brahmana, p. 401.

slaughter the consecrated (victim) as one that, in its nature as Prajapati, represents all the deities. But the Ashvamedha, in truth, is he that shines yonder (the sun), and the year is his body." [3]

Summary. On the whole the Fire-altar symbolism and that of the Ashvamedha are much the same in their cosmic meaning as the Dance of Shiva described above. In all the space-time universe is portrayed in a concrete symbolic form; but in the Fire-altar ritual the symbolism is much more detailed. Space-time is the concrete content in all, the generation of the entire universe of living and non-living things. The purpose of the ritual for the sacrificer in the Fire-altar ritual is not only long life in this world (a life-span of 100 years), but immortality—eternal life—through identification of himself with the Divine, Agni-Prajapati. This identification with and absorption into the Godhead understood at a far more profound and philosophical level becomes true Freedom and the final goal of man in the great yogic philosophies of Hinduism, Buddhism, and Taoism, and in the mystical philosophies of Judaism, Christianity and Islam. These profound philosophies in relation to the meaning and goal of human history will be treated explicitly below. For the present we need to describe the theory of cosmic cycles, everlastingly recurrent, in Buddhist thought.

---

[3] *Ibid.*

Chapter IV

Development of the Cyclical View in
India: Buddhism

Since Buddhism developed within Hinduism, the philosophy of history is similar, a cyclical view. In Buddhaghosa's [1] treatise on Buddhist doctrine called the *Visuddhi-Magga* (Way of Purity) there is a description of the six "high powers" possessed by the Buddhist monk who has arrived at the higher stages in meditation in the progress towards Nirvana. One of these six powers is the ability to recall to mind previous existences as far back as one hundred or "even one thousand world-cycles." [2] However, the eighty great disciples of the Buddha have greater power still and can "call to mind former states of existence for one hundred thousand world-cycles; the two chief disciples, for one immensity and one hundred thousand world-cycles; Private Buddhas, for two immensities and one hundred thousand world-cycles . . . But the Buddhas have their power unlimited." [3]

A world-cycle is an enormous length of time. The Samyutta-Nikaya, xv.5, tells us:

> It is as if, O priest, there were a mountain consisting of a great rock, a league in length, a league in

---

[1] Buddhaghosa lived in the fifth century A. D. and is an authority on Buddhist doctrine.

[2] Henry Clarke Warren, ed., *Buddhism in Translations*, Harvard Oriental Series, Vol. 3 (Cambridge: Harvard University Press, 1922), Visuddhi-Magga xiii, p. 316.

[3] *Ibid.*

width, a league in height, without break, cleft, or hollow, and every hundred years a man were to come and rub it once with a silken garment; that mountain consisting of a great rock, O priest, would more quickly wear away and come to an end than a world-cycle. And many such cycles, O priest, have rolled by, and many hundreds of cycles, and many thousands of cycles, and many hundreds of thousands of cycles. And why do I say so? Because, O priest, this round of existence is without known starting-point, and of beings who course and roll along from birth to birth, blinded by ignorance, and fettered by desire, there is no beginning discernible. Such is the length of time, O priest, during which misery and calamity have endured, and the cemeteries have been replenished; insomuch, O priest, that there is every reason to feel disgust and aversion for all the constituents of being, and to free oneself from them.[1]

The world of time is plainly beginningless and its periodic division, world-cycles, innumerable. A world-cycle takes this pattern: (1) Period of destruction, (2) Period of continuation of the destruction, (3) Period of renovation, (4) Period of continuation of renovation after which follow the destruction periods again, then renovation periods — the entire sequence is endlessly repeated.

If the destruction is by fire (it may be by water or wind) the Destruction takes place in this way: A great cloud appears and much rain falls but when the crops have "grown just large enough for cow-fodder" all rain is cut off. "There comes a time . . . when, for many years, for many hundreds of years, for many thousands of years, for many hundreds of thousands of years, the god does not rain."[2] All living creatures eventually die and are reborn in the Brahma-world. Then a second sun appears in the world so that when one sun sets the other immediately rises. This causes scorching heat. After another long

---

[1] *Ibid.*, footnote, p. 315 f.
[2] *Ibid.*, p. 321.

period a third sun appears and then four more after very long periods —seven suns in all. When the seventh sun makes its appearance,

> "the whole world breaks into flames; and just as this one, so also a hundred thousand times ten million worlds. All the peaks of Mount Sineru, even those which are hundreds of leagues in height, crumble and disappear in the sky. The flames of fire rise up and envelop the Heaven of the Four Great Kings . . . Having thus burnt up three of the Brahma-heavens, they come to a stop on reaching the Heaven of the Radiant Gods." [3]

Thus end the two periods of Destruction. The renovation begins after the lapse of another long interval. Rain begins the Renovation. Water is massed by the wind and begins to descend to a lower level. "As the water descends, the Brahma-heavens reappear in their places, and also the four upper heavens of sensual pleasure." [1] Then it descends to the surface of the earth and life is renewed by peopling the planet with beings who had meanwhile been living in the Heaven of the Radiant Gods which escaped destruction. These beings have now exhausted their merit which enabled them to reside in this heaven; they must now be reborn on earth. They shine like stars by their own light when they come down to earth, but fall to eating ravenously of the sweet earth. This causes them to lose their divine light. The sun and moon then appear to give them light and the stars also. At first these beings live a life of primeval innocence and bliss without greed or lust because grains grow spontaneously and abundantly and because there is no sex as yet nor private property. Then the Fall begins. Because of appetite for certain foods excrements form which necessitate the forming of sex organs. Then all the evils of man begin. The "fever of lust springs up," houses are built for concealment of sexual intercourse, food is

---

[3] *Ibid.*, p. 323.
[1] *Ibid.*, p. 324.

stored by the lazy so that it no longer grows spontaneously. Then men "institute boundary lines, and one steals another's share. After reviling the offender two or three times, the third time they beat him with their fists, with clods of earth, with sticks, etc." Then someone suggests, "What if now we elect some one of us, who shall get angry with him who merits anger, reprove him who merits reproof, and banish him who merits banishment. And we will give him in return a share of our rice."[2] In this way government, or the state, was born.

The Visuddhi-Magga summarizes the entire cycle:
> Now from the cycle-destroying great cloud to the termination of the conflagration constitutes one immensity, and is called the period of destruction. And from the cycle-destroying conflagration to the salutary great rains filling one hundred thousand times ten million worlds is the second immensity, and is called the continuance of destruction. From the salutary great rains to the appearance of the sun and moon is the third immensity, and is called the period of renovation. From the appearing of the sun and moon to the cycle-destroying great cloud is the fourth immensity, and is called the continuance of renovation. These four immensities form one great world-cycle.[1]

When a world-cycle perishes by water the destruction proceeds up to the Heaven of the Completely Lustrous Gods so the repeopling in the renovation era begins with beings from this heaven; when a world-cycle perishes by wind, destruction continues as far as the Heaven of the Richly Rewarded Gods, a still higher heaven, and renovation begins from this realm.

Reasons are given in the Visuddhi-Magga for the particular mode of destruction. The mode is related directly to the particular vice characteristic of the cycle. If the vice

---
[2] *Ibid.*, p. 326.

is predominantly passion the world is destroyed by fire; if hatred, then water destroys all; if infatuation, then wind destroys the world.

Sequences of destruction are described next:

> Now the world, in perishing, perishes seven times in succession by fire, and the eighth time by water; and then again seven times by fire, and the eighth time by water. Thus the world perishes each eighth time by water, until it has perished seven times by water, and then seven more times by fire. Thus have sixty-three world-cycles elapsed. Then the perishing by water is omitted, and wind takes its turn in demolishing the world; and when the Completely Lustrous Gods have reached their full term of existence of sixty-four world cycles, their heaven also is destroyed.[2]

However there are higher heavens which have a longer life-span than sixty-four cycles. The Abhidhammattha-Sangaha (v.2-6, and 10) describes thirty-one "grades of being," but we shall begin with the beings of the Brahma heavens:

> The term of life for the Gods of the Retinue of Brahma is the third part of a world-cycle, for the Priests of Brahma it is half a cycle, for the Great Brahma Gods a whole cycle, for the Gods of Limited Splendor two cycles, for the Gods of Immeasurable Splendor four cycles, for the Radiant Gods eight cycles, for the Gods of Limited Lustre sixteen cycles, for the Gods of Immeasurable Lustre thirty-two cycles, for the Completely Lustrous Gods sixty-four cycles, for the Richly Rewarded Gods and for the Gods without Perception five hundred cycles, for the Aviha Gods a thousand cycles, for the Untroubled Gods two thousand cycles, for the Easily Seen Gods four thousand cycles, for the Easily Seeing Gods eight thousand cycles, and for the Sublime Gods sixteen thousand cycles . . . The length of life of the gods who make their abode in the realm

---
[1] *Ibid.*, p. 327.
[2] *Ibid.*, p. 329.

of the infinity of space is twenty thousand cycles, of the gods who make their abode in the realm of the infinity of consciousness forty thousand cycles, of the gods who make their abode in the realm of nothingness sixty thousand cycles, and of the gods who make their abode in the realm of neither perception nor yet nonperception eighty-four thousand cycles.[1]

Even more staggering in temporal-spatial immensity is the later view of Buddhism (and later Hinduism) that there are innumerable worlds each of which goes through a cosmic cycle similar to that described above. A Tibetan authority on Mahayana Buddhism, Lobsang Phuntsok Lhalungpa, writes:

> The conception of the universe in Tibetan Buddhism is the same as that held in other Buddhist lands . . . The Abhidharma and the Kalachakra tantra agree that the universe is so full of worlds that it is impossible even for a Buddha to enumerate them all. Wherever the universe reaches, there worlds and beings exist . . .
> The duration of one particular world system is equal to one great cosmic period. One cosmic period consists of twenty intermediate cosmic periods. Twenty periods are required for the evolution of a world system, twenty for its duration, twenty for its gradual destruction, and twenty for its annihilation. The twenty cosmic periods of gradual destruction are equal to the time it takes for the length of human life to decrease from eighty thousand years to ten years at the rate of losing one year at the end of every century. The origination and destruction of a world system both start with the lowest world.[2]

All world systems observe the same pattern of evolution and dissolution though not simultaneously; and since the

[1] *Ibid.*, p. 290.
[2] Lobsang Phuntsok Lhalungpa, "Buddhism in Tibet," *The Path of The Buddha*, ed. by Kenneth W. Morgan (New York: Ronald Press, 1956), p. 285 f.

pattern is the same everywhere, man need not feel utterly lost in these immensities.

Buddhism has anticipated contemporary Western views in scientific astronomy, *viz.*, such theories as the immensity of the space-time continuum, of the enormous number of galaxies in the continuum, and the similarity in the evolution-dissolution pattern of a universe (spiral nebulae) within each galaxy. The significance of the cyclic evolution-dissolution pattern of universes in relation to human history is discussed in chapter VII below. In chapter VII it will be seen that human bondage lies in subjective involvement, i.e. ego-involvement, in the cycle which is itself meaningless except insofar as it provides the necessary stimulus towards release from such finite involvement. This release is spiritual freedom, the freedom which sees the Time or Samsara world as one with, or finite manifestation of the Eternal or Nirvana plane of being. It is this spiritual freedom — release from the finite, transient, phenomenal world into the Eternal Being, the Buddha Essence or plane of Nirvana which is the goal of all human existence.

Perhaps in many of its aspects earlier, but in many ways similar to the Buddhist cyclical view of time, is the time-philosophy of the Jainas; it is the cyclical philosophy of history of this group which will occupy us in the following chapter.

Chapter V

Development of the Cyclical View
in India: Jainism

The Wheel is one of the symbols used frequently to stand for a cyclical view of time in Hindu and Buddhist thought. It is the perfect symbol for the Jaina view of time. The Jainas represent time as the Kalacakra or Wheel of Time. Each spoke of the Wheel represents a period in each of two ages called Avasarpini and Utsarpini. A complete revolution of the wheel, which revolves at a constant speed, is the total period of the two ages, Avasarpini and Utsarpini. Unlike the cosmic wheel of Hindu and Buddhist cycles, the Jaina wheel continues its revolution without any period of cessation at the same speed eternally in a continuous succession of Avasarpini and Utsarpini ages. There are no "quiet" periods, no "nights of Brahma." The Wheel moves continuously and forever. Time is the continuously "moving image of eternity" as in Greek thought.

The serpent symbol, according to Heinrich Zimmer, is revealed in the very words used as names of the cycles. The root "sarpin" (which appears in Avasarpini and Utsarpini) means "serpent," and "ava" means "down while "ut" means "up." The image, therefore, is that of the "serpent-cycle of time (the 'world-bounding serpent, biting its own tail),"[1] endlessly "revolving through these alternating 'ascending' and 'descending' periods . . ."[2]

The Jainas believe that there are two ages in each cycle equal in length and alike in pattern except that one is the

[1] Heinrich Zimmer, *op cit.*, n. 44, pp. 224 f.
[2] *Ibid.*

reverse of the other. The Avasarpini era begins with a "best" period and ends with a "worst" period, while the Utsarpini begins with a "worst" and ends with a "best."

The following table quoted from Professor Finnegan's *Archaeology of World Religions* [1] makes clear one complete revolution of the Kalacakra:

AVASARPINI

1. Sushama-sushama, "best" period. [Its length] 4 kotikotis of sagaras
2. Sushama, "good" period . . . 3 kotikotis of sagaras
3. Sushama-duhshama, "good-bad" period, 2 kotikotis of sagaras
4. Duhshama-sushama, "bad-good" period, 1 kotikoti of sagaras less 42,000 years
5. Duhshama, "bad" period, 21,000 years
6. Duhshama-duhshama, "worst" period, 21,000 years

UTSARPINI

1. Duhshama-duhshama, "worst" period, 21,000 years
2. Duhshama, "bad" period, 21,000 years
3. Duhshama-sushama, "bad-good" period, 1 kotikoti of sagaras less 42,000 years
4. Sushama-duhshama, "good-bad" period, 2 kotikotis of sagaras
5. Sushama, "good" period, 3 kotikotis of sagaras
6. Sushama-sushama, "best" period, 4 kotikotis of sagaras

To appreciate the liberal time spans in these periods, the reader needs to know that one kotikoti equals in our number system 100,000,000,000,000; and one sagara equals 100,000,000 palyas. One palya equals "the length of time required to empty a receptacle one yojana (9 miles) wide and deep, which is filled with new lamb's hairs grown with-

---

[1] *Op. cit.*, Finegan, *The Archaeology of World Religions*, pp. 203 f.

in seven days, when one hair is taken out every hundred years." [2] From the point of view of the humans of this period, the length of a complete cycle or revolution of the Wheel of Time is inconceivable and might almost as well be infinite; the humans of the Sushama-sushama period, however, might be able to grasp these gigantic time spans. This is because in Sushama-sushama or the "best" period, there is the god-like life of primeval Eden similar in beatitude to the first quarter of a world cycle in Hindu popular cosmogony. Mrs. Stevenson, who studied Jainism with Jaina scholars early in the twentieth century gives us a picturesque description of this "Eden" epoch which seems to have been a universal belief in the ancient world:

> Avasarpini, the era in which we are now living, began with a period known as *Sushama Sushama*, the happiest time of all . . . when every man's height was six miles, and the number of his ribs two hundred and fifty-six.
> The children born in this happy period were always twins, a boy and a girl, and ten Kalpavriksa (desire-fulfilling trees) supplied all their need; for one tree gave them sweet fruits, another bore leaves that formed pots and pans, the leaves of a third murmured sweet music, a fourth gave bright light even at night, a fifth shed radiance like little lamps, the flowers of a sixth were exquisite in form and scent, the seventh bore food which was perfect both to sight and taste, the leaves of the eighth served as jewelry, the ninth was like a many-storied palace to live in, and the bark of the tenth provided beautiful clothes . . . The parents of the children died as soon as the twins were forty-nine days old, but that did not so much matter, since the children on the fourth day after their birth had been able to eat as much food as was equal to a grain of corn in size, and they never increased the size of this meal, which they ate only every fourth day. The children never committed the sin of killing, for during their whole lives they never saw a cooking vessel or touched cooked food, and on their deaths they passed

---

[2] *Ibid.*, p. 191.

straight to Devaloka, without ever having heard of religion.[1]

The Sushama period is only one-half as blissful as the first. The twins are only four miles in height and live only two palyas of time, parents live longer, and human appetites increase so that a larger meal is necessary.

The third period, Sushama-duhshama, is one in which sorrow appears to mar happiness. The twins are now only two miles in height, live only one palya, but nevertheless go to Devaloka upon death. The first Jaina Tirthankara is born, since sorrow and evil are now entering the picture and men will need a teacher to cope with them. This first Jaina saint (or Tirthankara) called Rishabhadeva "taught the twins seventy-two useful arts, such as cooking, sewing, &c.; for he knew that the desire-fulfilling trees would disappear, and that human beings would then have only themselves to depend on."[3] He taught men also the art of government and established a kingdom. His daughter, Brahmi, the Jaina patroness of learning, invented eighteen alphabets.[4]

The fourth period, Duhshama-sushama, increases in evils. Stature decreases still more, men and women eat more. As an aid to man's salvation the remaining twenty-three tirthankaras are born. Human beings in this era do not all go to Devaloka upon death but some are reborn in hell, heaven, or on earth again as a human being or an animal.[2]

The fifth period, Duhshama, is the present epoch. It is "entirely evil."[5] Length of life is at most one hundred and twenty-five years, and no one can be taller than seven

---

[1] Mrs. Sinclair Stevenson, *The Heart of Jainism* (London, Edinburgh, New York, Toronto, Melbourne, Bombay: Humphrey Milford, Oxford University Press, 1915) p. 273. (Devaloka is one of the heavenly abodes).
[2] *Ibid.*, p. 274.
[3] *Ibid.*, p. 274.
[4] Ibid.
[5] *Ibid.*, p. 275.

cubits. Evil is rampant everywhere. No tirthankara can be born in this period and Jainism itself will disappear in this age.[1]

The sixth period, Duhshama-duhshama, is still more evil, the worst of all the epochs. Man's stature decreases to one cubit and his life span to between sixteen and twenty years. Disease will plague man, his lusts will overwhelm him in an extreme degree so that chastity will be nonexistent. Natural disasters will add to man's misery; for at the end of this era horrible tempests will sweep over the earth. Men and animals will be driven into the ocean, the river Ganges, or into caves for refuge from the incessant storms.[2] After this sixth period has come to an end, the second half of the cycle, Utsarpini, begins. The pattern is much the same as in the Avasarpini epoch. The tirthankaras are identical in form and function, but their jivas (souls) are different since the tirthankaras of the previous age have obtained *moksa* (release from the cycle of births and deaths on the wheel of Time). In Utsarpini the first tirthankara will come in Duhshama-sushama and his name will be *Padmanabha*. This saint-to-come was, in our age, a king of Magadha "and at present he is expiating his bad karma in the first hell."[3] The rest of the tirthankaras will be born in Sushama and similar knowledge is given about their present and future status. Most of them are now in one of the heavens.

Summary of the Jaina cyclical philosophy. The Jaina cycles are repeated everlastingly in form, though not in every detail, since a very few souls win release in each cycle so do not reappear. Their forms (or types) do reappear, however, to aid others in release from the Kalacakra, for the purpose of life is to win such release. Time has no other meaning or value than as an opportunity to escape

---
[1] *Ibid.*
[2] *Ibid.*
[3] *Ibid.*, p. 276.

from it into the eternal. A very compact shorthand symbol [2] expresses this entire philosophy perfectly:

(c) crescent with dot above.
(b) three dots
(a) the swastika

Mrs. Stevenson explains that the ancient symbol (a) the swastika (originally signifying the daily cycle of the sun as explained in chapter III) is used here to symbolize the entire cycle of rebirth in time; it represents the "state in which a jiva may be born as either a denizen of hell, or of heaven, a man, or a beast."[3] The three dots (b) signify the Three Jewels: right knowledge, right faith and right conduct through which the jiva (soul) may reach *moksa* (release from the Kalacakra) symbolized by (c).[4]

The way of release is very difficult. The Digambara sect of this religion recommends starvation so that one will not sin by causing injury to any of the jivas which are in plant and animal life and in liquids such as water.

There are, fortunately for most humans, less ascetic and more glamorous ways of overcoming the Wheel of Time. One of these features the use of diagrams (mandalas) which are replicas of the entire space-time cosmos. The Jaina cosmic diagram (or mandala) symbolizes the realization of the distinction between the matter-world of the Kalacakra — the world of subjective involvement in endless reincarnation — and the eternal world of spirit, the world in which the individual's eternal spirit is released from such bondage. When such self-realization is achieved the saint's karma is close to being exhausted and will be exhausted in this present life-span. There will be no rebirth— the eternal spirit now free forever from the bondage of the temporal or samsara world of the Kalacakra knows itself as it truly is, ever free and immortal — the plane of eternity is now its home forever. To attain such a goal there

[2] *Ibid.*, pp. 251-252.
[3] *Ibid.*
[4] *Ibid.*

must be strict observance of reverence for all life because every living thing has its jiva or soul, and like one's own soul each jiva is a candidate for realization of its eternity; all jivas, from this point of view, are of infinite worth. The Jaina saint of the Digambara, the more extreme sect, therefore enters nirvana—the eternal state free from the bondage of the finite samsara world — by means of a literal starvation. He does not even drink water lest he inadvertently swallow some tiny living creature. (He out-Schweitzers Schweitzer in this extreme reverence for life.)

A point of similarity with Western thought is the goal of man as spiritual freedom. We shall find this a dominant emphasis in the Western one-cycle and culture-cycle ideas of history, and we have already noticed how important a goal this is in Hindu and Buddhist philosophies. At this time we need to elaborate further upon Oriental views of human and cosmic history and the spiritual goal of eternal life and freedom. Our next step will be a presentation of a fascinating diagramatic art form, the Oriental mandala, as an approach to the comprehension of Oriental views of the cycle-pattern in relation to the nature and meaning of human and cosmic history. To anticipate, we shall see that the cycle-pattern time world is an organic part of the total samsaric organism which in its turn is a reflex or thought-created world of the Eternal One.

Chapter VI

CYCLICAL TIME AND THE PHILOSOPHY OF THE MANDALA

The word *mandala* suggests immediately to the uninitiated Westerner a "magic circle," but as one of the great contemporary Buddhist scholars, Bhiksu Sangharakshita, tells us only "uncomprehending observers" think of the *mandala* as a magic circle. Actually it is a symbol of profound significance both in its meaning and in its function. The most general and significant type of *mandala* is in meaning a visual representation in diagram form of the Mahayana Buddhist's philosophy of the total universe; in function its purpose is reintegration of the devotee with this cosmic reality. This practical psychological function of the *mandala* has already been given impressive recognition by one of the greatest Western psychologists, Carl Gustav Jung.

The *mandala* plays a major role in the Tantric form of Mahayana Buddhism prevalent in Tibet, although it is important elsewhere among Mahayana Buddhists. The origin of the Tantric Buddhism of Tibet was India where yoga practices prominent in Tantra were probably very ancient, perhaps as old as the prehistoric Indus Valley culture of 2000 B.C. Tantric Buddhism in India was probably earlier than Tantric Hinduism and gave to the latter a philosophy. This seems to be the opinion of recent Buddhist scholarship which reverses the earlier view that Buddhist

Tantric practices and doctrines were borrowings from Tantric forms of Hinduism.[1]

The Tantric yoga practices of Buddhism in Tibet, as well as those of Hinduism are often misunderstood by Westerners. A good antidote for such misunderstanding has been supplied by Evans-Wentz in the books he has edited on Tibetan Buddhism. The most attractive of these is the biography of the great Tibetan yogi and saint, Milarepa. Milarepa attained the heights of a saintly spiritual life judged by any standards including the Christian. The *mandala* is a graphic representation of this Tantric yogic philosophy followed by such great saints as Milarepa.

The Buddhist mandala is similar in function though not quite the same in meaning as the Hindu Tantric *mandala* called a *yantra*. Since Heinrich Zimmer in *Myths and Symbols in Indian Art and Civilization* provides us with a very lucid account of the design and meaning of a simple Shaivite Tantric *yantra*, we shall begin our presentation of *mandala* symbolism with this example which is called the *Shri Yantra*.[1]

The Shri Yantra has an outside border which is a square with four gateways. Inside the square there are four concentric circular lines, and inside these a circular ring of sixteen lotus petals enclosing another circular ring of eight lotus petals; then within this innermost circle is a symmetrical geometrical pattern of interlocking triangles. There are five cone-shaped triangles pointing upward and five pointing downward all of the same shape and size. In the very center of the intersecting upward and downward pointing triangles is a single tiny triangle pointing downward which has no other intersecting it.

---

[1] See Anagarika Govinda, "Principles of Tantric Buddhism," *2500 Years, of Buddhism*, ed. P. V. Bapat (Delhi: Publications Division, Government of India, 1959). See also the essay by H. V. Guenther, "Mantrayana and Sahajayana," in the same volume.

[1] Heinrich Zimmer, *Myths and Symbols in Indian Art and Civilization* (New York: Pantheon Books, Bollingen Series, VI, 1946), pp. 146-8.

Zimmer's explanation of the yantra makes clear its cosmic meaning. The triangles pointing downward symbolize the *yoni* or female creative energy; the triangles pointing upward symbolize the *lingam* or male creative energy. The five female and five male triangles intersecting and expanding from small to large symbolize the procreation of the phenomenal dynamic world of force, matter and life through the union of opposites, the male and the female energies. The single female triangle in the exact center is very significant. It has a male counterpart which is not represented because it is the Absolute itself, and invisible because the Absolute is beyond the space-time world. The lone central triangle represents the "Primal Shakti" which unites with the invisible Absolute (the impersonal Shiva). This transcendental Shiva is not shown because its essence is, as we said, non-spatial and non-temporal, i.e. its essence is eternity; and in uniting with the Primal Shakti it unites with itself — the two are ever one. The invisible Real, the Core of the spiritual and material cosmos is the Center from which—in interaction with its shakti—emanates the phenomenal world, spiritual (symbolized by the circular regions) and material (symbolized by the square or earth-element region).

To Zimmer's description we might add that it seems probable that the four projections, or gateways, one on each side of the square enclosing the diagram make of this frame a swastika. The swastika, a sun symbol, signifies the *samsara*, i.e., all of the everlasting cycles of earthly time. This same swastika-square is prominent also in practically all Tibetan mandalas, and in all it is one of the symbols of the orderly integration of the entire universe of time and space within the borders of the diagram. The four gateways, apart from their significance as symbols of the space-time universe, are stairways to the upper spiritual planes of the cosmos, the paradises of the gods which are represented by the circles of the *yantra*.

The central point of the diagram, the invisible Absolute

itself, casts out the space-time or *maya* world of subtle spiritual forms and gross bodily forms. These are symbolized by the square and the circular regions; the dynamic energies of the evolution-expansion of the *maya* world are represented by the intersecting triangles (male and female energies—the positive and the negative).

The Tantric devotee who uses such a *yantra* for intense concentration is enabled to realize experimentally his identity with the Center, the Absolute Reality or transcendental Shiva, the Being of being, whose *maya* is the *samsara* world of physical and spiritual finite existences. Both of these worlds, the Absolute and the Relative or *Nirvana* and *Samsara*, are enclosed within the diagram. Therefore in intense concentration upon the yantra, the devotee, the microcosm, reintegrates himself with the macrocosm who is both the Absolute and the Relative worlds.

The Tibetan Buddhist *mandala* is to be understood also as a cosmic diagram and as such is the analogue of the Tantric *yantra* of Hinduism just described. In the Tantric Buddhism of Tibet as in Tantric Hinduism the general significance of the *mandala*-form is the same, viz., the interpenetration of the material and spiritual worlds—of *samsara* and *nirvana* — but with this difference: *samsara* and *nirvana* are symbolized in Buddhist Tantra as Compassion and Wisdom, not the Shiva and Shakti of the Hindu Tantric symbolism of which the *Shri Yantra* is an example. The philosophical basis for the representation of this interpenetration of the material *(samsara)* and spiritual *(nirvana)* worlds is found in three sources [1] which are the following: (1) the teaching of the Yogacara school that all things are manifestations of Absolute Mind; (2) the fundamental tenet of the Madhyamika school that the Absolute Mind in its transcendental form is *Shunyata* (Void); and (3) the central idea of the Avatamsaka Sutra, viz., the idea of the interpenetration of the Transcendental Void

---

[1] Bhikshu Sangharakshita, *A Survey of Buddhism* (Bangalore, India: The Indian Institute of World Culture, 1957), pp. 409 f.

and the *samsara* world (the world of phenomenal objects). In the *Avatamsaka Sutra* the *Gandavyuha* is the significant section which brings out this idea. The theme is the pilgrimage of the young man, Sudhana, towards the goal of entering into the *Dharmadhatu* (the Absolute reality). Sudhana finds that he can attain this goal only by looking within himself. In doing this he realizes that the human mind is the Buddha-mind and that the Buddha, Mind and all existences are one. He learns that each is the All and that the All is in each. A favorite analogy often used to make clear this teaching is that of Indra's net: the god, Indra, has a net made of myriads of individual jewels each of which reflects all the others. This analogy makes plain the basic philosophical teaching of the Avatamsaka that each in knowing truly himself knows the All, for the All — the Unconditioned — penetrates the phenomenal or Conditioned world. In this way Time and Eternity, the Conditioned and the Unconditioned, *Samsara* and *Nirvana* are reconciled.

The peculiarity of the Tantric emphasis falls upon actual living realization of the truths just described. Such realization may be equated with the faculty of Vigour, one of the five Buddhist spiritual faculties (the other four are Faith, Concentration, Mindfulness and Wisdom). It is actually this spiritual faculty of Vigour or experimental realization which prevents Buddhist and other religions from petrifying into empty formalisms. It is this emphasis upon Vigour, practical actual realization of the profound philosophico-religious beliefs just described, that makes it evident as Bhiksu Sangharakshita and other well-known scholars insist, that "it is a serious blunder to represent, or rather misrepresent, the Tantra as a corruption or degeneration of Buddhism, or as being connected with it only by accident, or because of historical circumstances." [1] Tantric Buddhism differs from other schools only in its emphasis upon practice, the faculty of Vigour. The Tantric

---
[1] *Ibid.*, p. 412.

disciple aims to experience directly the transcendental unity and the interpenetration of all things. The idea of interpenetration, so important a theme in the *Avatamsaka Sutra*, is understood as interpenetration of the static and the dynamic elements of the Absolute. The dynamic element, called *Upaya*, is represented as masculine, the word *Upaya* means "device" and signifies the device by means of which sentient beings are saved; this device is Compassion. In this way *Upaya* became equated with Compassion. The quiescent element of the duality is called *Prajna* which means Wisdom. *Prajna* is represented as female. In Tibetan Buddhist iconography the yab-yum representations of deity show these male and female aspects, *Upaya* and *Prajna* in indissoluble union and interpenetration. This plainly and dramatically signifies the unity and interpenetration of the material and spiritual worlds — the worlds of Time and Eternity, of *Samsara* and *Nirvana*.

Bhiksu Sangharakshita describes what he calls the "four main reflections of this 'duality.'" These four are the cosmic, the Buddhological, the individual and the social.[2] The cosmic can be represented most emphatically in the essential teaching of Amoghavajra which forms the basis of Shingon Buddhism. This teaching asserts that the cosmos consists of two fundamental elements, a passive and mental womb-element called *Taizokai (garbha-dhatu* in Sanskrit), and an active and material diamond-element called *Kongokai (vajra-dhatu* in Sanskrit). Each element has its own *mandala*. This type of symbolism seems to be evident in the architecture of *Borobudur* discussed below.

The Buddhological reflection of Wisdom-Compassion is the representation in texts and in iconography of the union and interpenetration of Wisdom and Compassion portrayed as male-female human figures, since the human figure is the most fitting symbol of Enlightenment.

By the social reflection of the "duality" is meant the twin aspects of reality portrayed in the field of human re-

[2] *Ibid.*, pp. 424-426.

lations; this is the act of sexual union. However this union is performed symbolically, not literally (although "fools" may perform it literally [1]), because it is essential in such Tantric yogic techniques that the seminal fluid be retained. The sexual energy, an extremely potent force, is concentrated upon the Divine union and sublimated. This is the view of Bhiksu Sangharakshita and his interpretation is supported by other well-known scholars such as Evans-Wentz and Snellgrove both of whom have made careful studies of Tantric Buddhism. Added evidence is the testimony of the biography of Milarepa, Tibet's greatest yogi-saint.[2] No one could suspect Milarepa of gross sexual practices.

The fourth reflection, the individual, is the microcosmic counterpart of the cosmic reflection. In Buddhist Tantric yoga, as we shall see below in our discussion of the internal *mandala*, *Prajna* and *Upaya* are reflected in the individual as two psychic nerves, one at the left and the other at the right of the central psychic vein called Avadhuti. The union in the central vein, Avadhuti, of the subtle energies of which the left and right veins are the conductors takes place on three planes — the mental, the superconscious, and finally the transcendental.

As an aid in comprehending, directing, channeling and concentrating the psychic energies in their spiritual journey the *mandala* is very important. The external *mandala* is a symbolic pictorial representation of the planes of reality through which the yogin must travel to experience the ultimate goal, the Infinite Light, the Transcendental Absolute without qualities or distinction between subject and object. This ultimate goal is *Shunyata*, Void (Emptiness), the Dharmakaya, of which the superconscious, the mental and the material worlds are reflexes. The internal *man-*

---

[1] David L. Snellgrove, The *Hevajra Tantra*, 2 vols. London Oriental Series, vol. 6. (London: Oxford University Press, 1959), vol. I, pp. 42 f.
[2] W. Y. Evans-Wentz, *Tibet's Great Yogi Milarepa* (London, New York, Toronto: Oxford University Press, 2nd ed., 1951).

dala is the microcosm, the representation of the universe within the yogin's body. We shall describe two examples of the external or macrocosmic form of *mandala* and then the internal form.

Before we begin our description of these *mandalas*, we should point out a significant difference between the meaning of the Tibetan *mandala* and the Hindu Saivite *yantra*. In the example of the *yantra* described above the Impersonal Absolute in its eternal quiescent state, though not shown, hints at being male, since the lone center triangle (its *Shakti*) with which it unites is female. The *Shakti* is the female sexual or creative energy of the male (or male-female) Absolute. In the Tibetan *mandala* the contrary is the case. The eternal or Absolute in its quiescent state is *Prajna* (Wisdom) and is female; whereas the dynamic element *Upaya* (Compassion) which corresponds with *maya-shakti* in the Hindu *yantra*, is male. The Absolute is the union of the two, female *Prajna* and male *Upaya;* the male is absorbed into the female, *Upaya* into *Prajna* or Wisdom and the state reached is called *Shunyata* (Void or Emptiness)— the Unborn, Uncompounded, Uncreated. It is this state, the goal of the spiritual journey of the Buddhist yogin, which is represented in the exact center of every cosmic *mandala*.

Our first example of such a *mandala* is the simplest, but its structure is basic to all *mandalas* of the cosmic type, as we shall see below. This *mandala* is named "The Fivefold Manifestation." (Fig. 1) Like all *mandalas* it is a circle of symbolic forms and may either be marked out upon the ground or produced mentally. The core of this *mandala* represents the Adi-Buddha, Vajrasattva. He represents the Absolute and symbolizes the unity of *Prajna* and *Upaya* from whence emanates the *samsara* world. The purpose of the yogin is realization of the state of Vajrasattva.

Around Vajrasattva in a circle at the Northern, Southern, Eastern and Western points are four Buddhas (called Tathagatas or Jinas) and with each at the intermediate

FIGURE 1

MANDALA

OF

THE FIVEFOLD MANIFESTATION

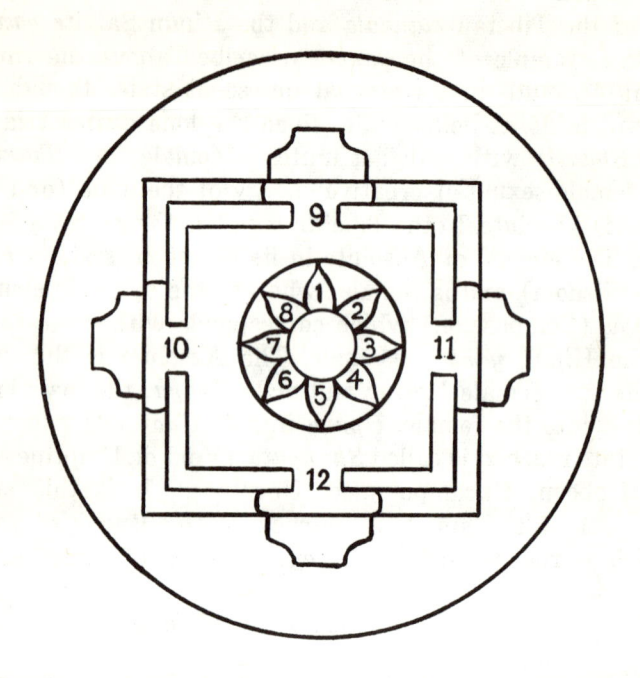

1. Vairochana: Form, East
2. Locana: Earth
3. Ratnasambhava: Feelings, South
4. Mamaki: Water
5. Amitabha: Perception, West
6. Pandaravasini: Fire
7. Amoghasiddhi: Impulses, North
8. Tarini: Air
9, 10, 11, 12: The Four Quarters of Earth
Center: Akshobhya (Vajrasattva), Consciousness

directions of space appears a female partner. Also in the center is the Jina named Akshobhya, the fifth member of the group of Five Jinas. Akshobhya has Vajrasattva marked upon his head which means that he (Akshobhya) the fifth Buddha is himself the essence of Vajrasattva. Vajrasattva is the sixth or Adi-Buddha in whom there is no duality but a perfect *advaita* unity. Akshobhya as Vajrasattva and the other four Buddhas from whom is emanated the space-time universe, or nirmana-kaya, have each a particular skandha, color, psychological quality, sound (consonantal) series and two time elements—one of which is the quarter of the day-cycle and the other the quarter of the year-cycle; these time elements symbolize the eternally recurrent daily, annual and cosmic cycles of time. The skandhas, of which there are five, on the microcosmic scale are the five component parts of every so-called individual. These skandhas are: (1) the body, (2) feelings, (3) perceptions, (4) impulses and emotions, and (5) acts of consciousness. In Buddhist philosophy man can be understood as this "heap" of characteristics; he has no permanent self or individuality. On the macrocosmic level the same five "heaps" or skandhas produce the universe of concrete particulars, i.e., the body of the universe. Then there are five evil psychological qualities and five kinds of knowledge related to each of the Buddhas. The five evil psychological qualities are those which are the source of the *samsara* world of egoistic individualism: wrath, delusion, passion, envy, malignity. Opposing these evil qualities are the five kinds of wisdom which release man from egoistic individualism. These five are: (1) revealed knowledge, (2) mirror-like knowledge, (3) knowledge of sameness, (4) perceptual knowledge, and (5) knowledge of needful activity.

Another major symbol of the samsara world which appears in the *mandala* is the alphabet in its two divisions, the male consonantal series and the female vowel series. Each Jina has his own set of consonants and his female partner her particular vowel series. The significance here is the symbolic inclusion of the entire cosmos of objects.

The complete alphabet is included in the *mandala* in the consonantal and vowel series; therefore all names are included, since all names must be made up of these letters; and names not only signify the objects named, but properly uttered conjure them forth. From this point of view every object in the universe is included.

Vajrasattva, to continue the description of his attributes, is characterized by the evil psychological quality of wrath; the wisdom-quality of revealed knowledge; the skandha of consciousness, the color white, the consonantal series YA RA LA VA. The portion of the annual time-cycle belonging to him is Autumn, of the day-cycle the second half of the night—from midnight to dawn. His symbols are the Vajra (symbol of *Upaya* or Compassion) and the Ghanta (bell) symbol of Void (*Prajna*). He is absolute mind.

The Buddha of the Eastern quarter in this mandala is Vairocana.[1] His skandha is "form"; his evil psychological quality is delusion; his wisdom is the mirror-like knowledge; his color white; his quarter of the annual time-cycle Winter, and of the day-cycle the morning-watch; his consonantal series is the "KA series."

The Buddha of the Southern quarter is Ratnasambhava. His skandha is "feeling," and his psychological quality malignity; his wisdom is the knowledge of Sameness; his quarter of the annual cycle is spring and of the day-cycle the "third watch"; his consonantal series is the "TA series."

Amitabha is the Buddha of the Western quarter. He is red in color; his skandha is perception; his evil quality, passion; his wisdom is Perceptual knowledge; his consonantal series is the "TA series" also; his quarter of the annual cycle, summer; of the day-cycle, the evening watch.

The Buddha of the Northern quarter is Amoghasiddhi. In color he is dark green and he is shown with a crossed

---

[1] Edward Conze *et al* editors, *Buddhist Texts Through the Ages* (New York: Philosophical Library, 1954), "Note on the *Mandala*," and translation of text of "The Fivefold Manifestation" by D. Snellgrove, pp. 246-252. This translated text from the *Advayavajrasamgraha* is the authority for the above description of the "Fivefold Manifestation" mandala.

vajra as his spiritual symbol. His skandha is "impulses" and his evil quality envy; his wisdom is knowledge of Needful Activity; his consonantal series is the "PA series"; his quarter of the annual cycle is the "rainy season" and of the day-cycle the "first watch of the night."

The intermediate directions of space are symbolized by four goddesses: Locana, Mamaki, Pandaravasini, and Tarini. Each goddess represents one of the four elements—earth, water, fire, and air respectively; each has her vowel series so that the complete vowel series is included; each has her evil of the *samsara* world—delusion, wrath, passion and envy respectively. Each is the female partner of one of the four Jinas; the center Buddha Vajrasattva has Nayika as his female partner. Nayika is essentially the personification of Void (*Sunyata*). She is described as possessing "the true nature of Vajrasattva and is Queen of the Vajra-realm. She is known as the Lady, as Suchness, as Void, as Perfection of Wisdom (Prajnaparamita), as limit of Reality, as Absence of Self."[1]

A cosmic diagram of this kind is considered a truer picture of reality than that perceived in ordinary everyday human experience.[2] This is because the diagram shows the true nature of the spiritual and material worlds. In concentration upon such a *mandala*, the yogin is enabled to see reality as a whole, as the cycle of emanation-and-return of the Absolute, the *Dharmadhatu*. The yogin's aim is to return to this Absolute—this Unborn, Unoriginated Source of Being—source of all that exists in the *maya* world of emanation. The yogin's return is achieved through identification with the Adi-Buddha, Vajrasattva. When he attains this actual experience of identity, it is experience of *Shunyata*, the Void. The world of plurality, after this experience, is seen in a new light as the reflection or emanation of the distinctionless unity of the Absolute. Ego-consciousness is extinguished; the distinction between self and others is

---

[1] *Ibid.*, p. 252.
[2] Snellgrove, *op. cit.*, *The Hevajra Tantra*, vol. I, Introduction, p. 33, n. 3.

87

seen to be illusion; the reintegration of the yogin with the universe of reality has been accomplished.

Another example of a *mandala*, more detailed in its macrocosmic symbolism, is the *Demchog Mandala* of the *Demchog Tantra*. This *mandala* is of special interest and importance since it was used by Milarepa and the Kargyutpa Lamaist sect to which he belonged.

Before imagining the mandala or drawing it upon the ground, the yogin begins his meditation by calling upon Demchog (a wrathful manifestation of Akshobhya). The name *Demchog* means and signifies "supreme bliss" and refers to the bliss of the unitive state. After calling upon Demchog the yogin next dedicates all his good wishes and merits to the aid of all sentient beings in their struggle for non-attachment and release. Then he proceeds to purify and transmute the material elements of the cosmos as well as the sense organs and their functions by imagining them all as deities. The basic deities from whence these phenomena emanate are the five Jinas whose nature and functions have already been described in the Fivefold Manifestation Mandala. The yogin is now ready to visualize and meditate upon the Demchog Mandala.

The *Demchog Mandala* is typical of the *mandala* genre in being a symbolic replica of the universe of reality. As such a replica it has as its core Mt. Meru the traditional center of the universe. On the top of Mt. Meru a four-sided *Vihara*[1] with four entrances is represented. The *Vihara* has four tiers at the base, then a fourfold central wheel surmounted by a dome. Outside the *Vihara* are eight Great Cremation Grounds of the dead. The plan of this core of the *Demchog Mandala* conforms to the essential idea of the *mandala;* for, as Professor Snellgrove tells us, "The essential feature of a *mandala* is its regularity towards the various directions, for the first thing it must express is emanation from a centre into space."[2] The man-

---

[1] According to Buddhist and Hindu mythology Mt. Meru is the core or spinal column of the universe with lower heavens on its upper parts and higher heavens above its top.

[2] *Op. cit.*, p. 31.

dala itself represents the center of the universe; therefore Mt. Meru, the traditional center of the universe is appropriate as the center of this *mandala*. The *stupa* symbolism of the *Vihara* is very significant also and is probably the key to an understanding of great architectural works such as *Borobudur*. The four entrances to the Vihara signify the four main directions of space emanating from the center (Mt. Meru). Professor Snellgrove's view of the symbolism just described and its relation to *stupa* symbolism is made clear in the following passage from his Introduction to his translation of the *Hevajra Tantra:*

> The *mandala*, the primary function of which is to express the truth of emanation and return (*samsara* and *nirvana*), is the center of the universe. Hence it involves all previous tradition associated with this idea. Its core is Mt. Meru; it is the palace of the universal monarch, it is the royal *stupa;* it is even the fire-altar where one makes the sacrifice of oneself. This last idea finds expression in the figurative interpretation given to the rite of slaying (*marana*). It seems that all these notions were perhaps involved in the Buddhist *stupa* itself; . . . it is as a *stupa* that the *mandala* is primarily envisaged." [3]

Inside the *Vihara* with its stupa symbolism and in the central circle of the *mandala* is the God-head, Demchog. The yogin begins his meditation with thinking of himself as this deity, and eight lotus petals spring from him. As Demchog the yogin thinks of himself with four faces which symbolize such things as the four purified elements (earth, fire, air and water); the four Boundless Wishes (compassion, affection, love, impartiality); and the four Acts (the

---

[3] *Ibid.*, p. 32, n. 4. *Borobudur* as an architectural *mandala* is discussed below. The omitted part of Snellgrove's quotation is a reference to Paul Mus' study of *Borobudur* which defends this interpretation.

[1] Arthur Avalon (Sir John Woodroffe), *Tantrik Texts*, Vol. VII, *Shrichakrasambhara Tantra*, a Buddhist Tantra (the Buddhist Demchog Tantra), ed. Kazi Dawa-Samdup (London: Luzac & Co.; Calcutta: Thacker, Spink & Co., 1919). The description of the *Demchog Mandala* is taken from this work.

Peaceful, the Grand Upholding, the Fascinating and Producing, and the Fierce, Stern and Destructive.) The yogin's Demchog-body is blue to show the changeless condition of his knowledge. Each of his four faces has three eyes as symbols of the Three Times: Past, Present, Future; this means all the cycles of time and omniscience. As omniscient he has all the three worlds (*lokas*) under his vision: the six Kamalokas or sensuous worlds; the seventeen Bramalokas or form-worlds without sensuous craving; and the four Arupalokas or formless spiritual worlds. He has twelve hands which signify knowledge of the process of dependent causation, i.e., the process of Involution and Evolution of the Twelve Nidanas or twelve-fold chain of karma-causation.[2] He holds the *Vajra* (*Dorje*) as the symbol of Compassion and the *Ghanta* (bell) as symbol of the Void (*Shunyata*). To show the supreme state of Compassion-and-Wisdom-in-union his uppermost two hands embrace his female partner. There are also many other symbols held in other hands to show that pride and all sins of the *samsara* world are cut off, to show that ignorance is overcome, and that supreme knowledge is attained.

This supreme knowledge symbolized primarily in the union of Demchog as Compassion with his female partner, Vajra-yogini as Wisdom, is described as follows by the learned scholar Lama Kazi Dawa-Samdup in his Introduction to the *Demchog Tantra:*

> *Sunyata* is an inexpressible mystery in and behind the incessant flow of the stream of seeming, which can be described by no term borrowed from the world of appearance, for none of these terms has a meaning except in relation to its opposite. Thus "one" is an idea belonging to the world of numbers; freedom and permanence are only understood with reference to the phenomena of dependence and change. The Advaita

---

[2] This chain of twelve is: Ignorance, "aggregates" or personality, consciousness, the five skandhas, the six sense organs, contact, feeling, craving, grasping, becoming, birth, and finally old age, disease, and death.

Buddhist Tantra is thus the doctrine of *Sunyata*. This means that the universe and Nirvana are not two but one or *Sunyata,* just as mind and body in any individual are aspects of one unity.[1]

This statement of the nature of the supreme knowledge is fundamentally the doctrine of the Madhyamika school. In the *mandala* the center circle has the attainment of this knowledge (*Shunyata*) as the theme. Demchog in this circle is in indissoluble union with *Prajna* (Vajra-yogini) and this is realization of *Shunyata.*

The second circle from the center in the *mandala* is the circle of Great Bliss (*Mahasukha*), a unitive state of Joy which does not quite attain the absolutely *advaita,* nonconscious state of *Shunyata.*

The third circle from the center is the realm of Mind. The circle of Mind has eight lotus petals and in each is a female deity. It is blue and is in the sky. Its deities purify the spaces above the surface of the earth. Its *mandala* circle is protected by a fence of Vajras and a ceiling of Vajras. This Vajra-mandala "constitutes the very self of the incomprehensible secret of the Mind,"[2] i.e., the mind's creative powers.

The next of the concentric circles, which is the fourth from the center, is the *mandala* of Speech. This is red with eight lotus petals and a deity in each. From Speech is materialized the next or fifth circle the *mandala* of the Body. This too is represented as an eight-petalled lotus with a deity in each petal. Beyond this circle are ten female deities called "keepers of the doors." There are eight for each of the compass points plus two others which occupy the zenith and nadir. In addition the yogin summons innumerable other spirits particularly the powerful ones of the four cardinal points who are the guardian-kings of the world-system. Outside all there is a fence of "divine flames" surrounding the *mandala.*

---

[1] Arthur Avalon, *Tantrik Texts,* Vol. VII, *op. cit.,* p. xxxiii.
[2] *Ibid.,* p. 31.

The total universe of reality is in this way diagramed for the yogin's meditation. In the *Demchog Tantra* the *mandala* symbolism is interpreted at the metaphysical level as a representation of the three bodies of the Buddha. This is a further aid in the reintegration of the yogin with the Absolute state of realization. The *Nirmanakaya* is signified by the outer *Mandala* of the Body and by the guardian deities of the faith (the yogin's faith personified). The apparent-truth aspect of the entire world of objects is included in the *Nirmanakaya*. The *mandalas* of Speech and Mind and the Mahasukha *mandala* (the united aspect of Wisdom and Compassion in embrace) constitute the *Sambhogakaya*. The core-circle of the *mandala* which represents the final stage of perfection and the real truth of the nature of *samsara, nirvana* and the union of the two (*Shunyata*) is the *Dharmakaya*.

The next step the yogin must take is identification of himself as microcosm with the macrocosm represented in the *mandala* so that he can attain the final goal of realization of *Shunyata*. The method is one of internal reintegration. It is a process in which an internal *mandala* [1] as the microcosmic symbol of the macrocosmic reality is perceived within the yogin's body. The basis for identification of the microcosmic or internal *mandala* with the macrocosmic *mandala*-diagram of reality lies in the theory of the Three Bodies of a Buddha (*nirmanakaya, sambhogakaya* and *dharmakaya*) plus a fourth called the Self-Existent Body or Body of Great Bliss. Each body is identified with a *cakra* (radiating circle) of lotus petals of a certain definite number within the body. The *cakra* in the Head is identified with the Self-Existent Body; the *cakra* in the Throat with the *sambhogakaya;* the *cakra* in the Heart with the *dharmakaya;* and the *cakra* in the Navel with the *nirmanakaya*. In

---

[1] This account of the internal *mandala* and its philosophical and psychological significance is based upon Professor Snellgrove's description and interpretation in Vol. I of the *Hevajra Tantra, op. cit.,* pp. 35-39.

this way the total macrocosmic universe is a microcosm within the yogin's body.

The Five Buddhas of the Fivefold Manifestation Mandala described above from whom emanate the phenomenal world are in the Heart *cakra* with Akshobhya in the center as in the Fivefold Manifestation Mandala. The process which occurs in relation to the *cakras*—and this is the process of realization of *Shunyata*—is a psychic circulatory one carried on by three main "veins" called *Lalana, Rasana* and *Avadhuti*. *Lalana* is to the left of the central nerve-channel which is called *Avadhuti,* and *Rasana* is to the right. *Lalana* and *Rasana* correspond with Wisdom and Means in their separate condition; this symbolizes the *samsara* world. *Avadhuti* is the union of Wisdom and Means. By practising breath control the yogin is able to accomplish the union of Wisdom and Means in *Avadhuti*. He accomplishes this in the following way. The *bodhicitta* ("thought of enlightenment" and physiologically the seminal fluid) resides at the base of the genitals where all three of the psychic veins come together. Here the *bodhicitta* is in the relative condition; but at the top of the head (the Head *cakra*) it is in the absolute condition. Through strict breath control the yogin forces the two psychic veins to merge together in the central channel, *Avadhuti*. Here the *bodhicitta* is aroused by the merging of *Lalana* (Wisdom) and *Rasana* (Means). The contact of the two is Fire personified as the goddess, Candali. Candali burns. Her seed-syllable is the syllable A; she is identified also with the female partner of the central deity of the cosmic *mandala,* or may also be called *Avadhuti* or any name that signifies the bliss of the union of Wisdom and Means. She is then experienced as moving upwards, her blaze consuming all as she passes through the *cakras* from the navel to the heart and to the throat. Finally she enters the Head *cakra*. The *bodhicitta* in the head is given the mantra or syllable HAM. The HAM (called also the Moon) melts when *Avadhuti* (or Candali) enters. When it melts it flows downward pervading the entire body as it enters each of the cakras. Finally it reaches the lowest cakra of the seed-syllable A (Candali or Wisdom, the female partner) and A and HAM become AHAM. AHAM equals "I" and signifies the reintegrated self,[1] the *dharmadhatu* or Absolute state. This ends the account of the reintegration process as described in the *Hevajra Tantra*. The *Demchog Tantra* in which there is a similar reintegration process goes a step further and dissolves the syllable name into the Bindu, the center dot (a metaphysical point) in the *mandala* which stands for Absolute Being. "Then finally even the Bindu itself gradually becomes fainter and fainter until it fades away and disappears altogether; a process which is likened to salt dissolving in water."[2] The absolutely non-dual (*advaita*) state is experienced—the Unborn, the Unoriginated, the Uncompounded, *Shunyata*—ineffable, indescribable because beyond subject-object categories of the relative, phenomenal world. The philosophical goal has been attained in direct experience. The yogin can now say, "I had heard of thee by the hearing of the ear, but now my eye seeth thee."[3] He has experienced the philosophy which, until now, was a merely theoretical metaphysics. He has himself experienced in his own mind the nature of the cycle, ever recurrent, of emanation and reabsorption of the universe. In actual identification with this process he has, himself, as the central Absolute Buddha emanated from himself in meditative vision the five Tathagatas (or Jinas) each of whom personifies a particular wisdom and particular vice; and from the Five Jinas proceeds the phenomenal world. The *Demchog Mandala* shows the degrees of emanation from the central absolute *Dharmakaya*, through the *Sambhogakaya*—the world of subtle bodies—to the Nirmanakaya world, the world of gross bodies.[4] The deities beginning with the Five Jinas are perceived as vision-creations of the yogin's mind, but are none the less real because of their dream-world

---

[1] *Ibid.*, p. 37.
[2] Arthur Avalon, *Tantrik Texts*, Vol. VII, *op. cit.*, p. 55.
[3] *Book of Job*, 42:45.
[4] The subtle body is defined in the following chapter. The gross body is the fleshly body.

status. The Yogacara element in the metaphysics at the basis of the system affirms that the mind is the ultimately Real as in Western idealism; the phenomenal world of bodies, space, and time is the thought creation by emanation of the absolute mind. The Madhyamika ingredient of the metaphysics tells the yogin that the Absolute is strictly non-dual (*advaita*) in nature and beyond the categories of *samsara* and *nirvana* each of which has meaning only in relation to the other. The thought created world of the yogin therefore has only relative reality, a truth experienced when the yogin reabsorbs the mandala circles of phenomenal reality into himself and returns to the Center, the Absolute characterized by its non-duality.

The idea of the *mandala* is not only of great functional value in reintegrating the human personality and in clarifying philosophical concepts of the relation between time and eternity, but it has also been an inspiration for great art. *Mandalas* are painted in beautiful designs and colors on cotton and silken banners in Tibet; but even more impressive is the *mandala*-idea embodied in architecture. First of all we should point out the similarity between the symbolism of the Vedic Fire-Altar and the *mandala;* then the relationship between the Fire-Altar and the Buddhist *stupa* as architectural *mandalas.*

Historical background of the mandala-idea in architecture. The Vedic Fire-Altar we saw above (chapter III) has as its function the transformation of the devotee from a mortal-temporal plane to an immortal-eternal plane of being. Death is overcome by building the Fire-Altar the main purpose of which is identification of the builder-sacrificer with Agni-Prajapati, the Golden Purusa. The sacrificer through this identification or self-transformation makes the symbolic ascension through the three regions of the universe to the eternal *invisible* world, the world beyond the Year or cosmic time-process. This symbolism resembles that of the *mandala* with its three main regions (nirmanakaya, sambhogakaya, dharmakaya) progress through which leads to the experience at the Center of Eternity—

the ineffable state beyond the space-time universe. Dr. Kramrisch adds to our account of the meaning of the Fire-Altar an additional idea significant in understanding the bridge between this structure and Buddhist and Hindu temples. This is the function and meaning of the shaft in the Fire-Altar. Dr. Kramrisch explains:

> The shaft carried the 'breath' of the golden man beyond time; its highest ring-stone was placed above the top layer of the altar. The shaft was more imaginary than real, the perforated stones being laid between alternate courses of bricks. Similarly, at a later period, this more-imaginary-than-real internal shaft in the centre of the monument was enclosed by the walls of the temple and the pile of its towering superstructure. Above its sheath rose the uppermost section of the pillar . . . clasped by the ring-stone called 'stainless.' The *Amalaka,* the 'stainless,' represents the door of the sun and is pierced by the shaft . . . In the temples of Southern India, the shaft traverses a dome-shape, whose overvault signifies heaven . . . Beyond the *Amalaka* or dome, and above the high terrace of the mountain-like mass of the temple, gleams the finial, the highest point of which is co-axial with the inner imaginary pillar, which strikes the ground in the centre of the small cavity of the innermost sanctuary of the temple.[1]

It is this 'pillar' which is the central theme of the structure Dr. Kramrisch tells us; for it carries the transformed self through the planes of the cosmos to the Eternal, the Absolute plane. This symbolism holds for the Buddhist *stupa* as well as for the Hindu temple.

The Buddhist sacred building, the *stupa,* began when the great emperor, Asoka, started the practice of building a monument over a relic of the Buddha. This *stupa* was built in the same style as the royal sepulchers and signified that the Buddha was a world-ruler (*cakravartin*). The *stupa,* like the *mandala,* is a cosmic diagram; it is ani-

---
[1] *Stella Kramrisch, The Art of India* (London; The Phaidon Press, 1954), p. 19.

mated by a relic of the Buddha just as the more ancient Vedic Fire-Altar mentioned above was animated by the Golden Purusa (Prajapati). First, the orientation of the *stupa* was determined by elaborate geomantic ceremonies so that at the north, south, east and west square-shaped arms would project from the ground-plan of the structure as in the *Great Stupa* at Sanchi. These square-shaped arms are conspicuous in most *mandalas*. See the Fivefold manifestation diagram in this chapter. In the mandala diagram and in the *Great Stupa* the square shape with the arms at the Four Quarters is a swastika-form and symbolizes the course of the sun through the heavens.[1] The sun symbolism is made even more evident by the fact that circumambulation of the *stupa* is a ritual practice and is always performed in a clockwise direction, the direction of the course of the sun through the heavens.[2] The functional value of the circumambulation is identification of oneself with the total content within the circle, i.e., the cosmos in diagram form.

Professor Rowland informs us in his description of the Sanchi *stupa* that the building itself is a dome-shaped structure which simulates the dome of heaven enclosing the world-mountain, Mt. Meru. In the *Demchog Mandala* Mt. Meru is also the world-mountain, core of the universe. At the top of the Sanchi *stupa* is a balcony-like part which symbolizes the heaven of the Thirty-three gods which is traditionally located at the top of Mt. Meru (the highest peak of the Himalayas). Extending upward from the center is a mast or *yasti*, symbol of the world axis which has its source in the infra-cosmic waters and reaches through Mt. Meru up through all the celestial heavens. Beyond the heaven of the Thirty-three are three umbrellas on the mast which symbolize the heavens beyond that of the Thirty-three. These heavens culminate in the Brahma-heaven.[3] Dr.

---
[1] Rowland, *Art and Architecture of India, op. cit.*, p. 52.
[2] *Ibid.*
[3] *Ibid.*

Kramrisch illuminates further the meaning of the mast; it is the shaft which soars through the worlds of form and the formless worlds into the eternal realm beyond all worlds — the plane of the Absolute. The *mandala* symbolism is evident here again; the shaft leads into the Bindu or *Dharmadhatu*.

We described in a previous chapter (chapter III above) the symbols of the elements in *stupa* structure — earth, air, fire, water and ether are all represented. To summarize, the *stupa*-symbolism, like the mandala,[1] includes all space and time both earthly and celestial and points upward in its suggestiveness to the spaceless, timeless eternal Absolute which transcends all. All space is symbolized by the four quarters of the earth, the dome of heaven, the heavens beyond, and the axis or shaft of the universe which is the carrier of the devotee through and out of the spacetime world into eternity. All time is included in the swastika-symbol; this is cyclical time represented on the microcosmic scale by the everlasting course of the sun which sees all — present, past, and future; cyclic time is represented also in the spatial hierarchical levels of the structure symbolic of all the realms of the *samsara*, from earth through all the heavens. The total universe is here neatly tied into a very compact symbolic form which gives man a feeling of reintegration with it, therefore a sense of power over it, and of freedom and at-homeness in it.

A recent example of a similar construction of a cosmos in miniature in symbolic form is illustrated as late as the nineteenth century in one of the investiture ceremonies of King Chulalongkorn of Siam.[2] An artificial mountain was constructed to simulate Mt. Meru, the axis of the universe in the Himalayas; on each of the four sides of this mountain there were four animals—a lion, an elephant, a bull,

---

[1] See the quotation from Snellgrove's *Hevajra Tantra* above in this chapter, which asserts that the *mandala* itself is derived from the *stupa* since it is "as a *stupa* that the *mandala* is primarily envisaged."

[2] Rowland, *op. cit.*, pp. 44 f.

and a horse.[3] These animals symbolize the four quarters of the world and during the investiture ceremony the Prince received a baptism from each one. The gushing waters from each animal represented the four rivers of the world. The Prince circumambulated the structure as a replica of the universe in microcosm in order to integrate himself with and thus have power over the universe in macrocosm. Professor Rowland calls this an illustration of the principle of *pratibimba* which he defines as: "The reconstruction in architecture or sculpture of the imagined structure of supernatural things or regions, in order that men may have access to them or power over them through an imminent symbol."[1] But, as we have already said for Buddhist thinkers the symbolic world structure is neither imagined nor supernatural, it is a truer replica of the "real" universe than sense impressions can give us; but this structure and the deities from whom it emanates are also unreal — figments of the mind.[2]

The principle of *pratibimba*, if we wish to borrow the term, is illustrated on a magnificent scale and raised to the highest philosophical level in one of the most famous of all Buddhist structures, *Borobudur*, in Java. *Borobudur* is one of the greatest works of religious art in all Asia.

Borobudur: Cosmic mandala in stone. Borobudur is a temple building which is a complete *mandala* in stone in-

---
[3] *Ibid.* The symbolism of the four animals is at least as old as the *Sarnath Pillar* of Asoka's time (third century B. C.).

[1] *Ibid.*, p. 45.

[2] See also the *Bardo Thodol*. The Lama Anagarika Govinda in his Introduction to the translation of this work on the after death state says: "As the *Bardo Thodol* text makes very clear by repeated assertions, none of all these deities or spiritual beings has any real individual existence any more than have human beings . . . They are merely the consciousness-content visualized, by *karmic* agency, as apparitional appearances in the Intermediate State—airy nothings woven into dreams.

The complete recognition of this psychology by the deceased sets him free into reality. Therefore is it that the Bardo Thödol, as the name implies, is The Great Liberation by Hearing and by Seeing." (See *The Tibetan Book of the Dead*, ed. W. Y. Evans-Wentz, trans. Lama Kazi Dawa-Samdup. London: Oxford University Press, 1957.

BOROBUDUR: VERTICAL CROSS-SECTION
Figure 2

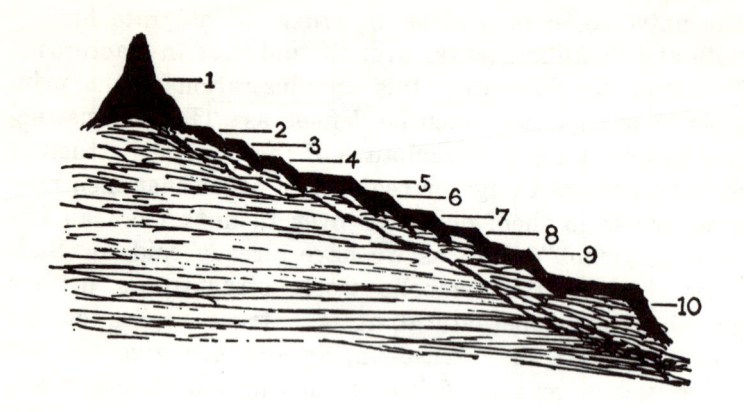

Explanation:

1. Central stupa
2, 3, 4. Three round terraces, mandala of the spiritual world (72 Dhyani Buddhas)
5, 6, 7, 8, 9. Five square (or pyramidal) terraces
5. Transitional terrace
10. Basement

FIGURE 8

BOROBUDUR: GROUND-PLAN

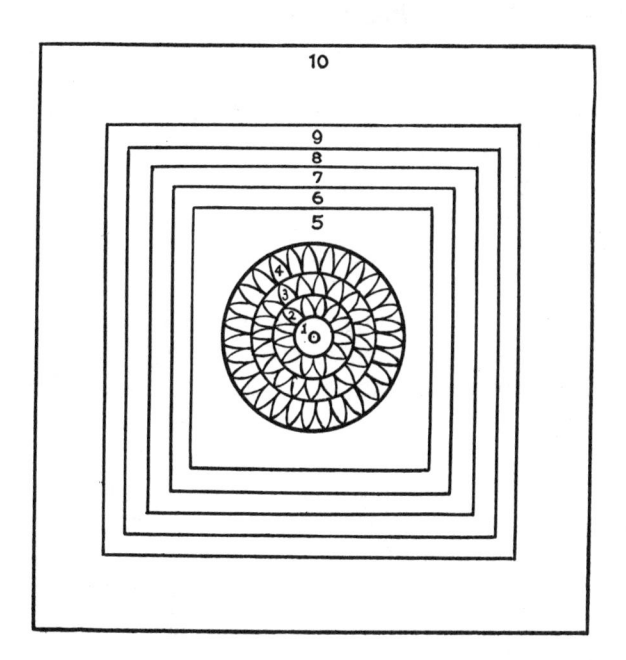

Explanation:

1. Small center circle with dot: Central stupa Akshobya (Vajrasattva)

2, 3, 4. Three round terraces: Mandala of the spiritual world. Each petal represents a Dhyani Buddha enclosed within a lattice-work stupa. There are 72 altogether.

5, 6, 7, 8, 9. Five square terraces: Mandala of the material world. Fifth terrace is transitional to the spiritual world.

10. Basement and enclosing terrace.

101

corporating "the complete world and its order, the succession of points visited by the sun in its round, the cycle of time materialized in space constituting the Law of the Buddha rendered visible in the geographic, political, and spiritual centre of the realm."[3] Figures 2 and 3 are simple diagrams of the ground plan and of a vertical cross-section respectively which will be of use in comprehending the meaning of this great cosmic *mandala* in stone.

Beginning at the bottom of the monument there is (1) a basement, now concealed, the reliefs of which represent scenes from the hells and the world of men; scenes from the heavens appear, also. The general theme is the world of karma, the world of bondage to desire which results in the endless round of birth and death in the hells, on earth, or in the heavenly paradises in accordance with the laws of karma. (2) The first gallery has for its main subject the story of Buddha who releases men from bondage to desire and thus from karma. (3) The second gallery portrays Buddha as a Bodhisattva in the Tusita heaven preparing himself for his task of saving men. (4) The third gallery (and part of the second) show reliefs describing Sudhana's search for enlightenment. He consults Maitreya, the Buddha of the future, who directs him to Samantabhadra. Samantabhadra directs him away from the temporal material worlds to the timeless eternal realm of the Jinas and Bodhisattvas; this is the theme of (5) in the series and is the fourth gallery. (6) The fifth gallery is transitional to these upper ethereal realms designed in three rising concentric circles and containing altogether seventy-two buddhas.[1]

Significantly, the relief sculpture of the basement and first gallery is done in realistic style, but the realism decreases until at the fourth level, the style becomes formal,

---

[3] Rowland, *op. cit.*, pp. 266f.

[1] *Ibid.* See also Heinrich Zimmer, *The Art of Indian Asia*, 2 vols. (New York: Pantheon Books published for Bollingen Foundation 1955), Vol. I, pp. 298-312.

and at the fifth level the style is still more abstract and static. This is because the fifth level is transitional to the circular terraces which have the same symbolic meaning as the circular regions of the *mandala* diagram, *viz.*, the *Sambhogakaya* and *Dharmakaya* "bodies" of the Buddha; and in the diagram and in *Borobudur* the square regions are the earth-regions or regions where karma and bondage to desire prevail. The circular terraces are three. These three circular terraces surround a central core which towers above them and points upward into the Void (see figure 2). In form it looks like a *stupa* within the structure; it symbolizes without much doubt the goal of human life for Mahayana Buddhists: the unitive state of Emptiness (*Shunyata*), of Absolute Mind where subject and object, *samsara* and *nirvana* are the same. It is a meaning analagous to the "mast" or "shaft" in Hindu architecture explained above in this chapter.

Further interpretation of the entire structure makes it evident that the basement and the square terraces probably symbolize two of the "three planes of existence" in Buddhist thought: (1) the *Kamaloka* or plane of enjoyment of the five senses, the world of sense experience; on this plane are the hells, the world of men, the realm of hungry ghosts, the realm of animals, and the heavens of the lower gods. This is the lowest of the abodes of beings. (2) The *Rupaloka* or second plane of existence, the realm of Form in which the senses of touch, smell, and taste are absent. This is the realm of Contemplation and is divided into four abodes of the higher gods. It is this realm that is probably suggested by the fifth level. It is transitional to the third plane of existence, the Formless world called *Arupaloka* where there is the sense of mind only. There are four "abodes" here which are four attainments: (a) the perception "space is infinite"; (b) the perception "consciousness is infinite"; (c) the perception "there is nothing"; and (d) the state of realizing neither consciousness nor non-consciousness.[1] Here the soul enters the great Void, the Absolute Mind, the pure unitive state beyond the relative world.

The Buddha images that cover the temple everywhere express most clearly its metaphysical and cosmic meaning. They represent the five Buddhas of the Fivefold Manifestation *Mandala* — Akshobhya, Ratnasambhava, Amitabha, Amoghasiddhi, and Vairocana. The significance of these Buddhas has been made clear already in our study above of the Fivefold Manifestation *Mandala*. These Buddhas in themselves comprehend the space-time universe.

The *mandala* form of *Borobudur* is more complicated than the Fivefold Manifestation diagram because it appears, as Professor Rowland points out, that there are two *mandalas* represented in *Borobudur,* one inside the other. Professor Rowland thinks that the key to the interpretation of the two *mandalas* is found in the symbolism of Shingon Buddhism. The ultimate reality in this Buddhist sect is Mahavairocana. He is the macrocosmic reality whose nature is symbolized in two complementary constituents represented symbolically by two *mandalas*, the *Kongokai* and the *Taizokai*. The *Kongokai* (Sanskrit *Vajradhatu*) is the active and material "diamond-element" which parallels *Upaya* or Compassion in Buddhist Tantric philosophies; the *Taizokai* (Sanskrit *garbha-dhatu*) is the passive and mental "womb-element" which parallels *Prajna* or Wisdom in Buddhist Tantric philosophies. Both *mandalas* have Vairocana as the central deity surrounded by the other four Jinas and other lesser deities. These two *mandalas* together represent the entire cosmos since every object, every event, all spiritual reality is an aspect of one or the other or both of these two basic "elements" of the transcendental cosmic Sun Buddha, Mahavairocana.[2] The interpenetration of the *Samsara* and *Nirvana* worlds, of

---

[1] Edward J. Thomas, *The History of Buddhist Thought*, sec. ed. (London: Routledge & Kegan Paul, Ltd., 1953), pp. 111-112.

[2] Bhikshu Sangharakshita, *op. cit.*, p. 425.

Upaya (Compassion) and *Prajna* (Wisdom) and their transcendental unity (Vairocana is the core reality of each) is graphically represented.

The Tibetan *Hevajra* Tantra is similar in its symbolism. The male deity, Hevajra, has a definite *mandala* of 'deities (fifteen in number) and his female partner, Nairatmya, has her own *mandala* of deities. The union of the two or superimposition of the two with absolute unity at the center diagrams *samsara* and *nirvana* as in the Shingon *mandalas*.

If *Borobudur* manifests a similar symbolism, the first five galleries show the *mandala* of the material world but with Akshobhya rather than Vairocana as the central deity, the root reality. The five upper terraces express the *mandala* of the spiritual world also presided over by Akshobhya. The fifth gallery is also transitional between the two mandalas, and may, Rowland thinks, symbolize the *Sambhogakaya* of Vairocana while the circular terraces beyond represent the *Dharmakaya*. In any case, it would appear from our study of the Fivefold Manifestation, the Demchog *mandala* and the *mandalas* of the *Hevaja Tantra* as typical examples of *mandala*-forms, that the three worlds symbolized by the three buddha bodies are intended in the symbolism of *Borobudur*. The square terraces are plainly the material world (*kamaloka*) of which the *nirmanakaya* would be the appropriate buddha-body; the circular terraces probably symbolize the *sambhogakaya* with the terminal core-stupa the representation of the *Dharmakaya*. Whether or not the transitional terrace alone represents the *Sambhogakaya*, the meaning of the *mandala*-form is the same; it is a cosmos in miniature.

The function of *Borobudur*, monumental cosmic *mandala* in stone, is that of all *mandalas* — reintegration of the devotee. Reintegration is accomplished by the worshipper in making the journey from terrace to terrace in emulation of Sudhana through the levels of the material world (the square terraces and the basement); then through the fifth terrace, the transitional level to the circular spiritual regions; finally through the circular terraces of the spiritual regions to the core reality, the *dharmadhatu*, whence issues the entire *samsara* world of multiplicity. Identification with this supreme reality is the goal of the spiritual journey — the Reality represented by the Buddha of the central *stupa* at the apex and top of the temple and by the mast ,or shaft) which ascends from it into the Void (*shunyata*).

With reference to the theme of this book, the time symbolism of *Borobudur* needs separate comment. We have already mentioned that the list of Buddhas appearing on the monument is that of the Fivefold Manifestation *mandala*. On the first four galleries the Buddhas of the four directions—Akshobhya, Ratnasambhava, Amitabha, Amoghasiddhi — are appropriately placed at the east, south, west and north respectively as in the Fivefold Manifestation *mandala;* and as in this *mandala* these buddhas symbolize also the cycle of time. On the fifth terrace, the transition to the non-material upper regions, there are on all four sides images of Vairocana alone in teaching *mudra*. The circular terraces of the spiritual regions have as a center Akshobhya surrounded by seventy-two Buddhas all hidden in latticework domes. The reason why Akshobhya is given this central place is clear again in the light of our study of the Fivefold Manifestation *mandala*, for this *mandala* has Akshobhya in exactly the same spot. The Fivefold Manifestation *mandala* explains that Akshobhya is "himself the essence of Vajrasattva, where there is no distinction between Void and Compassion."[1] The outer form of Akshobhya is, therefore given to the highest Buddha, the Adi-buddha Vajrasattva [2] who stands for the ultimate state — non-dual Being. This Being transcends all dualities even those of Void and Compassion, for he unites both and transcends both in himself. He is the transcendent source of Void and

---

[1] David Snellgrove, "The Fivefold Manifestation," *Buddhist Texts Through the Ages, op. cit.,* p. 250.

Compassion, *Samsara* and *Nirvana*, of the noumenal spiritual world and the phenomenal world of activity and material things. All is One in the ultimate Buddha-being, the *Dharmakaya*.

The seventy-two Buddhas surrounding Akshobhya (Vajrasattva) signify in another sense than that given in the Fivefold Manifestation *Mandala* the recurrent cycles of time. If Professor Rowland's interpretation is correct, the seventy-two Buddhas are related to cycles connected with knowledge of the precession of the equinoxes. Every seventy-two years marks a change in one degree in the precession "so the presence of seventy-two Buddhas — the number present in all the reckonings of the great cycles — would be a plastic-architectural representation of the existence of the Buddha Law throughout all the past and future kalpas of Time."[2] If this interpretation is not correct — but there is good reason to think that it is—we can be certain, at least, of the time symbolism of the Buddhas of the quarters and of the Center, which symbolize the sun-cycle and therefore all time in this world and in all other possible worlds, since all conform to the same pattern.

The philosophical Buddhist pilgrim in his meditative journey up the cosmic *mandala*-in-stone from the material worlds through the spiritual arrives at a true perspective of the space-time cosmos and its Source. He perceives all space and all time and all the mutiplicity of objects and living forms as integral parts of one cosmic reality. In reintegrating himself with the One eternal transcendent Source of all being, he experiences eternity; but at the same time the temporal world has new value, a new light illuminates it, for it too is but the temporal and finite manifestation of the One. All men, all nature are parts of oneself; the worlds of Time and Eternity, of death and life, *samsara* and *nirvana* are now in organic unity. The devotee in reabsorption into the eternal plane, the *Dharmakaya*, is himself the Real in the everlasting emanation-

---
[2] Rowland, *op. cit.*, p. 251.

and-return cycle; the ever-recurrent, ever the same time cycles are regarded in a new light as phenomenal mind-manifestations of that which is noumenally Identity and Eternity. All this is the yogic process of reintegration. The function of all *mandalas* is this sublime reintegration— this return of the alienated phenomenal self (which is really no self) — to the Source of its being. The Buddhist philosopher-pilgrim climbing up the terraces of *Borobudur* achieves this reintegration, an eternal state; this for him is the purpose and the goal of individual and collective human history.

In Mahayana Buddhism it is not sufficient to achieve such reintegration which is salvation for oneself alone; the saint who has arrived at the spiritual goal must not enter the eternal state but become a bodhisattva. In the bodhisattva body of celestial glory (the *sambhogakaya*) the saint emanates vibratory rays of altruistic love which are potent in the salvation of all other suffering creatures in the *samsara* world. Not until *all* are saved from the *samsara* will the bodhisattva himself enter the eternal Unity, the Absolute of Eternity. When all are "saved" all will be reintegrated with the One, the transcendent Eternal. This however, will not mean an eternal static condition. Evans-Wentz informs us that because the Eternal One is an Infinite, there is an inconceivably higher evolutionary goal after universal salvation is attained. The "Path of the Higher Evolution" will be entered upon and "lead to a Goal utterly beyond the conception of finite mind."[1]

Psychological value of the symbolism of the mandala in overcoming ideas and feelings of "alienation" through realization of meaning in recurrent time processes. The mandala-form as the symbol of total reality in both its phenomenal and noumenal aspects is a potent psychological aid in accomplishing the reintegration of the devotee. In deep

---

[1] Evans-Wentz, editor, *Tibetan Yoga and Secret Doctrines*, trans. Lama Kazi Dawa-Samdup (London, New York, Toronto: Oxford University Press, 1958), p. 149, n. 1.

meditation upon this rich symbolic form he grasps the unity of the cosmos, its hierarchic levels of truth and reality; in the internal *mandala* he perceives himself as identical with the external macrocosmic *mandala*. The endless repetition of creation and destruction of universes apparently meaningless to the unenlightened phenomenal ego under bondage to this cyclical world of karmic processes—for he finds only misery, suffering and alienation therein—takes on an entirely new light to the reintegrated yogin. All things that were perceived before the enlightenment experience as more or less separate entities in a time succession and space location are now perceived as organic parts of one whole, one self with whom the yogin has achieved identity. All men of all levels of vice and virtue, all animals and even the rocks and stones are the yogin himself since all have their reality in the Unconditioned, the Absolute. The yogin feels an entirely new Freedom because he is no longer bound to the fortunes or misfortunes of a private transmigrating ego; his enlightenment experience has demonstrated that his ego was an illusion as all separateness, which is the source of human vice and feelings of alienation, is illusion. The real is the identity of *Samsara* and *Nirvana*, the pure Unity without distinctions.[1] The yogin now rid of the ego-illusion is freed from the endless cravings from whence come endless sufferings and endless rebirths into suffering. He, as the Absolute, has become master of his fate instead of the selfish slave of an illusory ego. Ethically he can behave with the utmost spontaneity (cf. St. Paul's "freedom of the Christian man") and all of his conduct will be altruistic. His aim now is to help save all other beings from their ego-

---

[1] The very word, *tantra*, from which Tantric Buddhism gets its name means "weaving" or "loom, web, fabric." The philosophical connotation is that the "inner and outer worlds are only two sides of the same fabric, in which the threads of all forces and events, of all forms of consciousness and all objects are woven into one." Anagarika Govinda, "Principles of Tantric Buddhism," *2500 Years of Buddhism*, ed. P. V. Bapat (Delhi: Publications Division, Government of India, 1959), pp. 373 f.

illusion (*maya*); to help them attain also the state of a buddha (enlightened one).

The following chapter continues the theme of *mandala* symbolism as manifested in the great Hindu philosophies and in a Taoist form of Chinese yoga. At the end of this chapter Jung's evaluation of the idea of the *mandala* from both a psychological and philosophical view will be given, and finally a general summary of the relationships between the temporal world (*maya*), yoga and cyclical time.

Chapter VII

Maya, Yoga and Cyclical Time in Hindu, Buddhist and Later Taoist Thought

After our brief glance at Buddhist cyclical views both cosmic and biological-psychological let us return again to Hinduism and point out the likenesses between the two approaches to time and its phenomena. In both schools of thought cosmic time is cyclical and conforms to a pattern which is the same throughout the aeons. The great philosopher of the Advaita Vedanta school of philosophy in India, Shankara, summarizes this characteristic idea:

> As the various signs of the seasons return in succession in their due time, thus the same beings again appear in the different yugas. And of whatever individuality the gods of the past ages were, equal to them are the present gods in name and form.[1]

In Shankara's thought Brahman (who is eternally the same) casts out the web of maya from himself; he "breathes out" the same names and forms (idea-patterns) in each world-cycle, and therefore the phenomena are identical in each one. Heinrich Zimmer tells us that Indian myth is filled with this idea.[2] As an example he mentions the Puranic

---

[1] *The Vedanta-sutras with Commentary by Sankaracharya*, trans. George Thibaut, *SBE*, Vol. XXXIV (Oxford: Clarendon Press, 1890), p. 215.
[2] Heinrich Zimmer, *Myths and Symbols in Indian Art and Civilization*, op. cit., p. 18.

account of an event in the life of Vishnu during his incarnation as a boar. Vishnu as the Boar rescues the goddess Earth from the depths of the sea and says, "Every time I carry you this way . . ."[3] The repetitious character of the event is clear. The archetypal, the great events of history are cyclically repeated.

The pattern of evolution of each cycle of each cosmos is repeated also as would be expected. The earliest philosophical description of this pattern of evolution is probably found in the Taittiriya Upanishad. Radhakrishnan thinks that this Upanishad was written in the eighth century B.C. The evolutionary process begins when Brahman creates the material elements (ether, air, fire, water, earth). Bodies are composed of this Matter level of being, so it is called the "physical sheath of the Self." On the macrocosmic level, the material universe is the physical sheath of the cosmic Self and on the microcosmic level the body is the physical sheath of the individual man. Brahman next creates the Vital or Life level of being. This is the Vital Sheath of the cosmic Self and individual human soul. After this the level of Mind and Intellect are brought into being. In this way the manifold world has evolved. This world *is* Brahman, the Upanishad states, although Brahman is not to be equated with this world.

> Before creation came into existence, Brahman existed as the Unmanifest. From the Unmanifest he created the manifest. From himself he brought forth himself.[1]

The evolved world, however, will dissolve and reappear in endless cycles of similar pattern. It is not, therefore, the

---
[3] *Ibid.*

[1] Taittiriya Upanishad, trans. Swami Prabhavananda and Frederick Manchester, *The Upanishads*, Mentor ed. (New York: New American Library, 1957). Professor Radhakrishnan as noted below, chap. VI, Part III, points out the modern notion of the evolutionary development of the universe anticipated in this Upanishad.

Eternal Real, the essential, noumenal Brahman. Through yogic meditation the soul of the individual man returns full cycle to Brahman. The Upanishad describes the meditations on the physical sheaths (Matter), the Vital sheath (Life), the Mental sheath, the sheath of Intellect, and finally the return to Brahman, the Self. The Atman becomes the Brahman. The yogin in meditation completes the cycle of the return to Brahman; from the psychological and metaphysical point of view the universe has already been reabsorbed into Brahman in the yogic experience.

Probably the earliest systematic philosophy which posits precise evolutionary stages in the development of the cosmos is the Sankhya.

Section 1

Sankhya Yoga

The Sankhya philosophy is pre-Buddhistic, apparently, in origin although the earliest surviving treatise, the Samkhya-karika of Ishvarakrishna, Radhakrishnan thinks, was written in the third century A.D. In this authoritative and systematic treatise two ultimate kinds of reality are posited: purusha and prakrti. Purusha is spirit, and there is an infinite number of spirits; prakrti is matter. Matter (prakrti) is complex and consists of three gunas—sattvas, rajas and tamas. The sattwas guna is the lightest, most ethereal of the elements of matter; the rajas guna is the active element, the dynamic or energy component; and the tamas guna is the heavy, inert element which gives mass to things. Purusha is a simple substance: it is eternally the witness Self — Pure Being, Consciousness, Bliss (Sat-Chit-Ananda). It has intuitive knowledge-by-identity since it is itself the one, unitary quality the essence of which is eternal noetic spirit. There is an infinite number of such spirits, however, yet each is qualitatively alike.

The evolutionary process of the universe begins when the gunas of prakrti, in complete equilibrium during the quiescent involutionary period, start to separate. Then combinations begin which mix the gunas in unequal proportions and the particular things of nature appear. The first evolute is Mahat (the great) another name for which is Intellect (Buddhi). This is temporally and spatially the greatest in magnitude of all the evolutes.[1] Yet, this too is Matter (prakrti). Sattvas [2] is the dominant guna in buddhi, for its primary attribute is pure intelligence; and "in its cosmic character," buddhi "comprises all limited intellects with this difference that while the latter have felt reference to objects, the former is without any, since for it there is no object to be grasped." (Concrete objects have not yet evolved.)

The next evolute is ahamkara (egoity) or self-sense. From this evolves both an internal and an external series of evolutes. The internal series consists of eleven organs: five cognitive, five organs of action and Mind (manas).[1] The five cognitive organs are the ears, the skin, the eyes, the tongue and the nose; the five organs of action are voice,

---

[1] Satkari Mookerjee, "The Samkhya-Yoga," *History of Philosophy Eastern and Western*, 2 vols. ed. S. Radhakrishnan et al. (London: George Allen & Unwin, Ltd., 1952), vol. I, chap. XI, p. 250.

[2] In the microcosm, man, the sattvas guna is dominant in the man of wisdom or goodness. Such a man has power and shows nonattachment. On the other hand, if the tamas guna is dominant in the buddhi of a man, he shows the opposite qualities: vice, ignorance, passion, and weakness. See Sarvepalli Radhakrishnan and Charles A. Moore, *Source Book in Indian Philosophy* (Princeton: Princeton University Press, 1957), chap. XII, "Samkhya." Selections in this section of the chapter are quoted from *The Samkhya-karika* of Ismvara Krishna as given in this Source Book. The reference for the information in this footnote is in paragraph XXIII.

[1] Mind (manas) partakes of both sensory and motor functions. It is "an organ of sensation, as well as one of action, since the eye and the other sensory organs, as well as speech and other motor organs, are able to operate on their respective objects only when influenced by the mind ... *It is the observing principle* ... it is this observing, i.e., the perception of definite properties as belonging to the thing apprehended,—that is done through the mind." (*Ibid.* paragraph XXVII.)

hands, feet, and the organs of excretion and generation. The external series which evolves from ahamkara (egoity) consists of the five subtle elements (tanmatras) and the five gross elements. The five gross elements are earth, air, fire, water and ether. The subtle elements are uncompounded, non-specific and therefore lacking in the qualities of "calmness, turbulence, and delusiveness" which would make them perceivable by ordinary people.[2] As a famous Advaita Vedanta scholar explains:

> The rudimentary elements, when first evolved, are unmixed with one another. The gross ether is a combination of the original subtle ether with the other four subtle elements in a fixed proportion.[3]

The gross elements, all of them compounded by varying proportions of the subtle elements constitute the physical world of ordinary perception.

The individual, the microcosm, is composed of the same evolutes of prakrti as the macrocosm. The purpose of the evolutionary process is the emancipation of each purusha from the process.[1] Until emancipation each purusha is born again and again in the heavenly planes of existence, in some life-form on earth, or in the subterranean planes. The transmigration continues cycle after cycle until release (emancipation) is attained; for the Sankhya thinkers believe that the cosmos at definite periods dissolves, i.e. the gunas return to equilibrium; then the process is repeated without end. The body of the individual which transmigrates from birth to birth is called the "subtle body." The subtle body is composed of all the evolutes from buddhi down to the sub-

---

[2] *Ibid.* paragraph XXXVIII.
[3] Sadananda Yogindra, *Vedantasara* or *The Essence of Vedanta*, trans. Swami Nikhilananda (Almora, Himalayas: Advaita Ashrama, Mayavati, Swami Yogeshwarananda, 1949), pp. 46 f. Vedanta uses this same evolutionary process. See below.
[1] Ishvara Krishna, *Samkhya-karika, op. cit.,* LVI, LVII, LVIII.

tle elements. It is formed "primevally," which means at the time the emanations from prakrti begin the evolutionary cycle; and there is formed at this time a subtle body for each purusha. This subtle body acquires a gross body at birth. Through the operation of karma virtuous deeds performed in the world enable the subtle body to ascend to higher planes, while vice causes descent into lower. Transmigration continues until emancipation from prakrti and her cycles is obtained.

Release of purusha from prakrti may be gained through knowledge—ultimately of an intuitive kind. Ishvara Krishna says: "For the benefit of the spirit in the shape of experience and final release, she [Prakrti or Nature] releases herself by herself, 'by means of one form,' i.e., by wisdom — discrimination." [2] This wisdom or discrimination yields the knowledge that purusha is an eternal, simple substance, the Witness Self, pure immortal changeless Spirit that has nothing to do with the evolutionary cycles of prakrti. Kaivalya (isolation) of purusha (spirit) is then eternally achieved. Prakrti or Primal Nature never again weaves her web of involvement around the purusha which has gained this knowledge. "Primal Nature, . . . because of the realization 'I have been seen' never again comes into the view of the spirit." [1]

Yoga techniques are so closely associated with the Sankhya school that the *Gita* identifies Sankhya with Yoga; only fools, the *Gita* says, look upon them as different. Yoga is "applied Sankhya."[2] Nevertheless there is the difference that Yoga adds the category of Ishvara (Personal God) to those of the Sankhya. God brings the evolutionary cycle to an end and initiates each new cosmic cycle, solving in the Sankhya system the unsolved problem of how the universe dissolves and begins again. Patanjali, the most famous of yoga teachers and practitioners, in his *Yoga-sutra* men-

---

[2] *Ibid.,* LXIII.
[1] *Ibid.,* LXI.
[2] *Op. cit.,* Satkari Mookerjee, "The Samkhya-Yoga," p. 256.

tions meditation upon God (the omniscient Being) as an aid to release; but such meditation is not the only means. "Like the Samkhya, he holds the knowledge of the distinction of self from not-self as the sole and sufficient cause of emancipation."[3] This is clear from the following passage in the *Yoga-sutra:* "The means of the removal [of bondage] is discriminative knowledge undisturbed."[4]

The *Yoga-sutra* is famous for its eightfold method of gaining this discriminative knowledge. This method, or aspects of it, is used to gain the ultimate knowledge which wins release by many others than the followers of the Sankhya-yoga. It is used for example by the Advaita Vedanta school as we shall see below. Although the eightfold method is summarized in numerous books for Western readers, we beg the indulgence of the reader while we review the eight steps in order to relate them to the cyclical idea which is our major theme.

The entire eightfold method may be seen as the return half of a complete involution-evolution process on the psychological plane. Purusha has become involved in the descending categories of Nature (prakrti) until the furthest remove in quality from spirit, gross matter, is its (the purusha's) embodiment. This is the first half of the cycle for the spirit (purusha). The spirit in its embodiment suffers the extreme degree of self-alienation and ignorance (avidya), (and this is an *involution* for spirit) until it begins the journey of the "return." The return to its pristine, spiritual, simple nature uncontaminated even with the highest of the "evolutes," is difficult. The eightfold method of Patanjali's yoga is recommended as perhaps the most efficient and certainly the best known for achieving the cyclic return of the purusha to its pure Self. This return represents an introvert withdrawal of the purusha from its outer sheaths of the evo-

---
[3] *Ibid.*
[4] *Op. cit.* Radhakrishnan and Moore, *Yoga-sutra* of Patanjali, Chap. II paragraph 26.

lutes of prakrti into its isolated uncontaminated purity, and is an *evolutionary* progress for spirit.

The first stage of withdrawal from prakrti is concerned with control of the gross body and its desires. First there is a moral purgation in two stages: (1) Five restraints (*yama*): non-injury (ahimsa) to any living creature, truthfulness, non-stealing, chastity, and "abstinence from avariciousness."[1] (2) Five observances (*niyama*): "cleanliness, contentment, purificatory action, study, and the making of the Lord the motive of all action."[2] Next (3) there is concentration upon control of the body through certain postures (*asanas*). Then (4) one must master the vital forces through breathing, the stage of *pranayama*. The next stage (5) leaves the world of the gross body behind and is the second major step in the cyclic evolution of spirit in its return. This stage in the method is called *pratyahara* (withdrawal of the senses). It is the stage of withdrawal from the outer world of objects and is similar in idea-pattern to the transitional terrace in *Borobudur* between the phenomenal world of sense objects and the spiritual worlds.[3] Here the purusha sheds the sheath of the gross body and its world of objects for the world of the "subtle body," the intermediate stage between the gross physical and the subtle-physical or idea-worlds. Stages (6) and (7) in the cyclic return belong to the evolute buddhi (pure intelligence) closest in the realm of prakrti to spirit. Stage (6) called *dharana* is that of concentration on one object. Stage (7), *dhyana*, is "continuance of the mental effort" of "one-pointedness,"[1] the effort to understand reality to attain the ultimate discrimination.

The final stage is the goal of the cyclical journey of purusha from its involution in gross matter to its evolutionary re-

---

[1] *Ibid.*, Chap. II paragraph 30.

[2] *Ibid.*, Chap. II paragraph 32. "Lord" is Ishvara.

[3] *Supra*, pp. 102-106.

[1] *Op. cit.*, Radhakrishnan and Moore, *Yoga-sutra* of Patanjali, chap. 3, paragraph 2.

turn through yogic methods. This final stage (8) is *samadhi*. Here the purusha achieves the return to its pristine purity, released forever from its illusory involvement with prakrti. In this trance state it has no object but is pure spirit—spirit has achieved its isolation from prakrti; and because this includes the evolute buddhi or intellect the subject-object idea world of intellect is also gone. Complete emancipation from the world of time and change is secured forever. The *Yoga-sutra* says:

> Absolute freedom comes when the qualities, becoming devoid of the object of the purusa, become latent; or the power of consciousness becomes established in its own nature.
> ... Absolute freedom is the becoming latent, by inverse process, of the qualities, when they are devoid of the object of the purusa, after having achieved the experience and emancipation of the self. Y.B.[2]

The "inverse process" is the cyclic return of the purusha to its original state. In Samadhi there is direct experience of this state. A residue of karma may continue the mundane involvement of the purusha until death, but he will be a *jivan-mukta*, one who is free while in this world. He will live in the knowledge, "I do not exist, naught is mine, I am not," [3] and when "the separation from the body has at length been attained, and by reason of the purpose having been fulfilled, Nature ceases to act, — then he attains eternal and absolute isolation." [4] The soul has but one complete cycle, from pure eternal spirit to pure eternal spirit. The cycle of involvement begins with the evolution of prakrti — spirit initiates the return cycle through the evolutes and out of the material world altogether. Spirit itself dissolves the world of prakrti

---
[2] *Ibid.*, chap. 4, paragraph 34. The second paragraph is commentary, the *Yoga-bhasya* of Vyasa (4th century A. D.)
[3] *Op. cit., Samkhya-karika*, LXIV.
[4] *Ibid.*, LXVIII.

as far as its own involvement in it is concerned. Purusha in the final state of discrimination learns:

> Verily no spirit is bound; nor does any migrate; nor is any emancipated. Nature alone, having many vehicles, is bound, migrates, and is released. Bondage, migration and release are ascribed to the spirit, in the same manner as defeat and victory are attributed to the king, though actually occurring to his soldiers, because it is the servants that take part in the undertaking, the effects of which—grief or profit—accrue to the king. In the same manner experience and emancipation, though really belonging to Nature, are attributed to the spirit, on account of the non-discrimination of spirit from Nature, as has been already explained...[1]

The spirit's cycle of Fall, or illusion of involvement in prakrti, and return resembles the Christian cycle of Fall and return to the spiritual City of God described below.[2] Avidya (ignorance) is the cause of the Fall, however, in Sankhya philosophy and Indian philosophy in general, whereas an ethical cause, Adam's (man's) intentional wickedness, is emphasized in Christian philosophy. *In both, however, there is but one complete historical cycle for the spirit.* This is true in Indian philosophy generally despite the belief in the endless cycles of evolutionary nature. The Vedanta philosophy is the most prevalent in India, and in Vedanta also there is but one cycle for the spirit. The cycle in Vedanta and its relation to the world of phenomenal appearance (maya) with its endless cycles is one of the most profound in any of the world's philosophical systems. To this we now turn.

---

[1] *Op. cit.*, Ishvara Krishna, *Samkhya-Karika*, LXII.
[2] *Infra*, Part II, chap. III.

Section 2: Advaita Vedanta, Maya, Cosmic Cycles and the Yogic Cyclical Return

In the Advaita Vedanta philosophic system as expounded by the great eighth century thinker, Shankara, the ultimate and the only Real Being is Brahman. Brahman is One-without-a-second and Existence, Consciousness, Bliss. The phenomenal world (maya) is to be understood as the super-imposition *(adhyaropa)* of the unreal on the real, as water is superimposed in a mirage. This maya is also called Avidya (ignorance). The origin, the purpose of maya and its relation to the One Real Being are all inscrutable. Maya, or the phenomenal world, is not Being but being-with-nothingness or dependent, phenomenal being; it is also, therefore not non-being. It has two powers, concealment and projection, i.e., it conceals the true nature of Brahman and projects the illusory world.

The evolutionary process of this maya world and its dissolution endlessly repeated is the following:

1. The primary substance of maya (equivalent to prakrti in the Sankhya) consists of the three gunas — sattvas, rajas and tamas as in the Sankhya. Evolutes are combinations of the three.
2. The primary evolute is Ishvara, popularly called God. Ishvara is the Brahman with qualities (*saguna* Brahman) whereas the Ultimate Being as Brahman is qualityless (*nirguna* Brahman). Ishvara has a preponderance of pure sattva which means that he is not deluded by maya (the Ignorance). Ishvara is omniscient because the witness of all objects in the cosmos; he is universal lord since he gives rewards and punishments to souls according to their merits; he is the all-controlling power, for he directs the mental propensities of all souls; and finally he is "Illuminator of the aggregate of ignorance"[1] because the Ignorance (maya) is manifest only to Ishvara, but Ishvara himself is never influenced by this maya.

[1] Sadananda Yogindra, *Vedantasara*, op. cit., p. 29.

On the microcosmic scale *prajna,* the state of the in-individual soul in dreamless sleep, is equivalent to Ishvara on the macrocosmic level. This state as described in the Mandukya Upanisad is something positive. Ignorance (maya) is present, as it were, in the dissolution state (the state when the cycle ends and all returns into Ishvara on the macrocosmic scale). The jiva (soul) perceives the bliss of the Atman (Brahman) and the Ignorance. This is experience of the "blissful sheath of the soul (*anandamayakosha*).[2]

3. The next evolute is ether (*akasa*), then air, fire, water, and earth. These five elements although having particles of sattva and rajas have a preponderance of tamas, but ether has most of sattvas and earth of tamas. These elements at this stage are unmixed with one another and are in the *"subtle"* form. They are called *tanmatras* or rudimentary elements as in the Sankhya.
4. Subtle bodies and the gross elements are produced from the tanmatras.
5. *Subtle bodies* are called *Linga Shariras* and have seventeen component parts as in the Sankhya: five organs of perception, five organs of action, the intellect (buddhi), the mind (manas), the five vital forces. Ahamkara (egoity) also belongs to them. Intellect (buddhi) with the organs of perception constitutes the *Vijnanamayakosha* or *sheath of intellect*. This sheath is called also the *jiva* or individual self which is subject to transmigration because "of its being conscious that it is an agent and enjoyer and that it is happy or miserable, etc." [1] The mind (manas) with the organs of perception make up the *mental sheath (manomayakosha)*. *Egoism (ahamkara)* is characterized by self-consciousness and is associated with mind (manas). The mind-stuff (citta) is

---

[2] *Ibid.,* p. 29. The *Vedantasara* says: "This aggregate of ignorance associated with Iswara is known as the causal body on account of its being the cause of all, and has the *Anandamayakosa* (the blissful sheath) on account of its being full of bliss and covering like a sheath; it is further known as the Cosmic sleep as into it everything is dissolved..."

[1] *Ibid.,* p. 51.

memory and is associated with buddhi, and the function of buddhi is to determine the real nature of an object (discrimination as in Sankhya). *Antahkarana* is the name given "the inner organ, of which Citta, Buddhi, Manas and Ahamkara are the different aspects."[2] The *vital sheath (Pranamayakosha)* is made up of five vital forces: Prana, Apana, Vyana, Samana, and Udana. Prana has its seat in the heart but its presence is felt at the tip of the nose. Apana is the vital force which goes downward with its source in the organs of excretion.[3] Vyana "moves in all directions and pervades the entire body."[4] Udana is the ascending vital force with its seat in the throat. It aids in the exit of the subtle body from the gross body at death. "Though at the time of death the subtle body may pass out through any part of the body, yet the throat is most often this exit."[5] Samana is the vital force "which assimilates food and drink and has its seat in the middle of the body."[6]

To summarize, the three sheaths are the basic aspects of the subtle body. The relation between the three are: the sheath of intellect is the agent with its power of discriminatory knowledge; the mental sheath characterized by will-power is the instrument; and the vital sheath "which is endowed with activity is the product."[7] All three together are the subtle body. The sum total of all subtle bodies when seen as one is called Samasti or aggregate, but when seen as many are called Vyasti or individuals. *The cosmic subtle body* is consciousness associated with the total aggregate of subtle bodies. This cosmic subtle body is named Sutratma, Hiranyagarbha, Prana, Prajapati or Brahma because it is "immanent everywhere and because it identifies itself with the five great uncompounded elements endowed with the powers of knowledge, will and activity."[8]

---

[2] *Ibid.*, p. 48.
[3] *Ibid.*, pp. 52-53.
[4] *Ibid.*, p. 53.
[5] *Ibid.*
[6] *Ibid.*
[7] *Ibid.*, p. 56.
[8] *Ibid.*, p. 57.

Hiranyagarbha is the Dream State at the cosmic level and the subtle individual body is in the dream state at the microcosmic level. In the dream state, the jiva enters the subtle plane in which the waking state of perception of gross physical objects is transformed into the subtle plane of mere ideas.

5. *Gross bodies* are made up of combinations of the gross elements. The gross elements are compounds of the subtle or rudimentary elements in definite proportions. Gross air, for example has a preponderance of subtle air mixed with small portions of the other elements.

6. From the gross elements have evolved the *seven planes*, the *world*, and the gross bodies contained in the world, and the *seven nether planes*. The seven planes are the heavens, one above the other: Bhur, Bhuvar, Svar, Mahar, Jana, Tapas, and Satyam. The four kinds of gross bodies in the world are those born of the womb, the egg, moisture and the soil.[1] The seven nether planes are one below the other: Atala, Vitala, Sutala, Rasatala, Talatala, Mahatala and Patala. Such is the gross body of the maya of Brahman. On the microcosmic level the gross physical body is the physical sheath of the atman and is called the *annamayakosha*. On the macrocosmic level consciousness associated with the aggregate of gross bodies (the cosmic Annamayakosha) is called Vaisvanara and Virat. In both cosmic and individual forms it is a waking-state consciousness and furthest from "reality."

The above is the outline of the evolutionary cycle in its procession from the One-without-a-second.

The wise man who desires release from transmigratory existence in this phenomenal world must through a reverse process "dissolve" this cosmos. He does this on the microcosmic scale in the same way as Ishvara dissolves the universe on the macrocosmic scale. He sheds the sheaths of prakrti one by one which envelop the Atman. This process — being the reverse of superimposition by which the maya world appears superimposed upon Brahman — is call-

[1] *Ibid.*, p. 86.

ed de-superimposition. It is the return half of the maya-cycle for the microcosm, the atman enveloped in the phenomenal world. The return into the Final Cause (Brahman) follows the reverse order to that of creation.[1] The return half of the cycle, de-superimposition, begins with the shedding of the *physical sheath, annamayakosha*. Since, in the return process effects must be reduced to their causes (and in reverse order from that of creation), the first step in the return is the perception that the entire physical world of gross bodies (food, drink, the seven heavenly planes, the seven nether planes, the world) can be reduced to their cause, the five gross elements. In this way the physical sheath is shed.[1]

The *vital sheath* — pranamayakosha, the *mental sheath* — *manomayakosha* (which includes egoity), and the *sheath of intellect* — *vijnanamayakosha*, all of which constitute the *subtle body*, are reduced to their cause — the tanmatras (uncompounded or rudimentary elements).

Next the tanmatras are reduced to their cause the gunas of prakrti (sattva, rajas, and tamas) which in their turn are reduced to their cause, viz., Consciousness (Ishvara) associated with Ignorance (avidya). Consciousness associated with Ignorance (Ishvara on the cosmic scale) is the *sheath of bliss* — *anandamayakosha*. This is the underblanket of dark Ignorance which ensheaths the entire universe on the macrocosmic scale and the atman still under the spell of the sheaths of maya. The sheath of bliss (experienced in deep sleep) is shed when it is perceived that this "causal body," i.e., Ishvara associated with Ignorance, can be "resolved into the transcendent Brahman unassociated with ignorance, which is the substratum of them all." [2]

---

[1] Shankara in the *Crest-Jewel of Discrimination*, trans. Swami Prabhavananda and Christopher Isherwood (Hollywood, California: Vedanta Press, 1947), pp. 68-79 explains the meaning of each sheath but the author finds the *Vedantasara* more illuminating for the Western reader since it elaborates much more on some difficult ideas.

[2] *Op. cit., Vedantasara*, p. 87.

A "mandala" diagram of a very simple kind will outline at a glance the cycle of the atman ensheathed in maya:

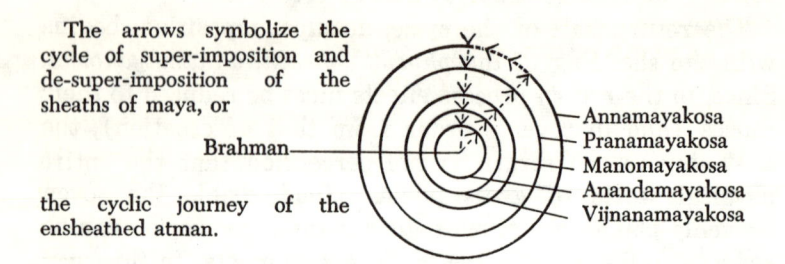

The arrows symbolize the cycle of super-imposition and de-super-imposition of the sheaths of maya, or

Brahman

the cyclic journey of the ensheathed atman.

— Annamayakosa
— Pranamayakosa
— Manomayakosa
— Anandamayakosa
— Vijnanamayakosa

The method recommended for shedding the sheaths and realization of the identity of the Atman with the Brahman is the eight-fold method of Yoga already described. The eighth and final step in the method, *samadhi*, has two stages. These are (1) *savikalpa samadhi* and (2) *nirvikalpa samadhi*. In *savikalpa samadhi* self-consciousness is present along with the presence of Brahman. One is aware of both; it is a state of dual consciousness. In *nirvikalpa samadhi* self-consciousness is eliminated; there is awareness of Brahman alone — the qualityless *(nirguna)* Brahman. In this state "the knots of the heart's ignorance are loosed completely and forever."[1] Identity with the essential, the real, the eternal, qualityless Brahman is realized, a state of complete freedom. He who has entered this state can say:

> I am that Brahman, one without a second, the ground of all existences. I make all things manifest. I give form to all things. I am within all things, yet nothing can taint me. I am eternal, pure, unchangeable, absolute.
> ... I am the truth. I am knowledge. I am infinite ...
> ... I am beyond action, the reality which cannot

---

[1] *Op. cit.* Sankara, *Crest-Jewel of Discrimination*, p. 107.

change. I have neither part nor form. I am absolute. I am eternal ... I stand alone. I am one without a second.[2]

The yogic return cycle in Tantric interpretations of Advaita Vedanta.

In Tantric interpretations of the Advaita (non-dual) Vedanta, maya is given a more positive position. Maya is the shakti of Brahman and is often personified as the goddess, Kali, the Mother. Kali takes the place of Ishvara in the systems described above. Kali is creator, preserver and destroyer of the cosmos in each cycle. Creation (maya or shakti) in its multiple glorious and terrible works is Kali. Kali is a great goddess therefore all created things are divine; the enlightened spirit adores the world as his beloved Kali. Nonetheless he seeks release from transmigratory existence and can secure this emancipation through the Tantric method called kundalini yoga. Great contemporary religious and philosophical leaders such as Sri Ramakrishna and Sri Aurobindo have high praise for kundalini yoga. The return cycle in this form of yoga resembles that of the "internal mandala" of Tantric Buddhism described in the previous chapter and takes the following pattern.[1]

The shakti of Brahman is imagined to lie asleep within the yogi coiled up like a sleeping serpent (kundalini) at the end of the spine, the muladhara. The devotee arouses the kundalini from slumber by means of mantras (sacred names or syllables). Meanwhile through pranayama (control of the breath) he clears the channel which is believed to run through the center of the spine called the sushumna. Now aroused shakti moves up the sushumna opening up as she passes an ascending series of "centers" or "lotuses" (*chakras, padmas*). Each "center" is the seat of an element of

---
[2] *Ibid.*, p. 137.
[1] *Op. cit.*, Heinrich Zimmer, *Philosophies of India*, pp. 584 ff.

the body. The muladhara is the seat of the element, earth, and is described as a crimson lotus of four petals. The next "center" is called *svadhisthana* (shakti's own abode) and is in the region of the genitals. It is the seat of the element, water, and is called the vermilion lotus of six petals. After this shakti rises to the region of the navel. This center is called *manipura*. It is the seat of the element, fire, and is the blue-black lotus of ten petals.

Most men in the samsara are guided by these inferior centers. The fourth center, which is in the heart and the seat of the element, air, begins the ascent to the superior divine world.[2] Here the sound OM is heard, not in its physical sense as sound, but the yogi hears the "fundamental OM of creation, which is the goddess herself as sound." [3] This center is called *anahata* and is the ruddy lotus of twelve petals. (This fourth center may be compared with the transitional terrace at Borobudur, the mandala-in-stone of yogic progress in Buddhism.) [4]

The fifth chakra or center is of smoky purple hue and is localized in the throat (where the subtle body usually makes its exit in Vedanta.) This chakra is called the *Visuddha* Chakra, "the completely purified." [1] It is the lotus of sixteen petals, and is the seat of the element, ether. The next two stages leave the realm of the subtle bodies.

The sixth chakra lies at the point between the eyebrows and is called the Lotus of Command *(ajna)*. It is the lotus of two petals and is white as the moon. At this stage the yogi beholds the Lord (Shiva who is equivalent to Ishvara in the Vedanta). The bliss experienced corresponds with the "sheath of bliss" in the Vedanta system. Here the de-

---

[2] *Ibid.*, p. 584.

[3] *Ibid.*, p. 585.

[4] *Supra*, pp. 103 ff. The first three lotuses parallel the Buddhist *Kamaloka* or world of enjoyment of the five senses. In the *Rupaloka* or transitional plane which is the realm of form (the subtle-body world) the senses of touch, smell, and taste are absent. The third world is the formless world wherein the soul perceives Reality.

[1] *Op. cit.*, Zimmer, *Philosophies of India*, p. 585.

votee, again as in Vedanta,[2] beholds the seed-form of the cosmos and of the Vedas, from which proceeds cycle after cycle the evolved universe. The trance state experienced here is of the savikalpa type since consciousness of self and of the Lord are both present.

The seventh and final chakra is located at the crown of the head called the Sahasrara and is the varicolored lotus of a thousand petals. This is the center where shakti is united with her Lord (Shiva) in pure Unity, a non-dual state. Nirvikalpa samadhi is experienced by the yogi, the goal of the return journey. Here the yogi has realized the identity of the Atman with the Brahman (or Shiva) and has attained release forever from transmigratory existence.

Tantric yoga is much more ancient than the more conservative and ascetic Vedantic type of yoga taught by such sages as the greatest Vedanta scholar, Shankara. Shankara was, however, a devotee of Shiva. The cult of Shiva and shakti as the mother-goddess, Kali, may be four thousand years old, perhaps five thousand.[3] The India of today with its more positive approach to life is reviving it in a profounder form in the life, the attitudes towards the world (maya), and the generous altruistic teachings of men like Sri Ramakrishna. The cycle of the return to Brahman is the goal to be fulfilled. This maya world, too, may be enjoyed as the Power or Shakti of the One Real Being if the person living in this world takes the disinterested selfless view of all things which Knowledge yields. The good and the ugly, pain and delight, brutality and gentleness, holiness and obscenity—all are aspects of shakti, and shakti has Brahman as its material and efficient cause; therefore the maya world, too, is Divine. Still, union with the Unmani-

---

[2] In the foregoing paragraphs, "Vedanta" refers to the Advaita school. There are, of course, two other main schools, but the Advaita is by far the most prevalent.

[3] See the discussion of Shiva and his cyclic cosmic dance, *supra*. chap. III, section 1. Paul Reps in an appendix to his *Zen Flesh and Zen Bones* (Charles E. Tpttle Co., Rutland Vermont, 1957) thinks the Shiva yoga cult is probably five thousand years old.

fested, Eternal and quiescent Brahman is the highest achievement of the soul — the cyclic return to the essential Brahman.

Section III

The Cyclical Return to the Center in a Taoist Form of Chinese Yoga: The Secret of the Golden Flower

Early Taoism, the Taoism of the Tao Teh King and of the Chuang-tzu is grounded in a mystical metaphysics similar to that of the Vedanta[1] in India, Sufiism in the Moslem world, and of the Plotinus and Meister Eckhart tradition in the Western world. In all of these mystical philosophies the purpose of the devotee is return to the Primal Source of Being. In early Taoism this Source is the Tao (translated variously as Way, the Great Meaning, and later under the influence of Confucianism, *T'ai Chi* or Great Ridge-Beam. The *T'ai Chi* in Confucianism signifies the great Ridge-beam or Pole of the Universe which is the handle of the Bushel (Great Dipper or Ursa Major). The origin and significance of this idea in the formative period of Chinese civilizaton — the Han Dynasty period — is explained more fully in the following chapter of this book. There are explanations also in the following chapter of many other terms and their possible origins; the reader unfamiliar with Chinese thought might wish, therefore, to read the following chapter before this section.

Richard Wilhelm in his introduction to *The Secret of the Golden Flower* tells us that:

> The character for *Tao* in its original form, consists of a head, which must be interpreted as 'beginning'; and, under that, the character for 'standing still' ...

[1] *Vedanta* as used in this chapter refers only to the Advaita School.

The original meaning, then, is that of a 'track which, though fixed itself, leads from the beginning directly to the goal.' The fundamental idea is the idea that *Tao*, though itself motionless, is the means of all movement and gives it law. Heavenly paths are those along which the stars move; the path of man is the way along which he must travel. Lao Tzu [2] has used this word in the metaphysical sense, as the final world principle, the 'Meaning' existing before there is any realization and not yet divided by the pulling asunder of polar opposites on which all realization depends.[3]

The universe is evolved from Tao, the quiescent source, the One who is the Core or Center (T'ai Chi) of evolved reality which proceeds from this Tao. The first evolute is positive Being which divides into two poles of opposite character: the *yang* which has the qualities of light, and the *yin* which is primarily darkness.[1] The *yang* is the active and masculine principle of nature and associated also with Reason (logos) similar to the sheaths of Intellect and Mind in Vedanta; the *yin* is the feminine principle and associated with Eros or the Life Force and parallels the Vital Sheath of the cosmos in Vedanta. From the Yang and the Yin forces all particular existent things are produced—"the Ten Thousand Things." Man is one of the ten thousand things and represents the cosmos in miniature, again as in Vedanta.

[2] Fung Yu-lan and other great scholars do not attribute the authorship of the Lao-Tzu to a sage by that name. Fung Yu-lan thinks that probably Li Erh, a sage of the early Warring States Period (403-221 B.C.) was the author. Most scholars think it a fourth century work and not by the traditional sixth century Lao-tzu, who may be a mythical character.

[3] Richard Wilhelm, *The Secret of the Golden Flower*, trans. and explained by Richard Wilhelm with a European Commentary by C. G. Jung, translated into English by Cary Baynes (New York: Wehman Bros., 1955), p. 11 f.

[1] Wilhelm denies the sexual origin of the *yang* and *yin* ideas as affirmed by scholars such as Granet and Fitzgerald (see next chapter).

The later Taoism of *The Secret of the Golden Flower*[2] affirms that the "central monad" or phenomenal form of Tao is enclosed in each individual as the life-principle. At conception, however, it separates into the impersonal bi-polar principles of *hsing* and *ming*. *Hsing* has its origin in the *yang* principle of *Tao*. *Hsing* is an impersonal logos — or very close to the Western idea of *logos* — since *hsing* is the formal principle, i.e., "man as a spiritual being is made human by essence (hsing)."[3] *Ming* is the impersonal principle of Life (eros) which with *hsing* enters into the individualizing process of phenomena. The Chinese character *ming*, Wilhelm explains, "really signifies a royal command then, destiny, fate, the fate allotted to a man, so too, the duration of life, the measure of vitality at one's disposal, and thus it comes about that *ming* (life) is closely related to *eros*."[4] The next evolutes proceed simultaneously also in opposing pairs. From *ming* evolves the personal individualized "psychic structure"[5] called the *p'o* which Wilhelm translates *anima*. This *anima* has its center in the abdomen and is the seat of irrational desire (compare the individualized "vital sheath" in Vedanta). From *hsing* evolves the personal individualized "psychic structure" called the *hun* which Wilhelm translates *animus*. The *animus* has its seat between the eyes; its dominant activity is thought and it is the active bright principle whereas the *anima* is dark and passive. The *animus*, if it succeeds in subjugating the *anima*, enables the ego to gain release from the phenomenal world. The ego is empowered to withdraw from this world by a process of introverted meditation (as in Indian yoga) and at death becomes a god (*shen*). He survives by a process of

---

[2] The *Secret of the Golden Flower* (*T'ai I Chin Hua Tsung Chih*) in written form can be traced to tablets of the seventeenth century, but the oral tradition, Wilhelm says, belongs to the eighth century A. D. and is identified with the eighth century sage, Lu Yen (Lu tung-pin) who founded the religion of The Golden Elixir of Life.

[3] *Ibid.*, p. 14.

[4] *Ibid.*

[5] *Ibid.*

"inner rotation" of the central monad. This process may continue for a very long time, and such shen can influence men's thoughts and lives in this world which they have left behind. "The saints and sages of ancient times are beings like these, who for thousands of years have stimulated and educated humanity."[1] If the *p'o* or *anima*, the outward-flowing, yin power of worldly desire gains control over the *animus*, at death the energy powers are so dissipated that the ego in the personal sense is almost lost; it becomes an "impotent phantom" and sinks to various heavens or hells in accordance with the degree of its disintegration. The fruits of its good and bad deeds are suffered but all of this takes place at the subjective or psychological level. Finally this ghost-being (*kuei* is the Chinese word for such a being) enters a new womb and begins another life out of what remains of its store of "images and memories."[2]

The shen although enjoying a long and happy existence is not immortal. Only the Golden Flower is immortal. The Golden Flower or Immortal Body is attained when all ego-consciousness is lost, in the sense of desire for possession of anything. When freedom from attachment is gained individuality is transcended. The limitations of the central monad of hsing and ming, of yang and yin are burst and the devotee returns to *Tao*, the Center, the core of Reality and the only Eternal Being.

The process of attaining the return to the Center, the *Tao*, as described in the *T'ai I Chin Hua Tsung Chih* (The Secret of the Golden Flower) is essentially similar to that of Indian yoga already delineated. The Golden Flower is called the Light and the "true power of the transcendent Great *One*."[1] It is the "Elixir of Life."[2] Realization of the Golden Flower is obstructed by the *anima* in the body.

---

[1] *Ibid.*, p. 18.
[2] *Ibid.*, p. 17.
[1] *Ibid.*, p. 23.
[2] *Ibid.*, p. 25.

The *anima,* having produced consciousness, adheres to it. Consciousness depends for its origin on the *anima.* The *anima* is feminine *(yin),* the substance of consciousness. As long as this consciousness is not interrupted, it continues to beget from generation to generation and the changes of form of the *anima* and the transformations of substance are unceasing.[3]

The *animus* located between the eyes in the daytime and in the liver at night (when it dreams[4]) subjugates the *anima* by concentration which takes place through "circulation of the Light."[5] The Light is the *yang* principle, "in the physical world it is the sun, and in man the eye."[6] The circulation of the Light is "circulation of the true, creative formative powers."[7] If it is directed downward so that the *anima* gains control of it, the soul wanders through aeons of reincarnations unless in one of them it learns the secret of directing the Light in the "backward-flowing" direction. (The Buddhist idea of endless aeons of cosmic cycles is accepted here.) The backward-flowing direction is mastered through characteristic yogic methods such as regulated breathing (to gain control of the heartbeats and "vital sheath" in general) and contemplation. (The yogic methods were borrowed from T'ien T'ai Buddhism.)[8] Contemplation is accomplished through concentration upon the point between the eyes. [This is the "place" in Indian yoga where the dual (savikalpa) samadhi is experienced. Here Ishvara and Shakti are united.] Here the Light concentrates, not only the Light within but the Light without which permeates sun and moon, mountains and rivers, Heaven and Earth—all is the same Light (*yang* power) circulating not only in the body of the devotee but

[3] *Ibid.,* p. 28.
[4] *Ibid.*
[5] *Ibid.*
[6] *Ibid.,* p. 34.
[7] *Ibid.,* p. 35.
[8] *The Secret of the Golden Flower* shows not only Buddhist ideas which are mentioned as such, but also Nestorian Christian ideas.

rotating throughout the total universe. This yang power (Light) streams into the devotee in the point between the eyes which makes of this point the "third eye" of Indian yoga both Hindu and Buddhist.

The next step in the circulation of the Light causes the Light to penetrate downward to the "lower Elixir-field the place of power (solar plexus)" where the "spirit crystallizes and enters the center in the midst of conditions."[1] Here Light (*yang*) (also Fire, the Sun) unites with the "abysmal" the female element (*yin*—water and the moon) and the "new being" appears, the Golden Flower, the immortal body. This is mergence in *Tao*.

In stage three of the cyclical return to the One, the "new being" or Golden Flower (called also the spirit-body) separates from the human body and "ascends" in a state of "independent existence."[2] Its place is the place of the *Tao* "incorporeal space where a thousand and ten thousand spaces are one place . . . It is immeasurable time when all the aeons are like a moment."[3]

In stage four of the meditations the state of being "the center in the midst of the conditions" is realized in its full significance. The "center in the midst of the conditions" is the Tao realized by the devotee in his cyclical return to the primordial One; this Tao is the center of the phenomenal world as the Pole Star (the Tao) is the center or ridge-pole of the universe. The phenomenal world is seen as "empty" i.e., not the essential *Tao* and therefore a "delusion" (cf. Indian notions of the phenomenal world as *maya*). Yet the phenomenal world of emptiness and delusion (from the point of view of the eternal One, the *Tao*) has its origin in Tao, the Center. Therefore:

> Being on the way of the center, one also creates images of the emptiness, but they are not called empty, but are called central. One practices also contemplation of de-

---
[1] *Ibid.*, p. 40.
[2] *Ibid.*, p. 51 and p. 56 (explanation).
[3] *Ibid.*, p. 62.

lusion, but one does not call it delusion, one calls it central.[1]

The "delusion" or phenomenal world is seen as "central" which means it is seen as also the Tao. The world of nature and all men are part of oneself and oneself is part of all men and of all nature—all is Tao in phenomenal, emanated form; therefore all must be seen as "central." The characteristic Chinese emphasis upon identification with Nature, a positive attitude towards the world, is evident here as also in Ch'an contemplative, mystical Buddhism (called Zen in Japan). As in Ch'an the man who has attained the experience of the Golden Flower continues his life in this world in much the same way as before; the difference lies in his attitude which transfigures all things. *The Secret of the Golden Flower* describes the experience and attitudes of such a man:

> Long ago, the true man of the purple Polar-Light (Tzu-yang Chen Jen), made a saying: When a man lives in contact with the world, and yet still in harmony with the Light, then the round is round and the angular has angles; then he lives among men concealed, yet visible, different, and yet the same, and none can compass it; then no one takes note of our secret life and being. The living manner of the circulation of the Light has just this meaning: To live in contact with the world and yet in harmony with the Light.[2]

Unity with all men and all things is experienced when one has realized identity with the Center, the *Tao;* private personal consciousness (called egoity in Indian thought) is seen as delusion and transcended; this makes selfless action possible in this world.

Indian yoga, both Hindu and Buddhist, is founded upon a similar philosophy and the path of the cyclical return is much the same. The affinities with Ch'an Buddhism,

---
[1] *Ibid.,* p. 67.
[2] *Ibid.,* p. 58.

popular today in the Western world under the Japanese name, Zen, are still more pronounced. All forms of Chinese contemplative mysticism or yoga emphasize the characteristic Chinese aesthetic attitude of identification with nature in its *concrete* form. Macrocosm and microcosm are one, the true self is the timeless No-thing or reality of the One beyond the space-time world of transient objects and subjects. Yet,

> Dwelling in one's own abode, unconcerned with that without — The river flows tranquilly on and the flowers are red.[1]

The "comment" on these lines taken from the ninth of the ten Zen spiritual oxherding pictures by the twelfth century Chinese master, Ka Kuan, explains:

> From the beginning, truth is clear. Poised in silence, I observe the forms of integration and disintegration. One who is not attached to 'form' need not be 'reformed.' The water *is* emerald, the mountain *is* indigo, and I see that which *is* creating and that which *is* destroying.[2]

The tenth and last oxherding picture says:

> Barefooted and naked of breast, I mingle with the people of the world.
> My clothes are ragged and dust-laden, and I am ever blissful.
> I use no magic to extend my life;
> Now, before me, the dead trees become alive.[3]

---

[1] Paul Reps, *Zen Flesh and Zen Bones* (Rutland, Vermont and Tokyo, Japan: Charles E. Tuttle Co., 1957), p. 184.
[2] Comment is by Ka Kuan also.
[3] *Ibid.*, p. 186.

In this form of Buddhism (Ch'an or Zen) samsara and nirvana are one. The state realized is similar to that of "the center in the midst of the conditions" described in *The Secret of the Golden Flower*. The cyclical "return to the Center," which sees endless time as one ever-present moment, sees all things transfigured under the aspect of eternity—the entire world is "sacred." The beautiful nineteenth century Zen nun, Ryonen, expresses this idea in her identification with nature in the poem she wrote just before her death:

> Sixty-six times have these eyes beheld the changing scene of autumn.
> I have said enough about moonlight,
> Ask no more.
> Only listen to the voice of pines and cedars when no wind stirs.[4]

These Zen (or Ch'an) ideas reaffirm the philosophy of early Taoism. For example, the Chuang-tzu (fourth century B. C.), chapter VI, summarizes the cyclical return thus:

> I kept on speaking to him; after three days, he began to be able to disregard all worldly matters. After he had disregarded all worldly matters, I kept on speaking to him; after seven days, he began to be able to disregard all external things. After he had disregarded all external things, I kept on speaking to him; after nine days, he began to be able to disregard his own existence. Having disregarded his own existence, he was enlightened. Having become enlightened, he was then able to gain the vision of the One. Having the vision of the One, he was then able to transcend the distinction of past and present. Having transcended the distinction of past and present, he was then able to enter the realm where life and death are no more. Then, to him, the destruction of life did not mean death, nor the

---

[4] *Ibid.*, p. 66.

prolongation of life an addition to the duration of his existence. He would follow anything; he would receive anything. To him, everything was in destruction, everything was in construction. This is called tranquility in disturbance. Tranquility in disturbance means perfection.[1]

Such reintegration of the self with total Reality is a basic need of the human psyche. Great contemporary psychiatrist-psychologists such as Jung lay great emphasis upon this need. Jung informs us that several of his patients unacquainted with Oriental mandalas, spontaneously drew such diagrams.[2] The symbolism of these diagrams was the same as that of the characteristic Oriental mandala whether Hindu or Buddhist, viz., "centering." The patient, however, usually placed himself in the center of the diagram with symbols of the rest of the total universe around him. The purpose of the diagram was reintegration of the self with total nature, total reality in order to overcome the self-alienation from the universe which was the basic cause of the neurosis (distintegration of the psyche). Oriental yoga has much the same purpose and goal, but usually the Divine is in the center—the One or Brahman, or Nothingness, or the Tao—instead of the human as in the Western mandalas of Jung's patients. However, in both, Universe and self or the One and self are reintegrated in organic unity which shows the basic human need for such unity in all men whether of Eastern or Western culture.

Such reintegration, when accomplished, is of enormous psychological value. The great saints (or yogis) of East and West have achieved this in mystical experiences, and such experiences have revolutionized their moral and social attitudes. Contemporary man needs a similar experience of

[1] Quoted from the *Chuang-tzu* in Fung Yu-lan, *A History of Chinese Philosophy* trans. Derk Bodde, 2 vols. (Princeton: Princeton University Press, 1952), vol. I, pp. 238 f.
[2] *Op. cit., The Secret of the Golden Flower*, Commentary by C. G. Jung, section 2: "The Circular Movement and the Center."

reintegration, Jung thinks. He gives as reasons the religious, social, ethical, and political conflicts of our time and their unsatisfactory shallow solutions; but more scientifically and directly the evidence from his study of human individuals especially the patients he has treated. All of these patients over thirty-five years of age, Jung tells us, had as their root problem the philosophico-religious one of integrating themselves with some wider cosmic spiritual reality that would give their lives meaning.[1] Merely theoretical approaches to the problem, Jung writes, are not adequate. Only a liberating experience can give a man spiritual freedom which shows itself in four spiritual "gifts of grace."[2] These are (1) Love versus sexuality; (the yogis and saints have solved this problem); (2) Hope versus disillusionment by the world; (3) Faith versus fear; and (4) Understanding versus failure to know the meaning of existence. The yogis and saints of East and West have solved 2, 3, and 4 as well as 1. The mandala-idea of Centering, of reintegration with man and the cosmos in one organic totality is the general form of all the solutions, Eastern and Western. Therefore, Jung argues, the mandala motif is an archetypal idea mediated to us by the unconscious. These archetypal ideas when "perceived by consciousness seem to represent a set of variations on a ground theme." The theme of the mandala motif seems to be "central." Yet division and the periphery are important also in such diagrams. Therefore, Jung concludes, the archetype itself in its "real nature" is "not capable of being made conscious," but is "transcendent."[3] Its effects on the conscious psyche are "spiritual" Jung discovered in his studies of his patients. The centering process was the climax of their road to recovery and had "the greatest possible therapeutic effect."[4] The archetype is one pole, the *spiritual* pole of the

---

[1] Carl G. Jung, *Modern Man in Search of a Soul*, Harvest Book ed., trans. W. S. Dell and Cary F. Baynes (New York: Harcourt Brace, 1933), p. 229.

[2] *Ibid.*, pp. 225 f.

[3] Carl G. Jung, "A Philosopher Among Souls," chap. VIII of anthology, *This Is My Philosophy*, ed. Whit Burnett (New York: Harper & Brothers, 1957). Jung's essay is entitled" The Spirit of Psychology," and the quotation is from p. 157 of this essay.

[4] *Ibid.*, p. 147.

unconscious; the other pole is *instinct* (the biological) and the bridge to the world of inanimate matter; in the midst between the two is the psyche or conscious self characterized by will. The two poles, matter and spirit, "in archetypal conceptions and instinctual perceptions . . . confront one another on the psychic plane. Matter as well as spirit appear in the psychic realm as distinctive qualities of conscious contents. The ultimate nature of both is transcendent, that is, noumenal, since the psyche and its contents are the only reality which is given to us *without a medium.*"[1]

The purpose of Jung's analytical psychology is abrogation of the sovereignty of the "subjective ego and of collective consciousness" and its replacement with what is called the "self." The "self" is realized through what Jung terms the "individuation process," a reintegration of the whole person in which the collective unconscious contents both at the instinctual and spiritual levels are integrated with the conscious self. The individuation process is similar to the reintegration process of Eastern yogic philosophies described in this and the preceding chapters, and symbolized by the mandala. The person realizes the existence of the "shadow" the collective unconscious at the biological or instinctual level. As this level appears in himself this awareness has "the meaning of a suffering and a passion that implicate the whole man."[2] It is the "dark night of the soul" familiar to the Western world in the writings of mystics like St. John of the Cross or the recognition of the roots of ego-centricity (the cause of karma and rebirth) in the Eastern philosophies just reviewed. It is this aspect of the unconscious which lies in the biosphere, the sphere of the unconscious emphasized by Freud. In recognizing this element of the unconscious in oneself, Jung says, one loses his egoistic self-righteousness and has a broad sympathy with the vices of others even though one does not sanction them. The individuation process is a transformation process in which recognition of "sin" is essential. In

---
[1] *Ibid.*, p. 158.
[2] *Ibid.*, p. 151.

the Tibetan and Indian yogic philosophies these vices are recognized as aspects of the phenomenal cosmic consciousness, the basic causes of egoity. At the opposite pole of the collective unconscious is the archetype, the spiritual pole. It is this pole which yields salvation, the spiritual meaning of existence because its archetypal ideas, when they spill over into consciousness, reintegrate the person with all humanity and with the total cosmos. The person loses his former egocentricity; in the purgative dark night of the soul he annihilates not only the desires of the libidinous unconscious, but the selfish demands of the conscious ego. In the transformation process the source of which is the **Light of the luminous spiritual pole** (the archetype), the ego sees itself in broad and true perspective against its lower background (the biosphere, the instinctual stratum) and its higher spiritual Center, the ultimate Meaning which integrates the entire cosmos. Individuation (or realization of the *self*) has been achieved. Jung points to the self-realization of the great Christian mystics such as St. John of the Cross [1] and the great Eastern mystics, Hindu and Buddhist, and Taoist as examples of the achievement of individuation on the grand scale. His patients, for the most part, did not arrive at such a tightly unified harmonious integration; nevertheless their individuation processes were similar, even though as we said above they characteristically placed themselves (symbols of humanity) at the center of the mandala of reintegration instead of the spiritual Absolute.

Religions, Jung points out, are rich in transformation symbolisms the purpose of which is individuation. The Catholic Mass is an example in Western religion. The communicant recognizes his sins, loses or annihilates his egocentricity and unites himself with Christ in the bread and wine. This is a transformation and individuation process when really *experienced* as a St. Paul might experience it. Such religious rites, like the yogic mandala symbolisms have

---

[1] See "The Intuitive Element in Metaphysics," by the author in *Philosophy East and West*, Vol. IV, No. 1 (April, 1954), pp. 3-17.

the function of "centering" or reintegrating the person with the core of cosmic reality.

The *Divine Comedy*, mandala of the Christian philosophy of man's ultimate historical goal and destiny, at the spiritual level of its meaning has the form and transformation symbolism of the Eastern mandala-idea. The individuation process begins with the descent into the Infernal regions, the recognition of sin (desires of the libidinous unconscious which affect the ego), its purgation in Purgatory, and finally the journey in the spiritual heavenly (archetype) world to the Center or core-reality, God, to behold the vision of this Absolute Being, source of the unity of the cosmos. The "ascension mandala" of Mohammed's "night journey" through the planetary spheres to the throne of God has a similar meaning.

Neoplatonism, a source of Christian and Moslem mystical philosophies, has an alienation-and-return mandala symbolism also. From the ineffable One emanates the World of Ideas, then the World-Soul (which includes all souls), then Matter; the return mandala of the soul sheds the sheaths of Matter and enters the sheath of Intellect (buddhi in Oriental philosophies); then it sheds this sheath and is reabsorbed into the ineffable One.

Hegel's philosophy of history (discussed below in Part II) has a similar transformation symbolism and mandala of alienation and return which is the goal of history in Hegel's thought. The Absolute objectifies or alienates itself in the world of concrete particulars, of separate egos and returns to itself as the Individual. "Salvation" or human freedom, each man's historical goal, consists in a like process of realization of the human person's identity with the Absolute and its alienation and individuation process.

In Marxian philosophies (see the section below in Part II on the Marxian philosophy of history) Humanity is at the Center of the mandala. Class struggles cause egoism and alienation. The return to a unified whole of humanity will occur when class struggles cease. Inviduation here means social altruism, living the life of creative cooperation.

143

The Western philosophies are more humanistic, more man-centered; in the Eastern philosophies the Absolute ineffable Spiritual Reality is characteristically the Center. Jung comments on the significance and historical origins of this difference:

> The fact that all immediate experience is psychic and that immediate reality can only be psychic, explains why it is that primitive man puts the appearance of ghosts and the effects of magic on a plane with physical events ... When the primitive world disintegrated into spirit and nature, the West rescued nature for itself. It was prone to a belief in nature, and only became the more entangled in it with every painful effort to make itself spiritual. The East, on the contrary, took mind for its own, and by explaining away matter as mere illusion *(maya)* continued to dream in Asiatic filth and misery. But since there is only *one* earth and *one* mankind, East and West cannot rend humanity into two different halves. Psychic reality exists in its original oneness, and awaits man's advance to a level of consciousness where he no longer believes in the one part and denies the other, but recognizes both as constituent elements of one psyche.[1]

Professor Northrop gives an account of these characteristic differences from the point of view of the competent research of a great philosopher vitally concerned with the Meeting of East and West. Professor Northrop explains [1] that the East has always taken the aesthetic, non-technological, non-mathematical approach to nature; therefore Eastern philosophy never separates itself from nature as an outsider or attempts to exploit nature as does the West. Earth is Mother Earth in the East; earth, forests, plants and even the rocks are, like man, "fellow-members of an interconnected set of cycles." [2] Sensed particulars in their

---

[1] *Op. cit.*, Jung, *Modern Man in Search of a Soul*, p. 191.

[1] Northrop, F.S.C., "Man's Relation to the Earth in Its Bearing on His Aesthetic Ethical and Legal Values," *Man's Role in Changing the Face of the Earth,* ed. William L. Thomas et al (Chicago: University of Chicago Press, 1956).

[2] *Ibid.*, p. 1057.

cyclical sequence of perpetually being born and perishing is the law of karma in the East and "this is the concept of causality in a non-technological society." [3] Salvation from such causality can be had only by escape from the karma cycle; therefore this escape is the historical goal for all karma-bound souls. The West has developed a mathematical (theoretical), technological approach to nature, which, while it has led to many egoistic evils and alienation from nature and other men, has contributed much to the amelioration of human life in this world through technology; and even more important as an aspect of theoretical good it has contributed self-conscious abstract Law—ideas of Human Rights "contract-ideas" which must be guaranteed to all human beings as such. Nevertheless the West can learn from the East the aesthetic approach of organic unity of man with nature, with the cosmos; "immersion with, aesthetic sensitivity to, and harmony with nature," [4] which is the concept of the good in the East. The East, in its turn, needs to put to use the technologies and theoretical knowledge of the West (the East is actually doing this now).

Because of the non-technological, non-mathematical, subjective approach of Eastern philosophies which emphasize the "undifferentiated continuum" or distinctionless Absolute as the ultimate reality and goal of human existence, Western technological, mathematical approaches with their humanistic *Weltanschauungs* seem foreign perhaps to the characteristic Oriental world-views. The Western *Weltanschauungs* which take the phenomenal world as objectively real in an ultimate sense, are opposed in Eastern thought (in the yogic philosophies) with the view that the phenomenal world has the status of *maya*. Does this view of the phenomenal world lead essentially to rejection of, and emphasis upon escape from this world as the sole object of human life and human history on this planet? The problem of the world as *maya* (which Jung, Schweitzer and many others think is responsible for Asiatic misery) will be the

---
[3] *Ibid.*, p. 1058.
[4] *Ibid.*, p 1057.

subject of the following chapter. It will be seen that union with Brahman or the Buddhist absolute state, although it is the ultimate goal of human history, actually aids rather than inhibits altruistic creative action in this world; and the chapters in Part II on Sri Aurobindo and Professor Radhakrishnan support this view in a far more radical way.

Section IV
Yogic Experience, Maya, and Cyclical Time

In the Sankhya system, the nirvikalpa samadhi is an experience of the eternal state which is the Real; and it is this state which is the goal of the system of metaphysics and of yogic exercises. In the nirvikalpa samadhi spirit (*purusa*) is in its primeval pure state uncontaminated with the matter world (*prakrti*). This matter world, however, is real and not maya. The Sankhya metaphysics is dualistic. The maya concept is applicable only to the illusion that the self can be identified with aspects of *prakrti* such as intellect, mind and the sense organs, egoity, the vital sheath and the gross body.

In the Advaita Vedanta system however the metaphysics is monistic. All reality is Brahman, the one eternal Real Being. Brahman in his essential nature is experienced, we have seen, in nirvikalpa samadhi. In this experience Brahman is known as truth, i.e., "one mass of knowledge," but without specific cognitions (since this would imply parts and distinctions) and as Infinite, for It alone is real.[1] The phenomenal world of parts and distinctions, the evolutionary process of which we have described above as the Vedanta philosophy conceives it, is a maya world produced by Brahman as a magician produces an illusion or as a spider weaves a web out of its own substance. Shankara, the great-

---
[1] *The Vedanta-Sutras with Commentary by Sankaracharya*, trans. George Thibaut, SBE, Vol. XXXIV (Oxford: Clarendon Press, 1890), p. 281.

est metaphysician of the Advaita Vedanta school writes:

> As the magician is not at any time affected by the magical effect produced by himself, because it is unreal, so the highest Self is not affected by the world—[effects (or appearances)]. And as one dreaming person is not affected by the illusory visions of his dream because they do not accompany the waking state and the state of dreamless sleep; so the one permanent witness of the three states (viz., the highest Self which is the one unchanging witness of the creation, subsistence, and reabsorption of the world) is not touched by the mutually exclusive three states. For that the highest Self appears in those three states is a mere illusion, not more substantial than the snake for which the rope is mistaken in the twilight . . .
>
> . . . With regard to the . . . objection, viz., that if we assume all distinctions to pass (at the time of reabsorption) into the state of non-distinction there would be no special reason for the origin of a new world affected with distinctions, we likewise refer to the "existence of parallel instances." For the case is parallel to that of deep sleep and trance. In those states also the self enters into an essential condition of non-distinction; nevertheless, wrong knowledge being not yet finally overcome, the old state of distinction re-establishes itself as soon as the self awakes from its sleep or trance . . . [1]

Furthermore, the world of phenomena must be appearance and not reality or there could be no such thing as truth in its absolute meaning. In the absolute sense of the meaning of truth, truth and its object must be One. Reality cannot be a plurality nor even a duality; true knowledge must be knowledge-by-identity.

Many contemporary Hindu philosophers maintain this view of truth [2] which is truth on the spiritual plane beyond

---

[1] *The Vedanta-sutras with Commentary by Sankaracharya*, II.i.9, quoted in Radhakrishnan and Moore, *op. cit.*, p. 523.

[2] The views of Radhakrishnan and of Aurobindo are discussed in subsequent chapters so will not be treated here. Both, however, think of the world as a positive projection, a phenomenal and to that extent —real world produced by the One Absolute Reality.

the dualistic plane of discursive reason where object and subject are different from each other. V. Subrahmanya Iyer, for example, writes: "Non-difference is a necessity in attaining truth beyond doubt. Absolute non-difference in thought or knowledge is the same as non-duality in existence or being,"[3] and "to know is to be."[4] The ultimately Real, he says, transcends our "waking-state" categories of cause and effect, space and time:

> Causal relation is only characteristic of the thinking process, which enables the mind to know the world of experience ... Seeing that all Ideas and concepts are wiped out in deep-sleep, they are, as such, unreal. This universe, when viewed as unassociated with the concept of causal relation, is neither produced nor destroyed. Space and time which causality implies, share the same fate.[5]

Professor Iyer then goes on to show in this essay that science, psychology, art, ethics, sociology, religion—all aim at a unity which, if attained, would result in an absolute non-duality. The argument is similar to that of F. H. Bradley's *Appearance and Reality*. Almost exactly like Bradley, Iyer argues that the phenomenal world of terms and relations, of parts, distinctions, and differences is shown by Reason to be illogical and therefore unreal. Reason, Iyer says, removes the "intellectual misgivings" that the Real and the goal of truth is non-duality.[1] The deep-sleep state reveals a condition of distinctionlessness (non-duality) similar to the state of the Real, the Brahman. The other two states, the waking-self state and the dreaming-self state are phenomenal and unreal; of the latter two the dreaming

---

[3] V. Subrahmanya Iyer, "Man's Interest in Philosophy: An Indian View," *Contemporary Indian Philosophy*, S. Radhakrishnan and J. H. Muirhead, editors, rev. and enlarged ed. (London: George Allen & Unwin, Ltd., 1952), p. 606.

[4] *Ibid.*, p. 608.

[5] *Ibid.*, pp. 609 f.

[1] *Ibid.*, p. 618.

state is truer because the material world (world of the waking-self) has least reality. Professor Iyer in this essay is reiterating the idealistic philosophical views (combined with yogic experience as empirical verification) which are as old as the Upanishads. The Mandukya Upanishad describes the four states of consciousness on the macrocosmic scale which has its exact parallel on the microcosmic. These states are represented in the mantra (mystic syllable), *Om*. In the word *Om* the letter *o* was originally a diphthong *au* which makes three letters AUM. The "A" signifies the waking state of the universal person (physical sheath of the universe and of the individual as previously described)[2]; the "U" signifies the dreaming state and the sheaths which comprise the "subtle body" of the universe and the individual person (as described previously)[3]; and the "M" is the deep-sleep (dreamless sleep) state of the macrocosm and of the microcosm, the "sheath of bliss" and is described as "just a cognition-mass, consisting of bliss, . . . lord of all . . . the all-knowing . . . the inner controller . . . the source of all . . . the origin and the end of beings."[4] This is Ishvara ensheathed in the Ignorance, the dark deep layer of maya which underlies the phenomenal world.[5] This deep-sleep state is not the goal, however, but the fourth state called *turiya*. It is this fourth state which Professor Iyer is really describing perhaps, but in any case it is the fourth state which is knowledge-by-identity, the state in which the sedge of maya—all the sheaths—are stripped and the Eternal One in its changeless, distinctionless infinity is realized. The illuminated seer of the Mandukya Upanishad attempts to express the inexpressible, to describe the indescribable in these words:

> Not inwardly cognitive, not outwardly cognitive, not bothwise cognitive, not a cognition-mass, not cognitive,

---
[2] *Supra*, section 2.
[3] *Ibid.*
[4] *Mandukya Upanisad*, p. 56 translated in Radhakrishnan and Moore, *A Source Book in Indian Philosophy*, op. cit.
[5] *Supra*, section 2.

not non-cognitive, unseen, with which there can be no dealing, ungraspable, having no distinctive mark, non-thinkable, that cannot be designated, the essence of the assurance of which is the state of being one with the Self, the cessation of development, tranquil, benign, without a second (*a-dvaita*)—[such] they think is the fourth. He is the Self. He should be discerned.[1]

For Hindu, Buddhist and Taoist thought ignorance that the world of the sheaths, of the three states of consciousness, is maya is the fundamental sin of man which will send him bowling around the Wheel of Becoming for myriads of aeons in the everlastingly repeated cosmic cycles. Man must realize that the phenomenal world is the shakti of the highest Being, the transcendental Shiva, or the Brahman or Vishnu in Hinduism; or of the Adi-Buddha (such as Vajrasattva) in Mahayana Buddhism; or the yang-yin manifestations of the Tao in Taoism. In Hinayana Buddhism too, it is said that Buddha described a permanent world beyond this maya world as follows:

> There is an unborn, an unbecome, an unmade, an uncompounded; if there were not, there would not be an escape from the born, the become, the made, the compounded. But because there is an unborn, an unbecome, an unmade, an uncompounded, therefore there is an escape from the born, the become, the made, and the compounded. [2]

This negative description of what is beyond the maya world might be interpreted as annihilation. To this interpretation Buddha is said to have replied that there is no ego to be annihilated. [3] Belief in the ego is the basic ignorance from which all the rest of the maya world follows.

[1] *Mandukya Upanisad, op. cit.*

[2] E. J. Thomas, *The History of Buddhist Thought, op. cit.*, p. 129.

[3] The trance state in which nirvana is realized is qualityless, distinctionless, and in all ways seems identical with the nirvikalpa samadhi of Hinduism. In Hinayana Buddhism, the interpretation of this state is given a negative interpretation (Non-Being).

Here Buddhism, Hinduism, and Taoism are in agreement. All the yogas we have reviewed agree that it is the desire world of the karmic entity which gives the illusion of an ego born into the lifestream of *samsara* where illusory pleasures and pains of a private ego are evolved as psychic objects by the Lord of Shakti (or Yang-yin, Ming-Hsing polarities in the form of yogic Taoism described above) and the ego. Lust, anger and greed result from this narrow ego-consciousness because it alienates the self from its divine Source, its primeval unity with the One Real. Return to the Center, the aim of all the yogas, reabsorption into the One restores the bond of unity not only with the One but with the entire phenomenal world, Maya of the One. The world is not real in the same sense as Brahman or Tao or the Buddha essence, but it is a dependent "creation," a positive projection of the power of the One Real. Since this is true the yogi can return to the world with utter love but non-attachment—for the world, too, is Brahman. Having no illusion of a personal ego, the yogi conducts himself with complete equanimity in the world, for like Brahman with whom he now identifies himself, all men and things are viewed as organic parts of the one maya world, the one Shakti of the One Real. Why the Eternal One, spaceless and timeless, weaves the magic web of maya is in the last analysis an inscrutable mystery. The usual Vedanta view takes the maya or samsara world of particular space-time existence as the *lila*, the free play of the Eternal, for the Brahman is Infinite Being and needs nothing. He is not constrained to emanate the maya world in its endless cosmic cycles; his Pure Being is untouched by the involution-evolution cycles of the countless worlds. The yogi, if he attains his goal, is too this Infinite Being, this Brahman and like Brahman can in serene, detached fashion enjoy the drama of the maya world. But the unenlightened egos, slaves of maya, attached to the illusion of a private individuality for which worldly goods must be greedily grasped are bound throughout empty aeons on the empty Wheel of Time. The pathos of the *samsara* even though the state of a god-self such as an Indra is attained is brought out in a beautiful symbolic myth "The Parade of Ants" in the literature of the *Puranas*.[1]

The story begins when the god, Indra, hero of the tale, has just slain the dragon which held the life-giving waters of heaven captive. The waters are now released to nourish the world. Now that the combat is over Indra desires to have the public buildings of his heavenly city repaired. For himself he requests the craftsman of the gods, Visvakarman, to build a palace of such grandeur that it will be unrivaled anywhere. Indra's demands grew so enormously that the architect, Visvakarman, was in despair and went before a higher god, Brahma, for counsel. Brahma said that Indra would voluntarily give up the building enterprise very shortly. To accomplish this Brahma called upon Vishnu, the Supreme Being, for aid. Vishnu incarnated himself as a beautiful brahmin boy and appeared before Indra. This noble child told Indra that no previous Indra had completed a palace as magnificent as the one planned by the present Indra. Indra was surprised and asked the boy how many Indras he had known. The boy answered:

> O King of Gods, I have known the dreadful dissolution of the universe. I have seen all perish, again and again, at the end of every cycle. At that terrible time, every single atom dissolves into the primal, pure waters of eternity, whence originally all arose ... Ah, who will count the universes that have passed away, or the creations that have risen afresh, again and again, from the formless abyss of the vast waters? Who will number the passing ages of the world, as they follow each other endlessly? And who will search through the wide infinities of space to count the universes side by side, each containing its Brahma, its Vishnu, and its Shiva? Who will count the Indras in them all—those Indras side by side, who reign at once in all the innumerable worlds; those others who

---

[1] *Brahmavaivarta Purana*, Krsna-janma Khanda, 47, 50-161, quoted by Zimmer in *Myths and Symbols in Indian Art, op. cit.*, pp. 3-11.

passed away before them; or even the Indras who succeed each other in any given line, ascending to godly kingship, one by one, and, one by one, passing away? King of Gods, there are among your servants certain who maintain that it may be possible to number the grains of sand on earth and the drops of rain that fall from the sky, but no one will ever number all those Indras. This is what the Knowers know.

The life and kingship of an Indra endure seventy-one aeons, and when twenty-eight Indras have expired, one Day and Night of Brahma has elapsed. But the existence of one Brahma, measured in such Brahma Days and Nights, is only one hundred and eight years. Brahma follows Brahma; one sinks, the next arises; the endless series cannot be told. There is no end to the number of those Brahmas—to say nothing of Indras.

Put the universes side by side at any given moment, each harboring a Brahma and an Indra: who will estimate the number of these? Beyond the farthest vision, crowding outer space, the universes come and go, an innumerable host. Like delicate boats they float on the fathomless, pure waters that form the body of Vishnu. Out of every hair-pore of that body a universe bubbles and breaks. Will you presume to count them? Will you number the gods in all those worlds— the worlds present and the worlds past? [1]

Then a procession of ants in a column four yards wide paraded across the floor before the boy and Indra. The boy laughed. Indra insisted upon knowing why. The boy replied that the reason for his laughter was a profound secret that would merely injure worldly beings although it would be spiritual illumination for those seeking release from the samsara. Indra pressed the boy to yield the secret. The boy then revealed to him that each ant of the army had once been an Indra. By meritorious deeds in many lives each had won rebirth as Indra. However, by subsequent demeritorious and wicked deeds each had again become a much lower form of life — each was now an ant. This makes

---

[1] *Ibid.*, pp. 5 ff.

plain the futility of existence in the transient world of samsara.

The boy concluded his philosophical discourse with the notion that the phenomenal time-world is like a dream:

> Life in the cycle of the countless rebirths is like a vision in a dream. The gods on high, the mute trees and the stones, are alike apparitions in this phantasy. But Death administers the law of time. Ordained by time, Death is the master of all. Perishable as bubbles are the good and the evil of the beings of the dream. In unending cycles the good and evil alternate. Hence the wise are attached to neither, neither the evil nor the good. The wise are not attached to anything at all.[2]

Through non-attachment (loss of desire, greed, grasping, ego-consciousness) the escape from the Wheel of Time is won; for this makes possible the yogic trance experience in which such escape is actually realized. It is the trance-state, itself, it seems that has given rise to the idea of the Timeless Real since in this state only pure Consciousness is present of a richly noetic kind but without objects; absolute unity of Knower and known, subject and object is realized. This experience plus the view that evolution-cycles are ever the same in pattern and endlessly repeated, fosters the idea that time is meaningless. Yearning for release then becomes a dominant emotion, yogic methods of attaining this release are studied and practiced until samadhi is achieved, the fore-taste of the continuous eternal bliss of Brahman to be enjoyed after one's karma has been accomplished and the body dies forever.

The Vedanta of Shankara in its approach to the maya world has been accused of negativity, i.e., denial of any value to life in this phenomenal world. However, his view is really no more negative than the orthodox Christian

---
[2] *Ibid.*, p. 8.

view of St. Augustine who maintains that this world of the flesh, of the "Fall" which has alienated man from God, is a fleeting abode for the purpose of salvation of some souls for eternal life in the Heavenly City, the City of God.[1] The difference lies in the fact that the cosmic cycle is a unique one in Augustine's and Hebrew-Christian-Zoroastrian-Moslem thought generally whereas in Oriental thought world cycles are repeated. The new astronomy seems to affirm the latter theory — millions of galaxies with similar evolutionary patterns, although there may be a unique cycle of the total system of galaxies.

Heinrich Zimmer points out, nevertheless, that Shankara's attitude and the traditional classical Vedanta which followed his leadership was more negative towards this world than contemporary Hindu thought. Zimmer takes Sri Ramakrishna as a leading example of the change towards world-affirmation. Sri Ramakrishna (1836-86) was a follower of the Tantric (or kundalini) form of Yoga described above and was a worshipper of the Maya or Shakti of Brahman under the worm of Kali, the Mother. Sri Ramakrishna is quoted as saying:

> The Divine Mother revealed to me in the Kali temple that it was She who had become everything . . . She showed me that everything was full of Consciousness. The Image was Consciousness, the altar was Consciousness, the water-vessels were Consciousness, the door-sill was Consciousness, the marble floor was Consciousness — all was Consciousness. I found everything inside the room soaked, as it were, in Bliss — the Bliss of Saccidananda.[2] I saw a wicked man in front of the Kali temple; but in him also I saw the Power of the Divine Mother vibrating. That was why

---

[1] *Infra*, Part II, chap. III.

[2] This means Being-Consciousness-Bliss and is also written as three words *Sat, Cit, Ananda*.

I fed a cat with the food that was to be offered to the Divine Mother.[1]

The entire maya world is revered as the Divine Mother, Shakti of the Eternal. Ramakrishna, contrary to the yogi of the Shankara school, does not "like to say, 'I am Brahman,'" but he and the "lovers of God" take the attitude, "O God, thou art the Master, and I am Thy servant. Thou art the Mother, and I am Thy child . . . Thou art my Father and Mother. Thou art the Whole, and I am a part."[2] Yet Ramakrishna, too, accepted the Vedanta metaphysics and experienced the nirvikalpa samadhi in which he realized the Eternal One beyond maya; but it is evident that he loved the phenomenal world as also God. Twentieth century Hindu thinkers, the greatest of whom are Radhakrishnan and Aurobindo, also are world-affirming and believe that it is man's duty to embody the highest spiritual values in life in this world. A chapter is devoted to each of these thinkers in the next part of this book, so we need not elaborate here upon their ideas about the status of the world (maya).

Buddhism also in its Mahayana form took a far more positive attitude towards this world despite the emphasis upon the futility of cosmic cycles alike in pattern repeated forever[3] and the parallel emphasis upon the unreality, transiency and meaninglessness of the samsara wheel of the individual's transmigratory existence. The Bodhisattva ideal of the Mahayana of which Avalokitesvara is the prototype shows us a being who has overcome the maya world, has achieved freedom from it and is ready to enter Nirvana forever. Avalokitesvara, however (and others who follow his example and who, too, have become bodhisatt-

---

[1] Quoted in Zimmer, *Philosophies of India, op. cit.*, pp. 561-2, from The Gospel of Sri Ramakrishna, trans. with introduction by Swami Nikhilananda (New York, 1942), p. 858.

[2] *Ibid.*, Quoted from *The Gospel of Sri Ramakrishna*, pp. 133-5.

[3] *Supra*, chapter IV.

vas), took a vow not to enter Nirvana until *all* beings have been enlightened and thus saved from this maya world of transmigratory existence. This vow was taken because of the egolessness and compassion of the Bodhisattva who typifies perfected being. The significance of such a vow changes the value of the samsara world, Zimmer tells us, because the world is endless as we have seen in our review of Buddhist cosmic cycles. Therefore such a vow amounts to abandonment of nirvana since it cannot be entered as long as the cyclic aeons continue. The bodhisattva must remain in the state between time (the maya world) and eternity forever. "This is the reason," Zimmer writes, "why his vow is world-redemptive. Through it the truth is symbolized that time and eternity, samsara and nirvana, do not exist as pairs of opposites but are equally 'emptiness' *(sunyata)*, the void."[1] Samsara and nirvana are the same, it is paradoxically said.

Chinese Buddhism emphasizes this identity between samsara and nirvana in the Ch'an (Zen) school which directly influenced the later Taoist yoga school which began in the eighth century and fathered the doctrines we described as the content of *The Secret of the Golden Flower*. The basic idea, the return to the Center and "circulation of the Light" about this Center combines native Taoist thought with Buddhist yoga. In this Chinese yoga samsara and nirvana are again identified. One achieves the state of "the center in the midst of the conditions" described above.[2]

The conclusion is that Oriental philosophy does not negate the world. The purpose of the philosophies is rather the transfiguration of life in this world. As Aurobindo expresses it the yogi who has attained release, who has successfully made the return journey to the Center, the Source of Being, must become a Gnostic Being—a "poise of being" of the One and live both in time and in eternity, for both belong to the One Real Being. The yogi who has at-

[1] Zimmer, *Philosophies of India*, op. cit., p. 535.
[2] *Supra*, section 3.

tained this realization has gained true Freedom. Such Freedom, the core of which is egolessness, is the goal.

Freedom is the goal for the individual and society in many philosophies or mythologies of history both Eastern and Western as we shall see throughout this book, but the Hindu-Buddhist idea of freedom has a distinct flavor because emphasis is placed upon release from the bondage of the cyclic wheel of individual and cosmic repetitious history. Hindu-Buddhist views in Mahayana Buddhist forms reached China in the first century A.D. We have noticed the influence of such views upon the Chinese yogic later Taoism of *The Secret of the Golden Flower*. The Taoist background of this work, however, gives it a uniquely Chinese metaphysics. A cyclical philosophy of cosmic history is accepted but was derived from Buddhism. Historical cycles synthesized with nature cycles, however, were apparently pre-Buddhist and are purely Chinese. Not until the eleventh century it seems was there a fully developed theory of cosmic cycles, endlessly repeated; and even here the theory has an originality that has grown out of native Chinese concepts.

Chapter VIII

Organismic Cyclical Views of History in Chinese Thought

The cyclical approach to history is not characteristic of Chinese thought. The traditional dominant philosophy of history may be called a non-cyclical "chronological primitivism."[1] This is a view of history in which the Golden Age is always in the past of a culture and its subsequent history represents a decline. In China the Golden Age is the legendary era of culture heroes and legendary emperors such as Huang-ti, Yao, Shun, and Yu of the third millennium B.C.; all that later ages can hope for, as far as progress is concerned, is a close approximation to this primitive paradisiacal epoch. Nevertheless some of China's great thinkers have developed a cyclical philosophy of nature and of history which is grounded in the characteristic organismic nature-philosophy of this great culture. Since these cyclical philosophies are integral parts of the Chinese world view in general, we shall begin with a brief account of its formulation and development. The emperor (or Son of Heaven), Lord of the Calendar, Heaven itself, the Yin and Yang and the Five Elements of earth play essential parts in the organismic world view as we shall see below.

Yin-yang, the Five Elements, and the Son of Heaven. Just as in Mesopotamia and in India, the kingship in China developed out of cyclical seasonal fertility rites. The king became the key figure in keeping the seasons in proper

---
[1] Lovejoy and Boas, *op. cit,,* p. 1.

order so that crops would be plentiful. To perform this calendrical function, he had to be able to control the yin-yang forces of nature and read the astronomical signs in the heavens that predicted the crucial turning-points in the seasonal year, i.e., the solstices and the equinoxes. He was above all things, Lord of the Calendar, the son Celestial, and in later times, subject peoples showed his overlordship by accepting his calendar.

The notion of yin-yang forces gives Chinese culture its unique flavor. It is interesting to speculate about the origins of this idea. The sinologue, Fitzgerald, expresses a plausible opinion. He believes that the peculiar geographical conditions of the Yellow River valley culture gave rise to the yin-yang idea. He observes that a very delicate balance of nature forces is necessary for the fertility of this area. For one thing the farmer's crops depend upon the spring rains; at times these fail entirely or they may be insufficient for an adequate harvest. If the rains fail entirely, the summer sun withers the crops and there is famine. If this does not happen there may be excessive rainfall in midsummer which floods away the unripened crops; and again famine results. Fitzgerald says that one or the other of these calamities occurs in some part of the country every four or five years.[1] It is plain, then, that a delicate balance of nature forces, of seasonal rains and the proper amount of sunshine at the right time is necessary for adequate harvests. The Chinese called the watery (rain) element the yin and the sun element the Yang. These two must maintain a proper harmonious balance if famine is to be avoided. The yin-yang forces were given sex, also; appropriately the yin became female and was associated with the moon, the negative, the dark, the cold, and the even numbers; the yang with the sun, the positive, the light, the warm and the odd numbers.

The link between the association of seasonal nature

---

[1] C. P. Fitzgerald, *China: A Short Cultural History* (New York: Frederick A. Praeger, Inc., 1954) fourth rev. ed., p. 35.

forces with sex lies probably in the immemorial past when spring group marriages of youths and maidens were perhaps the ritualistic devices for control of these yin-yang forces to maintain the harmonious balance needed to avoid starvation. The places where these rituals were performed were called Holy Places; but by the time of the Shang dynasty (ca. 1700 B. C.) or earlier the marital relations between the prince and his wife came to be substituted for the spring group marriages.[1] The Prince personified and controlled the yang forces and his consort the yin powers.[2] The king now had the heavy responsibility for the seasonal harmony of nature. It was his function to promulgate the farmer's calendar which became the calendar for the realm.

Astronomical observations were essential for predicting the seasons; the king was the responsible head of this department since he was, himself, the essential figure in the harmony of the seasonal forces. To perform his calendrical functions, the king used a *Ming T'ang* or Hall of Light. This contained an observatory, and, at various times, from five to nine rooms (probably nine in the Chou Dynasty period—ca. 1122-256 B. C.). The king shed his magical power over the proper season in the five room Ming T'ang or proper month of the season in the nine room building. There was a direct correlation between the seasonal cycle and the directions of space: North was the winter season; east, the spring; south, summer; west, autumn. With the nine months style of *Ming T'ang* the intermediate directions were occupied by the monarch as in the following diagram:[3]

North—Winter—3 northern rooms of square { 10th mo. 11th mo. 12th mo.

---

[1] Marcel Granet, *Chinese Civilization*, trans. Kathleen E. Innes and Mabel R. Brailsford (London: Routledge & Kegan Paul Ltd., 1930), pp. 170-173 describe the spring group marriages.

[2] *Ibid.*, p. 185.

[3] William Edward Soothill, *The Hall of Light*, ed. Lady Hosie and G. F. Hudson (London: Lutterworth Press, 1951) p. 34.

West—Autumn—3 western rooms of square	9th mo. / 8th mo. / 7th mo.
South—Summer 3 southern rooms of square	6th mo. / 5th mo. / 4th mo.
East—Spring—3 eastern rooms of square	1st. mo. / 2nd mo. / 3rd mo.
West—Autumn—8th month Center room of West	Tsung Chang Shrine
North—Winter—11th month Center room of North	Hsuan T'ang: or Dark Shrine
Center shrine of square	Ling T'ai or Mid-Season
South—Summer—5th month Center room of South	Ming T'ang or Bright Shrine
East—Spring—2nd month Center room of East	Ch'ing Yang Shrine

The correlation between these directions of space and the seasons was apparently based on astronomical observations of the Bushel, most important star group in Chinese lore. This is our Ursa Major (popularly called the Dipper in the West). A Chinese text makes plain the method of telling the "time" of the seasons and directions of space by observing the Bushel handle:

> When the tail of the Bear points to the east (at nightfall) it is spring to all the world. When the tail of the Bear points to the south, it is summer to all the world. When the tail of the Bear points to the west it is autumn to all the world. When the tail of the Bear points to the north, it is winter to all the world. [1]

---
[1] *Ibid.*, p. 60 Professor Soothill is quoting Chalmers.

Professor Chalmers, who quotes this passage from the writings of Ho-kwantsze, adds: "It is well to keep in mind that the body of the Great Bear was in ancient times considerably nearer to the north pole than it is now, and the tail appeared to move round the pole somewhat like the hand of a clock or watch." [2]

The Pole Star itself is the axis of the celestial seasonal clock; therefore, since all the celestial bodies were thought of as deities, the Pole Star as the Center must be the Great Ruler of the Heavenly regions, [3] just as his counterpart on earth, the king, is the central or pivotal figure. This is another example of the *pars pro toto* type of thinking so universal in ancient cultures. Human social organization, the part, is extended on a macrocosmic scale to the universe, the heavens. This mythopoeic kind of thinking is far more pronounced in a work called the *Song of the Sky Pacer*, an astronomical rhyme attributed to Tan Hsuan Tzu (of the Sui dynasty—589-618 A.D.) but based on ideas popular at least as early as the Han period as we shall see below. Professor Soothill translates only the part of the rhyme that is concerned with the Polar (central) division of the heavens. The total plan of the celestial regions described is the following: The heaven is divided into five large regions, a central or Polar constellation area, and around this Four Quarters, the North, South, East and West. Each quarter has seven "mansions" or constellations (a total of 28 mansions) and in the poem each "mansion" or constellation has a verse which gives the name and position of the stars in that constellation.

Professor Soothill's translation makes obvious the mythopoeic *pars pro toto* approach to an understanding of the universe. "As below so above"; that is, the Pole Star and its accompanying constellation represent the Heavenly Ruler, the Supreme Spirit, and his family and officials.

---

[2] *Ibid.*

[3] Fung Yu-lan, trans. Derk Bodde, *A History of Chinese Philosophy* (Princeton: Princeton University Press, 1953) 2 Vols., Vol. II, p. 101, footnote 2

The Quarters represent lesser princes and their menages. The earthly world or microcosm is a replica of the heavenly world or macrocosm. The poem says:

> The North Pole Central Palace is the Purple *Wei* palace.
> The North Pole five stars are in its midst.
> The throne of the Great Ruler is the second pearl,
> The third star the abode of the concubine's son
> ....
> Left Pivot, Right Pivot keep the South gate,
> The Guards on both sides are fifteen;
> Prime Minister and Marshall face each other;
> Minor Minister, Senior Statesman, then Junior Statesman;
> ....
> East of the back gate is the Chief Assistant's office;
> ....
> Two yellow Yin-te stars assemble within the gate,
> In order come the Secretaries in their five places
> ....
> Kou-ch'en's tail indicates the head of the Pole.
> ....
> The Celestial Soverign is alone within Kou-ch'en.[1]

At the time this rhyme was composed (as in Chou dynasty times) astronomy and astrology were very closely related. Knowing the official position of each star in its constellation was very important in predicting events below, since changes in a star meant a change in the corresponding official or office below. Judicial astrology was a very important pseudo-science from earliest times. For example, Hsi and Ho (whose names mean respectively Sacrificer and Harmonizer) astronomers-royal of the legendary ruler Yao (24th century B.C.) are said to have supervised the arts of divination of which the first was astrology. The

---

[1] Soothill, *Hall of Light, op. cit.*, Appendix II, pp. 244-251.

I-wen Chih, the catalogue of the Imperial Han dynasty library now found in the *Ch'ien Han Shu* (chapter 30) tells us:

> Astrology is used to arrange in order the twenty-eight "mansions" and note the progressions of the five planets and of the sun and the moon, so as to record thereby the manifestations of fortune and misfortune. It is in this way that the Sage-king conducts government.[2]

The twenty-eight "mansions" (lunar), however, were not known until Chou times, probably somewhere between 1000-800 B.C.,[3] so the elaborate kind of judicial astrology described above was scarcely possible earlier. Nevertheless, observations of the Bushel in relation to seasonal cycles as quoted above in the passage from Ho-kwantsze were made between 1500-1000 B.C.[4]

By the time of the Han dynasty the Bushel constellation was of such significance that the Emperor's capital was planned to correspond with the pattern of the Great Bear (or Bushel constellation) and Little Bear joined together with the imperial palace itself in the position of the Pole Star.[1] Thus the Emperor is the core of the earthly organism and of its harmonious well-being, just as the Pole Star is the axis or core of Heaven. There is such a close organic relationship between Earth and Heaven that should the

---

[2] Fung Yu-lan, *op. cit.*, Vol. I, p. 26.

[3] H. D. Chatley, "Ancient Chinese Astronomy," *Occasional Notes,* No. 5, *Royal Astronomical Society,* 1939, pp. 65-74.

[4] *Ibid.*

[1] J. J. L. Duyvendak, "The Mythico-Ritual Pattern in Chinese Civilization," *Proceedings of the Seventh Congress for the History of Religions, Amsterdam, 4th-9th September 1950,* ed. C. J. Bleeker, G. W. J. Drewes, K. A. H. Hidding (Amsterdam: North-Holland Publishing Co., 1951), pp. 137-138. I am indebted to T. H. Gaster for drawing my attention to this article in his book review of *Iconography of Ancient Kingship* by Orange which appeared in *Review of Religion,* March, 1955.

Emperor conduct himself improperly, Heaven's anger would be felt in unseasonal weather phenomena plus other unpleasant manifestations. The ruler is responsible for announcing each season and for its "seasonableness." For example, when the stellar calendar clock, the Bushel, points its tail to the east at nightfall, the Ruler announces the arrival of spring and engages in a fitting ritual to "meet the spring." [2] The most ancient part of the ritual is a ritual ploughing; other parts are equally concerned with fertility such as the wearing of green as the ceremonial color, commands issued for sacrificing to hills, woods, and streams; and commands forbidding the sacrificing of female victims, or the disturbing of nests, or the destruction of the unborn, the newly-born, fledgelings, young animals or eggs.[3] The beginning of an offensive war is forbidden also.[4] All of these commands are obviously intended as mimetic magic to encourage the forces of the new life of spring; destructive acts by mimetic magic inhibit the life forces.[5] Suitable rituals and commands were issued for each of the twelve months of the year. It was in the Ming T'ang or House of the Calendar that the Emperor functioned as the pivotal figure in maintaining that harmony between Heaven, Earth, and Man upon which man's welfare was dependent. As Granet says, "The Son of Heaven extends to the entire Empire his regulating Virtue, because in the House of the Calendar he rules, in the name of Heaven, the course of Time . . ."[1]

The place of Earth in this organic cosmic harmony of Heaven, Earth, and man is presented in terms of a relationship between earth's Five Elements — earth, wood, fire, metal, and water — and human virtues:

> The Five Elements are the corporeal essences of the Five Constant virtues. [These are personal ap-

---
[2] Soothill, *op. cit.*, p. 36.
[3] *Ibid.*, p. 39. Soothill quotes from the *Yueh Ling* (*Monthly Commands*, a third century B C. almanac).
[4] *Ibid.*
[5] *Ibid.*
[1] Granet, *op. cit.*, pp. 381 f.

pearance, speech, vision, hearing, thought.] The Shu (Book of History) says: 'The first category is called the Five Elements. The second is called reverent practice of the five functions.' This means that the five functions should be used in consonance with the Five Elements. If one's personal appearance, speech, vision, hearing and thought lose their proper order, the Five Elements will fall into confusion and changes will arise in the five planets. For these all proceed from the numbers connected with the almanac, and are divisions of one thing (i.e., of the movements of the Five Elements). Their laws all arise from the revolutions of the Five Powers (i.e., Elements), and if they are extended to their farthest stretch, there is nothing (in the universe) which they will not reach to.[2]

Man's place in this organic scheme is brought out in the cosmology of the *Huai-nan-tzu* (written in the second century B.C., but probably reflecting much older views). Man's body is described as a replica of the universe and his spirit as having its origin in the ultimate formless reality itself, a notion derived from Taoist metaphysics.

About the body, the *Huai-nan-tzu* says:

Heaven has the four seasons, Five Elements, nine divisions, and three hundred and sixty days. Man likewise has four limbs, five viscera, nine orifices, and three hundred and sixty joints. Heaven has wind, rain, cold, heat, and man likewise has (the qualities of) accepting and giving, joy and anger. Therefore the gall corresponds to clouds, the lungs to vapor, the spleen to wind, the kidneys to rain, and the liver to thunder. Thus man forms a trinity with Heaven and Earth, and his mind is the master. Therefore the ears and eyes are as the sun and moon, and the humors of the blood as wind and rain.[1]

---

[2] Fung Yu-lan, *op. cit.*, Vol I, p. 27.
[1] *Ibid.*, p. 399.

About man's ultimate spiritual possibilities the *Huainan-tzu* says:

> If we look back to antiquity, to the Great Beginning, man was there born out of Non-being to assume form in Being. Having form he was regulated by things. But he who is able to revert to that state out of which he was born, so as to be as if he had never had physical form, is called the True Man *(chen jen)*. The True Man is he who is as if he had not yet separated from the Great Oneness.[2]

The Emperor was looked upon as such a True Man, the Unique Man, since he was, as we have shown above the hub of the wheel of the universal cosmic harmony. Shih Huang-ti (246-210 B.C.), the unifier of China after centuries of feudal strife, may have been the first Emperor to claim this role for himself on the grand scale of subsequent imperial rulers. As such a True Man he desired to master the physical elements so as to float in the air at will, enter water without getting wet, and invert the order of the seasons if he chose to do so. However, he could not invert the order of the seasons and remain the True Man since such inversion would disturb the harmony of the cosmos and this a True Man would not do. While the Emperor remains the True Man he commands all things in heaven and earth without acting, simply by permitting events to happen. The Virtue emanating from him is sufficient to order all things correctly. As celestial sovereign on earth his palace becomes a more adequate pattern of the universe than the *Ming T'ang* itself. The Ming T'ang had at various times from five to twelve rooms for the proper circulation of the King at appropriate months of the year, but Shih Huang Ti's palace had as many rooms as the year had days.[1] The Element under which he ruled was water;

---
[2] *Ibid.*
[1] Granet, *op. cit.*, pp. 392 f.

black (associated always with this element) was the dynastic color for official clothing, pennons and flags; six—the number of the element water — was the official number. Since water and black were associated always with Winter, the season of harshness and severity, everything was administered in accordance with a policy of stern justice.[2] The palace decorations, too, had cosmic significance and symbolized the celestial lordship of the Emperor. The Milky Way was represented; there was a glorious imperial chariot — again a microcosm in symbolism — the chariot had a square body symbolizing Earth while its round throne meant Heaven; star constellations were portrayed on flags; on the emperor's clothes the sun, moon, starry constellations, lighting, clouds and dragons were shown; the total scheme made of him and his surroundings the universe in microcosm.[3] The Emperor, axis and core of the universal organism, represented Celestial sovereignty brought to earth.

The Han dynasty, successor of the Ch'in, continued the functional apotheosis of the ruler which continued in greater or less degree as long as there was an emperor in China. Emperor Wu (140-87 B.C.) of the Former Han dynasty took his responsibilities as center of the world and universe very seriously. The historian Ssu-ma Ch'ien describes the building and inauguration of a new *Ming T'ang* (House of the Calendar) in 106 B.C. to celebrate the beginning of a new historical cycle. Ssu-ma Ch'ien writes:

> The period has revolved! . . . It begins again! . . . The divisions of the year were (from that time) correct; the note *yu* was again pure . . . the principles Yin and Yang were separated and united in a regular fashion.[1]

---

[2] Fung Yu-lan, *op cit.*, Vol. I, p. 163, footnote 1.
[3] Granet, *op. cit.*, p. 393.
[1] *Ibid.*, p. 388. Granet is quoting from *Les Mémoires Historiques de Ssu-ma Ch'ien*, traduit et annotés par Edouard Chevannes, 5 Vols. (Paris: Ernest Leroux, editeur, 28 Rue Bonaparte, 1895), Vol. III,

Wu raised the color yellow to honor and the number five, both symbols of the element, Earth; systems of measures were changed to harmonize with the number five; the musical pipes that determine the scale were appropriately adjusted. Emperor Wu took his place as Unique Man, the True Man, whose duty to human society, to Heaven and to Earth, and to himself involved the recommencement of Time and of History.

Ssu-ma Tan, official astrologer and annalist of Wu's reign was father of Ssu-ma Ch'ien who edited the *Historical Memoirs* of his father. It is symbolically significant that this history places the Yellow Emperor, Huang-ti, at the beginning of Chinese history. The Golden Age thus begins again with the new Yellow Emperor, Wu. The cyclical philosophy of history set by Ssu-ma Tan and Ssu-ma Ch'ien became standard for subsequent Chinese historians. Granet says:

> All his successors imitated him. The same spirit has continually inspired the choice of facts, the processes of exposition, the system of philosophic interpretation . . . It is engaged in noting in successive cycles the infallible repetitions. It only knows typical heroes and stereotyped events. At bottom it has only to occupy itself with one personage; the sovereign, the Unique Man, whose Virtue is typical of a particular moment of time. History does not differ from a Calendar, illustrated by generic pictures. Equally, it may be said, it is born of speculations about the Calendar.[1]

chapitre XXVI, "Le Calendrier," pp. 321-338. The passage quoted is on p. 331: "Dorénavant, les divisions de l'année sont de nouveau correcte; la note *yu* est de nouveau pure; les dénominations sont de nouveau modifiées exactement . . . alors la facon reguliére dont (les principes) *yn* et *yang* se séparent et s' unissent est en vigueur . . ."

The cyclical idea is applied in this same chapter "Le Calendrier" (chapitre XXVI): "Le principe des *Hia* fut le premier mois; celui des *Yn* fut le douzième mois; celui des *Tcheou* fut le onzième mois. Ainsi les principes des trois dynasties furent comme un cycle qui, une fois termine, revient a son point de depart . . ."

[1] *Ibid.*, Granet, pp. 46 f.

Systematic philosophies of history grounded in this organic-cyclical idea were developed by several great Chinese thinkers. Here we shall review only two of the greatest: Tung Chung-shu who represents the ideology of the Former Han dynasty (206 B.C.—24 A.D.) which we have just been describing, and Shao Yung (1011-77 A.D.) a Neo-Confucian philosopher of the Sung dynasty.

Tung Chung-shu (179?-104? B.C.)

Background of Tung Chung-shu's organic cyclic views of nature and human history: Tsou Yen and the Yin and Yang and the Five Elements School. Certain important cosmological ideas of Tung Chung-shu who lived in the second century B.C. are found earlier in the fourth and third centuries in what is called the Yin and Yang and the Five Elements School. Tsou Yen was the renowned leader of this school. The ideas of Tsou Yen relevant to a cyclical view of history are those which correlate the five elements with historical epochs. A third century document of various schools of thought compiled by Lu Pu-wei called the *Lu-shih Ch'un Ch'iu* states:

> Whenever any Emperor or King is about to arise, Heaven must first make manifest some favorable omen among the lower people. In the time of the Yellow Emperor, Heaven first made a large number of earthworms and mole crickets appear. The Yellow Emperor said: 'The force of the element earth is in the ascendancy.' Therefore he assumed yellow as his color, and took earth as a pattern for his affairs.[2]

The account continues with Yu, founder of the Hsia

---
[2] Fung Yu-lan, *op. cit.*, Vol. I, p. 161. Fung Yu-lan quotes this passage from the *Lu-shih Ch'un Ch'iu* (XIII, 2).

dynasty. Trees and grass appeared which denote the element wood in the ascendancy. Therefore green was the color honored. Next the element metal and color white came to power with the Shang dynasty (1766-1123 B.C.); after this the element fire and color red with the Chou dynasty (1122-256 B.C.) as the ruling house; finally the element water and color black with the Ch'in (255-207) or Han (206 B.C.-220 A.D.). The same cycle is repeated beginning with earth again in the ascendancy and this cyclical pattern continues endlessly. All changes in human history are correlated with the elements. The elements are, in fact, considered the causes of the rise and fall, and of the characters of dynasties. We mentioned earlier that Ch'in Shih Huang-ti adopted black as his dynastic color, acknowledged water as the element that brought him to power and under which he ruled. In consonance with this element he followed a "winter" policy of stern justice in ruling his empire. The idea of a "winter" policy in harmony with water was derived no doubt from the Yin-yang ideology in its synthesis with the five elements school. In this synthesis certain virtues have precise correlations with the four seasons, the five elements, and the five directions of space. In spring Yang is in the ascendancy, East the direction of space, the element is wood, the virtue pardon (of those who have given offense). In summer Yang is at its height, south the direction, fire the element and benevolence and pleasure the virtues. In autumn Yin is in the ascendancy, west the direction, the element metal, the virtues quietude, uprightness, severity, compliance. In autumn things are tightening up in nature, so the human world must be in harmony. In winter Yin is at a maximum, north the direction, water the element, and the virtues purity, mild anger, secret storing up. Resentments and punishments are appropriate here. The fifth element, earth, is represented at the center of space. Its influence is felt during all four seasons. Its virtues are harmony, equability, impartiality, for it assists all four seasons equally.

Rulers are supposed to administer punishments and rewards with regard to the suitability of the season. In general, pardon, benevolence, generosity, should be manifested in spring and summer to foster the expansive processes of growth; punishments, severity and strict justice in autumn and winter to aid the tightening up processes of nature. When this pattern is not observed, perversions of seasonal phenomena occur such as drought in spring, frost in summer, thunder in winter. Upon the shoulders of the sage-king falls the heavy responsibility for the harmony of the seasons and the universe (*cf.* Mesopotamia). In addition to the more specific pattern of virtues appropriate to the particular season, the ruler observes the general tone of virtues that belong to the organic complex of the Element under which his dynasty has come to power.

Tung Chung-shu. With this background of organic mythopoeic thinking about the cosmos and human affairs, Tung Chung-shu was able to develop a far more systematic and elaborate philosophy. His philosophy of nature and history is found in his major surviving work charmingly entitled *Luxuriant Dew of the Spring and Autumn Annals*. This, like most Chinese philosophies is an organic system, therefore it is necessary to present Tung's total system before his philosophy of history can be comprehended. The system is based upon the following key concepts: Yuan, Heaven, the Yin and Yang, the Five Elements, the Four Seasons, and the Correlations of Man with the Numerical categories of Heaven.

Yuan is the origin, the "great beginning" of all things. It is the source, the root, of all that exists; it exists before Heaven and Earth and is similar to the category, Being, in Western philosophy. From Yuan is derived Heaven, Earth, the Yin and Yang, Five Elements, and man, a total of ten. With these ten Heaven's number is made complete. (He distinguishes between the word "Heaven" used in its particular, more physical meaning and Heaven used as the name for the entire cosmos, physical and spiritual.)

The basic motive forces through which all things come into being are the Yang and Yin. He writes:

> Within the universe exist the ethers (*ch'i*) of the *yin* and *yang*. Men are constantly immersed in them, just as fish are constantly immersed in water. The difference between them and water is that the turbulence of the latter is visible, whereas that of the former is invisible. Man's existence in the universe, however, is like a fish's attachment to water. Everywhere these ethers are to be found, but they are less viscid than water. Thus in the universe there seems to be a nothingness and yet there is substance. Men are constantly immersed in this eddying mass, with which, whether themselves orderly or disorderly, they are carried along in a common current.[1]

Tung then proceeds to relate the yin-yang ethers to the rest of the universe. He says:

> Collected together, the ethers (*ch'i*) of the universe constitute a unity; divided, they constitute the *yin* and *yang;* quartered, they constitute the four seasons; (still further) sundered, they constitute the Five Elements. These elements . . . represent movement . . Their movements are not identical. Therefore they are referred to as the Five Movers. These Five Movers constitute five officiating (powers). Each in turn gives birth to the next and is overcome by the next but one in turn . . .[2]

The next step in the system is to make clear the relationship between the Five Elements and the Four Seasons. Tung, like earlier thinkers such as Tsou Yen, establishes the one to one correspondence between each element and each of the four seasons: Wood: spring; Fire: sum-

---

[1] Fung Yu-lan, *op. cit.*, Vol. II, p. 20.
[2] *Ibid.*, pp. 21 f.

mer; Metal: autumn; Water: winter; while Earth belongs to the Center and participates in all four seasons. The changes in the seasons which cause the growth and decay of all things is controlled by the *yang* and *yin* forces in the following manner:

> When the course of Heaven has been completed, it begins again. Therefore the north is the quarter where Heaven begins and ends (its course), and where the *yin* and *yang* unite with and separate from (one another). After the winter solstice the *yin* holds itself low and retires in the west, while the *yang* raises itself up and emerges in the east. Their places of emerging and retiring are always directly opposite to one another, but there is always a mutual concord in the equable blending of their larger or smaller quantities. The quantity (of the one) may be more, yet there is no excess. That (of the other) may be less, yet there is no deficiency. In spring and summer the yang is more abundant and the yin less, while in autumn and winter the yang is less abundant and the yin more. These amounts do not remain constant, for there is never a time when one or the other is not being divided and dispersed. As they emerge or retire, they mutually diminish or increase, and as they become more or less abundant, they mutually fructify and enrich. As the more abundant becomes dominant, the less abundant goes into retirement at an increasing rate. The one that retires is diminished by one, while that which emerges is augmented by two . . . In this way the ethers influence one another as they pass through transformations in the course of their mutual revolutions . . .
>
> As to metal, wood, water, and fire, they each take that over which they are to preside, so as, in accordance with the (movements of the) *yin* and *yang*, to join forces with them in the performance of the common work. Thus the resulting achievements are not solely (due to) the *yin* and *yang*. Rather it is a case of the *yin* and *yang* basing themselves upon these (four elements), so as to supply assistance to them in

those (seasonal tasks) over which (the elements) preside. In this way the lesser ... *yang* bases itself upon wood, thus assisting it in the germinating activities of spring. The greater ... *yang* bases itself upon fire, thus assisting it in the nourishing activities of summer. The lesser *yin* bases itself upon metal, thus assisting it in the maturing activities of autumn. And the greater *yin* bases itself upon water, thus assisting it in the storing-up activities of winter.[1]

Finally Tung makes plain the unity of man with Heaven and Earth, *yin* and *yang* and the Five Elements. He begins with a general eulogy of man:

Nothing is more refined than the (*yin* and *yang*) ethers, richer than Earth, or more spiritual than Heaven. Of the creatures born from the refined essence ... of Heaven and Earth, none is more noble than man. Man receives the Decree (*ming*) of Heaven, and therefore is loftier (than other) creatures. (Other) creatures suffer troubles and distress and are unable to practice love (*jen*) and righteousness (*yi*); only man is capable of practicing them. (Other) creatures suffer trouble and distress and are unable to match themselves with Heaven and Earth; only man is capable of doing this.[1]

Tung continues by showing the direct exact correspondences between man's body, emotions, spirit and cosmic phenomena:

In the physical form of man ... his head is large and round, like Heaven's countenance. His hair is like the stars and constellations. His ears and eyes, with their brilliance, are like the sun and moon. His nostrils and mouth, with their breathing, are like the wind. The penetrating understanding that lies within

---
[1] *Ibid.*, pp. 24 f.
[1] *Ibid.*, p. 30.

his breast is like the spiritual intelligence of (Heaven). His abdomen and womb, now full and then empty, are like the hundred creatures ... The body is like Heaven, and its numerical (categories) correspond with those of the latter, so that its life is linked with the latter. With the number (of days) that fills a year Heaven gives form to man's body. Thus the 366 lesser joints (of the body) correspond to the number of days (in a year), and the twelve divisions of the larger joints correspond to the number of months. Within (the body) there are the five viscera [heart, liver, spleen, lungs, kidneys] which correspond in number to the Five Elements. Externally there are the four limbs, which correspond in number to the four seasons. The alternating opening and closing (of the eyes) corresponds to day and night. The alternation of hardness and softness corresponds to winter and summer. The alternation of sadness and pleasure corresponds to the *yin* and *yang*. The mind possesses the power of thinking, which corresponds to (Heaven's) power of deliberation and calculation. (Man's) conduct follows the principles of proper relationship, which correspond to (the relationship between) Heaven and Earth [i.e. proper relationships between superior and inferior] ... In what may be numbered, there is a correspondence in kind. There is an identity in both (cases) and a single correspondence (of man) with Heaven.[2]

Not only are there these precise, intimate correspondences between man and the Universe, but the Universe would be radically incomplete without man. Tung says:

Heaven, Earth, and man are the origin of all things. Heaven gives them birth, Earth nourishes them, and man perfects them. Heaven gives them birth by (instilling) filial piety and respect for elders; Earth nourishes them by (supplying) clothing and food; man perfects them by (creating) ritual (*li*) and music (yueh).[3]

---
[2] *Ibid.*, p. 31.
[3] *Ibid.*, p. 32.

The central figure in this unity of Heaven, Earth, and man is the king. He is responsible for maintaining the unity and harmony of all three. To do this the ruler models himself on Heaven's four seasons. The ruler's:

> likes and dislikes, joy and anger, are equivalent to Heaven's spring, summer, autumn, and winter. Through the transformations it makes in their warmth, coolness cold and heat, it (Heaven) accomplishes its works. When Heaven brings forth these four (qualities) seasonably, the year is fine; when unseasonably, it is bad. (Likewise) when the ruler of men brings forth his four (qualities) in their correct relationship, the world is well-ordered; when he fails to do this, it falls into disorder. Therefore a well-ordered world is the same in category as a good year, and a world in disorder is the same in category as a bad year . . . When (the ruler) manifests a liking for something, this acts like the warm atmosphere (of spring), and births take place in the human world. When he manifests a dislike for something, this acts like the cool atmosphere (of autumn), and deaths take place in the human world. His joy acts like the hot atmosphere (of summer) . . . His anger acts like the cold atmosphere (of winter) and there is then a cessation (to human activities) . . .
> Beneficence, rewards, punishments, and executions match spring, summer, autumn, and winter respectively . . . Therefore I say that the king is co-equal with Heaven, meaning that Heaven in its course has four ways of government . . . The ruler's joy, anger grief, and pleasure, and his beneficence, rewards, punishments, and executions, are thus modeled on the four seasons. Let each operate in its proper degree, and then 'the world is well ordered.'[1]

When man, and especially the ruler, fails to observe proper human relations visitations and prodigies appear.

---

[1] *Ibid.*, pp. 47 f.

Wrong conduct and immorality, Tung says, cause the *yin* and *yang* ethers to become "twisted and perverse."

Having established all the above correlations between man and the cosmos, Tung is prepared to relate all that is significant in human history to the universe. This had already been done by Tsou Yen of the late fourth century B.C. in his doctrine of the sequence of the five elements which he correlated with types of dynastic rule in an unending cycle as described above.[2] This was the philosophy of history throughout the Han dynasty, though many who accepted it debated whether or not the Han was dominated by the element Water, or Earth, or Fire.[1]

Alongside this theory based on the Five Elements there was another philosophy, cyclical also, but quite different and more complicated which explains history as basically a cycle of Three Sequences, the Black, White, and the Red. Tung developed this idea into a systematic philosophy of history. He gives as the reason for assuming *Three* Sequences the fact that a sequence is a beginning or starting point. Heaven's starting point is the beginning of the year; there can be only three beginnings of the year: the eleventh month, the twelfth month and the thirteenth month. Any other beginning of the year would not synchronize with the seasonal weather and life processes dependent on such seasonal changes. The Beginning of the year or New Year inaugurates the advent of spring so cannot be placed earlier or later than the three months just mentioned, and these are therefore the three squences. Tung gives a rather detailed description of the general characteristics of each sequence. One sample will suffice to show the type of correlation he makes between a sequence and other phenomena:

> Among the Three Beginnings, the Black Sequence comes first. On the first day of its year, the sun and

---
[2] *Supra*, pp. 171 f.
[1] *Op cit.*, Fung yu-lan, Vol. II, p. 58.

new moon stand in the constellation of the Barracks [Pegasus] and the Big Dipper stands in *yin*. Heaven's all-embracing ethers then first begin to permeate and generate things, from which buds of growth appear. Their color is black. Therefore the clothes worn at court on the first day of the month are black, as are the pendants on official caps, the imperial chariots, and their horses. The cords that carry the great seals (of the officials) are black, as are their headdresses, the flags, the great precious jades, and the animals used in the suburban sacrifices. The horns of these animals are egg-shaped. The ceremony of capping (that takes place when a youth comes of age) is performed at the eastern steps (before the main hall). In the marriage ceremony (the groom) goes to meet (the bride) in the courtyard (of the ancestral temple of her home); in the funeral ceremony, the deceased is encoffined above the eastern steps (leading to the main hall) . . .[2]

In the White Sequence everything of importance is white and in the Red Sequence, red. A new dynasty is supposed to change the sequence in this exact order: Black, White, and Red, and then the next dynasty reverts to Black and the cycle is repeated. The heavenly Mandate given a new ruler must be made manifest by the proper sequence-change from that of the former dynasty from which Heaven has withdrawn its Mandate.[1] Historically speaking, the Hsia dynasty (2300-1800 B.C.) observed the Black Sequence, Shǎng (or Yin) — 1800-1150 B.C. — the White Sequence, and Chou (1150-250 B.C.) the Red Sequence. The dynasty succeeding Chou is again Black and the cycle repeats itself.

[2] *Ibid.*, pp. 58 f.
[1] Tung Chung-shu represents the synthesis of the *Yin-Yang* and Five Elements schools of thought typical of what is called the "New Text School" of Confucianism versus the "Old Text School" which began about the first century B.C. because of the supposed discovery of archaic Chou documents of Confucianism in the ancient language. The "New Text" school of Confucianism is based upon documents committed to writing during the Former Han Dynasty and therefore in the newer script of this era. The "New Text" documents are considered more authentic by scholars except in certain superstitious

Tung's philosophy of history contains other cycles, those of two, four, five and nine, which makes it somewhat complex. He summarizes the entire theory thus:

> Therefore for the kings (who found new dynasties), there are certain respects in which they should not change (their institutions from those of the pre-

excesses such as the belief that Confucius was a supernatural being. The New Text's synthetic philosophy of the Yin-Yang and Five Elements became so influential that when signs showed the decline of the Former Han dynasty, Wang Mang (6-23 A.D.) used this philosophy to justify his usurpation of the throne. This is shown in the article by Cheng Te-k'un "Yin-Yang Wu-Hsing and Han Art," *Harvard Journal of Asiatic Studies*, Vol. 20, June, 1957, Numbers 1 and 2, pp. 162-186. Cheng says that Wang Mang was "a good Confucian scholar and a great expert on rituals, but the progress of his career depended almost entirely upon the effectiveness of this theory. The drama of usurpation was enacted with the Five Elements as the background and supported at every turn with some heavenly signs in nature. He reinterpreted history along the same lines, and in order to justify his claim to the throne recognized Fu-hsi, Shen-nung, and a number of other legendary emperors. Chinese history was lengthened and enriched by his new scheme, which may be tabulated as follows:

Wood	1. Fu-hsi	6. Ti K'u	11. Chou
Intercalary			
Water	Kung-kung	Ti-Chih	Ch'in
Fire	2. Shen-nung	7. Ti-Yao	12. Han
Earth	3. Huang-ti	8. Ti-Shun	13. Hsin
Metal	4. Shao-hao	9. Hsia Yu	
Water	5. Ch'uan-hsu	10. Shang	

After presenting this chart Cheng continues, "According to this system, Chinese history had already passed through two and one-half cycles, instead of one as recognized in early Han times. Wang Mang even invented a stage of 'intercalary Water' to accommodate Kung-Kung, Ti Chih, and the Ch'in . . ."

Cheng adds more interesting details which bring out the centrality of the King in the macro-microcosmic organismic New Text ideology. Cheng says, "Wang Mang built a Ming-T'ang or Palace of Enlightenment [Soothill's 'Hall of Light' is a variant translation] and put the *Yueh Ling* or Monthly Commands into practice. The Ming T'ang was a square building with three halls on the four sides. The emperor was to live there, each month in one hall in which, according to the theory of the Five Elements, he was to dress in the appropriate color, eat the appropriate food, listen to the right music, sacrifice to the right deities, attend to the appropriate affairs of state, and so on. Thus the harmony of Heaven and Earth might be ensured."

ceding dynasty); certain respects in which they should revert (to those of a preceding dynasty) after (a cycle of) two (dynasties); certain respects in which they should revert after (a cycle of) three; certain respects in which they should revert (after a cycle of) four; certain respects in which they should revert after (a cycle of) five; and certain respects in which they should revert after (a cycle of) nine . . .[1]

An explanation is given of each of these cycles. First, however, he makes clear that there is one thing that is not cyclic, that remains the same in every cycle. This is moral virtue. The ruler changes his institutions in inaugurating a new dynasty, but never the fundamental Confucian virtues of love, righteousness, and wisdom. The change after a cycle of two dynasties is the polar oscillation between Simplicity and Refinement. This cycle of two, Simplicity and Refinement is explained in the *Po Hu T'ung* (a first century A.D. work) in somewhat fuller form than that presented by Tung. The *Po Hu Tung* says:

> How is it that the kings (who found new dynasties) must alternate between Simplicity and Refinement: It is in order that they may carry out (the work of) Heaven and Earth, and accord with the *yin* and *yang*. When the course of the *yang* has reached its apogee, that of the *yin* takes over, and when the *yin's* course has reached its apogee, that of the *yang* takes over. It is evident that there cannot be two *yin* and two *yang* each carrying on from the other. The fact is simply that Simplicity is modeled on Heaven and Refinement on Earth. Thus Heaven creates (things in their basic) Simplicity, which, being taken over by Earth, are then transformed, nourished, and given completed form, so that there is thus created (an elaborated) Refinement . . . When, upon the new arisal of emperors and kings, the first of them (follows) Simplicity and the next Refinement, this is done in order to accord with the course of Heaven and Earth, with the meaning of what

---

[1] Fung, *op. cit.*, Vol. II, p. 61.

is primary and what secondary, and with the sequence of what comes first and what afterward . . .
. . . 'There is a triple changing of the beginning of the year, while there is a dual alternation of Refinement and Simplicity.' [1]

In the list of cycles just mentioned above, the reference to "certain respects in which they should revert after a cycle of three" means following the Red, White, and Black sequence already described. "Certain respects in which they should revert (after a cycle of) four is explained thus. There is a cycle of Shang, Hsia, Simplicity, and Refinement. Shang and Hsia do not refer merely to the dynasties of this name but are abstract categories. Each member of this cycle of four has a definite character. Of Shang he says "The course of him who reigns, taking Heaven as his guiding principle and modeling himself on Shang, is that of the *yang* in all its fullness. It emphasizes family relations and exalts love and honest simplicity . . ." [2] The second member of this cycle, Hsia, is described as taking Earth as its guiding principle, therefore it is characterized by growing yin. It "emphasizes the honoring of superiors and exalts the regulations governing the proper relationships . . ." [3] The third member, Simplicity, represents *yang* in its fullness. "It emphasizes family relations and exalts simplicity and affection . . ." [4] The fourth member, Refinement, has Earth as its guiding principle and is a period of growing *yin*. "It emphasizes the honoring of superiors and exalts propriety and refinement." [5]

By way of summary, Tung says that these "four models" of Shang, Hsia, Simplicity and Refinement are "like the four seasons. When (their cycle) is completed, it begins

---
[1] *Ibid.*, pp. 63 f.
[2] *Ibid.*, p. 66.
[3] *Ibid.*, p. 66.
[4] *Ibid.*, p. 67.
[5] *Ibid.*

again; when it reaches its conclusion, it returns to its starting point." In actual history the Shang period was in evidence "When Shun (legendary pre-dynastic ruler) reigned," and took "Heaven as his guiding principle"; the Hsia when Yu the founder of the Hsia began to reign with Earth as guiding principle; Simplicity when T'ang inaugurated the Shang (or Yin) era with Heaven as guiding principle. Refinement began with King Wen's founding of the Chou which took Earth as guiding principle and modeled itself on Refinement.[1]

The last two cycles mentioned (those of five and nine) are not as directly pertinent to a morphology of history. At these intervals descendants of the royal houses of previous dynasties are given estates and honors, the descendants of the most ancient are given the grandest titles, but smallest properties, while descendants of the recent dynasties are given larger holdings but lesser titles of honor.

The basic and most important of all these cycles is that of the Three Sequences, Black, White, and Red, since these are related to the beginning of the year, a thing of tremendous significance from the most ancient times. In this notion there is recognition of the importance of the Ruler as Lord of the Calendar, hence responsible for the harmony of the seasons, of the Elements proper to each season, hence the Ruler as Center of the Universe. When, for lack of virtue, he is unable to maintain this harmony and thus loses the Mandate of Heaven, a new dynasty must be founded which shows its intention of inaugurating a New Era by changing the Beginning of the Year. Since there can be but three beginnings (the eleventh, twelfth, or thirteenth month), there can be but three main types of dynasties, endlessly repeated. (The cycles of two — Simplicity and Refinement — and of four — Hsia, Shang, Simplicity, and Refinement — are subordinated to the major three, since they involve less radical changes; they are concerned more with correcting excesses of qualities that are

[1] *Ibid.*, pp. 67 f.

virtues in themselves, than with the total renovation signified by the change in the beginning of the year.) We noted above [1] Ssu-ma Ch'ien's comments on the supreme importance of such a cyclical renewal as that indicated by the change in the beginning of the year. "The period has revolved! It begins again!... The divisions of the year were (from that time) correct; the note *yu* was again pure... the principles Yin and Yang were separated and united in a regular fashion."
The *Po Hu T'ung (Comprehensive Discussions in the White Tiger Hall)* tells us that Confucius when he "fell heir to the abuses of the Chou, ... put into operation the calendar of Hsia, knowing that he, as successor to (a dynasty that had used) the eleventh month as the (year's) beginning, must himself use the thirteenth month." [2] Derk Bodde (translator of Fung Yu-lan's two volume *A History of Chinese Philosophy* from which we have been quoting extensively) adds a footnote to this quotation about Confucius' cyclical ideas. Bodde says:

> I.e., since the Hsia, Shang, and Chou calendars had already been successively used, the next phase in the cycle would be a return to the Hsia calendar. This has reference to the belief elaborated by Tung Chung-shu ... according to which Confucius was an 'uncrowned king' who by rights should have become founder of a new dynasty, even though, through force of circumstances the Chou dynasty actually continued after his time for several centuries. We know from *Analects*, XV, 10, that Confucius did indeed advocate a return to the Hsia calendar.[3]

Our footnote above [4] describes the functional value of the cyclical idea as applied by Wang Mang in his usurpa-

[1] *Supra*, p. 169.
[2] Fung, *op. cit.*, Vol. II, p. 65. Fung is quoting from the *Po Hu T'ung*.
[3] Fung, *ibid.*, p. 65, note 7, by translator, Derk Bodde.
[4] *Supra*, pp. 180 f.

tion of the throne in the first century A.D. It is evident that a cyclical view of history was an integral part of Han dynasty culture, the culture which in many ways set the pattern for all subsequent civilization. Buddhism, however, which entered China in the first century A.D. added some new ideas. The Buddhist cyclical view of cosmic history is reflected perhaps in the cyclical theory developed at the cosmic level by Shao Yung, a great Sung dynasty philosopher.

Shao Yung (1011-1077 A.D.)
and the Great Cyclical Year of the Cosmos

A cyclical view of history similar in many ways to the Han pattern set by Tung Chung-shu is that given us by Shao Yung. His philosophy of history, like the Han, is inspired by reflections on the ancient calendrical theme, the cycle of seasonal changes. Shao lived during the formative period of Neo-Confucian philosophies. He and a fellow Neo-Confucian contemporary, Chou Tun-yi, were much influenced by religious Taoism in their metaphysical views. Both borrowed ideas in metaphysics from a Taoist work at least as old as the early eighth century called *Shang-fang Ta-tung Chen-yuan Miao-ching T'u (Diagrams of the Truly First and Mysterious Classic of the Transcendent Great Cave.*[1])

The metaphysics of Shao, derived from this Taoist work, mentions the *Yi Ching* as its source. From the *Yi Ching* Shao develops a grand cosmology which he illustrates with diagrams that present the essential ideas in his system. The metaphysical system begins with the Ultimate Reality which he names the *Supreme Ultimate*. This Supreme Ulti-

---
[1] Fung, *op. cit.*, Vol. II, p. 438.

mate is Mind, Tao, or Spirit. This Mind produces numbers, numbers produce Emblems, and the Emblems produce Implements. By Mind producing numbers, he means that the Supreme Ultimate (Mind) is One, one produces two, two produces four by division, four produces eight by division in half, eight produces sixteen, sixteen produces thirty-two, and thirty-two produces sixty-four. These numbers then produce the Emblems. The Emblems are the Two Forms *yang* (—) and *yin* (- -); the group of four Emblems of Heaven greater *yang*, greater *yin*, lesser *yang* and lesser *yin*; and the four Emblems of Earth signified by the four remaining trigrams of the *Yi Ching* which Shao calls by the quality names "lesser hardness, lesser softness, greater hardness, and greater softness." From these Emblems all the Implements are produced. By Implements he means the concrete things of the cosmos. He explains how this comes about as follows:

> Movement in its major phase is called the greater *yang;* in its minor phase it is called the lesser *yang.* Quiescence in its major phase is called the greater *yin;* in its minor phase it is called the lesser *yin.* The greater *yang* constitutes the sun, the greater *yin* the moon, the lesser *yang* the stars, and the lesser *yin* the zodiacal spaces, [signs of the zodiac]. Through the interplay of sun, moon, stars, and zodiacal spaces, the bodily substance of Heaven is completely actualized. The greater softness constitutes water, the greater hardness fire, the lesser softness soil, and the lesser hardness stone. Through the interplay of water, fire, soil, and stone, the bodily substance of Earth is completely actualized.[1] . . . The intermingling of the eight trigrams with one another results in the production of all things.[2]

With this metaphysics as a basis Shao Yung goes on to construct a universal philosophy of history. The basis of

[1] *Ibid.,* p. 456. Quoted by Fung from Shao's *Observation of Things.*
[2] *Ibid.,* p. 457. Quoted from Shao's *Observation of Things.*

this construction is a correlation between yin-yang movements symbolized by the sixty-four hexagrams (complex variants of the eight trigrams), and the four seasons of the year. This scheme is then applied to a Great Year or cycle of the cosmos (probably under Buddhist influence). These cycles of the cosmos are repeated in identical patterns, each with the same types of objects and events.

The simplest and most fundamental application of the system is to the seasons of the year. Since this evolution of the seasons is the pattern applied to the evolution of the cosmos, the ancient importance of the Calendar idea is again manifested. Shao Yung begins the Calendar with the traditional beginning of the Chinese astronomical year, the winter solstice (which occurs in the eleventh month). At midnight of the winter solstice the single *yang* line of the appropriate hexagram (one *yang* line with five *yin* lines—a *yang* line is an unbroken line, a *yin* line is a broken line) symbolizes the rebirth of the *yang* after the apogee of the *yin* which has occurred in the tenth month. The apogee of the *yin* is represented by a hexagram of six *yin* (broken) lines. After the rebirth of the yang at the winter solstice, the yang influence gradually increases until it reaches its apogee in the fourth month. At midnight of the summer solstice the *yin* influence has its rebirth and continues growing until it reaches its apogee in the tenth Chinese month (our November); then Yang has its rebirth at the winter solstice (eleventh Chinese month) and the cycle begins again.

This cycle is applied to the growth and decay of all things in nature. For example a flower that begins to open is in the hexagram corresponding to the winter solstice with its one *yang* line, the rebirth of *yang* in the calendar; when it is in full bloom it corresponds to the apogee of *yang* (or month before the summer solstice in the calendar); with the hexagram corresponding to the rebirth of yin, the summer solstice in the calendar, the flower begins to drop its petals, and it dies at the hexagram corresponding to the apogee of *yin* in the calendar, the tenth month (November).[1]

Since the seasons and all individual things in nature — plants, animals, and men — undergo the *yang-yin* cycle symbolized by the sixty-four hexagrams, Shao thinks it certain that the cosmos as a whole undergoes a similar cycle. He writes:

> When the numbers of the *Changes* reach the end (of their revolution), Heaven and Earth complete a cycle. It may be asked: 'Do Heaven and Earth, then also pass through a cycle (like other things)?' I reply: 'Since growth and decay exist (for all things), why should they not have such a cycle? Although Heaven and Earth are large, they too consist of form and matter ... and thus constitute two objects.'[2]

Shao proceeds in his work called the *Cosmological Chronology* to describe the evolutionary process of World-Year of the total cosmos in terms of the sixty-four hexagrams which symbolize the *yang-yin* movements. The time divisions of his system are as follows. The period from the beginning to the total destruction of a world is called a cycle. A cycle has 129,600 years. Each cycle contains twelve Epochs just as a year has twelve months. Each Epoch has thirty Revolutions just as a month has thirty days. Each Revolution has twelve generations (thirty generations equal three hundred and sixty just as the human year has three hundred and sixty days according to the lunar calendar). Each Generation consists of thirty years; each year has twelve months; one month thirty days; and one day has twelve two-hour periods.

The relation between these time periods and the hexagrams is this: The world cycle begins with the hexagram which symbolizes the winter solstice and ends with the one

---
[1] *Ibid.*, p. 463.
[2] *Ibid.*, p. 469. Quoted from Shao's *Observation of Things*.

which signifies the apogee of *yin*. In the first Epoch (1-10, 800 years) in which *yang* begins to grow, Heaven is born; in the second Epoch (10,801-21,600) Earth is born; in the third Epoch (21,601-32,400) Man appears; by the sixth Epoch (54,001-64,800) *yang* reaches its apogee: this is the midpoint of the cycle and the climax, the full flowering of human virtue, the Golden Age of Man under the rule of the great legendary sage-king, Yao, of the third millennium B.C. Now the decline begins; there is a gradual increase of *yin*, beginning in the seventh Epoch (64,801-75,600). This covers the dynasties of Hsia, Yin, Chou, Ch'in, Han, Chin, Three Kingdoms, Northern and Southern Dynasties, Sui, T'ang, Five Dynasties and the Sung (the Dynasty during which Shao lived). According to this time scale, the present year would correspond roughly to the 192nd Revolution of this same seventh Epoch. Decline continues until in the eleventh epoch, Revolution 315 (108,001-118,800) the Ending of Creatures occurs. In the twelfth Epoch (118,801-129,600) the *Yin* reaches its apogee and the entire cosmos comes to an end.[1] Then a new world arises to repeat the same cycle and the repetition of world cycles continues without end.

Within the Cosmic Cycle Shao gives us a pattern of human history which follows his basic and typically Chinese concept of the rise and decline of *yang* and *yin* powers. The human scene today is like the flower in full bloom, but past its first glory. All things human are related by him to government of which, he says, there are four main types: government by Sovereigns, by Emperors, by Kings, and by Tyrants. Each type of ruler has characteristic virtues: the Sovereign employs *wu wei* (non-activity: his virtue is so great that its potency harmonizes the *yang-yin* and all nature powers); the Emperor employs kindliness and good faith; the Kings are characterized by justice

---

[1] *Ibid.*, Translator's (Derk Bodde's) note, p. 473: "Equated with Western chronology Shao's table begins 67,017 B. C.; . . . Yao's rule 2337-2307 B.C.; end of creatures A.D. 46,023-46,383; end of entire cosmos 62,583 A.D."

and correctness; the Tyrant by scheming and force. These types are then related to actual history and the calendar of seasons:

> The Three Sovereigns correspond to spring, the Five Emperors to summer, the Three Kings to autumn, and the Five Tyrants to winter. The Seven States correspond to the coldest continuation of that winter.[2]

Shao does not list the dates and names of the three Sovereigns and five Emperors and accounts vary in the legendary tales of these times. Granet chooses Fu Hsi, Shen-Nung and Nu-kua as the Three Sovereigns and Huang Ti, Chuan-hu, Kao-Sin, Yao and Shun as the Five Emperors.[1] The dates given for this group are *ca.* 2450-2206 B.C. Fung Yu-lan in his "Chart of Traditional Chinese History Until Confucius"[2] gives the Five Emperors as Fu Hsi, Shen Nung, Huang-ti, Shao Hao, Chuan Hsu. These are followed by Yao and Shun (Yao seems to have been of the Sovereign type as defined by Shao Yung) who were not technically emperors since they did not found dynasties. After this Fung lists the Hsia dynasty founded by Yu the Great (also praised by Confucius as a ruler of golden virtue). The Three Kings mentioned by Shao Yung are the founders of the first three dynasties: Yu of Hsia, T'ang of Shang or Yin, and Wu of the Chou. The Seven States period is the Warring States period (404-221 B.C.) during which several leading feudal states were contending for power with Ch'in finally victorious under Shih Huang-ti.

Shang describes subsequent Chinese history up to his own time and concludes:

> From Emperor Yao until today there have been

---
[2] *Ibid.*, p. 475, quoted from Shao's *Observation of Things*.
[1] Granet, *Chinese Civilization, op. cit.*, chaps. I and II.
[2] Fung Yu-lan, *op. cit.*, Vol. I, facing p. 1.

more than 3,000 years, covering ... more than one hundred generations ... During this time ... there has sometimes been unity and sometimes division ... But never yet has there been anyone who could give a (real) unity to its manners and customs for a period of more than one generation.[3]

Though this sounds pessimistic, there is the great solace of believing that the entire universe will be repeated with a new beginning, and give rise to another Golden Age of culture, even though the decline of this culture is again inevitable, as the flower blooms and fades and dies. He does not say that individuals as such are repeated in every cycle but affirms types and the rise and fall pattern will always be the same cycle after cycle forever.

Shao's cyclical idea is based upon the notion of the cosmos as a great organism or macrocosm, eternally evolving from itself in a definite cyclic pattern the world of concrete existence. This world is brought into being and moved throughout, from inanimate to animate nature by the polar *yang-yin* forces. These yang-yin forces on the microcosmic level cause the seasonal changes organically related to the ever-repeated cycle of life and death of all things, on the microcosmic level and on the macrocosmic. On the microcosmic level, the *yang-yin* forces cause the seasonal changes of the year, the microcosmic fundamental cycle which gives rise to, and is the symbol of, the life cycle of all things in nature both animate and inanimate. Then, on the macrocosmic level, there is one grand world cycle or Great Year of the Cosmos perpetually repeated. "Between Heaven and Earth nothing goes away that does not return." [1]

---

[3] *Ibid.*, Vol. II, pp. 475f. quoted from Shao's *Observation of Things.*
[1] *Ibid.*, "The Appendices of the Book of Changes," p. 388 in Fung, Vol. I. These Appendices were written down by Han scholars around 175 B. C.

Shao's idea of the cyclic repetition of the entire cosmos in the same formal pattern was no doubt influenced by Buddhist ideas of cosmic cycles.

Chinese Cyclical Thought and Its Influence on the West

Chinese cyclical thought grounded in nature, especially the order of the seasons in their never-ending cycle, has provided the Chinese sages, especially of the Taoist school or those influenced by them (*e. g.* the Ch'an school of Buddhism), with a spiritual serenity and an at-homeness in the universe well represented in the thought of Chuang-tzu. Chuang-tzu's Taoist nature-wisdom is manifested in what he is purported to have said when he was reprimanded for singing when his wife died. The profound philosophical reasons he gave for this conduct which seemed so callous to his friends were:

> When she first died, how could I help not being affected? But then on examining the matter, I saw that in the Beginning she had originally been lifeless. And not only lifeless, but she had originally been formless. And not only formless, but she had originally lacked all substance. During this first state of confused chaos, there came a change which resulted in substance. This substance changed to assume form. The form changed and became alive. And now it has changed again to reach death. In this it has been *like the passing of the four seasons, spring, autumn, winter and summer.* And while she is thus lying asleep in the Great House (i.e., the Universe), for me to go about weeping and wailing, would be to show myself ignorant of Fate (*ming*). Therefore I refrain.[1]

This attitude is close to that of Spinoza's naturalistic pantheism in the West although Spinoza reached it by the more characteristically Western method, rationalism, versus the intuitive way of the Taoists and most Oriental philo-

---

[1] Fung, *op. cit.*, Vol. I, p. 237. Fung quotes this passage from chapter 18 of the *Chuang-tzu*. The italics are mine to draw attention to the basic importance of the four seasons in their ever-repeated cycle as the foundation, from the most ancient times out of which the cyclical view of history has developed.

sophers. Such nature mysticism can be defended, actually, from both points of view. Western science as we shall see in the next chapter and in the final chapter of this book is in harmony with it as well at the most profound intuitive thought of the East.

It is important for the West to realize the debt to Chinese thinkers. Japanese Zen Buddhism popular in the West today is one example because Zen is merely the Japanese name for the Chinese Ch'an Buddhism which has its roots in Taoism. The influence of Taoist and Confucian ideas of the organic Harmony of the Universe which involves the harmony between Heaven, Nature, and Man and upon which Chinese philosophy is founded, greatly impressed the Jesuit missionaries to China. These missionaries brought back these organic cosmic ideas to Europe where they were absorbed by Western philosophers such as Leibniz. Leibniz' organismic philosophy of the pre-established harmony of the universe was much influenced by Chinese thought.[1] Leibniz in his turn influenced Kant and German pantheistic idealism in general, although Indian thought was also another important influence upon the German pantheistic idealists. But there was contact between China and the West much earlier than the seventeenth and eighteenth centuries when such influences began to be important in the modern world. At least as early as Roman times (the period of the Former Han and Later Han dynasties in China) there was commercial traffic between China and the western Roman world; traffic in ideas probably occurred as well.[2] Fung Yu-lan points out, for example, the similarity between the Pythagorean number mysticism and the similar number philosophy of Han times.[3] In addition contact with India in Han times brought Greek ideas

[1] Adolph Reichwein, *China and Europe* (New York: Knopf, 1925), pp. 73-98.
[2] J. Needham, *Science and Civilization in China* 7 vols. (Cambridge: The Cambridge University Press, 1954-56), Vol. I, ch. 7, *passim*.
[3] Fung, *op. cit.*, Vol. II, pp. 93-96. See also translator's (Derk Bodde's) footnote which mentions that the musical scale of the twelve

into China via that country. However, the theoretical objective scientific approach to nature which the Greeks were first to develop seems never to have made real contact with the Chinese (or Indians) whose genius remained predominantly intuitive. Both approaches are necessary as Professor Northrop makes clear in his *Meeting of East and West*.

Greek thinkers were pioneers in the scientific or naturalistic approach to all problems including the problem of ascertaining the pattern of history. Like the Indian and Chinese thinkers they began with a mythopoeic approach but soon invented naturalistic and rationalistic if not really scientific solutions to the problem of ascertaining the pattern of cosmic and human history.

---

pitchpipes "total exactly one octave and thus comprise the twelve half tones of the untempered chromatic scale." This is "identical with that of Pythagoras" and "first appeared in China in the third century B.C." It "may well have been brought there as a result of the Asiatic conquests of Alexander the Great." (p. 11, note, in Fung, Vol. II).

Chapter IX

Mythical Cyclical Views in the Greek and Roman Worlds

In Greek thought Hesiod (eighth century B.C.) is the earliest witness to ancient notions of his countrymen about the pattern of history. His *Works and Days* reflects myths about the pattern of history already old among the Greeks. In Hesiod's pattern there are Five Ages, but this is a fusion of a pre-Hesiodic myth of the Four Ages and a legend about the Age of the Heroes "which Hesiod, or some precursor, interpolated between the third and the last of the other ages." [1] The Five Ages are the following:

(1) The Golden Age:

> First of all the deathless gods having homes on Olympus made a golden race of mortal men. These lived in the time of Cronus when he was king in heaven. Like gods they lived with hearts free from sorrow and remote from toil and grief; nor was miserable age their lot, but always unwearied in feet and hands they made merry in feasting, beyond the reach of all evils. And when they died, it was as though they were given over to sleep. And all good things were theirs. For the fruitful earth spontaneously bore them abundant fruit without stint. And they lived in ease and peace upon their lands with many good things, rich in flocks and beloved of the blessed gods.[2]

---
[1] Lovejoy and Boas, *op. cit.*, *Primitivism and Related Ideas in Antiquity*, p. 25.
[2] *Ibid.*, p. 27 trans. from Hesiod's *Works and Days*.

The Golden Age is similar to that in all myths of the ancient world, Mesopotamian, Egyptian,[3] Indian, Zoroastrian, Hebrew.[4] As in the Garden-of-Eden days of Adam and Eve as well as the primeval dawn of history described in all other ancient cultures, The Golden Race knew no moral or physical evil and did not have to labor.

The second race made by the "dwellers on Olympus" was the Silver, a race far worse than their predecessors. They lived "but a little while, and that in sorrow because of their foolishness; for they were unable to refrain from savage insolence towards one another, nor would they serve the immortals, nor sacrifice on the holy altars of the blessed ones . . ."[1] Zeus in anger destroyed them.

The third race was the Bronze. This race was "terrible and strong," delighting in the "deeds of Ares and violence"; but they were "destroyed by their own hands."[2]

The fourth race was the Heroic, a race of Demigods, "juster and more righteous, a divine race of hero-men."[3] These men were the god-like heroes of Homer's *Iliad* and *Odyssey*. These also died but they were sent to a heaven after death. In heaven they dwell "with hearts free of sorrow in the islands of the blessed."

The fifth race is the present species and is named the Race of Iron. Of this miserable race the poet says:

> Would that I were not among the fifth race, but had either died before or were born afterwards. For now the race is iron. Neither by day does it have an end of toil and sorrow nor by night of wasting away. But the gods shall give them toilsome anxiety. Nevertheless for these too good shall be mixed with their evils. But Zeus will destroy this race of men too when they reach the point of being born with greying temples. Nor will father agree with child nor child with

---
[3] *Infra*, pp. 233-5.
[4] *Infra*, pp. 235 f.
[1] *Ibid.*, p. 28. Quotations from *Works and Days*.
[2] *Ibid.*, p. 29 Quotations from *Works and Days*.

father, nor guest with host nor comrade with comrade, nor will brother be dear to brother as before. But soon men will dishonor their aging parents and will carp at them, scolding them with bitter words, merciless, knowing no fear of the gods. Nor will they whose right is in their fists, repay their aged parents for their nurture. And one man will sack another's city. Nor will there be any favor for the man who keeps his word nor for the just and good, but rather will men praise the evil-doer and his crime. . . And right will be in might, and modesty will no longer exist. And the evil man will injure the better man, speaking with crooked tales and swearing an oath thereto. And envy, foul-mouthed, of hateful visage, delighting in evil, will accompany all miserable men. And then Shame (Aidos) and Indignation (Nemesis), with their fair forms wrapped in white robes, will go from the wide-pathed earth to Olympus and to the people of the gods, abandoning men. And bitter sorrows will be left for mortal men, and there will be no help against evil.[4]

Hesiod's pattern of Five Ages is reduced to a Four Age pattern (the Age of Heroes omitted) in Hellenistic thought, for example in the *Book of Daniel*.[1] The Four Age version appears as late as Hegel's philosophy of history which is divided into four eras even though Hegel applies triads everywhere else in his thought. Hegel derives his pattern from the Bible which in turn derived it from sources pre-Hesiodic as discussed below.[2]

According to Lovejoy and Boas, Hesiod's theory of the Ages became most influential upon European thought in the version given by Ovid in his *Metamorphoses*. This version is "of especial importance in relation to primitivistic communism in medieval and modern times."[3] Ovid's notion

---

[3] *Ibid.*,p. 30. Quotations from *Works and Days*.
[4] *Ibid.*, pp 30-31. Quotations from *Works and Days*.
[1] *Infra*, pp. 245-7.
[2] *Infra*, p. 246.
[3] Lovejoy and Boas, *op. cit.*, p. 49.

of the Ages is influenced by the third century work by Aratus, the *Phaenomena*. Aratus simplifies the five age pattern ideas of Hesiod into a three-age version and features Justice as the central figure:

> And beneath both feet of Boötes behold the Maiden, who in her hands bears the Ear of Corn gleaming. Whether she be of the race of Astraeus, who they say was the ancient father of the stars, or of another, may she be borne on in safety. Now another tale is current among men, to wit, how formerly she was on earth, and met men face to face, and neither disdained the tribes of ancient men nor women, but sat amid them, immortal though she was. And they called her Justice; and assembling the elders, either in the market place or in the wide streets, she spoke aloud urging judgments more advantageous to the people. Not yet did men understand hateful war or vituperative disputes or din of battle, but they lived simply, and the cruel sea was concealed, nor did ships carry men's livelihood from afar; but oxen and the plough and Justice herself, mistress of the people, giver of just things, furnished all things a thousand fold. This continued as long as the earth nourished the Golden Race.[4]

The Silver Race followed and showed such deterioration that Justice withdrew to the mountains and predicted a worse race to come. The Bronze Race, successors of the Silver Race, fulfilled the predictions of Justice. These men were "more deadly than their predecessors, the first to forge the evil-working sword of the roadside and the first to eat of oxen who draw the plough.",[1] Justice so loathed this race that she "flew to Heaven. And she dwelt in that country where still at night she appears to men, the Maiden being near to far-seen Boötes." [2]

By the time Ovid composed his *Metamorphoses* the Ages

---
[4] *Ibid.*, p. 35 translated from the *Phaenomena*, 96-136.
[1] *Ibid.*, p. 35, translated from the *Phaenomena*, 96-136.
[2] *Ibid.*

had been practically reduced to two: the Golden Age of Cronus (or among Romans, Saturn) and the age of Zeus, the corrupt age of "modern" man.[3] The influence of Aratus is seen in Ovid's emphasis upon the supremacy of Justice in the Golden Age. Ovid does, in fact, describe four ages, Golden, Silver, Bronze, and Iron — but the emphatic contrast is between the Golden Age under Saturn (Cronus) and the subsequent eras of progressive degeneration under Jupiter (Zeus). The present race of men, however, is outside the scheme (though also degenerate) and originated out of the stones "which Deucalion and Pyrrha cast behind them to repopulate the earth after the Deluge." [4]

Ovid describes the Golden Age in these words:

> The first age was golden. In it faith and righteousness were cherished by men of their own free will without judges or laws. Penalties and fears there were none ... nor did the suppliant crowd fear the words of its judge, but they were safe without protectors ... Without the use of soldiers the peoples in safety enjoyed their sweet repose ... Spring was eternal ... Rivers of milk and rivers of nectar flowed and yellow honey dripped from the green oaks.[5]

Degeneration rapidly ensues with the reign of Jupiter. The Silver Race begins departures from virtue which reach a climax in the Iron Race (which succeeds the Bronze that followed the Silver). The Iron Race is extremely corrupt:

> ... Of hard iron is the last race. Immediately there broke out in the age of baser metal all manner of evil, and shame fled, and truth and faith. In place of these came deceits and trickery and treachery and force and the accursed love of possession ... And now noxious iron and gold more noxious still were produced: and these produced war — for wars are fought with

---
[3] *Ibid.*, p. 43.
[4] *Ibid.*, p. 43.
[5] *Ibid.*, p. 46, translated from Ovid's *Metamorphoses*, I, 76-215.

both—and rattling weapons were hurled by bloodstained hands. Men lived by plunder, guest was not safe from host, father-in-law from son-in-law, and the love of brothers was rare ...
Duty (*Pietas*) lay vanquished and the Virgin Astrea, last of the heavenly beings left the lands which ran with blood ...[1]

This race was destroyed. The present race of men, as stated above, arose from the stones left behind by Deucalion and Pyrrha to people the earth after the Deluge; this race too is corrupt.

Ovid, in this work, does not describe or theorize about a return to the Golden Age.[2] Virgil, however, does in his famous "Messianic" Eclogue. This Eclogue is influenced by the Stoic theory of world cycles [3] and by the idea found in Aratus and other writers about the Golden Age. Virgil follows Aratus in his association of the "Maid" (Justice) with the Golden Age, and like Ovid equates the Golden Age with the "reign of Saturn." Virgil's cyclical view of the return of the Golden Age has also been a great influence upon subsequent Western philosophies of history. Virgil, in his famous eclogue describing the return of the cyclic Golden Age, is anticipating the return of the age with the Era of Peace inaugurated by Augustus and a "wonderchild" successor. Virgil writes:

Now is come the last age of the Cumaean prophecy: the great cycle of periods is born anew. Now returns the Maid, returns the reign of Saturn: now from high heaven a new generation comes down. Yet do thou at that boy's birth, in whom the iron race shall

---

[1] *Ibid.*, pp. 47 f, translated from the *Metamorphoses*, I, 76-215.
[2] *Ibid.*, p. 48. Lovejoy and Boas comment: "It is noteworthy that Ovid does not suggest here the possibility of a return to the Golden Age. He is not touched, as far as one can see, by the Stoic theory of cycles, though the plan and purpose of his poem perhaps did not permit him to make use of that." Footnote on p. 7 adds: "There is a hint, however, of the great conflagration in lines 253-255."
[3] *Infra*, pp. 220 f.

begin to cease, and the golden to arise over all the world, holy Lucina, be gracious; now thine own Apollo reigns. And in thy consulate, in thine, O Pollio, shall this glorious age enter, and the great months begin their march: under thy rule what traces of our guilt yet remain, vanishing shall free earth for ever from alarm. He shall grow in the life of the gods, and shall see gods and heroes mingled, and himself be seen by them, and shall rule the world that his father's virtues have set at peace. But on thee, O boy, untilled shall Earth first pour childish gifts, wandering ivy-tendrils and foxglove, and colocasia mingled with the laughing acanthus: untended shall the she-goats bring home their milk-swollen udders, nor shall huge lions alarm the herds: unbidden thy cradle shall break into wooing blossom. The snake too shall die, and die the treacherous poison-plant: Assyrian spice shall grow all up and down . . . Begin, O little boy, to know and smile upon thy mother, thy mother on whom ten months have brought weary longings. Begin, O little boy: of them who have not smiled on a parent, never was one honoured at a god's board or on a goddess' couch.[1]

Christians noticed the similarity of this prophecy of a Golden Age inaugurated by a "wonder child" with that of Isaiah, hence the name "Messianic" given this eclogue. Since a chapter below is devoted to this kind of historical thinking, we shall not elaborate here upon its significance.

Virgil's cyclical idea, the return again of the Golden Age but with subsequent regression "new wars too shall arise, and again a mighty Achilles be sent to Troy . . ."[2] is inspired by the Stoic theory of cycles of Greek inspiration which attempts to be a naturalistic "scientific" historical theory. The Greeks were probably pioneers in taking an objective scientific approach to knowledge in all fields, including history human and cosmic. We shall ex-

---

[1] Virgil, *Virgil's Works, The Aeneid, Eclogues, Georgics*, trans. J. W. Mackail, Modern Library ed. (New York: Random House, 1934), pp. 274 f.
[2] *Ibid.*, p. 274.

amine some of these naturalistic views — all cyclic — and then return again to the mythological approach which is the immediate background of the one-cycle theories.

Chapter X

Greek Naturalism Applied to Cosmic Cycles

The first thinkers among the Greeks to offer purely naturalistic theories of the nature of the cosmos were the Ionians. Two of these Ionians, Anaximander and Anaximenes, were first to propose such a type of theory with relation to cosmic history. Anaximander conceived the ultimate substance of the universe to be *Apeiron* (the "Boundless"). This substance was without beginning or end. All the variety of the things in the world come forth by differentiation of its cold and warm parts. This differentiation gives rise to world-systems which progress to a certain point and then fall apart into decay. The process of formation and decay of world-systems is an everlasting one. It belongs to the nature of *Apeiron* which is this infinite cyclical process. Anaximenes' cyclical theory is similar except that he thinks the ultimate substance to be air instead of *Apeiron*.

Heraclitus (sixth century B.C.) taught that Fire is the ultimate substance of nature. This Fire element gives rise to earth, air, and water. All things are composed of these four elements. The fundamental substance, Fire, however, has more than a material character. It is called the *Logos* (literally *Word* but with the connotation "Reason") and operates in accordance with "fixed measures kindling and fixed measures dying out." By this Heraclitus means that Change of which Fire is the essence is the all-pervading characteristic of nature, but there is law (*logos*) in the change. This *logos* operates in such precise fashion in the cosmos as a whole that there are regular cyclic periods of evolution of the elements and all other things out of Fire and *ecpyrosis* or conflagration in which all things return to Fire.[1] The length of the world cycle from the beginning of an evolutionary period to an *ecpyrosis* is given by one tradition as 18,000 years and by another as 10,800 years.[1] If the latter number, which is given by Censorinus, is correct it was derived apparently "by taking a generation of 30 years as a day and multiplying it by 360 as the number of days in a year."[2] Here we have a notion which may have been derived from Babylonian ideas of a Great or Divine Year, the mythological origin of which we have discussed above.[3] Heraclitus, if he actually held to the idea of regular world cycles of precise length provides an original version of the cyclical view in attempting to found it upon a more scientific nature philosophy than the usual mythopoeic cosmologies current in the ancient world.

The Pythagoreans and the Cyclic Great Year of the Cosmos. The Pythagoreans (sixth century B.C.) are also credited with a theory of recurrent world cycles. They wove a philosophy of nature out of their notion that number is the essence of all things. They were, therefore, much impressed with the regular motions of the heavenly bodies and connected these with the seasons and other periodic occurrences in the world. Unlike Heraclitus they did not believe in periodic destructions and evolutions of the universe. Their cyclical view was founded on the astronomical idea of a Great Year of the universe,[4] a time at which all the heavenly bodies and the earth would return to the same relative

---

[1] This idea of an *ecpyrosis* (and thus world cycles) is not found in Heraclitus' surviving fragmentary works, but was attributed to him by later classical writers such as Aetius and Censorinus. See Lovejoy and Boas, *op. cit.*, pp. 79 f.
[1] Lovejoy and Boas, *op. cit.*, p. 80 and footnote.
[2] Sir Thomas Heath, *Aristarchus of Samos, The Ancient Copernicus* (Oxford: Clarendon Press, 1913), p. 61.
[3] *Supra,* chap. II.
[4] Eduard Zeller, *A History of Greek Philosophy,* trans. S. F. Alleyne and others (London: Longmans Green, 1881-88), Vol. I, *The Pre-Socratic Philosophers,* p. 474.

positions. Since there is an intimate connection between astronomical and earthly events, all conditions upon the earth, too, must return to the state at which they were when these bodies were previously in their original conjunction; then again begin a cycle in congruence with the renewal of the heavenly cycle or Great Year. The events and persons of each new world cycle repeat exactly, numerically, the events of the preceding one, and this is because all is in definite relationship with the astronomical bodies.[1] This mathematical notion that the same events, the same things, and the same persons under the same circumstances would everlastingly recur in every cycle was probably first held by the Pythagoreans,[2] perhaps under the influence of Indian views.[3]

Empedocles of Athens, another pre-Socratic philosopher, also advocated the cyclical view. He offers the hypothesis that the elements of nature (earth, air, fire, and water) are unified into a One by the motive power of love, then scattered apart by Hate into a Many until a maximum of disintegration is reached after which Love again begins its integrating process. Cosmic history is an endless repetition of this cyclic pattern.

The cyclical view of history was common not only in early Greek thought; it remained characteristic of the most mature developments in Greek philosophy. It is found in the works of both Plato and Aristotle.

---

[1] Lovejoy and Boas, *op. cit.*, pp. 82 f.

[2] Eduard Zeller, *Stoics, Epicureans and Sceptics*, trans. Oswald J. Reichel (London: Longmans, 1870), p. 166 footnote.

[3] Gomperz in his discussion of Pythagoras and Pythagoreanism in *Greek Thinkers*, Vol. I, thinks that ideas of cyclical recurrence of births filtered through to the Ionian Greeks by way of the Persian empire which under Cyrus included a part of India. It was while Pythagoras was still in Ionia that he imbibed the cyclical ideas. Burnett, however, in his *Early Greek Philosophy* (1930 ed.) says that the earliest *known* Greek who came under the influence of Indian thought was Pyrrho of Elis (360-270 B.C.), the famous skeptic. Pyrrho accompanied Alexander's expedition to India.

Cosmic and Culture Cycles in Plato's Thought: The Great Year

The cyclical view of Plato is akin to that of the Pythagoreans, for it, too, is connected with the movements of the heavenly bodies. In Plato's *Timaeus* the Great or Cosmic Year is described as the interval of Time which must elapse before the planetary bodies return to the same relative positions from which they originated. Plato says, "And yet there is no difficulty in seeing that the perfect number of time fulfills the perfect year when all the eight revolutions having their relative degrees of swiftness, are accomplished together and attain their completion at the same time, measured by the rotation of the same and equally moving."[1] Plato does not in this connection give us the length of this cosmic year, but in the first part of the same dialogue, Critias relates Solon's tale of a great disaster which befell the Athenians of 9000 years ago; all were destroyed save a remnant in a great Deluge. Critias adds that this was but one of many destructions of mankind which have taken place caused mainly either by fire or water. Then there is the significant passage:

> Now this has the form of a myth, but really signifies a declination of the bodies moving in the heavens around the earth, and a great conflagration of things upon the earth, which recurs after long intervals; at such times those who live upon the mountains and in dry and lofty places are more liable to destruction than those who dwell by rivers or on the seashore.[2]

This passage shows that Plato connects the cycle of civilization on earth with the movements of the heavenly

---
[1] Plato, *Timaeus*, trans. B. Jowett, *The Dialogues of Plato*, trans. B. Jowett (New York: Random House, 1937), 2 Vols., Vol. II, p. 21 (Steph. 39).
[2] *Ibid.*, *Timaeus*, p. 8 (Steph. 22).

bodies. Perhaps, therefore, the length of the Great Year was 10,000 solar years or an approximate number such as 10,800 derived from Heraclitus (if Heraclitus gave this number). There is further evidence for a number of 10,000 years in the Phaedrus where Plato asserts that "ten thousand years must elapse before the soul of each one can return to the place from whence he came . . ."[3] that is, the time of a complete revolution of the heavens. In the *Timaeus* Plato says that the Creator made as many souls as there are stars and assigned each soul to its own star. At the beginning all enter the world as men, but those who free themselves from the bodily senses are to return to their stars and lead a blessed spiritual existence. Professor Taylor maintains that Plato nowhere gives any definite length to the astronomical Great Year and in the passage quoted from the *Timaeus* which describes it from a purely astronomical point of view, he does not. Zeller, on the other hand, thinks that the length of the Great Year was not fixed by astronomical calculation but by "arbitrary conjecture"; and that Plato "seems to connect with it, periodical changes in the condition of the world."[1] Gomperz, another great Plato scholar, thinks the length of Plato's Great Year 10,000 human years.[2] Gomperz relates this number convincingly to Plato's interest in Pythagoreanism. The Pythagoreans considered ten the perfect number. The reason is given by Sir Thomas Heath:

> The Pythagoreans (we are told) made ten the perfect number. Being the sum of the four numbers 1, 2, 3, 4, the number 10 formed the 'set of four (numbers)' called the *tetractys*. This set of numbers includes the numbers out of which are formed the ratios corres-

---

[3] *Ibid.*, *Phaedrus*, Vol. I, p. 253 (Steph. 248).

[1] Eduard Zeller, *Plato and the Older Academy*, trans. Alleyne and Goodwin, new ed. (London: Longmans Green and Co., 1888), p. 382.

[2] Theodore Gomperz, *Greek Thinkers*, trans. C. G. Berry (New York: Humanities Press, 1955), Vol. III, p. 223.

ponding to the musical intervals, namely 4:3 (the fourth), 3:2 (the fifth), and 2:1 (the octave). Such virtue was attached to the *tetractys* that it was for the Pythagoreans their 'greatest oath' and was alternately called 'Health.' It also gives, when graphically represented by points in four lines one below the other

```
      *
     * *
    * * *
   * * * *
```

a triangular number. Hence Lucian's story that Pythagoras once told someone to count, and when he had said 1, 2, 3, 4, Pythagoras interrupted 'Do you see? What you take for 4 is 10, a perfect triangle, and our oath.'

Speusippus observes further that 10 contains in it the 'linear,' 'plane,' and 'solid' varieties of number, for 1 is a point, 2 a line, 3 a triangle, and 4 a pyramid. This is easily seen by placing the right number of dots in the proper positions. We are thus brought back to the theory of figured numbers, which seems to go back to Pythagoras himself.[3]

Because Plato thought that the Demiurge made the world-organism (or world-soul) as perfect as possible, a large multiple of ten, the perfect, the holy tectractys number, ought to be the number of the length of one complete revolution of this world organism. In this way Plato may have decided upon a ten thousand year period as the length of his astronomical Great Year.

Other capable scholars argue, however, that Plato's Great Year was a period of 36,000 years. Sir Thomas Heath discusses this point of view rather fully. Here the perfect number of Plato's *Republic*, Book VIII, 546, is taken to be the square of 3,600 or 12,960,000. This figure signifies the number of daily rotations of the earth on its axis. Plato's

---

[3] Sir Thomas Heath, *A History of Greek Mathematics*. 2 vols. (Oxford: Clarendon Press, 1931), Vol. II, pp. 41 f.

small year as given in the *Laws* has 360 days. Thus the Great Year has 36,000 small years, i.e., 12,960,000 days divided by 360. Sir Thomas Heath does not find the evidence convincing and leaves the problem of the length of Plato's Great Year unsettled.[1] On the other hand, George Sarton accepts 36,000 years as the cycle length and thinks that Plato received this number from the Babylonians as 60^4 (36,000) supposedly the length of the Great Year (divine year described in chapter II of this book) in Babylonia. Sarton writes:

> Among the powers of 60, one occurs very frequently in the old tables, namely, $60^4 = 12,960,000$. Now this is the geometric number of Plato, and 12,960,000 days = 36,000 years of 360 days, the 'great Platonic year' (the duration of a Babylonian cycle). A man's life of 100 years contains 36,000 days, as many days as there are years in the 'great year.' The 'geometric number,' that is, a number measuring or governing the earth and life on earth, was thus clearly of Babylonian origin.[2]

Otto Neugebauer, a leading contemporary scholar in the history of astronomy, disagrees with Sarton's notion of the Babylonian origin of Plato's Great Year. Neugebauer comments:

> The lack of a notation which determines the absolute value of a number made it possible to misinterpret simple tables of multiplication or reciprocals. When Hilprecht, in 1906, published a volume of 'mathematical, metrological and chronological tablets from the Temple Library of Nippur' he was convinced that these texts showed a relation to Plato's number mysticism. In book VIII of the 'Republic' Plato gives some

---

[1] *Ibid.*, Vol. I, pp. 305-308.
[2] George Sarton, *A History of Science: Ancient Science Through the Golden Age of Greece* (Cambridge: Harvard University Press, 1952), p. 71.

cabalistic rules as to how guardians of his dictatorially ruled community should arrange for proper marriages. By some wild artifices, Plato's cabala was brought into relationship with the numbers found on the tablets ..."[1]

Since Hilprecht is one of the source authorities mentioned by Professor Sarton in the passage just quoted, the "Babylonian origin" of Plato's cyclic number is doubtful. The figure 36,000 is therefore uncertain since it is based upon the "Babylonian origin" theory. Neugebauer asserts that the Babylonian "Saros," taken by many to have an astronomical meaning of 3600 years, probably had no such astronomical significance until 1000 A.D. About this time we find such a connotation given the saros in the encyclopaedia of Suidas.[2] One of the original meanings of the cuneiform Sumerian sign *sar* was "universe," and "as a number word it represents 3600, thus being an example of the transformation from a general concept of plurality to a concrete high numeral."[3] The first appearance of the number applied to years (3600 years) is in Berossos (about 290 B.C.).[4] Neugebauer attributes the myths about the Saros and other astronomical cosmological Babylonian theories to the errors especially of Jeremias' *Handbuch der altorientalischen Geisteskultur*.[1]

[1] Otto Neugebauer, *The Exact Science in Antiquity*. op. cit. p. 26.
[2] *Ibid.*, p. 135.
[3] *Ibid.*
[4] *Ibid.*
[1] *Ibid.*, p. 132. Neugebauer condemns this work. He says: "With the use of an enormous learned apparatus, the author develops the 'panbabylonistic'doctrine which flourished in Germany between 1908 and 1914, only to be given up completely after the first world war. The main thesis of this school was built on wild theories about the great age of Babylonian astronomy, combined with an alleged 'macrocosm and microcosm.' There was no phenomenon in classical cosmogony, religion, literature which was not traced back to this hypothetical cosmic philosophy of the Babylonians. A supreme disregard for textual evidence, wide use of secondary sources and antiquated translations, combined with a preconceived chronology of

Plato discourses in half-mythical fashion about the nature of the world cycles. Unlike the Pythagoreans, he does not think that events and individuals are identical in each world cycle. In a vague and mythical way Plato suggests the pattern of three cycles in his dialogue, the *Statesman*. In the first cycle he describes, God himself is at the helm of the universe. This age is one of paradisiacal bliss, the Golden Age of Hesiod's *Works and Days:*

> In those days God himself was their shepherd, and ruled over them, just as man, who is by comparison a divine being, still rules over the lower animals. Under him there were no forms of government or separate possession of women and children; for all men rose again from the earth, having no memory of the past. And although they had nothing of this sort, the earth gave them fruits in abundance, which grew on trees and shrubs unbidden, and were not planted by the hand of man. And they dwelt naked, and mostly in the open air for the temperature of their seasons was mild and they had no beds, but lay on soft couches of grass, which grew plentifully out of the earth. Such was the life of man in the days of Cronos, Socrates; the character of our present life, which is said to be under Zeus, you know from your own experience.[2]

In the second cycle God lets go of the helm of the universe; this causes a reversal of all processes including the biological. The old become young, the young babies, and babies dissolve away. Then God, in his compassion, seeing that the universe is in such straits, takes the helm again and a third cycle begins.

The third cycle is the present one. There is no Golden Age again. Instead, God makes the World-Creature "imperishable and immortal" and animals as microcosms imi-

---

Babylonian civilization, created a fantastic picture which exercised (and still exercises) a great influence on the literature concerning Babylonia." (p. 132)

[2] *Dialogues of Plato, op. cit.,* Vol. II, *Statesman;* pp. 271-272.

tate the world-creature in its imperishability and self-sufficiency by generating their species out of themselves, sexually, instead of rising from the earth as before. Humans now must depend upon themselves instead of God and the demigods. In the beginning their condition was miserable:

> Deprived of the care of God, who had possessed and tended them, they were left helpless and defenceless, and were torn in pieces by the beasts, who were naturally fierce and had now grown wild. And in the first ages they were still without skill or resource; the food which once grew spontaneously had failed . . . For all these reasons they were in a great strait; wherefore also the gifts spoken of in the old tradition were imparted to man by the gods, together with so much teaching and education as was indispensable; fire was given to them by Prometheus, the arts by Hephaestus and his fellowworker, Athene, seeds and plants by others. From these is derived all that has helped to frame human life; since the care of the Gods, as I was now saying, had now failed man, and they had to order their course of life for themselves, and were their own masters, just like the universal creature whom they imitate and follow, ever changing, as he changes, and ever living and growing, at one time in one manner, and at another in another.[1]

Plato's description of this third cycle leaves the realm of myth in its affirmation of the progress of man by his own efforts (symbolized by the "gifts" of the gods Prometheus, Hephaestus and Athene).

Progress is not limitless, however. In the *Republic* Plato relates the human culture cycle to the cosmic cyclic period, the "geometric number" the length of which is so controversial as we have noted above.[2] The climax of perfection,

---

[1] *Ibid.*, p. 274. Plato's views of this first state of man and of culture cycles were basic in the development of Vico's cyclic theories described below.

[2] *Ibid.*, Vol. I, Republic VIII, 546 and discussion *supra*.

the ideal human community guided by philosopher kings will begin to decline because the guardian-rulers are "ignorant of the law of births," that is, the "geometrical figure which has control over the good and evil of births." The children born will not be as noble and intelligent as their predecessors. They will begin to neglect music and next gymnastic.

> In the succeeding generation rulers will be appointed who have lost the guardian power of testing the metal of your different races, which, like Hesiod's, are of gold and silver and brass and iron. And so iron will be mingled with silver, and brass with gold, and hence there will arise dissimilarity and inequality and irregularity, which always and in all places are causes of hatred and war.[1]

The ideal state, the aristocracy, degenerates to a timocracy, this to oligarchy which deteriorates into democracy, and finally the last degree of decline is reached in tyranny.[2]

The culture cycle idea is brought out again in the *Critias*. As in the *Statesman* the *Critias* describes a Golden Age of the gods as the first era. In this period the gods controlled human culture. Athene and Hephaestus guided Attica; Poseidon controlled Atlantis. Attica developed a social organization and culture like that of the ideal state of Plato's *Republic* mentioned above; Atlantis became a highly civilized maritime power of great wealth. The Atlantides remained uncorrupted by their power and luxury for "many generations."

> They despised everything but virtue, little esteeming their present state of life, and bearing lightly the burden of the gold and other property they possessed; neither were they intoxicated by luxury, nor did

[1] *Ibid., Republic*, VIII, 546-547.
[2] *Ibid.*, pp. 547-569.

wealth deprive them of their self-control and thereby cause their downfall. On the contrary, in their soberness of mind, they saw clearly that all these good things are increased by mutual good will combined with virtue, whereas to honor and strive after these goods destroys not only the goods themselves, but also virtue with them.[3]

The Atlantides, too, however, eventually degenerated. Greed and love for power gradually dominated their lives until Zeus resolved upon their destruction. As Lovejoy and Boas point out, the story is apparently continued in the *Timaeus*. The people of Atlantis became aggressors of the most vicious sort, warring on many peoples. The Athenians led the Hellenes in resisting the Atlantides and won a great victory; they freed not only the Hellenes but all peoples east of Gibraltar. Nevertheless, both peoples were destroyed in the same great Deluge occurring presumably at the end of the astronomical cycle as noted above. The remnant saved had to begin anew the development of a culture. Lovejoy and Boas comment: "These ancestors of the present Athenians, being assumed to have lost, or never known, the arts which had flourished among the vanished races, passed gradually through the same cultural phases until the existing — and inferior — social and political order was reached." [1]

Summary. Plato seems to have believed that there were astronomical cycles that were repetitive, probably because the divine heavenly bodies were thought to be more unchanging than earthly beings. Changes in human cultural history are correlated with these astronomical cycles, since all are part of one world-organism. Cultural history repeats a cyclic pattern of rise, climax, degeneration, and end with a remnant left at the end to begin the cycle anew. Events and persons are not repeated in identical form and some

[3] *Critias*, 120e, 121a. Quoted in Lovejoy and Boas, *op. cit.*, p. 161.
[1] Lovejoy and Boas, *op. cit.*, p. 161.

cycles reach a higher culture climax than others. The cause of decline is contempt for wisdom, greed and love for power. These vices result in the hatred and conflict which destroy the culture.

Great subsequent philosophers of history such as Aristotle in the ancient world, Vico in the Renaissance (who emphasizes his debt to Plato's cyclic culture theories), Rousseau and the "cultural primitivists" of the eighteenth century and many other thinkers such as Spengler, Toynbee and Sorokin in the twentieth century — all have used Plato as a source, directly or indirectly, for their theories of culture cycles.

Cycles in Aristotle's philosophy of nature and culture.

Like previous Greek thinkers, Aristotle takes the naturalistic position that the world must be everlasting. If it were not, we should have to assume creation out of nothing or some other supernatural beginning of the world, thus leaving the realm of human experience and logic. If we remain within the sphere of human experience and logic, the universe as a whole must always have existed, and if so its cause must be eternal. The eternal cause reflects itself as the everlastingness of the world. The fundamental dynamics of the world process, then, if everlasting, must be cyclical. Aristotle gives a somewhat systematic formulation of his cyclical approach to the dynamics of nature and of human culture in *De Generatione et Corruptione* and in his *Politics*.

In *De Generatione et Corruptione* Aristotle claims that coming-to-be and passing-away must be everlasting because their cause is eternal. Coming-to-be and passing away are dual or opposite movements and therefore caused by a dual movement. This dual movement is that of the sun in the inclined circle of the Zodiac which produces coming-to-be in its approach to the earth and passing away when it recedes. This eternal motion of the sun is caused in its turn by the constant and eternal motion of the outermost sphere which carries along with it all the concentric spheres, and the motion of the outermost sphere is constant and eternal because its unmoved cause, God, is eternal. Now this continuous dual movement of coming-to-be and passing away is the closest approach which the sublunar world can make to that which is eternal. Aristotle says,

> Now 'being' (we have explained elsewhere the exact variety of meanings we recognize in this term) is better than 'not-being,' but not all things can possess 'being,' since they are too far removed from the originative source. God therefore adopted the remaining alternative, and fulfilled the perfection of the universe by making coming-to-be uninterrupted; for the greatest possible coherence would thus be secured to existence, because that 'coming-to-be should itself come-to-be perpetually' is the closest approximation to eternal being.[1]

This passage appears modelled upon Plato's statement in the *Timaeus* that God made the world a "moving image of eternity," and placed within it every kind of creature in order that all possibilities should be realized and the temporal creature resemble the all-inclusive perfection of eternal being.

This dual movement of coming-to-be and passing-away is, then, perpetual, and since it is perpetual, Aristotle says it must be a circular or cyclical movement, not rectilinear. For example, Water is transformed into Air, Air into Fire, and Fire again into Water. Thus the change returns upon itself in circular form. If the movement were not circular, then the elements Earth, Air, Fire, and Water would in infinite time have been permanently separated from each other.

There is an Order, Aristotle thinks, controlling all things

---

[1] Aristotle, *The Basic Works of Aristotle*, Ross translation, single volume edition, ed. Richard McKeon (New York: Random House, 1941), *De Generatione et Corruptione*, 336b.

whereby each has a definite period of existence allotted to it.[2] The circle of coming-to-be and passing-away, of growth and decay is regular in accordance with the nature of each thing as well as continuous and recurrent. Such regular periodical appearance and disappearance of existents is caused, as we have said, by the approach and retreat of the sun. Although this movement of the sun regulates the length of life of each existent and makes its coming-to-be and passing-away, definite, necessary, and perpetual, it is not essential, Aristotle maintains, to assume that the ever-recurrent existences shall be *identical* in *concrete, particularized existence*. Every season of the year, for example, recurs in *form*, but seasons are not identical in concrete particularity. With reference to human existence, it is even more obvious that the same individual does not recur a second time through necessity; for although "your coming-to-be presupposes your father's, his coming-to-be does not pre-suppose yours." That individuals do not recur as such is owing, Aristotle says, to the perishability of their substance. Only those things, the substance of which is imperishable (and no sub-lunar substance is imperishable) can recur as numerically the same. However, all things do recur as "specifically" the same. By this is meant that the same types or *forms* of existence perpetually recur.[1] Here Aristotle is in agreement with Shankara, the great Indian thinker.

Aristotle carries this same cyclical conception to social life. The same cultural patterns recur, reach a climax and decay, analogous to the growth, maturation, decay, and death of the individual. Here he anticipates such modern thinkers as Vico and Spengler. The political life, the arts, and the sciences which make up any society follow this same pattern; there is no idea of a general and endless progress of humanity as a whole. Each culture discovers specifically the same cultural arts and sciences, progresses

---
[2] *Ibid.*
[1] *Ibid.*, 338b. See also Lovejoy and Boas. *op. cit.*, pp. 170-177.

to a certain point, and then decays. Aristotle gives a precise account of this cycle in the case of the political art.[2]

The family is the beginning of social organization and is caused by the sexual and parental instinct common to all animals. The second cause of social organization is the difference by nature in types of men, those whose nature it is to rule and those whose nature it is to be ruled — the slave-type. After the household, the second stage of social organization is the clan, ruled by the eldest of the several households. This is the origin of kingship. The next stage is the city-state formed by a union of clans in order to satisfy more adequately the social needs of protection and material goods, thus making possible a leisure class which can attend disinterestedly to lawmaking and the general good of the state. It is this class which cultivates the intellectual life. This is the natural pattern which any social group will follow if left to itself, but the last stage — the climax and full flower of the culture cycle — does not endure. When this climax is reached perversions begin to appear and the degeneration stage sets in. Aristotle thought that the Greek world of his day had reached its zenith of culture in every form; nothing was left for future discovery; all possibilities were exhausted. This is clear from the following passage in the *Politics:*

> We must not fail to keep in mind the length of time and multitude of years in which these things, if they had been good, would certainly not have remained unknown; for almost everything has been found out, though in some cases what is known has not been systematized, and in other cases men do not make use of the knowledge which they have.[1]

---

[2] Lovejoy and Boas, *op. cit.*, pp. 173 ff.

[1] *Basic Works of Aristotle, op. cit., Politics,* II, 1264a; quoted also in Lovejoy and Boas, *op. cit.*, p. 179.

It is plain, then, that Aristotle held to a definite cyclical view of all the forms and patterns which come-to-be and pass away in natural and in cultural-social life; the idea of a rectilinear progress was utterly foreign to his thought as well as to Greek thought in general.

Stoic cycles: the ecpyrosis. The Stoics took the most radical cyclical view of nature and culture cycles, a view similar to that attributed to the Pythagoreans. The Stoics believed that each world-cycle repeats in every detail, numerically, exactly what happens in every other cycle. According to Eudemus, in the account Simplicius gives of this writer in his *Physics*, the Stoics borrowed this notion from the Pythagoreans.[2]

The authorities, however, which inform us about the origins of the Stoic theory of cycles are late so we cannot be certain as to the source or date of such a doctrine in Stoic philosophy.[1] A second century writer, Tatianus, attributes the doctrine to Zeno[2] whereas Eusebius says that Zeno "suspended judgment concerning the *ecpyrosis* of all things."[3] Nemesius (fifth century A.D.) gives us a good account of the nature of the cyclical idea tradition attached to the Stoics:

> And the Stoics say that the planets will be restored to the same zodiacal sign, both in longitude and latitude, as they had in the beginning when the cosmos was first put together; that in stated periods of time a conflagration (*ecpyrosis*) and destruction of things will be accomplished, and once more there will be a restitution of the cosmos as it was in the very beginning. And when the stars move in the same way as

[2] Zeller, *Stoics, Epicureans and Sceptics, op. cit.*, p. 166 footnote.
[1] Lovejoy and Boas, *op. cit.*, p. 83.
[2] *Ibid.*, p. 84. A passage from Tatianus *Adv. graec.* c. 5, is quoted: "Zeno has shown that after the ecpyrosis these men will be resurrected as they were. And I say that this must imply that Anytus and Meletus will again bring their accusation, and Busiris slay the strangers, and Hercules perform his labors."
[3] *Ibid.*, pp. 83-84. Quoted from Eusebius, Praep. evang. XV, 18, 1-3.

before, each thing which occurred in the previous period will without variation be brought to pass again. For again there will exist Socrates and Plato and every man, with the same friends and fellow citizens, and he will suffer the same fate and will meet with the same experiences and undertake the same deeds. And every city and village and field will be restored. And there will be a complete restoration of the whole, not once only but many times, or rather interminably, and the same things will be restored without end.[4]

Seneca who writes much earlier (first century A.D.), though he does not give this much detail implies the same cyclical idea. He says that the first morning of creation writes what the last dawn shall read [5]; Marcus Aurelius takes a similar view. This is because the Stoics conceive of the ultimate substance of nature, Fire, as thoroughly rational, the Logos. Every event in nature follows in a mathematically logical order from the preceding event or events; there is absolutely no room for chance or the irrational; therefore everything must be repeated in its identical sameness.

Seneca follows a Hesiodic culture cycle pattern with a Golden Age of innocence and bliss at the beginning. However moral virtue is not greatest in this era since there is little opportunity for the conflicts which develop such virtue. Insofar as men have discovered the right pattern of moral virtue there has been progress, but even here there is no idea of a continuation of such progress to higher levels. Seneca thinks that the great moral truths have been discovered by the great Greek leaders of the Stoic and Cynic schools; no further progress is possible.[1]

At the end of the cycle Seneca thinks that man and all

---

[4] *Ibid.*, p. 84, quoted from Nemesius *De nat. hom.* c. 38.

[5] *Ibid.*, p. 285: "*a primo die mundi . . . quando mergerentur terrena decretum est.*" Quoted from Seneca's *Quaestiones naturales*, III, xxx-1.

[1] *Ibid.*, p. 264.

his works will be destroyed. Seneca sometimes describes the end of the world cycle in two stages. First there will be a great Deluge; then the *ecpyrosis*.[2] Then the world cycle and human culture cycle will begin again but follow exacty the same pattern. The primeval age of bliss will come again.

> Every species of animal will be created afresh, and the earth will once more be inhabited by men — men born under happier auspices, knowing naught of evil. But their innocence will endure only so long as they are new. Wickedness creeps in swiftly.[3]

Epicurean cyclical views. The Epicureans who flourished in the same era as the Stoics, also took a cyclical view of nature and culture, but for reasons different from those of the Stoics. Following the view of Democritus, they understood the universe as composed of an infinite number of atoms and the Void (empty space in which the atoms move). The sizes, weights, and shapes of atoms differ, and this gives rise to all the variety of phenomena in the world including such phenomena as body and soul. A world is formed in this manner: The scattered atoms fall and in their falling swerve into one another. This meeting causes a rebound. The lighter atoms are forced up and the heavier ones down. This gives rise to a rotatory motion and a consequent clustering of atoms which separate into groups by their own motion, thus forming a world. The atoms are everlasting and infinite in number and motion is inherent in them. This is a thoroughly materialistic naturalistic metaphysics.

Although the atoms are infinite in number, their kinds are few; therefore, thought Epicurus, our world and others were bound to be repeated in infinite time. The varieties of worlds are not endless. All imaginable combinations of

---
[2] *Ibid.*, pp. 285-286.
[3] *Ibid.*, p. 286. Quoted from *Quaestiones naturales*, III, xxx, 7-8.

atoms that have made the various worlds must already have occurred (in infinite time) and will recur again. From this point of view, Epicurus too believed that there is nothing new under the sun. Although the combination of atoms which our world illustrates has doubtless existed before and will exist again, yet there is no definite sequence of worlds. Just when our world will exist again is a matter of chance (there is no *logos*), but that it will exist again is as certain as it is that certain throws of dice will recur at intervals. (In modern philosophy a similar doctrine of "eternal recurrence" is found in the thought of Nietzsche described below.)

Lucretius, famous Roman disciple of Epicurus, does not follow the Hesiodic view of a Golden Age at the beginning of the human culture cycle. Man was like the beasts in the first era of his existence and produced from the earth like the other animals. Early he developed speech from animal cries, and invented agriculture, cooking and weaving; then the art of song and dance with which he made merry. Government next developed because of men's new interests in gold and accumulation of private property and wealth; war followed. Nevertheless progress continues for the world is still in its youth. Praise is given Athens for her "three great boons for mankind—agriculture, a new order of social life based upon established laws, and lastly the teaching of Epicurus, who, by making clear the true nature of things, freed men from supernatural terrors, 'set bounds to both desire and fear' . . . and showed the nature of the chief good which we all seek . . ."[1]

Despite this more optimistic view Lucretius does not think progress will continue indefinitely. The Earth itself is wearing out and will eventually disintegrate completely. He says:

> For the larger and broader a thing is, the more, when it ceases to grow, it ejects matter from itself and scatters it on all sides; and food is not easily absorbed

[1] *Ibid.*, p. 237.

into its veins, nor is it sufficient, in proportion to the copious streams that flow out, to enable an equivalent amount of substance to be formed in their place. Rightly therefore all things perish when they have become attenuated by this flux, and succumb to blows from without; since in great age nourishment at last is lacking, while external bodies, incessantly beating upon everything, disintegrate and overwhelm it with their blows.

So it is that the walls of the mighty universe shall be overthrown through all their circuit and collapse into crumbling ruins . . . And even now the force of life is broken and the worn-out earth scarce produces tiny creatures — she who once produced all animals of every kind and gave birth to the huge bodies of wild beasts . . . And now the ancient ploughman often shakes his head and sings that the labors of his hands have come to nought, and when he compares times present with times past, often praises the good fortune of his forebears. And the cultivator of an old withering vineyard rails at the work of time and importunes heaven and grumbles that the men of former days, rich in piety, easily supported life upon a scant domain — for in the olden time one man's portion of land was much smaller than it is now. He does not see that all things little by little wear away and, exhausted by the longdrawn span of time, approach their tomb.[2]

Lucretius on the whole seems to think that the happiest time for man was in the second era of his culture-history — the time when he had discovered enough of the simple arts to be able to enjoy his existence, and before greed for private wealth and power became dominant. He does, however, believe that further progress in science and technology are possible. Nevertheless all things must become senescent and eventually disintegrate; there is "no belief in an indefinite progress of the world as a whole."[1]

---

[2] *Ibid.*, pp. 238 f. Quoted from Lucretius *De Rerum Natura*, II, 1122-1174.

[1] *Ibid.*, p. 237.

Maternus Julius Firmicus: The Sothic cycle, the Five Planets and the Five Ages. Maternus Julius Firmicus, a Latin writer and astronomer who lived in the fourth century A.D. reflects the eclecticism of his time in his version of world cycles. He posits an astronomical Great Year of the universe of 1461 human years.[2] This time span is Egyptian in origin. The Egyptian Sothic cycle is based upon the heliacal rising of the star, Sirius. The day on which this occurs is New Year's day. The Egyptians had a 365 day year, but since the year has about 365¼ days, in four years New Year's Day was one day late; thus in 365 x 4 years which is 1460 years New Year's Day will fall again on the first original day. This Sothic cycle as a Great Year may have been known to the Egyptians as early as 4241 B.C. and in any case no later than 2781 B.C.[3]

Firmicus' second ingredient in his cyclic theory is the idea of the Five Ages of the World, a culture cycle idea as old as Hesiod.[4] Firmicus connects each age, however with one of the five planets.

The first age is controlled by Saturn but is not a Golden Age as in Hesiod's version (Cronus in Hesiod is equivalent to Saturn). On the contrary, in the age of Saturn men "live in a rude kind of association and inhuman and extreme savagery." This is similar to Lucretius' view of primeval man. The second age, controlled by Jupiter, purifies human manners; the third, controlled by Mars, is an era in which arts and crafts are cultivated; the fourth, controlled by Venus, the "happy and benevolent deity" is one in which men are governed "by the authority of foresight." The fifth and last age is dominated by Mercury. This is the age of degeneration, when the fickleness of man, his maleficent wiles, and general wickedness reach a cli-

---

[2] Sir George Cornewall Lewis, *An Historical Survey of the Astronomy of the Ancients* (London: Parker, Sons, and Bourn, West Strand, 1862), p. 282. Lewis quotes his source as the *Praef. ad astron.* of Firmicus.

[3] *Encyclopaedia Brittanica* (1957 ed.), Vol. 4, "Calendar," p. 575.

[4] *Supra*, pp. 196 ff.

max. Presumably Saturn takes control again and the Sothic cycle of five ages is repeated.[1]

Firmicus adds to this theory of world years an analogy between the world cycle of five ages and the life of the individual, the microcosm. He says, "That we may not appear to overlook anything, we must explain all as proving man to be formed in the image of the world."[2] This analogy receives great elaboration in modern philosophies of history as we shall see below.

Greek and Roman Naturalism and Modern Naturalism Applied to Cosmic Cycles

As we mentioned in our discussion of Lucretius, Nietzsche, a nineteenth century philosopher, teaches the doctrine of "eternal recurrence." He thinks that at chance intervals the world must repeat itself exactly down to the minutest detail. He has Zarathustra say:

> I come again with this sun, with this earth, with this eagle, with this serpent—*not* to a new life, or a better life, or to a similar life:
> — I come again eternally to this identical and selfsame life, in its greatest and its smallest, to teach again the eternal return of all things,—
> To speak again the word of the great noontide of earth and man, to announce again to man the Superman.[3]

---

[1] This description of the Five Ages is found in Lovejoy and Boas, *op. cit.*, pp. 76f.

[2] *Ibid.*, p. 76, quoted from Firmicus' *Mathesis*.

[3] Nietzsche, *Thus Spake Zarathustra*, Vol. XI of *The Complete Works of Friedrich Nietzche*, ed. Oscar Levy (New York: The Macmillan Company, 1913, copyright: Allen & Unwin, London) p. 270.

Nietzsche declares his doctrine scientific; he thinks it a necessary result of the scientific doctrine of the conservation of energy. He argues that because the amount of energy or matter in the universe is constant or finite, only a certain limited number of combinations is possible. The number of possibilities may be very great, but it must be a definite number. Time, on the contrary, is infinite. Therefore in infinite time all possible combinations must repeat themselves everlastingly, in no definite order but merely according to the laws of chance. This is the doctrine of "eternal recurrence." He adds also that energy must always remain constant and never reach a state of equilibrium. It must always remain constant because there is no way in which it can be dissipated; it cannot be dissipated because there is nothing but energy. Energy cannot be lost through radiation into space because there is no such thing as space. "Space like matter is a subjective form, time is not. The notion of space first arose from the assumption that space could be empty. But there is no such thing as empty space. Everything is energy."[1] Energy cannot reach a state of equilibrium, which would preclude the possibility of everlastingly recurrent combinations, because if such a state were possible, it would already have been reached since an infinity of time is behind us and the state would have persisted.[2] The present world, then, would not exist; but it does exist; therefore, a state of equilibrium is impossible. Thus "the whole process of Becoming consists of a repetition of similar states."[3]

Nietzsche's theory that all is energy has a modern ring since the era of Einstein's famous equation which shows the theoretical equivalence of "matter" and energy. The recurrence doctrine, too, is a possibility in cosmological theory though perhaps not as Nietzsche formulated it. One of the most generally accepted cosmological theories today

[1] *Ibid., Complete Works*, Vol. XVI, p. 240.
[2] *Ibid.*, pp. 241-242.
[3] *Ibid.*, p. 242.

227

is the one formulated by Professor Gamow but this is not cyclical. Gamow theorizes on the basis of the observed phenomenon of the expansion of the universe that this process began about five billion years ago with a core substance consisting mostly of radiant energy.

> During the first few minutes of the universe's existence matter must have consisted only of protons, neutrons and electrons . . . One can call the mixture of particles *ylem* (pronounced eelem) — the name that Aristotle gave to primordial matter. As the universe went on expanding and the temperature of *ylem* dropped, protons and neutrons began to stick together, forming deuterons (nuclei of heavy hydrogen), helium and heavier elements.[1]

In this way the universe began. The material masses called galaxies formed, and the galaxies are moving farther and farther apart. Eventually a maximum of expansion will be reached. Gamow says:

> Thus we conclude that our universe has existed for an eternity of time, that until about five billion years ago it was collapsing uniformly from a state of infinite rarefaction; that five billion years ago it arrived at a state of maximum compression in which the density of all its matter may have been as great as that of the particles packed in the nucleus of an atom (i.e., 100 million million times the density of water), and that the universe is now on the rebound, dispersing irreversibly toward a state of infinite rarefaction.[2]

The first part of this quotation mentions the hypothesis that there was a period of infinite rarefaction from which

[1] George Gamow, "Modern Cosmology," in *The New Astronomy* by editors of the *Scientific American* (New York: Simon and Schuster, 1955), p. 20.
[2] *Ibid.*, p. 23.

the universe collapsed into a state of maximum compression; now the universe is expanding again until a state of infinite rarefaction will again be reached. This ought to be a cyclical process, it seems. One astrophysicist, Professor Layzer of Princeton University, has been working on such an expansion-contraction everlasting cyclical process; but apparently he has not yet been able to demonstrate his theory. Professor Gamow thinks that the evidence implies irreversibility. He says, "Such motion is hyperbolic; it can be compared with the motion of a comet, which does not revolve around the sun as planets do but comes in from the infinity of space (in certain cases), sails around the sun in a bent path, developing a beautiful tail, and vanishes into infinity again without promise of return." [1]

This is far from an intellectually satisfying theory; we want to know whether or not there is sufficient evidence that it will not collapse again after infinite rarefaction is again reached. What is the difference between the previous rarefaction-contraction rhythm and the rarefaction process going on now which Gamow thinks will not have a contraction? If later theoreticians make a regular rhymthic contraction-expansion process everlastingly recurrent, the cyclical view of cosmic history almost precisely in the form first proposed by Empedocles will have proved the most plausible. In any case we are bound to wonder what the universe was like before the previous rarefaction occurred from which collapse and subsequent rarefaction followed.

Another rival theory for which there seems to be evidence also is the "steady-state" cosmological hypothesis defended by the astronomers Hoyle, Gold and Bondi. Hoyle claims that there is continuous creation of material particles out of nothing in the interstellar spaces; these form galaxies which evolve to a climax, then decline and die. There are galaxies of all ages in the universe. Cycles would be local phenomena of all particular galaxies with the universe as a whole having the same general pattern con-

---
[1] *Ibid.*, pp. 23 f.

tinuously. Gamow thinks the evidence weak for this theory. He comments: "As far as observations go, the weight of the evidence at present is definitely in favor of the idea of an evolving universe rather than a steady-state one such as is envisioned by Bondi, Gold and Hoyle."[2] But Hoyle points out flaws in Gamow's theory and adds that Gamow's is not open to experimental observational confirmation while the steady-state theory can be confirmed or refuted by further observation. More will be said in support of the steady-state theory in the last chapter of this book.

The significant thing to notice is that the Greeks attempted a naturalistic approach to cosmology similar to the "scientific" approach taken today by the astrophysicists such as the great astronomers mentioned. We have far more observational data and the size of the universe is far beyond anything imagined by the Greeks although not beyond the immensities conceived by Buddhist thinkers. Science does not yet have enough data to tell us whether or not the cosmos as a whole follows a cyclical recurrent pattern or the "hyperbolic" irreversible process defended by Gamow.

The next section presents a mediating point of view, in a sense, the theory that there is a one-cycle historical process for the entire cosmos or for human history or for both. The mythopoeic origins of this view will be given and then modern versions of the idea.

---

[2] *Ibid.*, p. 15.

PART II

ONE-GRAND-CYCLE

THEORIES

OF COSMIC HISTORY

Chapter I

Background of One-Cycle Theories:
From Eden to Eden: Idea of the Golden Age

Idea of the Golden Age in Ancient Egypt.

We are familiar from what we have reviewed in the foregoing chapters with the ancient notion of a Golden Age of paradisiacal bliss at the beginning of history. This idea appears early in Mesopotamian culture in the Uttu poem which we quoted in chapter II above. It is typical of Indian thought and of Chinese, and Hesiod established it in Greek thought. Egyptian culture shows a similar belief. We have not discussed Egyptian views thus far because there seems to be no evidence for a cyclical approach to history in this culture. The Egyptians did believe, however, in a Golden Age of the Gods at the beginning of their history though nothing seems to have been said about the return of this Age.

The great scholar, Maspero, informs us that the priests of Heliopolis

> changed the gods of the Ennead into so many kings, determined with minute accuracy the lengths of their reigns, and compiled their biographies from popular tales. The duality of the feudal god supplied an admirable expedient for connecting the history of the world with that of chaos. Tumu was identified with Nu, and relegated to the primordial ocean: Ra was retained, and proclaimed the first king of the world. He had not established his rule without difficulty. The 'children of Defeat,' beings hostile to order and light

engaged him in fierce battles; nor did he succeed in organizing his kingdom until he had conquered them in nocturnal combat at Hermopolis and even at Heliopolis itself. Pierced with wounds, Apopi the serpent sank into the depths of Ocean at the very moment that the New Year began. The secondary members of the Great Ennead, together with the Sun, formed the first dynasty, which began with the dawn of the first day, and ended at the coming of Horus, the son of Isis.[1]

This era of the reign of Ra was believed to have been one of bliss; at this time the Egyptians were born into the world happy and perfect, but their descendants gradually deteriorated into their present fallen state. Maspero documents this idea with inscriptions from the tomb of Seti I who reigned about 1319-1301 B.C.:

> In the tomb of Seti I, the words *flock of the Sun, flock* of *Ra,* are those by which the god Horus refers to men. Certain expressions used by Egyptian writers are in themselves sufficient to show that the first generations of men were supposed to have lived in a state of happiness and perfection. To the Egyptians *the times of Ra, the times of the god*—that is to say, the centuries immediately following upon the creation — were the ideal age, and no good thing had appeared upon earth since then.[2]

This notion of a primeval Age of the Gods appears in the history of Manetho, who, although writing in Hellenistic times (third century B.C.) reports well-grounded tradi-

---

[1] G. Maspero, *History of Egypt*, 2 vols., ed. A. H. Sayce, trans. M. L. McClure (London: the Grolier Society, 1901.) Compare this creation myth with the Mesopotamian in Chapter II. Tumu is close to Tiamat in name and idea. Conquest of the serpent by the hero with subsequent Creation is similar in pattern in both myths. This Osiris-Isis myth dramatized every year as a fertility ritual is similar in story and in function to the New Year's ritual myth and rites discussed in the chapter on Mesopotamia.

[2] *Ibid.*, p. 225.

tion. Manetho begins his chronology about 30,627 B.C.[2] He claims that there were first three dynasties of gods, then four dynasties of demigods [3] (an Age of Heroes). The first mortal king, Menes, reigned about 5702 B.C.[4] The prior age of gods and of demigods occupied 24,925 years.[5] Here again in the length of the Divine as compared with the human epoch of kingship we have a parallel with Babylonian thought.

A return of the Golden Age was not envisioned by the Egyptians probably because of the preoccupation with attaining an other-worldly bliss after death.

The Golden Age and the Wonder-Child in Hebrew Thought. Hebrew thought, too, has an account of a Golden Age in the story of the Garden of Eden. Before the Fall there was nothing but bliss and innocence for the first human pair; they did not need to work, there was no pain and nature and man were in harmony. Death was not yet and never would have been had not the Serpent incited Eve and Adam to eat of the wrong tree. If they had eaten of the Tree of Life (immortality), they would have lived forever.[6]

A famous idyllic passage in the *Book of Isaiah* seems to prophesy a return of the Golden Age:

> There shall come forth a shoot from the stump of Jesse,
>   and a branch shall grow out of his roots.
> And the Spirit of the Lord shall rest upon him,
>   the spirit of wisdom and understanding,
>   the spirit of counsel and might,
>   the spirit of knowledge and the fear of the Lord.
> And his delight shall be in the fear of the Lord.
> He shall not judge by what his eyes see,
>   or decide by what his ears hear;
> but with righteousness he shall judge the poor,

---

[2] Sir George Cornewall Lewis, *op. cit.*, p. 327.
[3] *Ibid.*
[4] *Ibid., Menes'* date c.2900 B.C.
[5] *Ibid.*
[6] *Gen.* 3:22.

and decide with equity for the meek of the earth;
and he shall smite the earth with the rod of his mouth,
and with the breath of his lips he shall slay the wicked.
Righteousness shall be the girdle of his waist,
and faithfulness the girdle of his loins.
The wolf shall dwell with the lamb,
and the leopard shall lie down with the kid,
and the calf and the lion and the fatling together,
and a little child shall lead them.
The cow and the bear shall feed;
their young shall lie down together;
and the lion shall eat straw like the ox.
The sucking child shall play over the hole of the asp,
and the weaned child shall put his hand on the adder's den.
They shall not hurt or destroy in all my holy mountain;
for the earth shall be full of the knowledge of the Lord
as the waters cover the sea.
In that day the root of Jesse shall stand as an ensign to the peoples; him shall the nations seek, and his dwellings shall be glorious.[1]

Earlier in the *Book of Isaiah* (chap. 9:6) the messianic ruler who will usher in this age is called "Wonderful Counselor, Mighty God, Everlasting Father, Prince of Peace," and Immanuel (God with us). One of the two main interpretations of the above messianic passages is that of Gressman. Gressman relates them to a widespread belief among the people that a divine redeemer would appear in the hour of the nation's need. Isaiah defined the time of the appearance of this redeemer. Gressman interprets the atmosphere of the belief in such a redeemer in the light of eschatological ideas widespread throughout the ancient East. The appearance of the Wonder Child as a redeemer is of central importance in these eschatologies. In India the Wonder Child is a Buddha or an avatar of Vishnu; and in previous chapters we have discussed the eschatological significance of

---
[1] *Isaiah* 11: 1-11.

these redeemers in relation to definite epochs in the recurrent cycles of history. In Zoroastrian thought there is a similar redeemer idea which may also have contributed to the Wonder Child myth and messianic ideas so important in early Christian thought and in subsequent Western philosophies of history.

Zoroastrian Beliefs about the Wonder Child and the Golden Age

Zoroaster, founder of Zoroastrianism, is difficult to date. Scholars vary in their estimates as to the time that he lived; some think he taught around 1000 B.C.; others place him in the sixth century B.C., but there is much more agreement about the doctrine Zoroaster taught. He taught that in the beginning there were two creative powers, Ahura Mazda and Ahriman. Ahura Mazda created light and all that is good in the universe; Ahriman created darkness, filth, death and all the other evils in the world. The history of the universe is the struggle between these two powers. Man is the key figure in this struggle. As the creation of Ahura Mazda, man is responsible to this deity, but since his Creator endowed him with freedom of will, he is open to the wicked influences of the evil spirit, Ahriman. By observing the ethical code of good thoughts, good words, and good deeds man can aid Ahura Mazda and his archangels in the ultimate victory over Ahriman and his demons.

The Zoroaster of the Gathas (the oldest sources for Zoroaster's thought) seems to have believed that he was sent as a prophet at this particular time to make a last appeal to men to take the side of Ormazd and righteousness; since the final conflict, he thought, was imminent and the kingdom of Heaven at hand. The victory of Ormazd was certain. There would be a resurrection of the dead and final judgment in which each man's good deeds would be weighed against his evil ones. Those whose virtue survived the judgment would live eternally in a new, renovated paradisiacal earth and in the heaven of Ormazd whose kingdom will be one undivided realm. Ahriman and Darkness and all evil will be exterminated forever. The Sons of Light will be completely victorious over the Sons of Darkness. These Zoroastrian ideas were a very important influence on post-exilic Hebrew thought in the development of the idea of Satan and his demons in conflict with the Lord and his angels. Hebrew and Christian apocalyptic literature is filled with these ideas.

Later Zoroastrian thought postponed the final Judgment and the advent of the Kingdom of Heaven until a later time. In the writings known as the Bundahish [1] the complete cycle of world history is described in order that men might know when the end is to be expected. The entire world cycle is 12,000 years in length. This number is based on the twelve zodiacal signs of 30 degrees each. But not until around 500 B.C. had the Babylonian astronomers (now politically under Persian rule) divided mathematically the celestial circle of the heavens into 30 degree sections to which the constellation names — themselves much older — were given.[2] The tradition, therefore, on which the notion of the world ages is based cannot be older than 500 B.C. Finegan thinks that the idea of world ages must have been "as old as the fifth century B.C., since belief in the preexistence of Zoroaster's spiritual body six thousand years before his birth on earth is a part of the theory and since this belief had evidently become known among the Greeks by the time of Xanthus."[3]

It seems probable, then, that by the fifth century B.C.

---

[1] The *Bundahish* in its present form is probably a ninth century work but contains much older traditional material, similar to our *Genesis*.

[2] Neugebauer, *The Exact Sciences in Antiquity, op. cit.*, p. 97.

[3] Jack Finegan, *The Archaeology of World Religions* (Princeton. Princeton University Press, 1952), pp. 78 f.

the notion of the world cycle took a form approximating that described in the *Bundahish*. Chapter XXXIV of this work is a good summary of this world history. As in Indian historical thought, history is divided into four quarters, but each is equal in length and a mere three thousand years compared with the enormous lengths of the Indian yugas (quarters). Within each quarter each millennium is dominated by its appropriate sign of the Zodiac.

The first quarter is a period prior to the appearance of the concrete world. In this period Ahura Mazda "produced spiritually the creatures" which "remained three thousand years in a spiritual state, so that they were unthinking and unmoving, with intangible bodies."[1]

The next three quarters are described in a general way thus:

> Auharmazd (Ahura Mazda) also knew this, through omniscience, that within these nine thousand years, for three thousand years everything proceeds by the will of Auharmazd (Ahura Mazda), three thousand years there is an intermingling of the wills of Auharmazd and Aharman (Ahriman), and the last three thousand years the evil spirit is disabled, and they keep the adversary away from the creatures.[2]

During the first of these three quarters during which all "proceeds by the will of Auharmazd," the world is created in the concrete and the primeval man, Gayomard, is placed on earth with the primeval ox. Gayomard and the ox led a Garden of Eden kind of existence for three thousand years. Ahriman was powerless to cause evil to the creation during this entire period.

In the second of these three quarters (the third in the entire scheme) Ahriman, incited by the female demon Geh, showed his power. He attacked the entire creation, material and spiritual. He diffused noxious, biting, venomous creatures over the earth; he caused a blight over the vege-

---
[1] *Sacred Books of the East*, Vol. V, Part I, *Pahlavi Texts*, trans. E. W. West (Oxford: Claredon Press, 1880), Bundahish, I, 8.
[2] *Ibid.*, I, 20.

tation and it withered away. "And avarice, want, pain, hunger, disease, lust, and lethargy were diffused by him abroad upon the ox and Gayomard." [3] Then the final enemy, death, attacked Gayomard and the ox. From Gayomard's seed Mashya and Mashyoi, the first human pair, were created, and from the seed of the ox, ordinary cattle. Thus was ushered in the third quarter of the Great Year of the World, the era of trials and tribulations caused by Ahriman and his demons. Yet man because he has free will can resist the moral evils to which Ahriman incites him. In this way man can aid Ahura Mazda in the ultimate victory over Ahriman and his demons.

The History of the world is described sketchily during this third trimillennium. The *Bundahish* begins with the observation that the "millennium reigns of Cancer, Leo, and Virgo had elapsed, [and presumably also Aries, Taurus, and Gemini] because it was six thousand years when the millennium reign came to Libra, the adversary rushed in, and Gayomard lived thirty years in tribulation." [1] Then Mashya and Mashyoi appeared but did not live together as husband and wife for fifty years; after "marriage" they lived together ninety-three years "till the time when Hoshyang came." [2] Hoshyang was thought to have been founder of the first Iranian dynasty. Other Iranian kings of this dynasty are also mentioned. In the second millennium of this third quarter Scorpio is the controlling sign of the Zodiac and during this time Dahak ruled the full thousand years.[3] Finegan takes this personal name as a symbol of an entire foreign dynasty. Then the "millennium reign came to Sagittarius" [4] and a list of kings is given up to "the coming of the religion," [5] by which is meant the coming of Zoroaster.

---

[3] *Ibid.*, III, 17.
[1] *Ibid.*, XXXIV, 2. Brackets by translator.
[2] *Ibid.*, XXXIV, 3.
[3] *Ibid.*
[4] *Ibid.*, XXXIV, 6.
[5] *Ibid.*, XXXIV, 7.

The advent of Zoroaster and his religion ushers in the fourth and last quarter of the world's history, the end of the Great Year of the historical universe. This is the era of the final battle against Ahriman. Zoroaster and his religion lead the fight, and as additional aids to man, lest he forget, at intervals of a thousand years three more messiahs will appear. These will be fathered by Zoroaster whose seed is miraculously preserved in a lake in Persia where virgins will bathe under the proper millennial sign of the Zodiac and conceive children through Zoroaster's seed. Aushetar will be born one thousand years after Zoroaster; two thousand years after Zoroaster Aushetarman will come; finally at the very end of the world when the 12,000 years have elapsed, the last messiah will appear—Saoshyant and there will be a general resurrection and final judgment.

In the resurrection all men beginning with Gayomard and then Mashya and Mashyoi will resume their material bodies. They will recognize one another and the wicked will stand out as conspicuously as "a white sheep among those that are black." [1] The wicked are cast into hell and suffer torture. After this fire and molten metal pour over the entire earth. To the righteous the molten metal will feel as if it were warm milk; to the wicked (apparently brought up from hell for this "purification") the molten metal will feel like molten metal.

After this purge by molten metal, families are reunited, the good and the wicked together, since the wicked have now been purged of their sins. All men are given *Hush*, a substance which makes them immortal. The mature are forever restored at forty years of age; children at fifteen. Every man has his wife but there is no more begetting of children.[2]

Ahuramazda next destroys Ahriman and his demons. Hell is then reclaimed "for the enlargement of the world".[3]

---

[1] *Ibid.*, XXX, 10.
[2] *Ibid.*, XXX, 26.
[3] *Ibid.*, XXX, 32.

and the world itself is made "immortal for ever and everlasting."[4] It will then be an "iceless, slopeless plain" where immortal ever-pure spirits will lead an eternally happy existence. Heaven, too, is open to all the immortal righteous. Thus there is to be a "new heaven and a new earth," as in Christian apocalyptic thought, a blissful end to world history.

Summary of Zoroastrian Views of the Cycle of World History, the Golden Age and the Wonder Child. In Zoroastrian thought history is one unique Great Year with an absolute beginning and absolute end. It begins with a Golden Age of bliss, the age of Gayomard and the primeval ox, then Ahriman and his demons enter the world to destroy righteousness, innocence, order, and truth. The critical turning-point comes with the appearance of the redeemer, Zoroaster the Wonder Child, who "brought the religion" to aid man in combatting the evil powers. Zoroaster's sons, three more redeemers, continue to aid man until the fight is won. Then there is the Golden Age again, only this time it is eternal. Thus the cycle comes around full swing to the beginning but to a paradise far more secure and blissful than the paradise of the beginning, because there is no longer any threat from opposing dark and evil powers.

These eschatological ideas in relation to a Great Year of the World were formulated after Zoroaster's time. Zoroaster seems to have thought the end of the world to be very close at the time he was preaching, but when the Last Days seemed delayed, the above theory of world epochs developed. This was probably during the Achaemenid (549 B.C. to Alexander the Great) and Sassanian dynasties (226 A.D.-651 A.D.).[1] The main ideas are in all likelihood as early as the Achaemenid era since, as we noted above,[2]

---

[4] *Ibid.*

[1] John B. Noss, *Man's Religions* (New York: The Macmillan Company, 1956), p. 457.

[2] *Supra,* p. 215.

Xanthus mentions the preexistence of Zoroaster six thousand years before his birth which implies the theory of world epochs of three thousand years each. The Zoroastrian eschatological ideas became known to the Hebrews during the Exile and influenced subsequent Hebrew religious thought just as the Persian angelology and demonology did; and it is through Hebrew-Christian thought that this one-cycle eschatological pattern of history has influenced Western Culture.

Chapter II

Hebrew-Christian One-Cycle Views
Cycle of the Return to Paradise: The Coming Kingdom of God

We have already mentioned early Hebrew ideas about the dawn of a Golden Age ushered in by the rule of a Wonder Child as Prince of Peace, an idea apparently widespread throughout the East. This means in Hebrew-Christian thought a one-cycle view of history which has the plan of (1) The Primeval Golden Age, (2) the Fall of Man, (3) period of Moral Degeneration after the Fall, (4) Return to the Golden Age — the Kingdom of God on earth, in Heaven or both.

In pre-exilic Biblical thought as illustrated by the "first" Isaiah (eighth century B.C.) mentioned above, God's Kingdom is to be an earthly one established by the "saving remnant", i.e. the virtuous few who will survive the destruction wrought by God upon the unrepentant sinners.[2] This remnant apparently is to be ruled by a wonder child, a

---

[2] According to R. H. Charles the bridge to apocalyptic eschatology is found in Is. lxv-lxvi. Here the writer abandons the idea of a rehabilitated kingdom in this world. He mentions a "new heaven and a new earth" which will come about through a gradual transformation of man in his spiritual nature. In this new Kingdom sinners will die at 100 but the righteous will live the full limit of his years, perhaps 1000. Canon Charles adds that this view appears "but twice more in Judaism in the Book of Jubilees, and the Testaments of the Twelve Patriarchs," (the latter two books belong to the second century B.C.) See R. H. Charles, *Religious Development Between the Old and New Testaments* (London, New York: Home University Library of Modern Knowledge, 1914), p. 70. The "first" Isaiah, however, of chaps. 1-39 was looking for the Kingdom to appear in this world.

"Prince of Peace," as God's anointed King. However, changes in the political situation during the next century and a half which reached a climax in the destruction of the Jerusalem temple in 586 B.C. gave rise to new versions of the plan of history. The most significant new version is to be found in the writings of the prophet Jeremiah. Jeremiah sees the coming Kingdom of God as a universal one. It is to be a worldwide society (including the Gentiles) in which external law and religious ritual will be unnecessary; the "law" will be written in the hearts of all human beings; all men will be spontaneously virtuous. Love for God and one's fellowman will become the universal inner motivation of conduct. This universalism of Jeremiah culminated in Christianity which affirms a similar idea but combined with apocalyptic thought.

Significant apocalyptic thought — significant because of its influence upon subsequent Western philosophies of history — begins with the *Book of Daniel* in Biblical thought.

The *Book of Daniel* belongs to the Hagiographa section of the Hebrew Old Testament and was written to strengthen the morale of the Jews during the persecutions of the Hellenizing Seleucid ruler, Antiochus Epiphanes. Since this was a subversive work at this time (c. 165 B.C.), the author had to veil his meanings; this is the reason for the apocalyptic style. He writes in the form of prediction of the future pattern of history and uses cryptic imagery to express his ideas, such as the images of the beasts and the horns, all of which is typical of the apocalyptic form of literature. The pattern of history given us by the author by way of hindsight consists of four epochs. Each is represented symbolically. The first is the era of the Chaldean empire, the second of the Median, the third the Persian, and the fourth the Seleucid. In the symbol of the image of Nebuchadnezzar's dream the four parts of the image represent each of these epochs, and the stone that strikes the image on the feet of iron and clay and then becomes a great mountain that fills the entire earth is the Hebrew nation. This means that the Jews will be established in a new kingdom through the intervention of God. Daniel's dream of the four beasts described in *Daniel*, chapter 7 has a similar significance.

Probable origin of the four-epoch periodization of history in Daniel. The clue to the origin of the four-epoch periodization lies in the materials of which the image in Nebuchadnezzar's dream is composed. The first epoch, the Chaldean world-empire is symbolized by the head of gold; the second epoch, the Median, by the breast and arms of silver; the third the Persian, by the belly and thighs of bronze; the fourth, the Seleucid, by the feet partly of iron and partly of clay. These metals are, in the order given, the names attached to the Four Ages in Hesiod's *Works and Days* (omitting the inserted Age of the Heroes). Also in Hesiod's work human history deteriorates morally from the Golden to the Iron age. Medieval writers were influenced both by Hesiod's views (which they received in the form given them by Ovid in his *Metamorphoses*)[1] and by the Four-Ages theory of the Book of Daniel. The philosopher, Collingwood, points out that this is the reason why Hegel as late as the latter part of the nineteenth century divides the epochs of history into four eras, despite the fact that the triadic pattern is used everywhere in everything else that pertains to the development of spirit.[2]

Hesiod's division into four eras, in its turn, is of ancient and unknown origin.[3] In the light of our study of time symbols in ancient cultures we might conclude that the four era pattern probably originated out of the Zoroastrian World-year which, as we have seen, was divided into quarters (like the seasons in the microcosmic year); or

---

[1] *Op. cit.* Lovejoy and Boas, p. 49.

[2] R. G. Collingwood, *The Idea of History* (Oxford: Clarendon Press, 1946), p. 57 footnote.

[3] *Op. cit.*, Lovejoy and Boas, p. 24.

the world-year idea could have been borrowed from the Babylonians or perhaps from Indian culture.

Apocalyptic eschatology of Daniel. In chapter 12 of this Book the author predicts a "time of trouble" such as there never was before; then the Ancient of Days takes his seat on His throne of fiery flames, the dead rise from their graves, the "books" are opened and there is a Last Judgment. The virtuous, the "Saints of the Most High" (which means apparently the Hebrews who refused to compromise their religious beliefs and were loyal to Mosaic religion) are given the gift of everlasting life in an everlasting Kingdom of God. The Book of Daniel, chapter 7, verse 27 says:

And the kingdom and the dominion
and the greatness of the kingdoms under the whole heaven
shall be given to the people of the saints of the Most High;
their kingdom shall be an everlasting kingdom,
and all dominions shall serve and obey them.

Cryptic reference is made to the time when these events will occur. The date is probably to be interpreted as 164 B.C.

Apocalyptic literature and the supernatural Messiah. The Book of Enoch. R.H. Charles tells us that the "germ" of the idea of a supernatural messiah is to be found in the *Book of Daniel* under the concept "Son of Man." However, in *Daniel* the Son of Man symbolizes the righteous of Israel, the "Saints of the Most High." [1] In the *Book of Enoch* written about a century later the notion of the Son of Man has developed into the idea of a supernatural Messiah who is to appear at the Last Judgment. This Messiah is given significant titles which appear subsequently in the litera-

---

[1] *Op. Cit.,* R. H. Charles, *Between the Old and New Testaments,* p. 85.

ture of the New Testament. These are: "the Christ," (xlviii. 10), the "Righteous One" (xxxviii. 2; Acts iii. 14), "the Elect One" (xl.5; Luke ix.55), and the "Son of Man" [2] *New Testament Apocalyptic thought.* The Messiah of the New Testament combines the notion in *1 Enoch* of the supernatural Son of Man with the idea of the "Suffering Servant of Yahweh" found in *Isaiah*, chapter 53.[3] The oldest of the New Testament writings, *I Thessalonians*, describes the eschatological concept common, apparently, among the first followers of Jesus:

> But we would not have you ignorant, brethren, concerning those who are asleep, that you may not grieve as others do who have no hope. For since we believe that Jesus died and rose again, even so, through Jesus God will bring with him those who have fallen asleep. For the Lord himself will descend from heaven with a cry of command, with the archangel's call, and with the sound of the trumpet of God. And the dead in Christ will rise first; then we who are alive, who are left, shall be caught up together with them in the clouds to meet the Lord in the air; and so we shall always be with the Lord.[4]

No one knows the time of the Second Coming. Paul says it will take men by surprise "like a thief in the night." [5]

The Little Apocalypse in chapter 13 of the *Gospel of Mark* is the next earliest version of the Second Coming. Here are mentioned the ominous portents associated with the Last Day: wars, false prophets, earthquakes, famine, eclipse of the sun and moon, falling stars; in general "such tribulation as has not been from the beginning of the creation which God created until now, and never will be." [1] Then "they will see the Son of Man coming in clouds with

---
[2] *Ibid.*
[3] *Ibid.*, p. 92.
[4] *1 Thessalonians* 4. 13-18.
[5] *Ibid.*, 5.2.
[6] Probably written about 70 A.D. or shortly thereafter.
[1] *Mark* 13:19.

great power and glory. And then he will gather his elect from the four winds, from the ends of the earth to the ends of heaven." [2]

The climax in apocalyptic is reached in the *Book of Revelation*, the very title of which is also known as the *Apocalypse*. The woes of the days of the "Judgment of Babylon" (Rome) are far worse than those of the "Little Apocalypse" of *Mark*. Thunder, lightning, fire, earthquake, hail, a falling star which turns one-third of the earth's waters to wormwood, an eclipse of one-third of the light of the sun and moon, one-third of the sea made blood, torture by the sting of scorpion-men for five months, are among the horrors which will bring the Roman Empire and all its idolatrous sinners to destruction. No one shall be able to withstand the wrath of God at this time. At the final Armageddon "Babylon" and the demonic spirits will be vanquished by the power of God. Satan, the Old Serpent (Dragon) will be chained in the pit for a thousand years. During this thousand years, the "millennium," all those "who had not worshipped the beast or its image [3] and had not received its mark on their foreheads or their hands" are to reign with Christ. After this millennium Satan is to be loosed from the "pit" and the rest of the dead will be resurrected. The books will be opened and all will be judged. Those whose names are not written in the "book of life" are to be thrown with Satan into a "lake of fire and brimstone" where they will be "tormented day and night for ever and ever." This is the "second death" from which there is no resurrection.

For the virtuous there will be "a new heaven and a new earth" with a new holy Jerusalem resplendent with precious jewels. The saints will dwell with God in the holy city. "God himself will be with them; he will wipe away every

---

[2] *Mark* 13:26-27.

[3] The "beast" whose number is 666 is variously interpreted to mean Nero, (perhaps first Caligula then Nero) or Titus, Roman emperor who destroyed the Second Temple, 70 A.D.

tear from their eyes, and death shall be no more, neither shall there be mourning nor crying nor pain any more, for the former things have passed away." And "there shall be no night there," for the "glory of God is its light." On either side of the river in this new Jerusalem is the "tree of life," and "blessed are those who wash their robes, that they may have the right to the tree of life." This is the return to Eden; the second tree of life is here, symbol of the immortality missed by Adam and Eve in the primeval paradise. The cycle of human history is now complete. From God has come man's soul and to God it returns as in Oriental yogic philosophies. History is a mere nightmarish interim in which certain souls are saved for the return to God. St. Augustine gives the most systematic and philosophical form to this idea of the purpose and meaning of history.

Chapter III

St. Augustine's Grand World Cycle: The Great Week of the World: Man's Journey from God to God, or from the Earthly to the Heavenly Paradise

In his famous work on the philosophy of history, the *City of God*, St. Augustine gives a more definite pattern and a more profound philosophical ideological approach to Christian apocalyptic thought of the type just discussed in the previous section. The core idea of history for St. Augustine remains the Biblical-apocalyptic one: the earthly Eden, the Fall by which death came to man, the Redemption, the Millennium, and the Last Judgment which ends in the return to Paradise and deathlessness for the saved.

The sophisticated philosophical mind of St. Augustine grapples first with the problem of Creation and Time. Influenced by Platonic thought (via Neoplatonism) Augustine declares that God is omniscient, knower of all that was, is, and will be; God's mind knows the entire world of Platonic forms. Since this is true, He knew from all eternity all the events that would occur in his created world; nevertheless He created it because He saw that it was good.[1] St. Augustine is here quoting *Genesis*. Scripture does not deal with the time problem involved in creation performed by an eternal, perfect, omniscient Being. As a philosopher, Augustine thought it necessary to tackle this problem. His solution is that the created world and time began simultaneously. Since there can be no change in an eternal being,

---
[1] *The Works of Aurelius Augustine*, ed. Rev. Marcus Dods, Vols. I and II, *The City of God*, trans. Rev. Marcus Dods (Edinburgh: T & T Clark, 1871-1872), Book XI, chap. 21.

God, creation adds nothing to God's knowledge. He creates but He does not alter his "eternal design," Augustine thinks.[2] This is the reason why the Providence of God controls all history. "The times of all kings and kingdoms are ordained by the judgment and power of the true God."[3] If this is not so God is not God — "For one who is not prescient of all future things is not God"[4] — declares Augustine. God's foreknowledge can have no temporal element whatsoever; things that emerge in time for us are all in an eternal NOW for Him:

> For He does not pass from this to that by transition of thought but beholds all things with absolute unchangeableness; so that of those things that emerge in time, the future indeed are not yet, and the present are now, and the past no longer are; but all of these are by Him comprehended in His stable and eternal presence.[5]

This kind of omniscience in God would seem to make God the only responsible Being in history; the whole creation is apparently a mere puppet show with God pulling the strings. St. Augustine denies this, however, but the logic of the denial seems weak to some thinkers. In Augustine's view man has "free will" to love God (and be saved) or to love self (and be lost). God has foreseen that the archetypal first man, Adam, would sin so grievously in misuse of his freewill that the Redemption through Christ would be necessary to save the number predestined from all eternity. The only purpose of human history is the denouement of the cosmic drama the theme of which is the Fall and Redemption, but Redemption of only a limited number; the rest remain fallen. History since the original Fall thus divides men into two categories which Augustine calls "cities," the City of God (the Redeemed) and the City

---

[2] *Ibid.*, Book XI, chaps. 6 and 21.
[3] *Ibid.*, Book IV, chap. 33.
[4] *Ibid.*, Book V, chap. 8.
[5] *Ibid.*, Book XI, chap 2.

of Satan (the Lost). The plot of history takes the following form: God created the angels with freewill which means "able not to sin"; the angel Lucifer manifested the original and basic sin of Pride which means love of self even to the contempt of God. Lucifer gathered a following of angels who were attracted to the bad example of this form of sin. God then cast Lucifer, now become Satan, and the bad angels into Hell. Augustine says that this is the meaning of the passage of the creation story in *Genesis* which says that God separated Light from Darkness; Light symbolizes the good angels, Darkness the wicked.[1]

The next great act in the drama is the creation of man and his Fall. God created man, like the angels, "able not to sin." If man had used his freewill properly and had not sinned, he would have been rewarded with "angelic immortality"; but disobedience was rewarded with death.[2] Man chose disobedience but was incited to this sin of Pride by Satan who, because he was jealous of unfallen man, got the serpent to tempt the weaker of the human pair.[3] Death was the result to the human species. Augustine says, "Death is penal and had its origin in Adam's sin."[4]

Why did God in his omniscience and omnipotence "provide" for events to happen that mean so much misery for the human race? Augustine answers that God had foreknowledge of man's sin and could have prevented it. Nevertheless, He chose not to do so "to show what evil could be wrought by their pride, and what good by his grace."[5] God allowed Satan, an angel who envied and hated unfallen man to tempt him to his ruin also because "He [God] foresaw that by the man's seed, aided by divine grace, this same devil should himself be conquered, to the greater glory of the saints."[6]

---

[1] *Ibid.*, Book XI, chap. 19.
[2] *Ibid.*, Book XIII, chap. 1.
[3] *Ibid.*, Book XIV chap. 11.
[4] *Ibid.*, Book XIII, Argument.
[5] *Ibid.*, Book XIV, chap. 27.
[6] *Ibid.*

Subsequent human history is for the purpose of this conquest of Satan and all who follow him, the fallen angels and men unredeemed by God's grace. History, since it consists of human actions good or evil divides the universe of souls into two cities: the City of God and the City of Satan. To the city of God belong the Redeemed. These are the souls whose chief virtue is humility and love of God and neighbor — love of God to contempt of self. The City of Satan consists of egotists, those souls whose basic sin is Pride — love of self to the contempt of God and their neighbors. The salvation of those destined for the City of God is brought about by God's chosen people, the Hebrews. Therefore St. Augustine periodizes history in accordance with the epochal events of Hebrew history as mentioned in God's Word, the Bible.

In the Bible the holy day is the Sabbath. Augustine is inspired by this Day to divide Hebrew history, the only significant world history, into seven epochs. These are: (1) from Adam to Noah and the Flood; (2) from Noah to Abraham; (3) from Abraham to David; (4) from David to the Exile; (5) from the Exile to the birth of Christ; (6) the present epoch, indefinite in length; it is the Age of the Church which corresponds with the Millennium of the Book of Revelation. (Augustine thinks this period should be no longer than 1000 years, but says only the Lord knows); (7) the Sabbath, an age when God will give his redeemed, the Saints, rest in Himself; (8) the Lord's Day, "an eighth and eternal day, consecrated by the resurrection of Christ and prefiguring the eternal repose not only of the spirit, but also of the body. There we shall rest and see, see and love, love and praise. This is what shall be in the end without end." [1]

The pivotal event, the climax of history is the advent of Christ, God as Redeemer of fallen man. At the end of history the City of God will be immortal and eternal; the city of Satan a city of eternal torture for the fallen angels and

---

[1] *Ibid.*, Book XXII, chap. 30.

the great numbers of fallen men. At the Resurrection the Redeemed receive incorruptible bodies; the damned receive bodies also, but only to feel more intensely their eternal tortures.[2]

In conclusion Augustine's view of the meaning of human history as of the individual human life can be summed up in one sentence: Our whole life is nothing but a "race towards death." Man is never really alive "from the moment he dwells in this dying rather than living body," even though the source of sin lies not in the body but in man's soul. Adam's original sin of Pride (disobedience) left his soul without control over the body. Hence Adam and all subsequent men are in the fallen condition in which the flesh lusts against the Spirit. Only the grace of God in the Redemption by Christ suffices to regain mastery over the flesh. Those unredeemed die not only a first death after which they suffer torture until the Resurrection; but these victims of Adam's sin die in the second death when soul and body rejoined at this time are abandoned to torture for all eternity.

The cycle of human history for St. Augustine — from God to God; from Golden Age to Golden Age, i.e., from Earthly Paradise to Heavenly Paradise via the Fall and Redemption — is a cycle completed only by members of the City of God, the chosen few. Its symbol, versus the Great Year unit of Oriental cultures, is the Great Week the macrocosmic unit which corresponds with the microcosmic week of the original creation. Both the Year symbol and the Week symbol are borrowed from the creation stories, respectively of the Mesopotamian-Indic and Hebrew cultures. See the chapters on Mesopotamian and Indian cyclical views above. The cycle of the Great Week, like that of the Great Year, is a nightmarish interim of alienation of the soul from God.

[2] *Ibid.*, Book XXI, chap. 10.

Chapter IV

The One-Grand-Cycle in Moslem Thought

The Moslem religion, Islam, as is well known accepts the scriptures both of Judaism and of Christianity as revealed to authentic prophets of Allah. The revelation to Mohammed, the Koran, is nevertheless the latest, the final and therefore the most authoritative of all the revelations.

The Koran teaches a pattern of history in one cycle similar to that of the Hebrew and Christian apocalyptic thought we have already described. God creates the world out of nothing, "seven heavens" and the earth.[1] Adam was placed in Paradise when he was created, but because of the Fall he soon was lowered to earth. As in Augustine's thought, Satan was first to fall. Satan's sin, again as in Augustine's theology, was Pride. The pride was manifested when Allah requested the angels, of whom Iblis (Satan) was one, to "adore Adam."[2] Because of the inordinate pride manifested by Iblis in this episode, Allah counted him among the misbelievers. Iblis after his Fall caused the Fall of Adam as in the Hebrew-Christian tradition and the story is similar. Allah forbade Adam to eat the fruit of a certain tree in Paradise; Satan tempted Adam to disobey and eat of this fruit. Adam's disobedience was punished by his being cast out of Paradise. The Lord's compassion saved Adam at this time (and his descendants of the future who sin)

---

[1] The *Koran*, trans. E. H. Palmer with Introduction by R. A. Nicholson (London, New York, Toronto: Oxford University Press, 1900; World's Classics ed. reprinted 1953) II. 25-30.

[2] *Ibid.*, II. 30-35.

from the fires of Hell.³ No atonement is necessary as there is no doctrine of Original Sin.

Human history subsequent to Adam's "Fall" is sketchily reviewed and follows more or less strictly the Old Testament account of the epoch-making events such as the Flood, the Exodus from Egypt, the story of the convenant with Abraham from whose son by Hagar, Ishmael, the Moslems are descended (the Hebrews are descendants of Isaac). The covenant is emphasized as being made with Abraham and Ishmael which probably signifies that the Moslem faith is the ultimate one for salvation.⁴

As in Augustine's thought God is absolutely omniscient and omnipotent. Therefore he foresees every event in the world cycle from creation to the Last Day. Allah has provided for, has actually predestined everything that has happened, is happening or will happen. This includes the thoughts and actions of all men; it is Allah, Himself, who guides the virtuous in their virtue or the wicked in their wickedness. The *Koran* says, "Nought shall befall us save what God has written down for us; He is our Lord, and upon God believers do rely!"¹ The great theologian and philosopher, al-Ghazzali (1058-1111) writes in his best known work, *Resuscitation of the Sciences of Religion:*

> He knows all things knowable . . . "he knows the very tread of the blackbird in the darkest night upon hard stone" and notices the movement of the motes in the sunbeams . . . He knows the inward motives and impulses and the most secret thoughts, with an eternal knowledge which he has had before all time, not as though the knowledge were newly arisen in him or communicated to him . . . He wills all that exists, and determines events. Thus all things . . . good or bad . . . acts of obedience or disobedience, they all occur solely according to his decision and determination, his wis-

---
³ *Ibid.* II. 35-40.
⁴ *Ibid.* II. 115-135.
¹ *Ibid.*, IX. 50-55.

257

dom and will. What he wills, takes place, and what he does not will, does not take place . . . His will consists in his essence like his other properties and belongs to him always. From eternity he willed the existence of things in the times appointed for them, and they come into being at those times and no others, precisely in accordance with his knowledge and will.[2]

God's Providence directs all history, natural and human. The life each man lives is the life Allah planned for him. Orthodox Moslems generally accept this view. At the same time they accept the idea of reward and punishment (for virtue and vice) by a Just and Merciful God. Arthur Jeffrey, a well-known scholar in Islamic thought, tells us that the "favorite solution is a doctrine of *iktisab*, according to which, though each individual action is foreordained, the individual 'acquires' it by identifying himself with it in action and so becomes responsible."[1] Virtue is commonly centered around the Five Pillars [2] and failure to observe them unless circumstances prevent endangers the soul. Yet Allah is the Compassionate and Merciful; the only sin which He considers unpardonable is *shirk*, that is, associating other deities with him which is denial of his uniqueness. "There is no God, but Allah," is the essential belief without which it seems no one can be saved from eternal punishment, while if one truly believes this from the heart salvation is practically certain.

Mohammed seems to have thought that the Last Day was soon to come although he did not presume to know exactly

---

[2] Al-Ghazzali, *Resuscitation of the Sciences of Religion*. This is quoted from a brief excerpt from this book in *Philosophers Speak of God* by Charles Hartshorne and William L. Reese (Chicago: University of Chicago Press, 1953), p. 107.

[1] Arthur Jeffery, ed., *Islam*, Library of Religion (New York: The Liberal Arts Press, 1958), p. 147.

[2] Briefly these are: Profession of the creed (There is no God but Allah and Mohammed is the prophet of Allah), prayer at definite intervals, fasting during the month of Ramadan, giving the legal tithe *(zakat)*, the pilgrimage to Mecca if possible.

the date of the end of human history on this earth. God alone knows this secret. The *Koran* gives details of the catastrophes of the Day, but one of the collections of the *Traditions* (*Hadith*) gives interesting and important information about "ten preliminary signs" that will precede the "Hour." The *Sunan* of Abu Dawud (died 888 A.D.) lists these ten signs:

> The Hour will not come till ten preliminary signs have been fulfilled, viz., the rising of the sun from its place of setting, the appearance of the Beast,[3] the coming of Gog and Magog,[4] of ad-Dajjal,[5] of Jesus son of Mary, and the smoke,[6] and three eclipses,[7] an eclipse in the West, an eclipse in the East, and an eclipse in the Arabian peninsula. After that a fire will break out in the Yemen, from the hollow of Aden, and will drive all men to the place of assembling [where they wait for Judgment].[8]

The *Koran* itself set the style for such apocalyptic thought. The Koran paints a terrifying picture of the Day of Judgment:

---

[3] Professor Jeffery explains in a footnote to this passage: "This is said to be an enormous beast, made up of parts of many beasts, which will come forth from a cleft on Mt. Safa near Mecca and will brand all men on their faces so that it will be visibly apparent who are believers and who are not.

[4] Professor Jeffery explains: "These barbarian hosts will break through the barrier Alexander the Great set up against them . . . and cause great destruction and distress until Allah, at the intercession of Jesus, sends destruction on them. The Descent of Jesus is thus to end the troubles caused by both the False Messiah and the hosts of Gog and Magog.

[5] Professor Jeffery's note tell us: ad-Dajjal is "the False Messiah, who will work miracles and perform wonders and deceive many, pretending that he is the Lord. Jesus will be sent down to earth again from heaven to put an end to him.

[6] Professor Jeffery's note: "This dense smoke will cover the earth for a period of days."

[7] Professor Jeffrey's note: "*Khusuf*, which some say means not 'eclipses' but 'earthquakes.'"

[8] Quoted from the *Sunan* of Abu Dawud in Jeffery, *Islam, op. cit.*, p. 144.

> When the heaven is cleft asunder,
> And when the stars are scattered,
> And when the seas gush together,
> And when the tombs are turned upside down...[1]
> ....
> And when the trumpet shall be blown with one blast,
> And the earth shall be borne away, and the mountains, too,
> And both be crushed with one crushing...
> And the heaven on that day shall be cleft asunder...[2]

The appearance of Jesus [3] at the end of the world to end the career of the False Messiah, ad-Dajjal, seems borrowed from Christian apocalyptic thought (Jesus conquers the anti-Christ). The *Sunan* of Abu Dawud mentions also the coming of the Mahdi, the Moslem equivalent of messiah or deliverer who, before the Last Day "will fill the earth with justice and equity as it has been filled with injustice and oppression. He will reign seven years." [4] The *Koran* and the earliest Traditions know nothing of the Mahdi, but this being plays a major role in the unorthodox sects, the Shi'ites.

On the Last Day, the Koran tells us, the dead will rise from their graves (resurrection of the body is insisted upon) and the Last Judgment will take place before Allah seated on a throne borne by angels. Each resurrected person will be handed his "book" which is a careful record of his life. The virtuous are handed their books in their right hands; the wicked are given theirs in their left hands. The fate of each group the *Koran* describes in vivid language:

> When the earth shall quake, quaking! and the mountains shall crumble, crumbling, and become like motes dispersed!

---

[1] *Koran*, LXXXII, 1-5.
[2] *Koran*, LXIX. 10-20.
[3] The *Koran* affirms the virgin birth of Jesus, but not divine Sonship. Jesus was created as Adam was created, by the Divine Breath. The Koran is not clear on this matter, but there is a strong tradition that Jesus will appear again before the Last Day.
[4] Quoted by Jeffery in *Islam, op. cit.*, p. 146.

And ye shall be three sorts;
And the fellows of the right hand — what lucky fellows!
And the fellows of the left hand — what unlucky fellows!
And the foremost foremost![1]
These are they who are brought nigh,
In gardens of pleasure!
A crowd of those of yore,
And a few of those of the latter day!
And gold-weft couches, reclining on them face to face.
Around them shall go eternal youths, with goblets and ewers and a cup of flowing wine; no headache shall they feel therefrom, nor shall their wits be dimmed!
And fruits such as they deem the best;
And flesh of fowl as they desire;
And bright and large-eyed maids like hidden pearls;
A reward for that which they have done!
They shall hear no folly there and no sin;
Only the speech, 'Peace, Peace!'
. . . .
Verily, we have produced them[2] a production.
And made them virgins, darlings of equal age (with their spouses) for the fellows of the right!
. . . .
And the fellows of the left — what unlucky fellows!
In hot blasts and boiling water;
And a shade of pitchy smoke,
Neither cool nor generous!
Verily, they were affluent ere this, and did persist in mighty crime; and used to say, 'What, when we die and have become dust and bones, shall we then indeed be raised? or our fathers of yore?'
Say, 'Verily, those of yore and those of the latter day shall surely be gathered together unto the tryst of the well-known day.'
Then ye, O ye who err! who say it is a lie! shall eat of

---

[1] E. H. Palmer's note reads: "i.e. the foremost in professing the faith on earth shall be the foremost then." *(Koran, op. cit.*, p. 466).

[2] E. H. Palmer's note reads: "The celestial damsels." *(Ibid.*, p. 467).

[3] Arthur Jeffery quotes this passage as illustrative of the eschatology of Islam in *Islam (op. cit.).* His footnote (p. 141) elucidates the significance of the Zaqqum tree. It is a tree which provides "food for the Damned which is as hot in their insides as molten lead."

the Zaqqum tree![3] and fill your bellies with it! and drink thereon of boiling water! and drink as drinks the thirsty camel.
This is their entertainment on the judgment day![4]
. . . .
Or, if he be of the fellows of the right! then 'Peace to thee!' from the fellows of the right!
Or, if he be of those who say it is a lie,— who err! then an entertainment of boiling water! and broiling in hell!
Verily, this is surely certain truth![5]

This description of the Last Judgment and the fate of the virtuous and the sinners resembles both the Zoroastrian and Christian (Book of Revelation) apocalypses. The inclusion of the maidens (houris) in the Moslem reward for the virtuous is a delight omitted from the other two accounts. The great Moslem philosophers, however, such as Avicenna and Averroes like the great philosophers in other great world religions, had different and more spiritual views of the final destiny of man.

Avicenna (d. 1037), influenced by Aristotle and Neoplatonism, rises well above what he considers the ignorant superstitions and desires of the masses of people. He comments acutely that the majority of men can be incited to virtue only by what they understand, viz., physical pleasures as a reward; "true happiness and spiritual pleasure are not comprehended by them at all and have no place in their understandings, even though some may make a verbal pretence of it."[1] Mohammed, therefore, was really greatest of all the prophets since he portrayed reward and punishment in the most concrete terms. By contrast, the Christian notion of the resurrection is anemic with its picture of the afterlife that of the angels. Privately and in their

---
[4] *Koran*, LVI, 1-60.
[5] *Koran*, LVI, 89-95.
[1] Quoted from Avicenna's essay, *al-Risalat al-adhawiya fi amr al-ma'ad* in A. J. Arberry, *Revelation and Reason in Islam* (New York: The Macmillan Co., 1957), p. 53.

hearts the masses of Christian believers, Avicenna says, think that the angels have a most miserable existence: "They have no pleasure and no repose at all; they neither eat, drink, nor marry; they are at their alleluias and devotions every hour of the night and day, never flagging for a moment, and at the end of it all they are not even rewarded." [2] This offers Christians food for thought; perhaps this is why there are so very few *true* Christians.

The initiated, the men of wisdom and knowledge, Avicenna says, cannot believe in a physical resurrection at all, not even the more spiritual version of Christianity (such as we described in Augustine's philosophy). The spirit of the individual is alone immortal; there is no kind of bodily resurrection whatsoever; metempsychosis is rejected also. It is the rational soul of man that is immortal because it is this alone that does not depend for its being upon matter. The proof is that the rational soul actually gains greater power in older men whose bodies are declining. Since this is true the rational soul is not an aspect of the body. The substance of the rational soul alone is eternal and immortal and therefore an angelic substance. The goal and eternal destiny of the rational soul is the angelic kind of happiness. Avicenna writes: "Happiness in the world to come, when the soul has become free and stripped of the body and of physical impressions, is perfect pleasure, being the intellectual contemplation of the Essence of Him to whom belongs the kingdom most mighty, the spiritual beings who worship Him, the world most sublime, and the attainment of one's perfection thereto. Misery in the world to come is the opposite of that." [1]

Souls who have not attained the bliss of the contemplative life and have been dominated by passions and appetites in their worldly existence continue to be dominated by such passions and appetites after death but at the imaginative, dream level without a body although they "dream" that

[2] *Ibid.*, p. 53.
[1] *Ibid.*, pp. 54-55.

they have a body. Imagination creates a Hell of punishment for them and reward of the heavenly gardens, palaces, houris, and wine.[2]

Further description of the goal of the rational soul (primarily that of the philosopher) is derived from Neoplatonism tinged with Aristotelianism. Here we find ideas similar to the Indian and Chinese pantheistic yoga systems, viz. the idea of the cyclic Return to the Center. Avicenna describes this return in the following passage in his *Book of Salvation:*

> Now the peculiar perfection towards which the rational soul strives is that it should become as it were an intellectual microcosm, impressed with the form of the All, the order intelligible in the All and the good pervading the All: first the Principle of the All, then proceeding to the Noble Substances and Absolute Spirituality, then Spirituality connected in some fashion with corporeal things, then the Celestial Bodies with their various dispositions and powers, and so continuing until it realizes completely within itself the shape of all Being, and thus converts itself into an intelligible cosmos of its own in correspondence with the whole existing Cosmos, contemplating perfect Comeliness, absolute Good and true Beauty, and united therewith. So it will have become graven after its idea and pattern, and strung upon its thread as a pearl is strung upon a necklace, being refashioned into the self-same substance thereof.[1]

This reads very much like a yogic Hindu or Buddhist cosmic mandala in which the yogi identifies himself (sheaths of the soul) with the "sheaths" of the macrocosm and in this way gains entrance to the core or Center of Being. The *Divine Comedy*, too, may be considered the same kind of mandala pattern with God as the core or Center of Being, Pure Infinite essential Being. Dante's spiri-

---
[2] *Ibid.*, p. 55.
[1] *Ibid.*, p. 49, quoted by Arberry from the *Book of Salvation*.

tual journey, too, symbolizes the cyclic return to the Source of Being. (Scholars, led by the research of Professor Asin, think that Moslem ideas of the journey to Heaven and the throne of God taken by Mohammed in his famous "night journey" was the source of much mystic thought about, and fantastic descriptions of the heavens and Hell; it was this kind of literature which was one of the sources for the *Divine Comedy.*)[1]

The philosopher-theologian who curbed such intellectualism for all of subsequent orthodox thought in Islam was Al-Ghazzali (1058-1111). Al-Ghazzali's view of the afterlife returns to the Koran's literal teaching. He rejects the rationalistic philosophers' (especially Avicenna's) allegorizing of the eschatological passages in the *Koran.* Such allegorizing implies that the Prophet directly falsified the truth and "the office of prophecy is far too sacred for that."[1] The physical resurrection is made clear in God's revelation to Mohammed, the *Koran,* and it is no more repugnant to reason than the creation of the world out of nothing. If one assumes God the eternal Being, existing in his infinity without any world, the same when all worlds are destroyed, then Creation, a mystery to us, is no difficult task for such a Being. Equally, resurrection of the physical body of each man and the establishment of the

---

[1] Emile Dermenghem, *Muhammad and the Islamic Tradition,* Men of Wisdom series (New York: Harper & Bros., n. d.) p. 33. A quotation from another great Islamic scholar, Alfred Guillaume, also vindicates Asin's view: "To the fascinating studies of the late Professor Asin of Madrid we owe the discovery of the enormous influence of Ibn 'Arabi on Dante. The Arab first described the infernal region, the heavens of the astronomers, the Paradise of the blessed, the choirs of angels round the divine light, and the beautiful woman who was his guide. Curiously enough both Arab and Florentine were forced to write a commentary on their first works to show that their love-songs had an esoteric and not an amatory significance. The link between the two writers has since been discovered, and the fact of affiliation has now passed into the history of European literature. The significant point is that the narrative is based on the legend of Muhammad's ascent to Paradise." (Alfred Guillaume, *Islam,* Penguin ed., Baltimore: Penguin Books, Inc., 1954), p. 148.

[2] Arberry, *op. cit.,* pp. 63-64.

Paradise for men (and Hell for the wicked) when this world is brought to a close poses no problem for the omnipotence of God. The Paradise which is the Destiny of Man, the goal of the entire panorama of human history, Al-Ghazzali declares is exactly as "physical" in its luxuries and pleasures as the *Koran* states. Al-Ghazzali goes even further and quotes one of the stories told about saints who have been afforded glimpses of Paradise. In this story a saint, Utba al-Ghulam, had a dream in which he beheld a beautiful houri out of Paradise. The houri said, "O Utba, I am in love with you. Beware lest you do anything so that I cannot come to you, and they hold me back from you!" Utba replied, "I have triply divorced this world and will not go around after it any more, so that I may come to you."[1] Orthodoxy was thus vindicated by this great thinker-theologian called the "Proof of Islam." He was given this appellation because of his learned "refutation" of rationalistic philosophers (his great work *Incoherence of the Philosophers* attempts this) and defense of Revelation given man in the Koran. Al-Ghazzali attempted to join science with Revelation it is clear, in his acceptance of the Ptolemaic world view that the earth is a globe and around it revolve the spheres of the planets and the fixed stars. Revelation is brought into the picture in the declaration that all the universe was produced by the will of God and will be annihilated again by his will in accordance with the eschatological passages of the *Koran*.

Sufi influence is apparent in al-Ghazzali's doctrine of the nature of man. Al-Ghazzali had been a Sufi after his disillusionment with philosophy, and the mystical identification with God, the heart of Sufi doctrine and practice, remained in Al-Ghazzali's theology in the emphasis upon the closeness between man and Allah. There is a spark of the divine in the human soul which is restless until it rests in the primal Spirit — God, a view like that of St. Augustine (Al-Ghazzali is often compared with St. Augustine).

---
[1] *Ibid.*, p. 64.

This divine spark, the spirit in man, rules man's body as God rules the world. *Will* is common to man and God and through the will man knows God. Man is created in the image of God, in short, and is a microcosm; God is the macrocosm. There is no doctrine of Original Sin in al-Ghazzali's thought nor in Islamic thought in general. Adam's free will caused his personal Fall but he was forgiven without any atonement, although it is true his descendants were put out of Eden. Each man, like Adam, has free will and is responsible for his eternal Destiny in Paradise or Hell assigned him on the Last Day. At the same time Al-Ghazzali strongly emphasizes the omniscience and omnipotence of Allah as we mentioned above at the beginning of this chapter which makes it difficult to see why anyone should be either rewarded or punished for his actions. Al-Ghazzali has no answer to this dilemma except that man cannot have knowledge of the absolute and infinite but only of the relative and finite. Revelation alone gives us knowledge of God; the Koran therefore must be accepted in its version of the destiny of the individual soul and of the human race. The omnipotent, omniscient Allah foreordains, predestines in the most literal sense, every event in the history of the individual and of the human race collectively.

The Sufis. The idea of personal and cosmic history is very different among the Sufi pantheists or monists.[1] This group of Sufis which was predominantly Persian derived its philosophy mainly from Christian and Neoplatonic sources, but was influenced also by Zoroastrian, Buddhist, Hindu and Gnostic ideas.[2]

The central doctrine of this mystical philosophy is the unity of God affirmed so strongly by Mohammed. The unity

---

[1] There are differing theological opinions among Sufis from mere forms of devotional pietism, asceticism, feeling of the Divine closeness as in Al-Ghazzali's orthodox Sufiism to monistic pantheism.

[2] H. A. R. Gibb, *Mohammedanism*, Mentor ed. (New York: New American Library, 1955), p. 101. See also *Encyclopaedia Brittanica*, 1957 edition, Vol. 21, article "Sufiism," pp. 523 f.

of God means that all is God; there is nothing apart from God's being, therefore man and the entire universe are manifestations of God. God in his essential Being is unknowable as in Neoplatonism, but unity with God may be experienced in *fana* (annihiliation) — annihilation of the individual consciousness in union with the ineffable One—God.

There is no separation between God and the "created" world — such separation denies God's unity — the world is an everlasting process, a Divine self-manifestation. There is no such thing as real Time or creation in Time. "While the *forms* of the universe change and pass and are simultaneously renewed without a moment's intermission, in its *essence* it is co-eternal with God." [3] As in Mahayana Buddhist thought, Taoist Chinese Yoga, and Ramakrishna's Vedanta *samsara* and *nirvana* are the same; and as in these mystical philosophies the cyclic return to the *Center*, the soul's journey, is the only purpose and significance of human history.

As in the yogas already described, (and also in Christian and all mysticism) there are purgative and meditative stages. An eary Sufi of the ninth century set these stages as: repentance, abstinence, renunciation, poverty, patience, trust in God and satisfaction. Corresponding with these stages or "way-stations" are spiritual states such as fear, hope, and love which lead to the supreme state of Knowledge (union with the Divine Mind) and then the ultimate intuitive knowledge-by-identity of reabsorption in the Divine Essence.

The highest phenomenal manifestation of the One is the Divine Mind. This Mind is the "Indwelling Rational Principle (Logos)" which pervades total nature but reveals itself preeminently and fully in the Perfect Man.[1] The archetypal Perfect Man is the "preexistent Reality or

---

[3] Reynold A. Nicholson in his Introduction to *Rumi: Poet and Mystic* (London: George Allen and Unwin, Ltd., 1950), p. 23.

[1] *Ibid.*, p. 23.

Spirit of Mohammed, whose 'Light' irradiates the long series of prophets beginning with Adam and, after them, the hierarchy of Muslim saints, who are Muhammad's spiritual heirs."[2] The Perfect Man corresponds with the yogi who has achieved next to the final stage of self-realization in Indian and Taoist Chinese thought; both identify themselves with the Macrocosm. I am Brahman as Isvara, or I am the active Tao, or I am the Buddha-Mind are similar to the Sufi idea expressed in the following lines of Rumi:

> From the pure star-bright souls replenishment is ever coming to the stars of heaven.
> Outwardly we are ruled by these stars, but our inward nature has become the ruler of the skies.
> Therefore, while in form thou art the microcosm, in reality thou art the macrocosm.[3]

In the macrocosm the Logos or Universal Reason with which the Perfect Man is one, "animates and rules" the entire phenomenal world of nature as the spirit in the microcosm (man) animates and rules his body. The Logos or Perfect Man is the Final Cause of "creation" because the purpose of the phenomenal manifestation of the One is self-consciousness. Only through the Perfect Man "does God become fully conscious of himself."[1]

The ordinary man has the potentiality of becoming one with the Perfect Man. Private ego-consciousness and all of its phenomenal manifestations must be overcome before union with the Perfect Man *(Logos)* can be attained. The next step takes the devotee beyond the Logos (Universal Reason) into the Center of Being. The analogy which is most in accordance with Moslem tradition is the well known story of Mohammed's Ascension or Night Journey which

---
[2] *Ibid.*, pp. 23 f.
[3] *Ibid.*, p. 124.
[1] *Ibid.*, Introduction, p. 24.

as we have already said provides an esoteric mystic mandala for Moslem mysticism. Gabriel took Mohammed on this journey. In the first and lowest heaven Mohammed met Adam; in the second heaven, the third, the fourth, the fifth and the sixth Mohammed met Idris, Moses, Jesus and Abraham but the narrator of the story does not know in which heaven these saints were encountered except that Abraham was in the sixth. Beyond in the seventh heaven Mohammed entered the presence of Allah where the Divine Voice informed his Messenger (Mohammed) that all Moslems were to say fifty prayers a day (finally Allah agreed upon five as more realistic). The stages of mystic progress towards union with God are also six as we mentioned above; the seventh takes the initiate into the Divine Center itself. This is the stage beyond the Universal Reason (the Logos or Perfect Man) and is realized as an ineffable ecstatic union with the One — *fana*. The mystic knows then that "the circle of existence begins and ends in a single point, the Essence of God . . ."[2] The phenomenal world as in Oriental thought is God's maya. To quote again from the Sufi poet Rumi.

THE WORLD OF TIME (Rumi)

Every instant thou art dying and returning. "This world is but a moment," said the Prophet.
Our thought is an arrow shot by Him: how should it stay in the air? It flies back to God.
Every instant the world is being renewed, and we are unaware of its perpetual change.
Life is ever pouring in afresh, though in the body it has the semblance of continuity.
From its swiftness it appears continuous, like the spark thou whirlest with thy hand.
Time and duration are phenomena produced by the rapidity of Divine Action,

---

[2] *Ibid.*, p. 117 n.

As a firebrand dexterously whirled presents the appearance of a long line of fire.[1]

The world must be viewed under the species of eternity as in Spinoza's thought; but the knowledge-by-identity of the ecstatic trance-state in which man *is* God in His very core of Being is beyond Spinoza's system, but in harmony with the Oriental philosophies already reviewed. History as a genuinely "creative" time-process in which unpredictable events can happen is negated by this kind of thinking. History, instead, becomes a phenomenal appearance of the One Being who eternally IS. The purpose of human history in Sufiism is cyclic: self-revelation of the One in the Perfect Man or archetypal man, the Active Intellect which in turn embodies itself in the lesser forms of phenomena the animal and plant worlds and finally inorganic matter. The cycle of the return is through lesser states of soul to greater (man can live at the vegetative or animal levels of soul as Aristotle says); the stage of union with the Active Intellect (Perfect Man) is very high in the "ascension mandala" of the return; but coincidence with the Center of Being itself, its very core is the ultimate goal. The devotee then has totally reintegrated himself with all that is since He Is All That Is — the atman has become the Brahman as the Advaita Vedantists express this glorious and final state. This is the meaning of human history.

The Isma'ili Theory of the Cycle of Cosmic and Human History

The Moslem sect of Isma'ilis is an offshoot of the Shi'a, the opposition group of the orthodox Sunnis. (The views of Al-Ghazzali, the greatest theologian of the orthodox Sunnis have been discussed above.) The Shi'a began as a poli-

---
[1] *Ibid.*, p. 117.

tical movement when Mohammed's son-in-law, Ali (husband of Mohammed's daughter, Fatima) was denied the right to the caliphate. His sons, too, were similarly wronged; the older was pressed by his opponents to resign his rights to the caliphate for a mere pension, and the younger son was martyred in an attempt to secure by force of arms the caliphate to which he was entitled. Friends of the sons of Ali rallied around them and parties formed which regarded the descendants of Ali's sons as the rightful heirs of the caliphate and of Mohammed's power which he had allegedly transmitted to Ali. The idea developed that Mohammed had bequeathed his spiritual power and the leadership of Islam in the caliphate upon Ali and his blood descendants, the Imams. The Shi'ites quote a *hadith* accepted by Ali partisans in these early days which quotes Mohammed as saying: "I shall soon be called back to heaven; I leave you two important bequests, the Koran and my family." [1] The Shi'a believe Mohammed conferred divine authority upon Ali in these words, for the phrase "back to heaven" implies that Mohammed is a preexistent divine being; he was, therefore, passing on his divine authority to Ali, the first Imam. The second and third Imams were Ali's sons and the later Imams descendants of these men. The three most important Shi'a sects differ about the number of these "divine" Imams. The Zaidites name only two after the sons of Ali, the Isma'ilis seven and the Twelvers twelve. All hold that the Imams are sinless, infallible beings who possess secret and superhuman knowl-

---

[1] John Clark Archer, *Faiths Men Live By*, second ed. rev. by Carl E. Purinton (New York: The Ronald Press, 1958), p. 483. *See also* A. S. Tritton, *Muslim Theology* (London: Luzac & Co., published for The Royal Asiatic Society, 1947), p. 33. Later, Tritton says, the imams "were more excellent than all prophets and angels; they have the books of the prophets, the staff of Moses, the seal of Solomon, the shirt of Joseph, the ark, the tablets of the law, etc. They are the purpose of the creation of the world, the means by which God acts here and hereafter, and the necessary ambassadors between God and men." (p. 33).

edge.[1] The Twelvers, dominant in Persia, believe that the twelfth Imam, Mohammed al-Mahdi, disappeared in 880 and will reappear to public view again as the Mahdi at the end of the world. He will inaugurate a reign of justice and righteousness in the world under Moslem auspices before the final end of the world. In the sixteenth century when the doctrine of the Twelvers became the official religion of Persia, the Safavids always kept two horses saddled for the use of Jesus and the Mahdi upon their Second Coming.

The Isma'ilis differ about the identity of the Mahdi and think that the seventh Imam was Isma'il and the Mahdi and second only to Allah himself. (The Twelvers think that Isma'il was an imposter.) The Isma'ili movement by the eleventh century had become so powerful that there were followers throughout the entire Moslem world. It still has a following of about twenty million Moslems who live mainly in Pakistan, India, Afghanistan, Iran, Arabia, Syria, Morocco and Zanzibar.

The doctrinal teachings of the Isma'ilis became a secret teaching and remains so to this day. Scholars have, however, had access to some of the literature of this sect. It seems that the philosophy of their beliefs is "fundamentally Neoplatonic,"[2] but with added elements derived from Gnosticism, Hermetism and Manicheism.[3] The *Koran* is used allegorically and esoterically.

The metaphysics is integrated with the philosophy of cosmic and human history. The ultimate reality is God (Allah) without attributes as in Neoplatonism; all the other categories of being emanate from Him, again as in Neoplatonism. The first emanation is Universal Reason which creates the Universal Soul which in turn gives rise to Primal Matter whence comes the final elements Space and Time. All of this is Neoplatonic. The prominence of the

---
[1] Alfred Guillaume, *Islam*, Penguin ed. (Baltimore: Penguin Books, Ltd., 1954), p. 120.
[2] *Ibid.*, p. 123.
[3] Arberry, *op. cit.*, p. 84.

number seven in the metaphysical chain of categories (there are seven when man is included) is probably derived from the "ascension mandala" described above. Man is a microcosm composed of all the categories up to and including Universal Reason. Universal Reason has "science" (intelligence) as its only attribute. Primal Matter takes on the forms given it by Universal Reason. Space and time interact with Universal Soul and all the categories act upon Matter.

Universal Reason became incarnate in seven prophets: Adam, Noah, Abraham, Moses, Jesus, Mohammed, and Mohammed ibn Isma'il, son of the seventh imam (Isma'il). There is a prophet for each epoch of history; closely associated with each of these epochal prophets just listed is his Executor, the "Imam" of the age. The imam of Mohammed, for example, was Ali. Arberry tells us that "Ali was believed by his partisans to have been privy to all the esoteric teachings of the Koran and the Prophet; his position vis-a-vis Mohammed was the same as that of Abel to Adam, Shem to Noah, Ishmael to Abraham, Aaron to Moses, and Simon Peter to Christ."[1] Isma'il's son, Mohammed, who has opened the seventh (presumably the last) prophetic cycle was followed by the imams believed to be his descendants, the Fatimids of Egypt. The Fatimid dynasty ended in the twelfth century in Egypt but meanwhile a branch of the Fatimid (Isma'ili) sect had established itself in Persia and northern Syria. This group was known as the Assassins since they believed in and used violent methods to disestablish ruling powers in the name of the legitimate ruling house, that of Ali. The famous contemporary head of the Isma'ili sect, the Aga Khan recently a young Harvard student) is a descendant of the leader of the Assassins.[2]

Arberry, *ibid.*, p. 70.

[2] The father of this young man, the late Aga Kahn, was once a president of the All India Muslim League. He showed wisdom in choosing as his successor the son who was an A student at Harvard rather than the older sons who apparently had less serious interests.

As we have already said the esoteric teachings of this sect are still officially secret. Recently some of these have become known. Arberry gives examples from the *Kitab Jami' al-hikmatain* by Nasir-i Khusrau sub-titled by its French editor very appropriately "Harmony of Greek Philosophy with Isma'ilian Theosophy." A typical example of the type of esoteric teaching given by Arberry is the following:

> The Universal Intellect is the same as the Pen mentioned in the Koran; the Universal Soul is the Tablet; the physical world is as it were God's written book ...
> "In the world of religion, the Prophet is also the Pen of God; the noble Koran is God's Book inscribed by the Pen — that is, the Prophet — upon the Tablet, i.e. the Executor ...
> Therefore the visible Book (the world of creation) and the audible Book (the noble Koran) are two writings of God's executed by two Pens upon two Tablets for the benefit of men having a share of understanding." [1]

Another example which is more pertinent to our main theme:

> The sun occupies in the macrocosm which is the physical world the same positions as the heart in the microcosm which is man; the moon is the brain; the five planets are the five senses. "Since man is corporeally the child of the macrocosm, and spiritually the child of the Universal Soul, it follows that the macrocosm is as it were the body of the Universal Soul, having the instruments we have mentioned. It was in this sense that Jesus the son of Mary — upon him be peace — said, 'I go unto my father, and my father is in heaven'; that is, 'My particular soul is returning to the Universal Soul which is in heaven.'" [2]

---
[1] Arberry, *op. cit.*, pp. 79-81. The passages enclosed in quotation marks are quoted by Arberry from Khusrau's book.
[2] *Ibid.*, p. 78. Passages in quotation marks quoted from Khusrau's book.

275

Appropriate passages of the *Koran* are quoted with allegorical interpretations.

It seems that there are *seven* degrees of initiation into such secret doctrines. The belief about Paradise is that it is perfect knowledge or union with the Universal Reason; Hell is the state of ignorance and belongs to man's passionate and appetitive nature. Hell is only temporary, however. The soul is reborn as in Hindu-Buddhist thought until it is able to rise to union with the Universal Reason.

Evil will finally disappear when this cycle ends and all men plus the rest of the entire system of emanated creation will be merged again into the Universal Reason from whence they originally issued. The microcosmic cycle and the macrocosmic cycles are thus alike.

The microcosmic cycle is the familiar one of emergence from the Divine Source in an involutionary series of "sheaths." Then there is the evolutionary cycle of the return in which the "sheaths" are shed and the devotee returns to the Divine Source. The familiar yogic mandala pattern is again described.

The macrocosmic cycle is exactly similar. Universal Reason emanates its lower "sheaths" and after seven epochs reabsorbs all into itself. Cosmic history describes the same cycle as that of the individual human soul. There is one cycle for each — from the Divine to the Divine.

The majority school of Moslem thought (the Sunnis), however, accept the apocalyptic one-cycle view of history in its exoteric interpretation. Their greatest theologian, Al-Ghazzali, follows this view also; and in this respect Moslem thought and orthodox Christian thought are in agreement. We have pointed out above the resemblance between St. Augustine's ideas and those of Al-Ghazzali.

Chapter V

The Influence of Augustine's One-Cycle Philosophy of History upon Subsequent Western Thought

St. Augustine's philosophy of human history was prevalent during the Middle Ages; it was reaffirmed by St. Thomas Aquinas in the thirteenth century, and in this form it is today the accepted view in Roman Catholicism. In the *Catholic Encyclopaedia* under the article "Predestination," we read that there are three qualities that belong to predestination. These are: (1) immutability of the divine decree based on the infallible foreknowledge of God that certain souls will leave this life in a state of grace; (2) definiteness of the number of the elect, which follows from the preceding statement; (3) the subjective uncertainty about election; for the soul may relapse into sin after believing itself among the elect. The will of man is free to remain in grace or to relapse into sin. Nevertheless, because God is omniscient He foresees what the individual will do. To allay excessive anxiety the individual may feel he is probably among the saved if he has purity of heart, receives the sacraments regularly, takes pleasure in prayer, has patience in suffering, loves Christ and the Church, shows devotion to the Blessed Virgin and leads an exemplary life in general.

The Encyclopaedia quotes St. Thomas further on the number of the elect. St. Thomas, states the Encyclopaedia, in his *Summa*, I, Q xxiii, a. 7, deals with the problems whether or not the number of the elect will equal the number of fallen angels, while the number of the predestined will equal the number of faithful angels. St. Thomas' reply is that God alone knows the number of angels, faithful or fallen; therefore God alone knows the number of the elect. The *Catholic Encyclopaedia* adds that the number of the saved must be at least half of the human race since it is necessary for the glory of God that his Kingdom be at least as large in population as the Kingdom of Satan.

The emphasis on Reason and Science which began in the Renaissance began to undermine the Providence theory; but the Reformation reaffirmed it more strongly than ever especially in Calvin's theology where Predestination was very explicitly formulated as a central doctrine. In the field of history, Sir Walter Raleigh completed part of a work called *The History of the World*. In this book he asserts that the Providence of God is the controlling factor in human history.

By the seventeenth century the influence of the scientific approach begun by such thinkers as Copernicus and Descartes (d. 1650) created skepticism about the part played by Providence in history. The last great historian before the twentieth century to defend this theory was Bossuet whose *Discourse on Universal History* again revived Augustine's Providence approach to the course of human history. Again in the middle of the twentieth century, Arnold Toynbee has reaffirmed it in his famous *Study of History*.

Augustine and Toynbee. Toynbee believes that the Hindu and Buddhist and ancient Greek cyclical views of history make life in this world meaningless. "Humanity," he says, "is not an Ixion bound for ever to his wheel nor a Sisyphus for ever rolling his stone to the summit of the same mountain and helplessly watching it roll down again."[1] This dreary spectacle is Toynbee's interpretation of cyclical philosophies of the multi-cycle pattern.

A careful study of history leads Toynbee to reaffirm St.

---

[1] Arnold J. Toynbee, *A Study of History*, abridgement of Vols. I-VI by D. C. Somervell (New York and London: Oxford University Press, 1947), p. 254.

Augustine's Providence theory. There are cyclic patterns, he admits, in the rise and fall of great civilizations; nevertheless there has been linear progress on the whole in Religion. The purpose of human history, Toynbee thinks, is that all men might come to know the One True God and become as like Him as possible. This purpose is God's plan, the Providence of God in history.

Since a chapter in Part III is devoted to Toynbee we shall not elaborate upon his theories here. It will suffice to comment that Toynbee's philosophy of history emphasizes a spiral progress pattern — civilizations of mankind rise and fall but the cause of the "falls" of civilizations and of individual men is alienation from God the Creator. The one-cycle view similar to St. Augustine's is implied. There is alienation-from and return-to-God at higher and higher levels until the appearance of Christ (the Incarnation) is reached. Subsequent history is for the purpose of spiritual conversion of the world to real Christianity. Man's destiny as an individual and as a race is the return to God — the individual soul to the eternal Presence of God and the race to a Heavenly City of earth. The return of the soul to God is exactly the aim of all history individual and social in the Oriental religions. In these religions history is not meaningless repetition, but repetition of the outward forms is the school for souls which makes them turn to God. This is exactly the purpose of secular history according to Toynbee's view; there is a repetitious form-pattern to culture-cycles and will be unless the human race returns to God and inaugurates a Heavenly City on earth; even then man's home is the eternal one with God, and not of this world. The yogic cycle of the return is actually Toynbee's, St. Augustine's, and Al-Ghazzali's view of the meaning of human history.

Influence of the Apocalyptic-Providential One-Cycle View on Modern Secular Historical Thought: The Hegelian and the Marxian Cycles

Background: The Idea of Progress. Collingwood in his book *The Idea of History* comments upon the significance of the Hebrew-Christian view of history for all subsequent Western historians and philosophers of history. This influence, he says, is brought out in four ways which he lists as follows: "Any history written on Christian principles will be of necessity universal, providential, apocalyptic, and periodized."[1] The Hegelian and the Marxian cycles of history have all four of these characteristics, but in their secular transformations. The trend away from the traditional religious approach to the universe and human affairs which began in the Renaissance reached a climax in the Enlightenment era. In historical thought this secularism is manifested in the Enlightenment Idea of Progress expressed in its most eloquent form in the work by the Marquis Antoine-Nicolas de Condorcet *Sketch for a Historical Picture of the Progress of the Human Mind.* In this work Paradise is brought down from Heaven to earth. The goal of man becomes achievement of the bliss of the heavenly Jerusalem here on this earth. This was not a new idea, for Dante in his Divine Comedy thought it possible for man, unaided by supernatural grace, to achieve an earthly paradise. Dante symbolizes this by placing the Garden of Eden at the top of the Mount of Purgatory. This means that man when purged of his vices with the aid of natural reason (Virgil) can attain the blissful state of Adam (Eden) before the Fall. Condorcet as an Enlightenment thinker makes this goal sound more modern and convincing by utilizing the promise of the new scientific knowledge which was beginning to grow so rapidly in his time. Through

---

[1] R. G. Collingwood, *The Idea of History* (Oxford: The Clarendon Press, 1946), p. 49.

science, Condorcet writes, man can eventually make his own Heaven here on this earth.

Progress towards this final goal of man, says Condorcet, can be systematized as a linear series in ten stages. These are: (1) The stage in which tribal organization develops out of enlarged family units; (2) the pastoral or nomadic stage which gave man more economic security; (3) the agricultural stage and the invention of writing; (4) Greek culture especially the development of the sciences up to the time of Aristotle; (5) the division of the sciences beginning with Aristotle to their decline; (6) the "decadence of knowledge to its restoration about the time of the crusades"; (7) the "early progress of science from its revival in the West to the invention of printing"; (8) "from the invention of printing to the time when philosophy and the sciences shook off the yoke of authority"; (9) "from Descartes to the foundation of the French Republic"; (10) "the future progress of the human mind." This tenth stage will see the "abolition of the inequality between nations, the progress of equality within each nation, and the true perfection of mankind." [1] By the perfection of mankind Condorcet means continuing amazing progress in the arts and sciences and in ethics—War will be abolished, education will be free and equal, there will be a universal language, all men will have their economic needs abundantly satisfied, intellectual ability will increase enormously, and finally death itself will be conquered and man will attain a noble immortality.[2]

The Dialectical Cycle of History in Hegel's Thought. This idea of secular progress was given a cyclical formulation by Marx under the influence of Hegel's dialectical one-cycle philosophy of history. In Hegel's dialectical cycle human history reveals the thesis-antithesis pattern as follows: the

---

[1] Antoine-Nicolas de Condorcet, *Sketch for a Historical Picture of the Progress of the Human Mind,* trans. June Barraclough (New York: The Noonday Press, 1955), p. 173.

[2] *Ibid.,* "The Tenth Stage," pp. 173-202.

Infinite as Pure Being is its negation, Nothing; to be real the Infinite must be concrete, therefore it must manifest Itself in the myriad forms of the existential world ("secular" manifestation) and return to itself as the One Real Individual, the Absolute Idea. The concrete process of development shows a spiral progress of developmental accretion from lower to higher levels, but the dynamic of the entire process is the dialectical logic in which a stage (thesis) is negated (antithesis). Then this negation is negated (this is the synthesis); then the synthesis becomes another thesis which gives rise to its antithesis, and so on, *ad infinitum*. The goal of the historical process is the complete concrete realization of the Absolute Infinite Spirit. This means the realization of Freedom.

Hegel defines Freedom as the self-awareness of Spirit that all its limitations or negations are simply self-manifestations of the One Absolute and Infinite Spirit under its concrete aspect; but without this concrete aspect the Infinite Spirit would be an empty abstraction without content and therefore equivalent to Nothing. Yet in becoming concrete the Infinite Spirit must negate itself as Infinite and become finite, since every determination is a negation, i.e., every determinate (concrete) entity is bounded, limited, or negated by other entities. Each is finite and temporal since only the Absolute all-inclusive Whole can be infinite, unlimited and eternal. Nevertheless in the dialectical development of Spirit under its concrete forms the ultimate purpose (and here is the Christian idea of Providence) is the realization by Spirit that its concrete finite manifestations are not alien to it (e.g. as finite vs. infinite; spirit vs. matter); but that It is limited only by Itself. This is the idea of Freedom; Spirit is free when nothing outside itself limits or compels It, when It is absolutely and completely self-determined. This ultimate self-awareness of Spirit (the metaphysical state of Freedom) can be achieved only at the human level and at the human level only in an organized community of persons, the State. This is because one cannot achieve *self*-consciousness unless he first becomes conscious of an Other-consciousness. The polar dialectical opposites of Self and Other are essential to give meaning to the synthesis of self-awareness or self-consciousness at the highest level; for here it is seen that all selves (persons) are real only with reference to their opposites (Other Selves), therefore they are the Other Selves and vice versa. Self and Other are then seen as essential dialectical moments in self-awareness of the only ultimately real Individual, the Absolute Spirit.

All selves are other selves in a still more concrete and obvious way. A self is a self or personality only because of its concrete content, says Hegel. This concrete content comes to the individual self only in interaction with the society (the State). The social whole (other selves of past and present) supply concrete idea content such as religion, art, literature, music, philosophy, science. Thus in a rather literal sense a Self (personality) in its content contains, in a sense *is* Other Selves. Thus through the social whole (the State) Self and Other are seen as essential dialectical moments in the self-awareness of the only ultimately real Individual, the Absolute Spirit. It is the self-realization by Spirit of this truth that it is Itself its own Other which is Freedom, and the entire dialectical temporal-historical process is for the purpose of this self-realization.

The matter-world of nature shows the dialectic of this process as it is revealed in Space; history is the manifestation of the process in Time. The core-idea of the space world (matter) is *gravity*. Gravity, however, negates itself because as a force it draws all particles into a unity which, if achieved absolutely, would annihilate the matter world, since matter for its very existence depends upon the existence of separate, discrete particles. External relations characterize this matter world as such, but gravity as the drive towards internal relations gives rise dialectically to "chemism" wherein relations become more internal and organic; then further development of internal relations is achieved at the organismic (biological) level of nature. At the stage of life (organisms) each element of the organism is what it is and does what it does with reference to the Whole. Here Spirit is approaching ultimate self-realization which lies, as we have said, in the self-awareness on the part of Spirit that all relations are internal, i.e., that all concrete finite realities are organic parts of the One ever-living dynamic concrete all-inclusive Whole. The mind-level in man realizes this truth through the historical process. State organisms as we noted above provide the basis for such self-realization; this is also, at the same time, realization of the consciousness of absolute Freedom on the part of Spirit.

The unfolding of this concrete historical process begins in Asia. "In Asia arose the Light of Spirit, and therefore the history of the World." [1] for "the History of the World travels from East to West, for Europe is absolutely the end of History, Asia the beginning." [2] In Asia (India and China) history begins and Asian historical consciousness reveals itself as the Childhood of the development of Spirit. This is the stage of "unreflected consciousness." [3] At this level *One* is free, "the One Individual as that substantial being to which all belongs, so that no other individual has a separate existence . . ." [4]

This is the stage of absolute emperorship. The second stage is the stage of the adolescence of Spirit and is represented by the Greek World. Here and in the Roman World *some* are free (slavery still exists.) The Greeks realized the stage of "Beautiful Freedom." Here "the Idea is united with a plastic form." [1] for it is "bound up with the Real, as in a beautiful work of Art; the Sensuous bears the stamp

---

[1] Georg Wilhelm Friedrich Hegel, *The Philosophy of History*, trans. J. Sibree, rev. ed. (New York: Willey Book Co., 1944), p. 99.
[2] *Ibid.*, p. 103.
[3] *Ibid.*, p. 104.
[4] *Ibid.*, p. 105.
[1] *Ibid.*, p. 106.

and expression of the Spiritual."[2] Morality is not yet self-conscious since "the individual will of the Subject adopts unreflectingly the conduct and Habit prescribed by Justice and the Laws."[3] Reflective self-consciousness, i.e., true morality begins with Socrates, but this means liquidation of classical culture. This is because Socrates represents a departure from the characteristic Greek manifestation of Spirit. This characteristic manifestation is revealed best in Greek art wherein Spirit as felt is revealed adequately in and as an objective concrete form. The gods are revealed in human form. But in the next developmental level of Spirit, it is perceived that Spirit is Infinite and cannot be represented in its essential nature in any finite concrete form. Socrates represents the beginning of this realization in the reflective inwardness of his approach to Spirit. The Spirit develops further in its third stage in the Roman State.

The third stage is the manhood of Spirit and is manifested in the Roman World. It is the stage of "abstract Universality (in which the Social aim absorbs all individual aims)."[1] The State in its abstract universality assumes importance; the individual sacrifices himself for national interests. At the same time the individual's personality is recognized; he becomes the abstract object of definite rights. These two opposite principles come into conflict when the individual personalities assert themselves to such a degree that the State deteriorates into atomistic individualism. The strong individual despot then takes control of the State and is accepted as a means of keeping order; but the misery of Spirit under such brutal tyranny gives rise to the fourth and final stage of world history, the *German* world.

The German world is the *Old Age* of the Spirit. In this stage is the recognition that all men — man as man — is

[2] *Ibid.*, p. 106.
[3] *Ibid.*, p. 106.
[1] *Ibid.*, p. 107.

free. It begins with the Christian religion that developed out of the degeneracy of tyranny in the Roman world. Spirit has now reacted against the brutal Roman despotism by returning deep within itself. "Within the soul therefore arises the Spiritual pacification of the struggle, in the fact that the individual personality, instead of following its own capricious choice, is purified and elevated into universality; a subjectivity that of its own free will adopts principles tending to the good of all — reaches, in fact, a divine personality." [2] With the rise of the Church the division between the holy life divine and the secular world takes shape. This is institutionalized by the Catholic Church. Yet the secular world *ought* to be in harmony with the spiritual. This harmony, Hegel says, has been accomplished by the corruption of the Church in the Middle Ages, its negation or secularization. This threw men back upon "realizing the Ideal of Reason from the Secular principles alone." In this way the

> "antithesis of Church and State vanishes. The spiritual becomes reconnected with the Secular, and develops this latter as an independently organic existence . . . Freedom has found the means of realizing its Ideal — its true existence. This is the ultimate result which the process of History is intended to accomplish, and we have to traverse in detail the long track which has been thus cursorily traced out. Yet length of Time is something entirely relative, and the element of Spirit is Eternity. Duration, properly speaking, cannot be said to belong to it." [1]

The historical dialectical progress of the Idea towards the concrete realization of Freedom — the state of self-conscious realization that Reason (Spirit) and its Works (concrete manifestations) are one all-inclusive Whole in which

---

[2] *Ibid.*, p. 108.
[1] *Ibid.*, pp. 109-110.

all relations are internal (organic) — both is and is not a time-process. From the relative finite point of view of the individual human spirit, history is real as a temporal process. From the point of view of Spirit in its infinite eternal nature, however, there is nothing but an eternal Present. This is seen in the above statement which claims that length of time and duration cannot belong to Spirit in its essential nature. Even more emphatic is Hegel's statement in his Introduction to the *Philosophy of History*: "Spirit is immortal; with it there is no past, no future, but an essential *now*." [2]

The essential manifestation of Spirit as concrete life (History) is the cyclical dialectic of thesis, antithesis, synthesis. And so

> the life of the ever present Spirit is a circle of progressive embodiments, which looked at in one aspect still exist beside each other, and only as looked at from another point of view appear as past. The grades which Spirit seems to have left behind it, it still possesses in the depths of its present.[3]

In conclusion, history from the point of view of Spirit in its eternal infinite nature is One Grand Macrocosmic Dialectical Cycle in which the Infinite Spirit posits itself as abstract Infinite; dialectically this immediately gives rise to its negation, the whole infinitude of finite particulars of the concrete world; and the negation of the negation (synthesis) which is the concrete infinite (Absolute Whole-Idea).

The dynamic logic of concretion is non-temporal from the point of view of the Infinite Spirit (Absolute Idea). One grand overall cycle of concretion of the Infinite and its myriad sub-cycles of concretion all of the same form (macro-microcosmic thinking again) are real *now* and all at

---
[2] *Ibid.*, p. 79.
[3] *Ibid.*

once for the Absolute. The entire content of the Cycle with all of its "developmental" subcycles is thus, from the point of view of the Absolute, really non-developmental and non-historical—an eternal NOW.

As in Indian philosophy man's goal is Freedom (mukti), and as in Indian philosophy freedom means self-realization, i.e., the realization that the private ego in its particularity is unreal — the only reality is the infinite Absolute (Brahman or the Hegelian Absolute). The difference lies in the conception of the Absolute if one compares the Hegelian Absolute-Idea with the Absolute of the Advaita Vedanta school of Indian thought. For the Vedantists the Absolute is qualityless, the concrete world is an inessential maya manifestation of Brahman; whereas for Hegel the concrete world is an essential manifestation of the Absolute.[1] In both Indian (Advaitist) and Hegelian schools of thought the goal of man is the Freedom which comes when it is realized that *I am Brahman* or *I am the Absolute*. This realization is Freedom and the goal of individual and collective human history. Indian thinkers, both Hindu and Buddhist, differ from the Hegelian in their greater awareness of vast numbers of cosmic cycles, of varieties of "planes of existence," all of which seemed fanciful in Hegel's time, but possible, even probable today.

Hegel's man-centered philosophy of history is significant today especially because of its influence upon Karl Marx father of theoretical Communism. The Marxian philosophy of history, dialectical materialism, is the secular "scientific" version of Hegel's dialectical idealism.

The Marxian Apocalyptic One-Cycle Idea of History. As we have already mentioned above the Marxian and Hegelian philosophies of history borrow the Christian characteristics enumerated by Collingwood: universality, apo-

---

[1] Ramanujah (eleventh century A.D.), founder of the *Visistadvaita* school of Vedanta, is a famous and still popular Indian thinker whose idealism is similar to Hegel's. Ramanujah, long before Hegel, argued that a qualityless Absolute is non-being.

calypticism, periodization, and the idea of providential control (the dialectic of Spirit or Reason in Hegel treated materialistically by Marx). All of these ideas have pre-Christian ancient origins which we have already discussed in previous chapters: universality, periodization and providential control are characteristic of Greek cyclical views; apocalypticism of Zoroastrian thought; Marx's contribution lies in the attempt to give a more modern scientific foundation to these principles.

The aspect of Marxian philosophy most relevant to the thesis of this book is the cyclical periodization. Whereas Hegel's periodization is overtly biological (childhood, adolescence, manhood, old age of the concrete manifestation of Spirit),[1] Marx's periodization is cyclical. The major epochs of man's history are (1) the stage of primitive communism, (2) the stage of slavery, (3) feudalism, (4) capitalism, and (5) communism, a return to the beginning and thus the cycle is completed. Stages (1) and (5) have property in common public ownership and thus a classless society. The difference is in the dialectical dynamics whereby stage five does not precisely repeat stage one, but is a "higher synthesis" which includes the previous stages of production within itself. Stage five is merely a repetition of one in *form,* not in concrete matter. For comprehension of this type of cycle we must understand the Hegelian dialectic as applied by Marx. The Law of the cycle (which corresponds with the operation of Providence in Augustine's and the Stoics' philosophy of history, and with the dialectic of Spirit or Reason in Hegel's) is dialectical, but belongs to the Marxian materialistic verson of dialectics.

Marx borrows and accepts the Hegelian view that nature animate and inanimate operates dialectically and as an organism; there are no atomic entities for Marx as there were none for Hegel. Marx disagrees only with Hegel's

---

[1] As we noted above Hegel was probably motivated by writers who borrowed the periodization of the *Book of Daniel* to divide history into four epochs whereas his dialectical pattern elsewhere is the triad.

idealistic interpretation of the dialectic. All reality in the Marxian view reduces itself to matter in motion, but emphasis is upon motion (energy-developmental dynamics) rather than upon matter. Dialectics is simply the "science" of the laws of motion "both of the external world and of human thought."[1] Matter and motion are prior to thought rather than the reverse. Logic itself is "merely the conscious reflex of the dialectical motion of the real world..."[2]

The major categories of the motion of the real world (borrowed from Hegel's logic) are three: (1) quantity, (2) quality, and (3) negation of negation. A contemporary accurate elucidation of the meaning of these categories by the British Communist, Maurice Cornforth, is valuable in showing us their significance for the Communist world today. Cornforth clarifies the first category, the "law of development" of quantity into the second category, quality, with an example taken from the writings of Marx's cotheoretician, Engels: Water has certain qualitative properties, but when a certain definite amount (quantity) of heat is applied to it, which causes the molecules of water to move farther apart from each other, a definite point is reached — called the nodal point at which the quantity of motion caused by the increased temperature causes the molecules to separate so that they become volatile. At this point water becomes steam and a new *quality* is produced. The nodal point is the *leap* from one quality to another caused by an increase in quantity. All significant evolutionary changes in nature are explained similarly, e.g., the emergence of living from non-living matter.

It seems that philosophers of science and scientific method in the non-Communist world do not accept this Hegelian dialectic as a valid description of the mode of operation of the developmental changes in nature, organic or inor-

---

[1] Karl Marx and Friedrich Engels, *Selected Works*, Vol. II (London: Lawrence and Wishart, 1950) essay: "Feuerbach and the End of Classical German Philosophy," p. 350.

[2] *Ibid.*

ganic. However, in a restricted way these laws can be applied to certain historical phenomena. For example, the law of development of quantity into quality may be applied in the economic field thus: capitalism comes into being when there are *quantitatively* a sufficient number of capitalists to dominate the economic life of a country. The "nodal point" at which the "leap" from feudalism to capitalism takes place might be hard to ascertain, yet the idea of the leap is of crucial importance, apparently, in Communist theory as Stalin makes plain in the following passage which describes the "leap" from capitalism to socialism:

> Further, if the passing of slow quantitative changes into rapid and abrupt qualitative changes is a law of development, then it is clear that revolutions made by oppressed classes are a natural and inevitable phenomenon.
> Hence, the transition from capitalism to Socialism and the liberation of the working class from the yoke of capitalism cannot be effected by slow changes, by reforms, but only by a qualitative change of the capitalist system, by revolution.[1]

This passage dramatizes the "leap" and shows the difference between Menshevik democratic peaceful evolutionary socialism and Bolshevik socialism (Communism).

The third dialectical law is "negation of negation." Cornforth begins an explanation of this "law" by first making clear the difference between the meaning of this phrase as it is applied in formal logic and as it is applied to historical development. He points out that in formal logic the negation of the negation of a proposition yields merely the original proposition. For example, the negation of the proposition *This is a rose* is *This is not a rose;* the negation of the negation merely yields the original proposition *This is a rose.*

---

[1] Joseph Stalin, *Dialectical and Historical Materialism* (Moscow: Foreign Languages Publishing House, 1951), p. 16.

Next, to make clear the difference which he thinks exists between negation of negation in formal logic and in what he and the Communists generally call concrete logic (or historical development), he reviews the main stages of human history as Marx[1] and all subsequent Communists have understood it. The quotation from Cornforth which follows summarizes not only negation of negation and the other two "laws" but summarizes all the essential ideas of Communist theory mentioned above. *Let us notice especially his description with reference to the one grand cycle view of human history and the apocalyptic climax of the cycle.*

Society develops from *primitive communism* to the *slave* system. The next stage is *feudalism*. The next stage is *capitalism*. Each stage arises from the previous one, and negates it. So far we have simply a succession of stages, each following as the *negation* of the other and constituting a *higher* stage of development. But what comes next? *Communism.* Here there is a *return to the beginning* but at a higher level of development. In place of primitive Communism based on extremely primitive forces of production comes Communism based on extremely advanced forces of production and containing within itself tremendous new potentialities of development. The old, primitive classless society has become the new and higher classless society. It has been raised, as it were, to a higher power, has reappeared on a higher level. But this has happened only because the old classless society was negated by the appearance of classes and the development of class society, and because finally class society, when it had gone through its whole development was itself negated by the working class taking power, ending exploitation of man by man, and establishing a new classless society on the foundation of all the achievements of the whole previous development.[1]

[1] Marx and Engels, *op. cit.*, Vol. II, "Socialism: Utopian and Scientific," pp. 107-142.
[1] Cornforth, *op. cit.*, pp. 112 f. My italics.

First let us examine the logic of the law of "negation of negation" as it is illustrated in this passage. A critic might point out that there was never a negation of any total system mentioned but that elements of one were carried over into the other. Where these elements were carried over they were not negated and where they were negated they were not carried over but lost or destroyed. For example, in the change from capitalism to socialism the actual negation is concerned only with the character of the ownership of the means of production. It is not true that they are both privately and publicly owned in the same sense under both systems taken in their "pure" forms. The negation (public ownership) of one set of relations private ownership, if it is really a negation, destroys that set even though the way is made clear for public ownership, the new and directly opposed set of relations.

It seems bad logic to take a system as complicated as feudalism or capitalism and call it negated as a totality, then call the facts obviously not negated the negation of negation in a "higher synthesis." The truth seems to be that some elements of a system and culture are "negated," destroyed, or lost, and some are carried over into the succeeding socio-economic system either because of cultural lag or because they remain useful under the new conditions. The family, for example, has remained as an institution throughout many cultural epochs and is still found a valuable institution in contemporary Russia, the "socialist" state.

The Communists themselves are under no obligation to follow the dialectic; Lenin, himself, long ago abandoned it. In criticism of the dialectic he wrote:

> It is clear to everybody that the main burden of Engels' argument is that materialists must depict the historical process correctly and accurately, and that insistence on . . . selection of examples which demonstrate the correctness of the triad is nothing but a relic of Hegelianism . . . And, indeed, once it has been cate-

gorically declared that to attempt to prove anything by triads is absurd, what significance can examples of 'dialectical' process have . . . Anyone who reads the definition and description of the dialectical method given by Engels will see that the Hegelian triads are not even mentioned, and that it all amounts to regarding social evolution as a natural-historical process of development . . .

What Marx and Engels called the dialectical method is nothing more nor less than the scientific method in sociology, which consists in regarding society as a living organism in a constant state of development, the study of which requires an objective analysis of the relations of production which constitute the given social formation and an investigation of its laws of functioning and development.[1]

Cornforth comments on the above quotation: "As regards the study of society, and the estimate we make of the real social changes on which we base our political strategy, Lenin ridiculed those who took some abstract preconceived scheme as their guide." At the same time Stalin holds to the dialectic in his *Dialectical and Historical Materialism* and until the Malenkov regime even biologists had to use the "preconceived scheme." Cornforth himself as we have seen takes great pains to explain and illustrate the dialectical laws. The only conclusion that one can draw is that Lenin and subsequent Communists hold to concreteness as the essential element in dialectical materialism. This is because their main interest lies in seizure of power by whatever means or at whatever time is possible without regard to any preconceived dialectical pattern worked out by Marx and Engels. Lenin set the example by showing, contrary to Marxist laws of dialectical development, that socialism was possible in Russia without the prior developmental stage of capitalism.

But let us repeat, concreteness (which means political

---

[1] Lenin: *What the Friends of the People are and How They Fight the Social Democrats*, Part I. Quoted in Cornforth, *op. cit.*, p. 89.

and ideological expediency) is the important and decisive factor. Where the law of dialectical development interferes with the progress and victory of Communism it is abandoned, but where it aids the Communist cause it is played up as an essential element in Marxism. It is an aid to Communist theory and morale especially in its doctrine that the dialectic as applied to human history makes the victory of Communism inevitable. Marx's exposition of the reasons for this victory is given in terms of the dialectic. First he points out that the bourgeoisie as a class at once posits its negative, the proletariat. The one class cannot exist, cannot be a reality, without its other. These two main and opposing classes face each other. The proletariat is bound, inevitably, to win the struggle against the bourgeoisie because of the contradictions inherent in capitalism. War, trade unions, colonial expansion alleviate the situation as temporary remedies, but eventually the entire capitalistic system is doomed to collapse. Then social ownership, planned production for use, will come into being as the only solution of the contradictions. Social ownership (or socialism) is the negation of the negation and the final end or goal of the dialectical cycle. Thus the law of the dialectic makes Communism inevitable.

The picture of the state of man when the cycle of the dialectic is fulfilled resembles the Kingdom of Heaven idea of Christianity. It is man's return to Eden (primitive Communism for the Marxist) but at a much higher developmental level. It is like the apocalyptic goal painted by Condorcet which we described above. Engels in his essay: "Socialism: Utopian and Scientific" speaks of this heavenly era as one dominated by the ethical principle of brotherly love, a time when the productive forces of the world are owned by all humanity in common, a time when "the free development of each is the condition for the free development of all."[1]

---
[1] Marx and Engels, *op. cit.*, Vol. II, "Socialism: Utopian and Scientific" and Vol. I, "Manifesto of the Communist Party," p. 51.

It is the time when all men will become truly free for the first time. Freedom is much emphasized and eulogized as the goal just as in Hegel's philosophy. Engels writes:

> With the seizing of the means of production by society, production of commodities is done away with, and simultaneously the mastery of the product over the producer. Anarchy in social production is replaced by systematic definite organization. The struggle for individual existence disappears. Then for the first time, man, in a certain sense, is finally marked off from the rest of the animal kingdom, and emerges from mere animal conditions of existence into really human ones ... The laws of his own social action, hitherto standing face to face with man as laws of nature foreign to, and dominating him, will then be used with full understanding, and so mastered by him ... The extraneous objective forces that have hitherto governed history pass under the control of man himself. Only from that time will man himself, more and more consciously, make his own history — only from that time will the social causes set in movement by him have, in the main and in a constantly growing measure, the results intended by him. It is the ascent of man from the kingdom of necessity to the kingdom of freedom.[1]

Here we find the complete secularization of the Hegelian dialectic functioning to achieve the Enlightenment goal so nobly conceived by Condorcet. It is important to notice that the "laws" of the dialectic operate mechanically and absolutely before the stage of freedom is achieved. Not only is this true in the sphere of nature and in the functioning of economic causes as described above, but in all phases of human culture. This is because the entire cultural superstructure of every economic era is merely the ideological aspect of the economic substructure. This idea is brought out by Marx in a famous and oft-quoted passage:

> In the social production of their life, men enter into

---
[1] *Ibid.*, Vol. II, Essay, "Socialism: Utopian and Scientific," pp. 140-141.

definite relations that are indispensable and independent of their will, relations of production which correspond to a definite stage of development of their material productive forces ... The mode of production of material life conditions the social, political and intellectual life process in general. It is not the consciousness of men that determines their being, but, on the contrary, their social being that determines their consciousness ... With the change of the economic foundation the entire immense superstructure is more or less rapidly transformed. In considering such transformations a distinction should always be made between the material transformation of the economic conditions of production, which can be determined with the precision of natural science, and the legal, political, religious, aesthetic or philosophic — in short, ideological forms in which men become conscious of this conflict and fight it out.[1]

This passage makes it plain that the economic determinism operating in accordance with dialectic law is absolute in all phases of human activity and culture throughout the historical cycle from primitive communism to the return to communism. It is only after the cycle is complete that man becomes free of this absolute determinism by economic causes which themselves are an aspect of impersonal natural law operating at the biosociological level. Emancipation from the cycle when the inevitable return to communism occurs, enables man for the first time to become truly free, for now "the extraneous objective forces that have hitherto governed history pass under the control of man himself ... It is the ascent of man from the kingdom of necessity to the kingdom of freedom." [2] The new Communism of freedom like the Hegelian idea of freedom is the new and higher grand concrete synthesis of all the

---

[1] Karl Marx, "Preface to the Critique of Political Economy," Marx and Engels, *Selected Works, op. cit.,* Vol. I, pp. 328 f.

[2] Frederick Engels, "Socialism Utopian and Scientific," Marx and Engels, *Selected Works, Ibid.,* Vol. II, p. 141.

lower stages of development. The Kingdom of Freedom is the end and goal of history. In form it corresponds with the new Eden, the millennium and Kingdom of God or Heaven which is the goal of human history in Zoroastrian and Hebrew-Christian philosophies; all are paralleled by the Oriental ideas of Freedom to be attained by the soul liberated from the determinism of the Wheel of Karma. Progress of the spirit of man out of the determinism of cycles (whether one or innumerable) has a definite direction: Freedom from the determination of mundane physical, psychological and sociological causes, freedom for self-determination. The Marxian self-determination remains more within the empirical limited sphere, the human, whereas the Hegelian and Oriental Hindu and Buddhist self-determination is that of the One cosmic and infinite Being. The Western Marxian and Hegelian as well as the Oriental cycles already described have very significant goals beyond the determinism of the cycle. But a real rapprochement between East and West is far more pronounced in the one-cycle theories of history proposed by the two greatest Indian philosophers of the twentieth century, Sarvepalli Radhakrishnan and Sri Aurobindo. Of the two Sri Aurobindo is somewhat closer to Marx, Radhakrishnan to St. Augustine and Toynbee.

Chapter VI

Sri Aurobindo's One-Cycle Theory of History: The Involution and Evolution of the Infinite

Sri Aurobindo sees cosmic history as the process of Involution and Evolution of the Infinite Spirit. This resembles Hegel's philosophy of history but with the very important exception that the concrete manifestation of Spirit shown in cosmic history is not an essential one in Aurobindo's thought as in Hegel's. Aurobindo's more characteristically Hindu concept of the Infinite is that of a Being whose reality is manifested only in a partial manner by the cosmos; there is an infinite depth unmanifested.

The basic cosmic historical process, the involution and evolution of the Infinite is not caused through any kind of necessity. It occurs simply because the Infinite One in delight or play *(lila)* chooses to manifest a richly creative activity which is a revelation of an aspect of Himself in the Many, the multiple world of concrete existence.

The Involution of the Infinite is its descent into the lowest level of Being, Matter. Matter is called also the Inconscient level. Then Evolution begins and the Inconscient rises to the Subconscient or Life level of Being. Next evolves the self-conscious or Mental level, the human. Beyond this, and the final goal of the evolutionary process is the Gnostic level, the Supramental, but this level has not yet been reached.

In defense of his theory of cosmic and human history understood as the Involution and Evolution of an aspect of the Infinite Being, Aurobindo appeals to Western empirical evolutionary theories of man and nature; he appeals also to the typically Eastern intuitive Yogic type of empiricism. Only the latter needs elaboration for Western readers.

The Yogic experience, as interpreted by the Tantric schools, Aurobindo tells us, can be looked upon as parallel to the macrocosmic Involution-Evolution cycle. Involution is represented in this experience by the Kundalini, "eternal Force coiled up in the body in the bottom root vessel or chamber, *muladhara*, pedestal, earth-centre of the physical nervous system." [1] This corresponds to the Involution at the macrocosmic level. Evolution begins when the Kundalini "is struck by the freely coursing breath, by the current of Life which enters into search for her." [2] When awakened by Life she "rises flaming up the ladder of the spinal chord and forces open centre after centre of the involved dynamic secrets of consciousness till at the summit she finds, joins and becomes one with the spirit. Thus she passes from an involution in inconscience through a series of opening glories of her powers into the greatest eternal superconscience of the spirit." [3] In this way the microcosmic Yogic experience confirms the macrocosmic Involution-Evolution cycle.

This cycle in its main outline resembles St. Augustine's philosophy of history. In both there is a procession of the world from the Infinite; in both there is a "fall" and subsequent return to the Divine World. The Fall of Augustine's philosophy is paralleled by the "descent into Matter" in Aurobindo's idea of cosmic history, but with marked ethical differences. Augustine's Fall is due to the Pride of God's created beings whereas Aurobindo's "descent into Matter" and the evolutionary ascent is conceived much more from the point of view of a Hegelian spiritual naturalism. There are affinities also in Aurobindo's cyclic

---

[1] Sri Aurobindo, *The Problem of Rebirth* (Pondicherry: Sri Aurobindo Ashram, 1952), p. 76.

[2] *Ibid.*

[3] *Ibid.*

theory of history with the Marxian one-cycle view, as we shall see later in this chapter.

Aurobindo sees the human psyche at the Mental level of Being striving in birth after birth [4] towards the next and final evolutionary level, the level of the Gnostic Being. The advent of this new level, Sri Aurobindo claims, is the only permanent cure for man's social ills. All cosmic history and all human history has functioned and is at present functioning to usher in this new evolutionary development which is the goal of history. Aurobindo sees the present era of human society not merely as a transitional one but as bringing to an end a whole evolutionary level. Socialist, Communist, and Capitalist — even religious remedies — offered as solutions for the crisis which prevails in the human world can merely be temporary stop-gap palliatives. The real and the only permanent solution is the advent of the Gnostic Being, the new evolutionary level.

Aurobindo's description of this level which he calls by the names Gnostic, Supermind, Superman, Supramental is based largely upon the state attained by yogins in the trance called *Samadhi*. The Gnostic level of being will have all the powers experienced in *Samadhi* but in perfection and permanently and continuously. The Gnostic being will know all levels of existence — matter, life, and mind — intuitively. This means that his knowledge will be knowledge by *identity* (noumenal knowledge) instead of the phenomenal, subject-object knowledge of discursive reason characteristic of the present Mind level of evolutionary nature. The subliminal depths of the psyche are even at this present evolutionary level in subconscious contact with the Matter, Life, Cosmic Mind and Supermind levels of Being; but at the Supermind level this subconscious will

---

[4] Aurobindo accepts the Hindu-Buddhist theory of the soul's rebirth. He argues that if there is some element in us which cannot be accounted for by heredity (evolutionary) and environment but "presupposes a past or admits a future evolution other than that of the race mind and the physical ancestry, then some kind of soul birth becomes a logical necessity." *(Ibid.,* pp. 36-37.)

become completely conscious; there will be *noumenal* knowledge of Matter, Life, and Mind. Such knowledge will obviously give control over physical nature — all energy problems will be solved for the benefit of all beings; it will yield control over biological nature which means that all disease and even death will be conquered (Gnostic Beings will be immortal or change bodies by choice); and finally there will be complete control at the Mind level, because Supramental beings will have noumenal k n o w l e d g e of mind-processes and complete control over them. All this is possible since Supramental beings will know intuitively the Infinite, the Absolute Being or Spirit whose concrete manifestation *is* the evolution of the levels realized in this and in other universes. With noumenal knowledge of and identity with the Infinite, the Gnostic Being will see himself both as Macrocosm and Microcosm, as the One and the many, as Infinite and Finite. Aurobindo describes this pantheistic identity of the One and Many in numerous passages of which the following is typical:

> The Master and Mover of our works is the One, the Universal and Supreme, the Eternal and the Infinite. He is the transcendent unknown or unknowable Absolute, the unexpressed and unmanifested Ineffable above us; but he is also the Self of all beings, the Master of all worlds, transcending all worlds, the Light and the Guide, the All-Beautiful and All-Blissful, the Beloved and the Lover. He is the Cosmic Spirit and all this creative Energy around us; he is the Immanent within us. All that is he, and he is the More than all that is, and we ourselves, though we know it not, are being of his being, force of his force, conscious with a consciousness derived from his; even our mortal existence is made out of his substance and there is an immortal within us that is a spark of the Light and Bliss that are forever.[1]

Such realization of Self as One and yet become Many in

---
[1] Sri Aurobindo, *On Yoga, Book I, The Synthesis of Yoga, op. cit.*, p. 279.

the universes is the realization state which Aurobindo calls Sachchidananda. Sachchidananda means Being-Consciousness-Bliss; it is this state which is reached by the Gnostic Being. Aurobindo describes it as follows:

> It is this Chit [consciousness] which modifies itself so as to become on the Truth-plane, the Supermind, on the mental plane the mental reason, will, emotion, sensation, on the lower planes the vital or physical instincts, impulses, habits of an obscure force not in superficially conscious possession of itself. All is Chit because All is Sat [Being]; all is various movement of the original Consciousness because all is various movement of the original Being.
>
> When we find, see or know Chit, we find also that its essence is Ananda or delight of self-existence. To possess self is to possess self-bliss; not to possess self is to be in more or less obscure search of the delight of existence. Chit eternally possesses its self-bliss; and since Chit is the universal conscious-stuff of being, conscious universal being is also in possession of conscious self-bliss, master of the universal delight of existence. The Divine whether it manifests itself in All-Quality or in No-Quality, in Personality or Impersonality, in the One absorbing the Many or in the One manifesting its essential multiplicity, is always in possession of self-bliss and all-bliss because it is always Sachchidananda.[1]

The progress of the soul towards such self-realization is described in terms of the general yogic pattern already delineated,[2] which itself as we noted represents in microcosm the cyclic pattern of the macrocosm, but there are some differences in emphasis in Aurobindo's yoga. Aurobindo calls his yoga the integral yoga and believes that through practice of this yoga man can expedite the advent of the new Gnostic or Supramental level of being. He claims that the integral yoga is based upon "true Vedanta"

[1] *Ibid.*, p. 445.
[2] *Supra*, Part II, chaps. VI and VII.

versus what he takes to be the mistaken Vedanta of Shankara. "True Vedanta" says Aurobindo, does not, as in Shankara's thought, make the universe a merely phenomenal appearance of the Infinite Being, but a real, a concrete manifestation of the Infinite. If this "true Vedanta" is accepted the individual is induced to take a positive constructive approach to life in this world instead of the negative escapist attitude which supposedly follows from Shankara's view. (Other great thinkers such as Radhakrishnan do not agree with Aurobindo's criticism. See above Part I, chapter VII).

Aurobindo eulogizes his interpretation of Vedanta as having a very positive, creative approach to life in this world. His system makes clear that this world and its living beings are all concrete and real manifestations of the Infinite as it shows itself in the Involution and Evolution of the universe. Life in this world has, therefore, noumenal value. In the integral yoga this is manifested in the importance attached to all three yogas — the yogas of action, of love and of knowledge. The yoga of action means egoless action, action without attachment to the rewards or punishments of action; the yoga of love means egoless love for man and the Infinite Being; the yoga of knowledge means the intuitive knowledge (knowledge by identity) already described above.[1] All three yogas are integrated into one harmony. God is realized as present in every aspect of nature — material, biological, mental, spiritual — all is divine. Such an integrated yogic consciousness of the Divine Harmony, unity and Gnosis in all things can expedite the birth of the Gnostic Being; the activity of the Infinite in its evolutionary ascent is, however, even more necessary. The Infinite descends to us from above, we strive through an integral yoga from below; both in cooperation can bring in the age of the new Gnostic Being. This interplay between the divine and the human resembles Augustine's idea of

---

[1] Aurobindo is simply following here the three yogas described in such classic Indian philosophical works as the *Bhagavad-Gita*.

the grace of God coming to man to redeem him for life in the City of God and man's response.

When the Gnostic level of evolutionary development arrives, there will be a new social order; for the new Gnostic beings with their direct, immediate and intuitive knowledge of their own and the mental, vital, and material levels of Nature will be able and anxious to use all aspects of Nature for the enrichment of the spiritual life of all beings, unlike present man (a mental-level being) who is tyrannized over by his subconscient biological drives, physical wants and by material Nature. The new human society as Aurobindo glowingly conceives it will be a spiritual socialism, although he himself does not call it by this name. In this new social order there will be no source of conflict between individualism and altruism. The self of each Gnostic Being will be one with the self of all; for each will see the other as a "poise of being," a center for concrete action and creativity of the Infinite Spirit. Each will know and feel intuitively his fellow beings since he has the Gnostic Knowledge-by-Identity versus the confused kind of knowledge we now have of other persons. All will have a continuous yogic consciousness (similar to but surpassing the consciousness and knowledge of angels in Christianity). There can be no conflicts, therefore, because of misunderstanding or of overlapping fields of action and creativity. In the society of Gnostic Beings there would be no such thing as "war with its spirit of antagonism and enmity, its brutality, destruction and ignorant violence, political strife with its perpetual conflict, frequent oppression, dishonesties, turpitudes, selfish interests, ignorance, ineptitude and muddle."[1] With the advent of this new and final evolutionary level of Being, the Involution-Evolution cycle will be complete. The concrete universe will then in the Gnostic Being have returned self-consciously to the Infinite from whence it came.

---

[1] Sri Aurobindo, *The Life Divine* (Pondicherry: Sri Aurobindo Ashram, 1955), p. 1267.

To recapitulate, the Divine Being, the One, through self-alienation has manifested itself in an opposite, Matter, then has evolved Itself through stages of Life and Mind to the level of the Gnostic Being, the return to pure Spirit. Yet the Gnostic Being, though realizing its unity with the one infinite Spirit, realizes itself also as one of the many concrete "poises of being" of this Infinite because Gnostic Beings will still have material bodies over which, however, they will have complete control.

Aurobindo's one-cycle view of history is a cycle from the Divine to the Divine and from this point of view similar to St. Augustine's idea of the cyclic odyssey of the human soul which has come from God and Eden (earthly Paradise) and returns (with difficulty because of the Fall) to God and the Heavenly Paradise. Aurobindo places his "angels" in this world but spiritually there is little difference in the ultimate divine society which is the goal of the One-Grand-Cycle of human and cosmic history.

The affinity with Marxism is not only the one-cycle notion of history but the consummation of the cycle in a society of freely cooperating beings whose maxim will be in Marxian phraseology "All for each and each for all." This society will be a paradise in *this* world; and here Aurobindo and Marx are in agreement. There is a similarity also in the view that the process of development in history evolves from deterministic stages (the Matter, Life, Mind levels in Aurobindo's thought) to Freedom. The difference lies in the emphasis upon the priority, the absoluteness of Spirit in Aurobindo's system versus the priority of Matter in Marxian philosophy. Indian thought is characteristically idealist, however, and Aurobindo's only originality lies in his theory that evolution on this planet is about to achieve a new and final stage, the level of the Gnostic Being; and this will mean a Paradise on this earth of indefinite duration.

We turn now to Radhakrishnan's philosophy of history based also upon classical Indian idealist thought.

Chapter VII

Radhakrishnan's One-Cycle Idea of History

The great Indian philosopher and statesman Radhakrishnan also sees human history and the history of this universe as one cycle versus the usual Indian multi-cycle view discussed in Part I of this book. Like Aurobindo Radhakrishnan offers a metaphysical system grounded in a typically Indian idealism, but with full and critical knowledge of the best achievements in Western philosophy. Both Sri Aurobindo (also a master of Western lore) and Radhakrishnan think that Indian thought is in many ways superior to that of the West because of the major emphasis of Indian philosophy upon the life of Spirit as man's goal. Western philosophical thought is too often mere criticism, or skepticism or materialism, and at best Intellect rather than Spirit is given the place of the highest category.

Radhakrishnan posits Being as the primal reality. Being is the Absolute, the source of all that exists, although it is not Itself any existent thing like an animal or an individual.[1] The Absolute (Being) is pure Spirit and Freedom. Why the Absolute freely chose to realize the particular possibility which is this world is to us a mystery which we can only acknowledge as the "will of God."[2] The Absolute has two aspects: the impersonal, timeless, spaceless Brahman in eternal calm and peace; the personal Ishvara, which

---
[1] Sarvepalli Radhakrishnan, "The Religion of the Spirit and the World's Need," (Fragments of a Confession), *The Philosophy of Sarvepalli Radhakrishnan*, ed. Paul Arthur Schilpp (New York: Tudor Publishing Co., 1952), p. 38.
[2] *Ibid.*, p. 39.

307

is the "Absolute in action as Lord and Creator."[3] Ishvara is the Absolute in "conscious active delight creatively pouring out its powers and qualities."[4]

The Absolute is infinite "because it possesses infinite possibilities" and it abides in Freedom. It has chosen to enter "into the world of non-spirit to realize one of the infinite possibilities that exist potentially in Spirit."[5] In this way the Unconditioned Being has become conditioned (limited) by creation of the specific possibility which is this world. The Absolute may be said to be Creator, Preserver, and Destroyer (that is He ultimately resolves the universe) for which the Indian names are respectively Brahma, Vishnu and Shiva. "The Ideas of Brahma" Radhakrishnan says, "are seeking concrete expression and Vishnu is assisting the world's striving for perfection."[1]

The world is real in status; it does not have the character of an illusion. It does, however, have dependent conditioned reality unlike the Absolute upon which the world depends. This, Radhakrishnan explains is what is meant by the doctrine of maya. The doctrine of maya "does not mean that the temporal process is a tragedy or an aberration. The reality of the world is not in itself but it is in the thought and being of the Creator."[2] Radhakrishnan interprets Shankara's idea of the classical doctrine of maya, unlike Aurobindo in as positive a sense as the Christian's doctrine of the God-dependent reality of the world. As in the Christian doctrine, also, Radhakrishnan posits a beginning and an end to the world and to time. What happens between the beginning and the end, in other words the history of the cosmos and of man especially, is full of significance. Radhakrishnan writes:

> Every moment in the temporal process is a moment of decision. It is charged with extreme tension. History

---
[3] *Ibid.*
[4] *Ibid.*
[5] *Ibid.* p. 40.
[1] *Ibid.* pp. 40 f.

is not a cyclic movement. It is full of new things, because God works in it and reveals Himself in it. The end of the time process is the triumph of the World-Spirit or to use the phrases of Greek classical thought, the triumph of *Nous* over chaos.[3]

Radhakrishnan sees the historical world process as an involution-evolution cycle similar to that posited by Aurobindo. Radhakrishnan points out that the evolutionary idea is an ancient one in Indian thought. It is found, he says, in an ancient Upanishad the *Taittiriya* (eighth century B.C.), and in the chapter on Indian cyclical views in Part I of this book[4] we have seen that the evolutionary concept of nature is probably older (ninth century B. C.) if the reverse process may properly be called evolutionary.[1] The *Taittiriya* does describe a true evolutionary process equivalent to Aurobindo's and the Western theory of universal evolution, that is, a process beginning with matter, evolving in the next stage to life then to consciousness of a perceptual-instinctive kind, then to the stage of reflective consciousness and ultimately achieving spiritual consciousness.[2] Radhakrishnan comments that in this Upanisad there is "the successive emergence of the material, the organic, the animal the human and the spiritual orders of existence."[3]

Radhakrishnan's view of the evolutionary cycle is a similar one. He begins however with the Sankhya[4] concepts of

---

[2] *Ibid.* p. 41.
[3] *Ibid.*, p. 42.
[4] *Supra*, Part I, Chap. III.
[1] Each cycle begins with a Paradise Age and evolves into a final fourth age of extreme moral chaos. However Prabhavananda and Isherwood use the phrase "evolutionary cycle" with reference to the Sankhya cosmology which begins with the highest creative manifestations and descends to the lowest. (See their trans. of the *Bhagavad Gita, Mentor ed.* (New York, New American Library, 1951), p. 134.
[2] *Op. Cit.*, Radhakrishnan, p. 27.
[3] *Ibid.*
[4] *Ibid.*, p. 81.

309

Purusha and Prakrti. Prakrti is in a sense non-being, the potentiality of all things. "It is the unmanifested imperceptible, all but nothing, capable of receiving, though not without resistance, existence, form and meaning." Purusha (Spirit) is the positive principle which informs prakrti with meaning, and guides it in creative progress towards higher and higher evolutionary forms. Radhakrishnan writes:

> The splendour of Spirit, which in Greek philosophy was identified with the transcendental and timeless world of Ideas, or in Christian thought is reserved for the divine supernatural sphere, is making use of natural forces in the historical world. The highest product of cosmic evolution, ananda or spiritual freedom, must also be the hidden principle at work, slowly disclosing itself. Spirit creates the world and controls its history by a process of perpetual incarnation. Spirit is working in matter that matter may serve the Spirit.[5]

Radhakrishnan points out in the above quotation the likeness to Greek ideas in the relation between matter (prakrti) and form (Spirit *Nous*, or the World of Ideas) and the Christian idea of Incarnation. He adds also a Hegelian-Marxian dialectical notion to his metaphysics when he says that "the world process can only be conceived as a struggle between two antagonistic but indispensable principles of being and non-being."[1] Prakrti nevertheless is throughout a dependent aspect of the Absolute, the One, and equivalent to Maya. Prakrti (maya) is the matter of the object world given form in its evolutionary stages by the Purusha (Spirit or the Absolute manifesting itself in the creative process).

---
[5] *Ibid.*
[1] *Ibid.*, p. 31. The Marxian school as the reader knows differs from Radhakrishnan and Indian idealism and from Hegelian idealism in metaphysics. Spirit is the absolute and prior reality in idealism whereas matter is prior and "spirit" a later evolutionary development out of and dependent upon, matter in Marxian materialism.

The goal of the creative process has not yet been reached. Like Aurobindo, Radhakrishnan believes that the stage of Spirit is next in evolution; this is the goal of the entire cosmic historical process.

> The meaning of history is to make all men prophets, to establish a kingdom of free spirits. The infinitely rich and spiritually impregnated future, this drama of the gradual transmutation of intellect into spirit, of the son of man into the son of God, is the goal of history. When death is overcome, when time is conquered, the kingdom of the eternal spirit is established.[2]

Man is now as a race at the level of intellect, the stage of Spirit is next and when this is reached history and time come to an end. Man has the freedom to rise to the level of Spirit even now, for it is apparent that saints and sages have achieved liberation into the spiritual plane. The human will is free, but is subject to the mechanical forces of Karma when dominated by selfish motivations (egoity). Freedom from Karma and liberation into the spiritual plane is achieved through prayer and meditation which opens the self to communion with the Eternal Spirit, "the very power to which necessity or Karma is in subjection."[3] The Spirit illuminated in us can help us create a new world for all men. This is necessary, for ultimate Freedom in the absolute sense (union with the Absolute) cannot be attained until the entire human race achieves the level of Spirit. The individual who achieves this level must retain his individuality until all others have reached this condition. The reason is:

> ... Complete liberation implies not only harmony within the self but also harmony with the environment. Complete freedom is therefore impossible in an imperfect world. Those who have attained to the con-

---
[2] *Ibid.*, p. 30.
[3] *Ibid.*, p. 43.

sciousness of the Eternal work within the world to set other men forward in their journey toward the goal. In a true sense the ideal individual and the perfect society arise together.[1]

When all men have reached the level of Spirit, the level of knowledge of and enjoyment in the absolute values, the *Brahmaloka* or Kingdom of God on earth will have arrived. This will be the end of the historical cycle. Radhakrishnan says, "There is a coincidence of the beginning and the end."[2] The process of history has come from the Divine Spirit and to the Divine Spirit it returns. "When everyone achieves his fulfilment, the cosmic purpose is fulfilled."[3] Then, "the end of the process is in continuity with the beginning and when the two coincide, cosmic existence lapses into Absolute Being."[4] *The historical cycle as in Augustine's and Aurobindo's views is one unique creative process in a circle from God to God, an alienation from and return to the Absolute.*

Radhakrishnan is certain that the world-cycle must come to an end. He argues:

The meaning of time is beyond the confines of time. Time has meaning because it comes to an end. If it is unending, it is meaningless. Time process can be understood only in the light of the end it aims at; the victory over time, the victory over this disrupted, fallen condition, victory over alienation, estrangement, enslavement by the objective. We conceive the end as taking place in historical time, though it is illogical to relate to history in simply historical terms what is beyond history. Though it may not be possible for us to think of the end of time except in terms of time, yet the end is not a term in the time series. It belongs to another order of existence, inasmuch as it marks the

[1] *Ibid.*, p. 43.
[2] *Ibid.*, p. 45.
[3] *Ibid.*, p. 46.
[4] *Ibid.*

end of time itself. It is victory over time. It is life eternal.[5]

The more fundamental and basic evidence given for the swallowing up of time in eternity is derived from "integral insight" a mode of knowledge beyond the subject-object categories of intellect. As in Aurobindo's Gnostic level of being and knowledge, the soul who attains "integral insight" has "knowledge by identity,"[1] which, of course, "transcends the distinction of subject and object."[2] The intellectual level (discursive reasoning), Radhakrishnan affirms, "is an instrument for attaining to the truth of the spirit, but the inward realisation of the truth of spirit transcends all intellectual verification, since it exists in an immediacy beyond all conceivable mediation."[3] This "inward realisation" achieved through integral insight is direct "unmediated apprehension of the primordial Spirit."[4] Such apprehension can be reached only by the twice-born soul, the soul who has renounced its ego-desires (karma), overcome *avidya* (ignorance), and thus achieves a changed consciousness which opens it to direct knowledge of the Eternal. It is this kind of direct knowledge which yields certainty that time will be swallowed up in eternity; in the experience of integral insight this eternal state has already been tasted. This ecstatic experience of God is "the fulfilment of man."[5] In our hurried lives such divine moments may be few but they shed joy over our being and change our lives into centres of divine action.

Radhakrishnan is emphatic in denying the charge of "escapism" often directed against the saints who have centered their lives upon the Eternal Spirit and live in almost

[5] *Ibid.*
[1] *Ibid.*, p. 60.
[2] *Ibid.*, p. 61.
[3] *Ibid.*
[4] *Ibid.*
[5] *Ibid.*, p. 63.

continuous consciousness of the One Supreme. He describes these emancipated beings who have achieved the level of Spirit thus:

> Selfish action is not possible for them. Ignorance and craving have lost their hold. They are dead to pride, envy, and uncharitableness. The world in which they live is no more alien to them. It is hospitable, not harsh. It becomes alive, quakes, and sends forth its greetings. Human society becomes charged with the grace and grandeur of the eternal. These free spirits reach out their hands towards the warmth in all things. They have that rarest quality in the world, simple goodness, beside which all the intellectual gifts seem a little trivial. They are meek, patient, long-suffering. They do not judge others because they do not pretend to understand them. Because of their eager selfless love they have the power to soothe the troubled heart. To those in pain their presence is like the cool soft hand of some one they love, when their head is hot with fever. The released individuals are artists in creative living. With an awareness of the Eternal, they participate in the work of the world. Even as the Supreme has two sides of pure being and free activity, these liberated souls, who are the vehicles of divine life, have also two sides: the contemplative and the active.
> ... Their life is socially minded. We are members of a whole, parts of the brahmanda (the cosmic egg), which is one, which is perpetually in transition until its final purpose is achieved ... Their attitude is not one of lofty condescension or patronising pity to lift a debased creature out of mire. But it is a conviction of the solidarity of the world *loka-samgraha* and a recognition that the low and the high are bound together in one spirit. Vicarious suffering, not vicarious punishment, is a law of spiritual life. The free spirits bend to the very level of the enslaved to emancipate their minds and hearts. They inspire, revive and strengthen the life of their generation.[1]

---
[1] *Ibid.*, p. 65.

Such is the description of the spirit-level beings towards which the creative historical process is directed. Those who have achieved this level lead an active life (as well as a contemplative) to emancipate the others who also belong to the one organic Whole. The others are still in a "fallen" condition. Radhakrishnan thinks that the Christian doctrine of the Fall of Man is best understood when explained as man's tasting of the tree of knowledge of good and evil (the dawn of ethical consciousness), an act which entailed the "unhappy consciousness" that man alone has of needing to get out of the fallen condition. To get out of the fallen state man has withdrawn from his animal condition of integration with the environment. This withdrawal is not purposeless but drives man on to "integration at a higher level," ultimately the Spiritual Level.

When all have achieved the level of Spirit, the cosmic process will have achieved its purpose and goal and history and time will end. Cosmic existence then "lapses into Absolute Being."[1] However, this means an end of this particular universe only; Radhakrishnan maintains that God is "infinite possibility," and is not to be identified with this particular evolutionary process. He is "not merely the past, present, and the future of this world, he is the transcendental principle of this and all possible worlds, whether they are to be realised or not."[2] Besides, Radhakrishnan adds, if this universe according to the scientific views, is manifesting a degradation of energy it must once have been wound up at the beginning and will show an energy-end; if so, "if it was wound up once, what prevents it from being wound up again, if another possibility requiring this type of structure is to be started?"[3] Here Radhakrishnan affirms the possibility of a cyclical repetition of the "name and form" pattern of this particular universe, a view in

---
[2] *Ibid.*, p. 49.
[1] *Ibid.*, p. 46.
[2] *Ibid.*
[3] *Ibid.*, pp. 46 f.

315

harmony with Shankara's, and traditional Indian philosophy but with the very significant qualification that such a repetition is a possibility rather than a characteristic process.

Similarities between Radhakrishnan's and the Christian-Augustinian and Hegelian one-cycle theories of history. As in Augustine's version of the Christian philosophy of history, Radhakrishnan posits a one-cycle process directed by Spirit throughout, which begins with bondage, the self-alienation of Spirit, (symbolized by the Fall) and ends with the return to Spirit (Brahmaloka or the Kingdom of God), the kingdom of Freedom. In Hegel's philosophy of history there is a similar theory of the meaning and purpose of history. History begins for Hegel also with the self-alienation of Spirit in its dialectical opposite, Matter, then develops (as in Radhakrishnan's view) dialectically through the stages of Life, of Mind, and Spirit (the highest level of Mind or Reason.) Spirit is the goal of the development and at this level Freedom is realized. This Freedom is the self-conscious realization of the individual's identity with the Absolute as a partial and essential concrete manifestation of the Absolute's eternal being. The cycle from Spirit and the goal and end of the concrete process, the return to Spirit is the same in both Radhakrishnan's and Hegel's philosophies of history. F. H. Bradley in his great work *Appearance and Reality* shows that Hegel's concept of Spirit in terms of Reason — discursive reason with its mode of thought in terms and relations, subject-object categories — leads by its own logic (or any logic) beyond itself to an Absolute in which subject-object, terms and relations become one, immediate, eternal (timeless) Reality.[1] Such a Reality is what Radhakrishnan and the classical Indian idealists mean by Spirit. Radhakrishnan's interpretation of Spirit in relation to Western philosophy and religion (Christianity especially with its concept of Incarnation) bridges the gulf between Eastern and Western philosophy

---

[1] F. H. Bradley, *Appearance and Reality* (New York: Macmillan, 1908).

(idealist) and Eastern and Western religion in general including the philosophies of history which are integral parts of these systems. Radhakrishnan's bridging of the gulf is affirmed by such noted journals as the Times Literary Supplement (London) of May 3, 1934 in the following passage:

> The metaphysics of Radhakrishnan's Absolute Idealism represents a real fusion of East and West in so far as it boldly confronts the problem which haunted Bradley — that of the relation between the Absolute and the God of religious experience — and answers it in the form of an eschatology at which Bradley may have hinted in his denial of ultimate reality to the finite self, but which he never made fully explicit. Radhakrishnan suggests a solution of the problem which is, in essentials, derived from Indian Idealism endorsing the hypotheses of pre-existence and palingenesis, and envisaging a consummation wherein, all spirits being perfected at last and set free from the cycle of Karma, the purpose of God will be achieved and God Himself will lapse into the Absolute, creation being thus at once ransomed and annulled by the cessation of the impulse to individuate. This is no place to discuss the case for and against a subtle and elevated philosophical system; but it at least behoves every inquirer to ask himself whether the gulf between this eschatology and that which asserts the 'value and destiny of the individual' is or is not one which is ultimately bridgeable. Those who feel able to reply in the affirmative may well accept Radhakrishnan, not merely as the distinguished exponent of a lofty spiritual philosophy (as he assuredly is), but as the initiator of a new synthesis.[1]

Radhakrishnan's one cycle theory compared with the Marxian view. Radhakrishnan points out that Marxian dialectical materialism posits self-movement, dialectical in pattern, in nature which gives rise to creative activity, intelli-

---
[1] *Ibid.*, p. 47. Quoted by Radhakrishnan.

gence and the qualities which might be called spirit. However these developments emphasize the priority of matter rather than spirit which is a mere product of matter, a kind of conscious reasoning activity of matter. Radhakrishnan says that the Marxians affirm that "the way in which matter behaves is 'objective dialectic' and its reflection in consciousness is 'subjective dialectic.' "[2] Radhakrishnan thinks that the Marxians give no explanation of the relation between these two, what they give is merely "a method of interpretation, not a philosophy of history."[3] On the positive side they emphasize our kinship with nature "which implies a source of unity"[4] However the dualism between man and nature "cannot be abolished by making nature a form of spirit as in Hegel or spirit a form of nature as in Marx."[5] Both the Hegelian and the Marxian dialectic of nature, man and history, Radhakrishnan thinks, need to posit the Absolute Spirit from which has come and to which returns the entire concrete universe.

There does appear to be some likeness between the Marxian and Radhakrishnan's idealist view in the notion that the human society of this world is an organic one in which the maxim will be in the Kingdom of God (Brahmaloka) Age "All for each, and each for all." This goal (Freedom) is the end of human history in both views. The same goal is the end of history in the Augustinian-Christian theory of history. This organic society of all spirits (or men in Marxian language) is the reason and the goal of all the suffering, the agony and the toil of existence. The new Kingdom of God age, however, will be swallowed up in eternity for Radhakrishnan and the Christians whereas for Marx and Hegel the Kingdom will be one in this world, which is true also of Aurobindo's new kingdom of Gnostic Beings. Aurobindo in this respect is closer to bridging the gap be-

---
[2] *Ibid.*, p. 33.
[3] *Ibid.*
[4] *Ibid.*
[5] *Ibid.*

tween Marxian and Idealist thought than Radhakrishnan who, however, is closer to Christian ideas about the end of history.

All the modern views, however, discussed in this section—the Christian as classically formulated by St. Augustine, the Zoroastrian, the Hegelian, the Marxian, and the contemporary Indian idealist views of Aurobindo and Radhakrishnan — have in common a one-cycle view of human history, the goal of which is the emancipation of man in a new organic society in which the good of one is the good of all, the suffering of one the suffering of all, but because of this there will be little or no suffering; "there shall be no night there," for Love the bond of organic unity among these free spirits will rule. Will time then be swallowed up into eternity, will all be dissolved again into Absolute Being, the purpose and goal of the time process having been achieved? Radhakrishnan defends the classical Indian idealist position and the Christian in maintaining that this must occur; the other one-cycle thinkers discussed in this section deny such a consummation. No one can say with absolute certainty what will happen, but Radhakrishnan makes the classical Indian view [1] very plausible.

The next and final section of this book will be concerned with cyclic views which limit themselves to the much narrower range of human culture cycles. Only twentieth century theories and two great precursors of these theories will be sampled.

---
[1] The classical Indian idealist view is, of course, the multi-cycle philosophy of history; but in this view and in Radhakrishnan's this world-cycle ends in reabsorption into the Absolute; both views have this in common.

PART III

CULTURE CYCLES: TWENTIETH CENTURY VIEWS

Chapter I

Great Forerunners of Twentieth Century Culture Cycle Theories: Ibn Khaldun and Vico

Section 1

Ibn Khaldun: *The Muqaddimah* (completed 1377)

The first great name in twentieth century culture cycle theories is Oswald Spengler. Spengler sees history as a rise and decline cycle of human culture organisms, the macrocosms which have the same pattern of life cycle as the microcosmic human organisms. The stages of spring or childhood, summer or adolescence, autumn or maturity, and winter or senility each with characteristic phenomena has been anticipated at the more mythological level as early as the Great Year symbolism described in Part I of this book. But a more Western objective philosophical and sociological approach in which the organismic macrocosmic-microcosmic symbolism is applied was anticipated in the philosophy of history of the great Moslem historian, Ibn Khaldun, as we shall see below.

In his great introduction to his History, the *Muqaddimah*, Ibn Khaldun almost four centuries before Vico explicitly calls history a *science* and a social science.[1] The subject matter of this "independent science"[2] he informs us

---

[1] Ibn Khaldun, *The Muqaddimah*, An Introduction to History, trans. from the Arabic by Franz Rosenthal, 3 Vols., Bollingen Series XLIII (New York: Pantheon Books, 1958), Vol. I, p. 77.
[2] *Ibid.*

is information about human social organization, which itself is identical with world civilization. It deals with such conditions affecting the nature of civilization as, for instance, savagery and sociability, group feelings, and the different ways by which one group of human beings achieves superiority over another. It deals with royal authority and the dynasties that result (in this manner) and with the various ranks that exist within them. (It further deals) with the different kinds of gainful occupations and ways of making a living, with the sciences and crafts that human beings pursue as part of their activities and efforts, and with all the other institutions that originate in civilization through its very nature.[3]

He begins his study with the "positivist" theories of such later Western thinkers as Montesquieu and Buckle, viz., that geographical influences are largely responsible for the rise of higher cultures. Climate, he says, is very significant. In the temperate zones men are "more temperate (well-proportioned) in their bodies, color, character qualities, and (general) conditions."[1] They are in fact temperate in everything — houses, clothing, food, crafts — and have the best tools. The temperate zones he lists as the Maghrib, Syria, the two Iraqs, Western India, China, Spain, the lands of the European Christians, the Galicians. In the non-temperate zones such as Africa below Egypt and the cold north, home of the Slavs, men are like "dumb animals."[2]

Food, too, is significant in stimulating men to higher levels of activity. For example a milk diet makes animals and men healthy in body and acute in mental perceptions.

After this attempt to show that cultures are possible only in the temperate zones and among healthy people, Ibn Khaldun outlines the rise, the course and the fall of a civilization.[3] Actually he traces only the rise and fall cycle of a dynasty, but his generalizations by implication apply to the

[3] *Ibid.*, p. 71.
[1] *Ibid.*, p. 167.
[2] *Ibid.*, p. 168.

course of an entire civilization as such recent philosophers of history as Toynbee, Spengler and Sorokin use this term.

Man is the only animal who can think, Ibn Khaldun asserts, following Aristotle; and again following Aristotle Ibn Khaldun tells us that man is a political animal — his intelligence sees the advantage of cooperation in groups. Group living begins with the family which expands to tribal proportions. The nomadic stage (Bedouin) of human culture begins here and out of this stage higher civilizations develop. The pattern of such development is traced on the analogy of the life cycle of the microcosm, the human individual.

The human individual has a "natural life (span)" of one hundred and twenty years "in the opinion of physicians and astrologers," even though the "life of a Muslim lasts between sixty and seventy years."[4] The dynastic cycle of a civilization, too, has the same duration. Its duration is three generations and a generation is forty years.[1] In the fourth generation the end is reached (winter). Such a life cycle of a dynasty (civilization) follows the life cycle pattern of all things in nature, but especially man. Ibn Khaldun says:

> It should be known that the world of the elements and all it contains comes into being and decays. This applies to both its essences and its conditions. Minerals, plants, all the animals including man, and the other created things come into being and decay, as one can see with one's own eyes. The same applies to the conditions that affect created things, and especially the conditions that affect man. Sciences grow up and then are wiped out. The same applies to crafts, and to similar things.[2]

---

[3] By a civilization Ibn Khaldun means any stage beyond the savage state of human organization.

[4] *Ibid.* p. 343.

[1] *Ibid.*, p. 344.

[2] *Ibid.*, p. 278.

Civilization arises out of Bedouin tribal life; royal power (a dynasty) comes into being which lasts four generations — usually. In the first generation, which is the first stage of the rise of a civilization, there are the desert qualities of courage, toughness, rapaciousness, and therefore "the strength of group feeling continues to be preserved."[3] In the second generation, the second stage of the civilization, wealth is accumulated which makes a sedentary culture come into being. The desert qualities of strength begin to wane because one man (the ruler) now "claims all the glory for himself while the others are too lazy to strive for (glory), and from proud superiority"[4] their attitude is changed to a subservient one. This lessens the vigor of group feeling. Nevertheless some of the former strength of character remains in the men of this generation because they had direct, personal contact with the first generation.

The third generation has forgotten completely the desert qualities. Sedentary culture flourishes and reaches a zenith. "Luxury reaches its peak."[5] The ruler's government is one of force and people acquire dependent, subservient attitudes. They become "more cowardly than women upon their backs." The ruler must take men outside the blood or relative group for defense of the dynasty. "Group feeling disappears completely."[1] The outsiders have the status of mere paid workers, and the paid worker will not give life and limb for the group. These outside clients and supporters, therefore, are not sufficient to save the dynasty. Only where "group feeling" exists is there enough stimulus to risk life for the dynasty. With group feeling gone, the dynasty is "senile and worn out."[2] The fourth generation witnesses utter destruction of the "(ancestral) prestige." This is the end of the civilization. Then a provincial family rises to royal power and takes over the territory of the

[3] *Ibid.*, p. 344.
[4] *Ibid.*
[5] *Ibid.*
[1] *Ibid.*, p. 345.
[2] *Ibid.*, p. 345.

former House, or a foreign power invades. The new royal power, however, goes through exactly the same dynasty-cycle.

Ibn Khaldun has much to say about each of the stages in the cycle especially about the first and the third or sedentary stage when civilization is at a climax.

In the first stage group feeling is a prime phenomenon essential to the rise of royal power. Such group feeling characterizes Bedouins whose type of life is the basis for and always precedes sedentary or city life.[3] Group feeling "results only from (blood) relationship or something corresponding to it."[4] This "(respect for) blood ties is something natural among men, with the rarest exceptions."[5] It leads individuals to risk life and limb for a close or even distant relative and is the natural source for mutual support and aid in groups.[6] Group feeling also "increases the fear felt by the enemy."[7] The rise of a House to royal authority and large dynastic power can be attained only through the group and group feeling. "This is because . . . aggressive and defensive strength is obtained only through group feeling which means (mutual) affection and willingness to fight and die for each other."[1] Nobility and a House from whence royal authority is derived are possible only for those who share in the group feeling. A House possesses an original nobility through the outstanding personal qualities of its ancestors which pervades the group feeling and such a house may rise to royal authority. "The goal to which group feeling leads is royal authority."[2] Chieftainship comes first[3] and then royal authority in the real sense of the term. Royal authority (in the sense of some type of rulership), Ibn Khaldun thinks, "is natural to mankind."

[3] *Ibid.*, pp. 252-3.
[4] *Ibid.*, p. 264.
[5] *Ibid.*
[6] *Ibid.*, p. 263.
[7] *Ibid.*
[1] *Ibid.*, p. 313.
[2] *Ibid.*, p. 284.

The reasons he gives are exactly those of Hobbes in the *Leviathan*. Ibn Khaldun writes:

> Royal authority is an institution that is natural to mankind. We have explained before that human beings cannot live and exist except through social organization and cooperation for the purpose of obtaining their food and (other) necessities of life. When they have organized, necessity requires that they deal with each other and (thus) satisfy (their) needs. Each one will stretch out his hand for whatever he needs and (try simply to) take it, since injustice and aggressiveness are in the animal nature. The others, in turn, will try to prevent him from taking it, motivated by wrathfulness and spite and the strong human reaction when (one's own property is menaced). This causes dissension. (Dissension) leads to hostilities, and hostilities lead to the destruction of the (human) species. Now, (the human species) is one of the things the Creator has especially (told us) to preserve.
>
> People, thus, cannot persist in a state of anarchy without a ruler who keeps them apart. Therefore, they need a person to restrain them. He is their ruler.[4]

Chieftainship the lowest level of rulership is not royal authority in the more precise definition of the term. "Royal authority, in reality, belongs only to those who dominate subjects, collect taxes, send out (military) expeditions, protect the frontier regions, and have no one over them who is stronger than they."[5] Such royal authority is the political form that belongs to civilization — civilization belongs to the cycle of the rise and the fall of such authority.

Families, with the head as ruler, may rise to domination of other houses by conquest either because of superior numbers or because of the decadence of the other houses. However, "dynasties of wide power and large royal authority

---

[3] *Ibid.*
[4] *Ibid.*, pp. 380-381.
[5] *Ibid.*

have their origin in religion based on prophecy or on truthful propaganda."[1] The importance of religion as the basis of a civilization is another modern insight. (We shall see in the following chapters the significance of this institution in the cultural structures of civilizations.) The significance of religion in the opinion of Ibn Khaldun lies in its power to unite diverse tribes of diverse group feelings. By means of religion these tribes, as in the example of the Arab tribes under the Moslem faith, overcome their envy, jealousy and haughtiness and join together as one community. Such a large united group fired by the zeal of a common religious faith can — and did in the case of the Moslem Arabs — overcome enemies much greater numerically and territorially. The religion provides a much wider basis for group feeling. Group feeling makes the community feel superior and the religion of the Arabs gave them a still greater basis for feelings of superiority[2]; such superiority gives rise to royal power.[3] Religion, like the tribal group feeling, provides a rallying point around which men will risk life and limb. Only religion was a powerful enough bond to unite the proud, individualistic Arab tribes, Ibn Khaldun observes. Yet religion itself, he adds, depends upon group feeling for its successful development; some family group as in Mohammed's case must support the prophet. Religious propaganda cannot spread without group feeling because "every mass (political) undertaking by necessity requires group feeling."[4]

United by the religious bond the Arab tribes were soon able to establish royal authority in the Near East and the Mediterranean countries as far as Spain. In most of these countries there was little or no group feeling among the populations — their rulers were in the decadent stage. (Compare Toynbee's parallel idea described below of the internal and external proletariats of the decline-stage of

---
[1] *Ibid.*, p. 319.
[2] *Ibid.*
[3] *Ibid.*
[4] *Ibid.*, pp. 322-324.

every culture.) This lack of group feeling made it easy for the Arabs to found dynasties in these countries.

When a dynasty is founded it goes through the cycle mentioned above but a fuller account needs to be given of each stage. Ibn Khaldun later in his *Muqaddimah* lengthens the stages to five.[1]

1. The first stage is that of the successful overcoming of all opposition and "the appropriation of royal authority from the preceding dynasty."[2] The ruler now becomes an exemplary leader of his people. He is just in his taxation policies, in his defense of property, and he provides military protection. "He does not claim anything exclusively for himself to the exclusion of (his people), because (such an attitude) is what is required by group feeling, (and it was group feeling) that gave superiority (to the dynasty), and (group feeling) still continues to exist as before."[3]

2. "The second stage is the one in which the ruler gains complete control over his people, claims royal authority all for himself, excluding them, and prevents them from trying to have a share in it." The glory and egotism of the one ruler who appropriates all for himself and his family checks the ambition of others who then become lazy, humble and servile.[4] The ruler and his own family by appropriating all power begin the destruction of group feeling.[5] Outsiders are given the government jobs; relatives are kept away.

3. This is the last stage in which the ruler is in complete authority. This is the climactic stage in which general tranquility in the realm enables the ruler to expend large amounts on city construction, large buildings and monuments. He pays his soldiers liberally, gives gifts to embas-

---
[1] *Ibid.*, p. 353.
[2] *Ibid.*
[3] *Ibid.*
[4] *Ibid.*, pp. 339-340.
[5] *Ibid.*
[6] *Ibid.*, p. 354.

sies of foreign countries, and in general dispenses "bounty to his own people." [6] The money he has been able to collect in taxes has enabled him to pay "hired help" to run the country.

4. The fourth stage is one of "resting on one's oars." Ibn Khaldun says that in this stage "the ruler is content with what his predecessors have built." Traditional patterns established by the former rulers are followed carefully.

5. This is the age of senility. Ibn Khaldun's description is the following:

> The fifth stage is one of waste and squandering. In this stage, the ruler wastes on pleasures and amusements (the treasures) accumulated by his ancestors, through (excessive) generosity to his inner circle and at their parties. Also, he acquires bad, low-class followers to whom he entrusts the most important matters (of state), which they are not qualified to handle by themselves, not knowing which of them they should tackle and which they should leave alone. (In addition,) the ruler seeks to destroy the great clients of his people and followers of his predecessors. Thus, they come to hate him and to conspire to refuse support to him. (Furthermore) he loses a number of soldiers by spending their allowances on his pleasures (instead of paying them) and by refusing them access to his person and not supervising them (properly). Thus, he ruins the foundations his ancestors had laid and tears down what they had built up. In this stage, the dynasty is seized by senility and the chronic disease from which it can hardly ever rid itself, for which it can find no cure, and, eventually, it is destroyed.[1]

This is the course of a dynastic culture. Ibn Khaldun sometimes names three stages, four stages or five stages. He gives no absolute number of years, but we saw above that one-hundred and twenty is a favored number. He men-

---

[1] *Ibid.*, p. 355.

tions dynasties of longer duration, however. The general pattern is the same regardless of the number of stages or the number of years of the dynasty in power; and the senile stage is the same in all. The beginning of the breakdown is really when the ruler takes all the glory for himself and his immediate family, for this is the beginning of the breakdown of group feeling.[2] But there is another factor, a crucial and inevitable one which causes the decline of a dynastic power or of any civilization in general. This is sedentary culture. *"Sedentary culture is the goal of civilization."* [1] But it also "means the *end of its life span and brings about its corruption."* [2] As the microcosm, the human individual ceases to grow and increase his powers at the age of forty, so a civilization ceases to grow when it becomes sedentary; and "excessive sedentary culture" causes the ruin of the culture.

Sedentary culture is dominant in stages 3, 4, and 5 listed above. It is defined as "the adoption of diversified luxuries, the cultivation of the things that go with them, and addiction to the crafts that give elegance to all the various kinds (of luxury), such as the crafts of cooking, dressmaking, building, and (making) carpets, vessels, and all other parts of (domestic) economy."[3] The simple desert life needed none of these things. However, when such luxurious living is tasted and becomes popular in the culture religion and morality become undermined. Luxury customs usually corrupt the person. The sedentary person is too weak to take care of his needs personally or else too proud. "Man is a man only in as much as he is able to procure for himself useful things and to repel harmful things . . ."[4] Man is the child of custom, Ibn Khaldun wisely observes. He imitates the habits of his group and if these

[2] *Ibid.,* pp. 372-373.
[1] *Ibid.,* Vol. II, p. 291.
[2] *Ibid.,* p. 291.
[3] *Ibid.,* p. 292.
[4] *Ibid.,* p. 296.

331

are luxurious and pleasure-loving the individual follows this pattern.

Too much luxurious living, high taxes, high prices and general inflation make living in the customary manner more and more precarious. Morality deteriorates further and people use trickery, lying, gambling, cheating, fraud, theft, usury to gain or to retain the luxuries. The city soon "teems with low people of blameworthy character."[5] Men in high places and even members of the dynastic family suffer corruption. "If this (situation) spreads in a town or nation God permits it to be ruined or destroyed."[6] For, "when the strength of a man and then his character and religion are corrupted, his humanity is corrupted, and he becomes, in effect, transformed into an animal."[1] Therefore, Ibn Khaldun says, "It has become clear that the stage of sedentary culture is the stopping point in the life of civilization and dynasties."[2]

Ibn Khaldun then goes on to survey in more detail all the facets of sedentary civilization. His observations in the field of economics have a modern ring. He has a labor theory of value which anticipates Marx.[3] If the laborer's profits equal his needs they are his sustenance; if the profits exceed his needs then these profits in excess are capital accumulation. Agriculture, the crafts, and commerce are "natural" ways of making a living, and of these agriculture has first place since it was Adam's occupation. Being a servant is not a natural way of making a living and Ibn Khaldun has contempt for it. No one should make his living in this way, if possible.

Music at the professional level is one of the better pleasures of life in the luxury or sedentary stage. Music is a form of beauty, which in its turn is harmony:

The object that is most suited to man and in which

---

[5] *Ibid.*, p. 293.
[6] *Ibid.*, p. 294.
[1] *Ibid.*, p. 297.
[2] *Ibid.*
[3] *Ibid.*, p. 311.

he is most likely to perceive perfect harmony, is the human form. Thus every man desires beauty in the objects of vision and hearing, as a requirement of his nature. Beauty in the objects of hearing is harmony and lack of discordance in the sounds.[4]

His account and criticism of the "sciences" of sedentary culture are worth noting. The ability to think, which man alone of all the animals enjoys, gives rise to the sciences or intellectual activities. He lists the sciences of his own contemporary civilization as follows: the philosophical sciences (logic, physics, metaphysics, and mathematics — mathematics includes geometry, arithmetic, astronomy and music); the conventional or traditional sciences all of which depend upon the "authority of the given religious law." These conventional or traditional sciences are Koran interpretation, Koran reading, Tradition *(hadith)* study, Jurisprudence, Philological sciences (such as lexicography, grammar, and literature), and Speculative Theology.

He approves strongly of the Koranic studies and of Sunna tradition. He paints the Shi'ite sects as in error and some of their "Mahdis" as deceivers. Ibn Khaldun takes the Moslem religious view of man tempered somewhat by Greek philosophy. The world of man, he says, is the most exalted and noble of the "worlds of existent things."[1] Man, himself, has four levels of existence: (1) waking, (2) dreaming, (3) prophetic, (4) Death (Purgatory and the Resurrection state). The waking level is that concerned with the world of the body such as external sense perception and activities directed towards making a living.[2] The dreaming state is the world of sleep visions. This is perception by imagination. In dream visions "human perceptions are the same as those of external sense perception."[3]

---
[4] *Ibid.*, p. 398.
[1] *Ibid.*, Vol. III, p. 69.
[2] *Ibid.*, Vol. III, pp. 70 ff.
[3] *Ibid*, pp. 71-72.

Yet the body does not move. Place and time elements are different from where the body is located. Such "perception in sleep is the clearest evidence (we have) for the fact that sensual perception operates at the subsequent levels." [4]

The third level, that of prophecy, is reached by very few such as Mohammed. This level is described thus:

> It is not known to us how sensual perception takes place on the third level — that of the prophets — but they themselves have a more than certain (knowledge of) perception through intuition. The Prophet sees God and the angels. He hears God's speech from God Himself or from the angels. He sees Paradise, Hell, and the divine throne and chair. He breaks through the seven heavens in his ascension. He rides al-Buraq and meets the prophets in (the seven heavens) and prays with them. He perceives all kinds of sensual perceptions, exactly as he perceives them at the levels of body and sleep, (but) through a kind of necessary knowledge that God creates for him, and not through ordinary human perception by means of the limbs of the body.[1]

The fourth level (Death) starts with the grave when the soul becomes free of the body or when it reassumes a body since the dead do have sensual perceptions. The dead person, for example, "sees two angels who question him," and also other things such as the "seat he will occupy in either Paradise or Hell". This is the state of Purgatory *(barzakh)* in which the soul is punished for its bad deeds or rewarded for its good deeds until the general Resurrection. On the "Day of Resurrection, the dead behold the different grades of bliss in Paradise and punishment in Hell with their own eyes and ears, exactly as they used to behold (things) during their life. They see the angels and they see their Lord".[2]

[4] *Ibid.*, p. 72.
[1] *Ibid.*, pp. 72-3.
[2] *Ibid.*, p. 74.

Ibn Khaldun has a profound religious belief, it seems, in the One God as a spiritual being. Man's goal is Paradise, eternal life in the presence of Allah and the corruption of soul engendered by sedentary culture which endangers this goal is very much deplored. Some of the intellectual sciences are held in high regard such as logic and physics and mathematics. Such studies as astrology, alchemy and philosophy (metaphysics) are condemned. Astrology is bad because it is a false science and even more because it undermines religion. The astrologers, if their predictions come true, attribute the events to the control of star-gods, not Allah, and this corrupts religion. Alchemy is fraud and deceit — base metals are coated with gold to deceive; this again is corruption. Philosophy is a very dangerous study for a man. Ibn Khaldun says, "No one who has no knowledge of the Muslim religious sciences should apply himself to it. Without that knowledge he can hardly remain safe from its pernicious aspects." [3] Some of these "pernicious aspects" are the beliefs of philosophers such as Avicenna about the afterlife, which contradict the word of the Koran.[1]

Sedentary culture in general corrupts man because it undermines his sterling character qualities of courage, truthfulness, usefulness, and group feeling; and because it undermines religion which also is the supernatural support for these character qualities. Religion provides the supernatural basis for group feeling on a very wide basis. Also, religion through the revelatory level of knowledge granted the prophets informs man about the eternal life of bliss (or misery) beyond this short existence. Ibn Khaldun accepts, too, the Koranic revelation about the one-cycle of history with God as creator at the beginning and God as bringing the temporal world to an end on the Last Day.[2]

[3] *Ibid.*, pp. 257-258.
[1] Avicenna's criticism of the physical resurrection is discussed above in Part II in the chapter "The One Grand Cycle in Moslem Thought."
[2] *Muqaddimah, op. cit.*, Vol. I, p. 387.

Sedentary culture with its sensuous luxuries, its pleasures, its over-intellectuality de-spiritualizes man. It is an age of skepticism, criticism and emptiness with its extreme specimens manifested in the last days of this stage of civilization — the days when man's "character and religion are corrupted, his humanity is corrupted, and he becomes, in effect, transformed into an animal." [3]

Vico's stages of the rise and decline of a culture are similar with his Age of the Heroes, and the Age of Men. (Vico's Age of the Gods is omitted by Ibn Khaldun.) In Vico's thought, too, the Age of Men sees the rise and flourishing of skepticism and materialism which is the cause of the decline and fall of a people. In Spengler's, Sorokin's, and Toynbee's thought skepticism and materialism also cause the corruption of morale which causes the disintegration of the civilization. Ibn Khaldun is, therefore, astonishingly modern in his philosophy of history. Actually, the translator of the Muqaddimah — Franz Rosenthal — tells us, Ibn Khaldun was not studied by European scholars until the beginning of the nineteenth century. Since Vico lived 1668-1744 he could scarcely have been acquainted with his predecessor who much earlier placed history among the social sciences and attempted to ascertain the inner dynamics of a civilization which caused its rise and decline.[1] In European thought, Vico is first to establish a "science" of history in a pattern similar to twentieth century culture-cycle theorists.

---

[3] *Ibid.*, Vol. II, p. 297.

[1] Franz Rosenthal tells us that "the great period of the rediscovery of Ibn Khaldun began as early as the sixteenth century and gained momentum in the seventeenth." A scholar of northwest Africa, al Maqqari, in the seventeenth century made much use of the *Muqaddimah*. The Ottoman Turks, however, showed most enthusiasm for this work and their scholars and statesmen "vied with each other in their interest." This was during the sixteenth, seventeenth and eighteenth centuries. But not until the nineteenth century did European scholars study Ibn Khaldun, Franz Rosenthal adds. (Translator's—Franz Rosenthal's—Introduction to the *Muqaddimah*, Vol. I, pp. lxvi-lxvii.)

Section 2

Giambattista Vico: The "Science" of the Culture Cycle

Vico's work *The New Science* defends the thesis, as the title indicates, that history is a science.[1] Like Ibn Khaldun he takes the modern sociological approach to the development of a civilization and tries to establish a definite pattern to such development based upon the nature of man as an individual and as a member of a group. As an individual man develops in the stages of childhood, adolescence and maturity. A nation or culture develops also in stages which are similar. First there is an Age of the Gods, next an Age of the Heroes, and finally the Age of Men. Vico borrows the names of the three Ages, he tells us, from the Egyptians whose traditional history according to Herodotus was divided into these three epochs. (See above Part II for a description of the Egyptian Age of the Gods.) Every Age of the Gods, Vico theorizes, is an age of the childhood of a human society. We can learn much about this stage from the study of the myths and fables of a people which symbolize their state of social organization (or lack of it) at this time, their religious beliefs and attitudes and their mode of life in general. The study of the symbolism of such myths belongs to the science of philology in general, Vico says; and philologians are defined as "historians, grammarians, and critics who study the languages and deeds of peoples." [2]

Fables and myths about giants and cyclopes in Greek literature and the literatures of other peoples are evidence that human history began with such beings. This original Age of the Gods at the dawn of human history, Vico thinks, began after the Biblical Deluge when the descendants of Ham, Japheth, and Shem "without the religion of their

---

[1] Vico's dates: 1668-1744.

[2] Giambattisto Vico, *The New Science of Giambattisto Vico*, trans. from the third ed. (1744) by Thomas G. Bergin and Max H. Fisch (Ithaca, N. Y.; Cornell University Press, 1948), p. 56.

father Noah, which they had repudiated (and which alone, in what was then the state of nature, could have held them by marriages in a society of families), were lost from one another by roving wild in the great forest of the earth, pursuing shy and indocile women, and fleeing from the wild animals with which the great ancient forest must have abounded. They were scattered further in search of pasture and water, and as the result of it all were reduced, at the end of a long period, to the condition of beasts." [1] Their stature was great because of their savage life; this is why they became known in myths as "giants." These beast-like men wallowed in sensuality and were without speech — only gestures were used for communication.

Awakening from the brute to the human level began with the religious fear and awe excited in these creatures by violent thunderstorms. They sought shelter in caves out of terror of the ominous "power" in the storm. Sex life, too, became ordered. Instead of the "community of women" characteristic of the beast-like state, "through fear of the apprehended divinity, in religious and chaste carnal unions they solemnized marriages under cover and begat acknowledged children and so founded families." [2] They began to bury their dead and so believed in the immortality of the soul. Religion, Vico declares, is fundamental to human cohesion and is one of the basic principles in the development of any civilization or nation. Another important result of awareness of the divine was the acquisition of self-consciousness by these men, i.e., they became moral, responsible beings. The first form of social organization — family life — and the religious awakening caused language to begin its development. The first words, Vico thinks, were monosyllabic and the first speech singing. Language was evolved slowly and the words were associated with myths,

---

[1] *Ibid.*, p. 8. Vico explicitly omits Hebrew history from this "natural history" treatment. The Hebrews did not develop out of this beast-like condition but were always high level men.

[2] *Ibid.*, p. 8.

an anticipation of Cassirer's views.[1] Poetry is more ancient than prose, for the childhood of the race is, as we have said above, like the childhood of the individual (cf. Spengler), filled with creatures of the imagination. Reason, at this stage, is as weak as imagination is strong. This divine age or Age of the Gods lasted about nine hundred years. Gradually it merged into a new age, the Age of the Heroes. In his "Chronological Chart" in which he diagrams his morphology of history, Vico lists as chronological contemporaries the "Call of Abraham," the Egyptian Age of the Gods, and the Greek Age of the Gods (the Greek Golden Age of Hesiod's *Works and Days*).

The Age of the Heroes is next. It began when the fathers of the primitive families subjugated the "beast-men" i.e., the "giants" still living in the savage state. These outsiders were made slaves and dependents. In this way communities of householders and their slaves and dependents were formed. As the number of dependents grew struggles began between the householders or ruling class and those ruled (the slaves and dependents). Gradually the power of the latter class grew until they won some democratic rights. They were excluded from actual ruling, however, because they were excluded from contact with the divinities. The dependent class were people without gods since they were drawn from outside the ancestral family groups. These dependents could not form families of their own, Vico says, because being without gods they did not have access to the sacred institution of marriage. (He appeals to Roman history in defense of this idea.) Government, therefore, was the business of the few "civilized" men, in direct contact with the divinities through the auspices.

In the previous age (Age of the Gods) government was by One, the father-despot who had powers of life and death

---

[1] Ernst Cassirer, *An Essay on Man*, Anchor Books ed. (Doubleday & Co., Garden City, N. Y., 1953). Cassirer says: "Language and myth are near of kin. In the early stages of human culture their relation is so close and their cooperation so obvious that it is almost impossible to separate them." (p. 142)

over his family. (Again Vico draws evidence for this stage from Roman history.) In the Age of the Heroes, government by the few (aristocracy) is characteristic. Force is used to establish the will of the aristocracy; and the force lies in the might of great heroes like the Greek Achilles, who, in their turn, reverence the gods. Language in the first age had been "mute" i.e., a gesture language which, when written was hieroglyphic. Hieroglyphic, Vico asserts, imitates in drawing the gestures of men and was written down for religious purposes; it is therefore a language of "sacred characters."[1] In the Heroic Age language is symbolic and metaphorical as in Homer, the typical Heroic Age poet.

In the Age of the Heroes cities begin with the nobles to rule and the dependents, the plebs, to obey. Feudalism is the characteristic type of organization and reappears again in the second Heroic Age, the Middle Ages. Trade and commerce also begin and the institution of war. Jurisprudence in this stage of culture-complex looked to "what the Roman jurisconsults called civil equity and we call reason of state."[2] (In the previous Age all was derived from the Divine in oracles). The Heroes thought they had a natural right to what was written or spoken in words:

> And if, as a consequence of this [civil] equity, the laws turned out in a given case to be not harsh but actually cruel they naturally bore it because they thought their law was naturally such. Furthermore they were led to observe their laws by their own highest interest, with which, we find, the heroes identified that of their fatherlands, of which they were the only citizens.[3]

In general. in this Heroic Age, "the natural law of force

---
[1] *Ibid.*, p. 31.
[2] *Ibid.*, p. 20.
[3] *Ibid.*

reigned supreme," and the peoples "looked upon each other as perpetual enemies, and pillage and piracy were continual because, as war was eternal between them, there was no need of declaration."[4] The relativity of morality to social organization emphasized by twentieth century sociologists is brought out also in Vico's comment: "Indeed as in the first barbarian times the heroes considered it a title of honor to be called thieves, so in the *returned barbarian times* the powerful rejoiced to be called pirates."[1] (The age of feudalism in Europe is a repetition in all the essentials of the pattern of the earlier Heroic Ages such as those of Egypt, Greece, and Rome.) The present era has some of these qualities which belong to Heroic Ages, perhaps, but even more our era has the characteristics of the Decline stage of a civilization, as Vico and twentieth century thinkers paint these characteristics.

The Age of Men follows inevitably upon the Heroic Age. It began earlier in Greece than in Rome because the Romans were preeminently a heroic people. In Greece it began with the Seven Sages; in Rome not until Carthage fell. The Age of Men is an age of *humanism* which corresponds with Ibn Khaldun's stage of "sedentary culture," and with Spengler's epoch of "civilization." In this era all men recognize themselves "as equal in human nature, and therefore there were established first the popular commonwealths and then the monarchies, both of which are forms of human government."[2] In the Age of Men language is epistolary with characters agreed upon by the people for their everyday usage. Jurisprudence and Law are based upon equity and truth as principles. Judgments become "ordinary" and in accordance with the merits of the case versus the "divine judgments" of the heroic age and Age of the Gods when duels were common the outcome of

---

[4] *Ibid.*, p. 17.
[2] *Ibid.*, p. 18.
[3] Scholarly research shows that the lands worked by the peoples of the early Mesopotamian states belonged to gods.

341

which depended upon the Divine. The kind of Authority found in the Age of Men is that of learned men who have a reputation for their wisdom, whereas "senate" control was the Authority in the Heroic Age, and the gods (property belonged to the goods) [3] in the Age of the Gods. Altogether, secularism and naturalism are dominant in the Age of Men. Reason and philosophy develop self-conscious knowledge of the laws of nature and of the nature of man and of human societies. This is the era of the great philosophers of Greece followed later by the same era among the Romans when they entered this Age of Men.

The Age of Men has two eras: (1) the era of the free popular commonwealth such as the democracies of Greece and Rome; and (2) the era of monarchy. It is inevitable, "an eternal natural royal law," that "nations come to rest under monarchies." [1] In the free popular commonwealth men become more and more engaged in their private concerns to procure luxury goods which have become customary. Because of this egoism of interests public affairs become less and less a matter of interest to the citizens who even employ "public arms at the risk of ruin to their nations." [2] (Compare Ibn Khaldun's similar argument for the necessity and inevitability of Royal Authority). Vico, like Ibn Khaldun, founds this "natural royal law" of the development of monarchy out of democracy on two principles: first, the Providence of God in His concern for the preservation of the human species; [3] second, human necessities and the utilities of social life. The latter he calls the "two perennial springs of the natural law of nations." [4]

The utilities of social life require resolution of the state of social and economic chaos that has resulted from the egotistic pursuit of private gain by the majority of citizens. Either the society must perish or yield authority to

---

[1] *Ibid.*, p. 340.
[2] *Ibid.*
[3] *Ibid.*, p. 91.
[4] *Ibid.*, p. 92.

one man. Ibn Khaldun, Vico, and Spengler agree that monarchy, "royal authority," or what Spengler calls Caesarism develops out of democratic societies, and very much as Vico describes the process. Vico tells us that Augustus, for example, was the inevitable monarch essential to the self-preservation of Rome which came to chaos under the dissoluteness of the late Republic. Monarchy is, however, praised by Vico. He says of it:

> Now in free commonwealths if a powerful man is to become monarch the people must take his side, and for that reason monarchies are by nature popularly governed: first through the laws by which the monarchs seek to make their subjects all equal; then by that property of monarchies whereby sovereigns humble the powerful and thus keep the masses safe and free from their oppressions; further by that other property of keeping the multitude satisfied and content as regards the necessaries of life and the enjoyment of natural liberty; and finally by the privileges conceded by monarchs to entire classes (called privileges of liberty) or to particular persons by awarding extraordinary civil honors to men of exceptional merit (these being singular laws dictated by natural equity). *Hence monarchy is the form of government best adapted to human nature when reason is fully developed* . . .[1]

The cycle is now complete. Vico writes that "the history of humanity is all contained between the family monarchies and the civil monarchies."[2] All nations by what we would call today the natural dynamics of human group living or what Vico calls the "principles of the ideal eternal history"[3] must develop in the following pattern: (1) Age of the Gods in which family monarchies arise; (2) Age of the Heroes, government by an aristocracy of noble family heads; (3) Age of Men in which there is first a free popu-

---
[1] *Ibid.*, pp. 340 f., my italics.
[2] *Ibid.*, p. 347.
[3] *Ibid.*, p. 338.

lar commonwealth—democracy which inevitably leads to a civil monarchy.[4]

Vico applies the abstract form of number, also, to his historical cycle.[5] History begins with the rule of ONE in the family monarchy, then the FEW rule in the heroic aristocracies; then the MANY and the ALL in the popular commonwealths; finally there is return again to the ONE in the civil monarchy, but at a higher level which is reminiscent of Hegel's philosophy of monarchy as the goal of historical development in social organization.

Vico implies that the decline and fall of a civilization or nation is the final stage, the dissolution, in the axioms he calls the "principles of the ideal eternal history."[6] These axioms are as follows:

> *241.* Men first feel necessity, then look for utility, next attend to comfort, still later amuse themselves with pleasure, thence grow dissolute in luxury, and finally go mad and waste their substance.
> *242.* The nature of peoples is first crude, then severe, then benign, then delicate, finally dissolute.
> *243.* In the human race first appear the huge and grotesque, like the cyclopes; then the proud and magnanimous, like Achilles; then the valorous and just, like Aristides and Scipio Africanus; nearer to us, imposing figures with great semblances of virtue accompanied by great vices, who among the vulgar win a name for true glory, like Alexander and Caesar; still later, the melancholy and reflective, like Tiberius; finally the dissolute and shameless madmen, like Caligula, Nero, and Domitian.
> *244.* This axiom shows that the first sort were necessary in order to make one man obey another in the family-state and prepare him to be law-abiding in the city-state that was to come; the second sort, who naturally did not yield to their peers, were necessary to establish the aristocratic commonwealths on the

---

[4] *Ibid.,* p. 338-339.
[5] *Ibid.,* p. 347.
[6] *Ibid.,* p. 338. Here he refers to axioms 241-245 (on pp. 70-71) as the axiomatic principles of the ideal eternal history.

basis of the families; the third sort to open the way for popular liberty; the fourth to bring in the monarchies; the fifth to establish them; the sixth to overthrow them.

245. This with the preceding axioms LXV-LXVII[1] gives a part of the principles of the ideal eternal history traversed in time by every nation in its rise, development, maturity, decline and fall.[2]

It is apparent that Vico agrees entirely with his remarkable predecessor, Ibn Khaldun, that sedentary culture weakens man because of its emphasis upon comfortable and then luxurious living with its pleasures and then dissolute living. On the intellectual plane philosophy too becomes corrupt and descends to skepticism.[3] "Learned fools" fall to "calumniating the truth."[4] The peoples have, in general, become slaves to their "unrestrained passions — of luxury, effeminacy, avarice, envy, pride and vanity,"[5] and fall into the "vices characteristic of the most abject slaves (having become liars, tricksters, calumniators, thieves, cowards and pretenders)."[6]

In the description of decline just quoted Vico is describing the Age of Men just before Monarchy comes into being; and he declares that Monarchy, the rise of a man like Augustus can once more restore order. The monarchy, providence ordains, "shall confine the will of the monarchs, in spite of their unlimited sovereignty, within the natural order of keeping the peoples content and satisfied with both their religion and their natural liberty. For without

---

[1] Axioms LXV-LXVII are those numbered 239-242. We have quoted all except 239 and 240. Number 239 traces the "order of human things: first the forests, after that the huts, thence the villages, next the cities and finally the academies." Number 240 relates the etymology of words to the cycle of the historical stages. (See p. 70.)
[2] *Ibid.*, pp. 70-71.
[3] *Ibid.*, p. 380.
[4] *Ibid.*
[5] *Ibid.*
[6] *Ibid.*, p. 381.

this universal satisfaction and content of the peoples, monarchic states are neither lasting nor secure."[1] The implication of the axioms seems to be that the monarchic states are not lasting and secure, but end in a state of decadence worse than that which needed the remedy of monarchy for survival. (See axioms 243-245.) The culture or nation then is either conquered by some other nation which makes of the conquered territory a subject province, or else the "extreme remedy" befalls the society. This extreme remedy has a very modern ominous ring:

> But if the peoples are rotting in this last civil illness and cannot agree upon a monarch from within, and are not conquered and preserved by better nations from without, then providence for their extreme ill has its extreme remedy at hand. For such peoples, like so many beasts, have fallen into the custom of each man thinking only of his own private interests and have reached the extreme of delicacy, or better of pride, in which like wild animals they bristle and lash out at the slightest displeasure. Thus in the midst of their greatest festivities, though physically thronging together, they live like wild beasts in a deep solitude of spirit and will, scarcely any two being able to agree since each follows his own pleasure or caprice. By reason of all this, providence decrees that, through obstinate factions and desperate civil wars, they shall turn their cities into forests and the forests into dens and lairs of men. In this way, through long centuries of barbarism, rust will consume the misbegotten subtleties of malicious wits, that have turned them into beasts made more inhuman by the barbarism of reflection than the first men had been made by the barbarism of sense. For the latter displayed a generous savagery, against which one could defend oneself or take flight or be on one's guard; but the former, with a base savagery, under soft words and embraces, plots against the life and fortune of friends and intimates. Hence peoples who have reached this point of premeditated malice, when they receive this last remedy of

---

[1] *Ibid.*, p. 380.

providence and are thereby stunned and brutalized, are sensible no longer of comforts, delicacies, pleasures and pomp, but only of the sheer necessities of life. And the few survivors in the midst of an abundance of the things necessary for life naturally become well behaved and, returning to the primitive simplicity of the first world of peoples, are again religious, truthful and faithful.[2]

This reads like a description of what might happen if World War III should materialize. Vico's "extreme remedy" the return to barbarism, means that the culture must evolve again through the same cycle described above. This is evident in the following passage:

The monarchs mean to strengthen their own positions by debasing their subjects with all the vices of dissoluteness, and they dispose them to endure slavery at the hands of stronger nations. The nations mean to dissolve themselves, and their remnants flee for safety to the wilderness, whence, *like the phoenix, they rise again.*[1]

This extreme remedy, the return to barbarism, thus begins a new culture which, however, evolves through the same cyclic pattern; there can be only one as long as human nature remains the same. Vico illustrates his idea of the "recurrence" of the pattern with the example of the rise and course of European culture after the decline and fall of Rome.[2] The Divine Age appears again with the period immediately following the barbaric invasions. Superstitious rites and religious wars dominated the mental and physical life of this period. There was a return to "mute language," the language of gesture; only very few could

---

[2] *Ibid.*, p. 381.
[1] *Ibid.*, p. 382, my italics.
[2] *Ibid.*, pp. 358-361 and *passim*.

write. There was a return to Divine Judgments in the form of "canonical purgations."

There was next the recurrence of the Heroic Age in feudalism. The feudal chiefs correspond to the Homeric heroes. There were heroic raids, heroic reprisals and duels. This recurrent Heroic Age has as its imaginative poet, Dante who is parallel with Homer in the Greek Heroic Age. Dante's *Divine Comedy* closed the European Heroic Age and initiated the present period the Age of Men characterized by monarchies and democracies. The implication is strong that this European civilization will likewise decay and give rise to a new but similar cycle. Vico points out that Egypt, Greece, Rome, China, India, as well as Europe have all followed the same pattern.

The reason for the inevitability of the one pattern, eternally the same is given us by Vico in the following passage:

> Our Science therefore comes to describe at the same time an ideal eternal history traversed in time by the history of every nation in its rise, progress, maturity, decline and fall. Indeed we go so far as to assert that whoever meditates this Science tells himself this ideal eternal history only so far as he makes it by that proof 'it had, has, and will have to be.' For the first indubitable principle above posited is that this *world of nations has certainly been made by men, and its guise must therefore be found within the modifications of our human mind. And history cannot be more certain than when he who creates the things also describes them.* Thus our Science proceeds exactly as does geometry, which, while it constructs out of its elements or contemplates the world of quantity, itself creates it; but with a reality greater in proportion to that of the orders having to do with human affairs, in which there are neither points, lines, surfaces, nor figures. And this very fact is an argument, O reader, that these proofs are of a kind divine, and should give thee a divine pleasure; since in God knowledge and creation are one and the same thing.[1]

---

[1] *Ibid*, p. 93, my italics.

Vico's method, in his opinion, yields knowledge of a kind not attainable in the physical sciences. In the physical sciences the human mind is attempting to comprehend things external to itself — things made by a Being other than itself. In the study of history man is at no such disadvantage; since man, himself, created history he can have intuitive and direct comprehension of the historical process. Theoretically this is true, as Vico says, but as contemporary historians point out, the billions of events which make up human history must be related in their significance as far as is possible. It is here that historiography runs into trouble; historians differ in their methods of choosing and relating what they believe to be the significant events. This problem will be discussed further in the last chapter of this book so we shall not discuss it further at this point. Vico's greatness, like Ibn Khaldun's, lies in his humanistic, sociological, psychological approach to human history which is the predominant one today.

Vico, however, (again like Ibn Khaldun, St. Augustine and Toynbee) brings the Divine into his theory of history under the aspect of Providence. By Providence Vico explains that he means conscious Mind or Intelligence, the Providence of the Stoic Cicero but even more so of the "divine Plato" and philosophical Christianity. Providence has given man his basic needs and motivations and has seen to it that by means of these, used selfishly by individuals, societies have developed at higher and higher levels until man has become a free and rational being. This idea is repeated in Hegel's philosophy (see the chapter on Hegel in Part II) where it is called the "cunning of reason." Hegel repeats Vico's idea that the Absolute (Vico's Providence) uses the selfish motivations of men — such as the personal ambitions of a Caesar or an Alexander — to advance man's self-consciousness and freedom by means of higher and higher forms of social organization (the State). Vico's version of this thesis (earlier by a century than Hegel's) is summarized compactly in this passage:

It is true that men have themselves made this world of nations (and we took this as the first incontestable principle of our Science . . .), but this world without doubt has issued from a mind often diverse, at times quite contrary, and always superior to the particular ends that men had proposed to themselves; which narrow ends, made means to serve wider ends, it has always employed to preserve the human race upon this earth. Men mean to gratify their bestial lust and abandon their offspring, and they inaugurate the chastity of marriage from which the families arise. The fathers mean to exercise without restraint their paternal power over their clients, and they subject them to the civil powers from which the cities arise. The reigning orders of nobles mean to abuse their lordly freedom over the plebeians, and they are obliged to submit to the laws which establish popular liberty. The free peoples mean to shake off the yoke of their laws, and they become subject to monarchs. The monarchs mean to strengthen their own positions by debasing their subjects with all the vices of dissoluteness, and they dispose them to endure slavery at the hands of stronger nations. The nations mean to dissolve themselves, and their remnants flee for safety to the wilderness, whence, like the phoenix they rise again.[1]

Providence, Vico writes, has guided man mainly through religion. Here again there is resemblance to Ibn Khaldun, St. Augustine, Toynbee and the other twentieth century philosophers of history discussed below. Religion provides a wide basis for what Ibn Khaldun calls "group feeling," or cooperation in society, but mainly through holding out to believers promises of reward in a sensuous paradise or of punishment in a Hell. Here Ibn Khaldun and Vico are in agreement. Vico's own words which express his view of the importance of religion in human history are represented in this brief paragraph:

> For in this work it has been fully demonstrated that through providence the first governments of the world

---
[1] *Ibid.*, p. 382.

had as their entire form religion, on which alone the state of the families was based; and passing thence to the heroic or aristocratic civil governments, religion must have been their principle firm basis. Advancing then to the popular governments, it was again religion which served the peoples as means for attaining them. And coming to rest at last in monarchic governments, this same religion must be the shield of princes. Hence if religion is lost among the peoples, they have nothing left to enable them to live in society: no shield of defense, nor means of counsel, nor basis of support, nor even a form by which they may exist in the world at all.[1]

Summary. Vico's cyclical pattern, guided by Providence, is an "eternal ideal pattern" of the "recurrence of human civil things." It is "the ideal of the eternal laws in accordance with which the affairs of all nations proceed in their rise, progress, mature state, decline and fall, and would do so even if (as is certainly not the case) there were infinite worlds being born from time to time throughout eternity." [2] Vico claims that the American Indians, also, "would now be following this course of human things if they had not been discovered by the Europeans." [3]

The human culture cycle is recurrent in exactly the same pattern, which is the reason why Vico calls his work Science, the New Science — history. The specific concrete content is not recurrent, however. The laws of the cycle do not yield, for example, "the particular history in time of the laws and deeds of the Romans or the Greeks," but rather "the substantial identity of meaning in the diversity of modes of expression." [4] All cultures, all nations follow the same pattern from their rise to their fall; but this does not exclude an overall progress for the human race

---

[1] *Ibid.*, pp. 382 f.
[2] *Ibid.*, p. 372.
[3] *Ibid.*
[4] *Ibid.*

as a whole. Vico's theory is compatible with a spiral progress pattern in total human history.

Oswald Spengler, whose Philosophy of History we shall study next has much in common with Vico, but is far more extreme in his Cultural Relativism; his Culture-Cycle Theory cannot be expanded into one of spiral progress as in Vico's thought.

Chapter II

Oswald Spengler's Theory of Culture Cycles: The Cycle of the Macrocosmic Organism

Spengler's purpose in his research into human history is the discovery of a definite pattern of such a sort that the future of our own or the course of any subsequent culture can be predetermined. In his great monumental work *The Decline of the West* he attempts to demonstrate such a pattern. The large features of this pattern are the same as in Vico's culture cycle which we saw was anticipated in its major features by Ibn Khaldun. Spengler's method is not as objective, however, as that of the aforementioned philosophers of history as we shall see. The main pattern of the cycle of the macrocosmic culture-organism which, as we said, resembles Vico's and Ibn Khaldun's is the following. First there is a Spring which corresponds to the childhood of the microcosmic organism, the human individual; then a Summer which corresponds with the youth of the individual; Autumn follows which parallels the period of ripe maturity of the individual; and finally Winter, the last phase, sees the end of the culture and corresponds with the decline and death of the individual.

The period of Childhood or Spring of a culture resembles Vico's Age of the Gods. It is marked by the awakening of a religious consciousness, "god-feeling," "world-fear" and "world-longing." Religion and myth characterize this age (cf. Vico) which is essentially a poetic one like the childhood of the microcosm, the individual. A typical architecture is begun, *e.g.*, the Doric in Classical culture, domed buildings in the Arabian, the pyramid type in the Egyptian, and the Gothic in the Western. Patriarchal or feudal politico-economic organization is typical of this era.

In summer, the period of youth, there is an awakening of the critical spirit. In religion there are reformations, *e.g.*, the Upanishads begin in Indian culture, Luther and Calvin appear in the Western, and Dionysian religion (as a reaction to the Apollinian type) in the Classical. In this nascently critical age metaphysics appears, a "purely philosophical form of the world-feeling." This is when the Ionian nature-philosophers and Eleatics appear in the Classical culture, and such men as Descartes, Boehme, Leibniz, in the West. The art-forms developed are: in the Classical, Ionic; in the Western, Baroque; in the Arabian, Islamic-Moorish. In the politico-economic sphere of culture city life begins.

In Autumn Culture reaches its full maturity. This is the age of Enlightenment, and the "zenith of strict intellectual creativeness." It is characterized by "belief in the almightiness of reason." Religion is approached rationally. In India this is the period of systematic development in Buddhism, the later Upanishads, the Sankhya and other philosophies; the period of discoveries in mathematics (especially the significant discovery of zero—related to the idea of the Nirguna Brahman). In Classical culture this epoch is marked by such mature thinkers as Socrates, Plato, and Aristotle. In Western culture the autumnal era gives rise to the Eighteenth Century English rationalists and French Encyclopaedists in philosophical thought, and in mathematics Euler and Lagrange. Then in the very last part of this period we have Kant and the romanticists Goethe, Schelling, Hegel, and Fichte. In Arabian culture, corresponding to the eighteenth century rationalists of the West, Spengler places the Mutazalites, Nazzam and Alkindi, and the Sufis. As morphological contemporaries of the Western romanticists Spengler names Alfarabi and Avicenna.

Winter sees the dawn of Megalopolitan Civilization. This

is civilization on the grand scale when great cities and empires become general. The people become formless aggregates, "masses," in the large cities. There is no bond to hold man to man. Every man tends to his own affairs and seldom knows even his next-door neighbor. Religious belief declines and becomes practically extinct. Skepticism dominates philosophical thought. Everywhere the pervading spiritual tone is one of disillusionment and world-weariness. In this declining period of a culture there is always a "materialistic world-outlook." It is the age of the "cult of science, utility, and prosperity." In India it is the age of Sankhya, Lokayata, and Buddhistic philosophies as living forms of thought, with the more theistic systems as mere lecture-room philosophies. In the West, Socialism, frankly materialistic, takes hold as a dominant philosophy. In the Classical culture Stoicism is popular. Generally speaking, creative philosophical thought is dead in this epoch and has become mere professional lecture-room mental gymnastics. The dominant political form of this age is first of all democracy, but this soon develops into Caesarism and imperialism. We find this occurring in Classical (Roman), Western, Egyptian, and Chinese cultures. The culture now is at the end of its life cycle.

Every culture has a life-period, Spengler claims, of about one thousand years (from birth to death). Each stage in the life cycle described above is essential and each follows in necessary chronological order just as in the life cycle of the individual, the microcosm. Each culture is an organic macrocosm, "a superlative human organism," with its own distinctive personality or *style*.[1] The instinctive goal of a culture is concrete expression of its soul or personality in all the forms which make a great culture-organism. This inner motivation of the culture-soul Spengler calls its Destiny-idea. The Western, Classical and Arabian culture-souls are compared and described fully as examples

---

[1] Oswald Spengler, *The Decline of the West*, 2 vols., trans. Charles Atkinson (New York: Alfred A. Knopf, 1932) Vol. I, p. 346.

of this thesis. **Dramatically significant names are given each of these three cultures:** the Classical is called Apollinian (after Nietzsche), the Arabian is called Magian (after the Zoroastrian wise men of the East), and the Western, Faustian (after the character, Faust, in Goethe's drama). Each of these macrocosmic personalities has its particular mode of expression of space and time forms; its own style of architecture, sculpture, painting, music; its unique style in literature, philosophy, and politics. We have space here only for a brief summary of some of the most significant parts of Spengler's rich treatment of this thesis.

Number and culture forms. Spengler's cultural relativism is manifest here as well as in every other aspect of a culture; there is not and cannot be number as such. The "style of a soul" comes out in its number world. Mathematics is an art (it needs inspiration), it is a metaphysics, and also a science like logic but is more comprehensive and portrays an *idea* (the Destiny-idea) of human existence in each culture form. Classical mathematics expresses the soul of its culture-organism in finite magnitudes the "sensuous element of concrete lines and planes." At bottom Classical mathematics is "solid geometry," and its ultimate significance is "measure in contrast to the immeasurable." [1] It is significantly a science of "perceivable magnitudes." The "Alpha and Omega of the Classical mathematics is *construction* . . . the production of a single visually-present figure." [2]

The soul of the Magian culture expresses itself in algebra which deals with *unknowns,* i.e., with magic or secret properties.

Indian culture invented zero, a typical metaphysical idea of this people. (The goal of Advaita Vedanta is union with the qualityless Brahman, of the Buddhist, the nirvana of the Void).

Faustian mathematics expresses the longing for the in-

---
[1] *Ibid.,* p. 65.
[2] *Ibid.,* p. 85.

finite so typical of its culture-soul in its replacement of the concrete line of the Greeks with the *point*, an *abstract* spatial element; its replacement of emphasis upon finite magnitude with emphasis upon the infinitesimal calculus. The Faustian love for infinite power shows itself in the number world in the replacement of static elements with those which are functional or variable. Spengler comments that "The history of Western knowledge is thus one of progressive emancipation from Classical thought, an emancipation never willed but enforced in the depths of the unconscious. And so the development of the new mathematic consists of a long, secret and finally victorious battle against the notion of magnitude." [3]

Time and culture forms. The Apollinian culture had no time sense; the pure present of the static eternal Platonic ideas or Aristotelian forms held the center of attention. The Faustian soul, on the contrary is extremely time-conscious. Faustian Care (anxiety for the future) shows the interest in time. In art forms this is manifested in the Virgin and Child which symbolize interest in the future.

Time is the tragic, Spengler says, and "it is by the meaning that it intuitively attaches to Time that one Culture is differentiated from another; and consequently 'tragedy' of the grand order has only developed in the Culture which has most passionately affirmed, and in that which has most passionately denied Time." [1] There is a characteristic difference between the treatment of tragedy in these two cultures: in Apollinian tragedy, tragic masks are used and situations and somatic attitudes are emphasized. Faustian tragedy is biographical with the emphasis upon character or inner development:

> The Classical form of the Destiny-idea I shall venture to call Euclidean. Thus it is the sense-actual per-

[3] *Ibid.,* p. 76.
[1] *Ibid.,* p. 130.

son of Oedipus, his 'empirical ego,' nay, his *soma* that is hunted and thrown by Destiny ... But the destiny of Lear is of the 'analytical' type — to use here also the term suggested by the corresponding number world — and consists in dark inner relationships ... Lear is at the last a mere name, the axis of something unbounded. This conception of destiny is the 'infinitesimal' conception. It stretches out into infinite time and infinite space.[2]

To conclude, Time is the directional fulfilment of the Destiny-idea of a culture.

Space and culture forms. What Spengler calls the "prime symbol" of a great culture is its space-form, its "kind of extension." It is this which underlies the symbolic forms which express the culture's interpretation of nature. The nature knowledge "discovered" in any human group is merely phenomenal, a function of its culture-pattern; there is nothing objective or noumenal about it. Basic to the culture's idea of Nature is its mode of intuition of depth (space), and this is a subjective experience. The Apollinian culture-soul experiences depth as finite, sensuously concrete. This is best expressed by sculpture, its characteristic art-form.

The Egyptian soul feels space and time as "one unchanging direction" to come before the judges of the Dead; the symbol is the Way. The Faustian soul (in a sense a synthesis of the foregoing opposites) intuits space as endless or infinite; infinite space is its prime symbol. This cannot be expressed satisfactorily in concrete material forms, but only in music — contrapuntal polyphonic music is the final characteristic and most adequate expression of the soul of Faustian man. The Chinese soul "wanders through his world" with Nature as his conductor; gardening is his "grand religious art" and not merely an accidental interest. The prime symbol of the culture dominates all as-

[2] *Ibid.*, p. 129.

pects of its style; its style is basically the expression of this symbol. "The *choice of prime symbol* in the moment of the Culture-Soul's awakening into self-consciousness on its own soil — a moment that for one who can read world-history thus contains something catastrophic — decides all."[1] The centrality of the prime symbol is most obvious in the art forms of the culture.

Art as the expression of the style of a culture. Spengler thinks that the expression of art can be classified as either *imitation* or *ornamentation*. Imitation belongs to Time, Direction, the living; it is spontaneous art expression as in poetry, the dance, song; in architecture it is the first art form of the culture, for example the home and the castle are spontaneous and unplanned. Self-conscious art forms in the grand style arise from this spontaneous foundation. Ornamentation is the more self-conscious and objective symbol of the generalized feeling idea; it requires knowledge and skill. Examples are the Doric column in the Apollinian culture, the cathedral in the Faustian.

Cycle of a grand style in the art of a culture. The first point of significance here is that "there can be but one style" in the history of a culture, "the style of the Culture."[2] "In the beginning there is a timid, despondent, naked expression of a newly-awakened soul which is still seeking for a relation between itself and the world that, though its proper creation, yet is presented as alien and unfriendly. There is the child's fearfulness . . ."[3]

Examples are: (1) In Faustian culture Romanesque architecture and sculpture. Spengler comments that sculpture is music even here. (2) In Magian culture there are the Early-Christian catacomb paintings. (3) In Egyptian culture there are the pillar-halls of the Fourth Dynasty.

---
[1] *Ibid.*, p. 180.
[2] *Ibid.*, p. 205. There are great anthropologists and sociologists who agree with this view, e.g., Kroeber and Sorokin. See also the essay, "Style," by Meyer Schapiro in *Anthropology Today*, ed. A. L. Kroeber (Chicago: University of Chicago Press, 1953), pp. 287-311.
[3] *Ibid.*, p. 206.

In the youth-period of the cycle "Being is understood, a sacred form-language has been completely mastered..."[1] This is the era of High Gothic in the Western soul-organism, of pillared basilicas of the Constantinian age in the Magian, and of relief-ornament in the Egyptian temples.

In the epoch of the Manhood of the Macrocosmic organism there is a change to the intellectuality characteristic of the great cities which are developed in this era. The art style also becomes intellectualized. "The artist appears, and 'plans' what formerly grew out of the soil."[2] In the Faustian culture Michaelangelo begins the Baroque "in wild discontent and kicking at the limitations of his art"[3]; In the Magian this is the age of Justinian in which Hagia Sophia and the mosaic decorated basilicas of Ravenna are characteristic; in the Apollinian this era is the period around 600 B.C., the archaic epoch; in the Egyptian this is the Twelfth Dynasty era of the Pylon-temple, Labyrinth, character-statuary and historical reliefs (2000-1788 B.C.).

The autumn of the Grand Style follows. The culture has reached the age of ripe maturity. There is conscious self-completion of the Destiny-idea, but with a presentiment of the end. "A perfectly clear intellect, joyous urbanity, the sorrow of a parting..."[4] characterize these last decades. The Apollinian organism expresses itself in the buildings and sculptures of the Acropolis of which the Parthenon is the most glorious. In the Magian this is the period of the Ommaiyad Caliphate during which there is the typical fairyland art form of delicate marble lace-work and effeminate Moorish arches. In the Faustian Rousseau with his Return-to-Nature idea heralds a presentiment of the end expressed in music by Haydn and Mozart, in painting, by Watteau and Guardi, and in architecture by the Viennese style.

---

[1] *Ibid.*
[2] *Ibid.*
[3] *Ibid.*
[4] *Ibid.*, p. 207.

Finally comes the Winter of the culture. Spengler's musical language describes it eloquently:

> Then the style fades out. The form-language of the Erechtheum and the Dresden Zwinger, honeycombed with intellect, fragile, ready for self-destruction, is followed by the flat and senile Classicism that we find in the Hellenistic megalopolis, the Byzantium of 900 and the 'Empire' modes of the North. The end is a sunset reflected in forms revived for a moment by pedant or by eclectic—semi-earnestness and doubtful genuineness dominate the world of the arts. We today are in this condition — playing a tedious game with dead forms to keep up the illusion of a living art.[1]

After this outline of the cycle of the style of a culture, Spengler goes on to show the organic unity and interrelationships of all arts of form. He begins with "music and plastic." He repeats the idea that "an art is an organism, not a system."[2] He says that learned pedants separate music, painting, drama, sculpture, then delimit and define these as particular arts:

> But in fact the technical form-language is no more than the *mask* of the real work. Style is not what the shallow Semper — worthy contemporary of Darwin and materialism — supposed it to be, the product of material, technique, and purpose. It is the very opposite of this, something inaccessible to art-reason, a revelation of the metaphysical order, a mysterious 'must,' a Destiny. With the material boundaries of the different arts it has no concern whatever.[3]

The choice of art-genus is the deepest expression of the

---
[1] *Ibid.*, p. 207.
[2] *Ibid.*, p. 221.
[3] *Ibid.*

soul of the culture as we have already said (*e.g.* sculpture of the Apollinian, music of the Faustian). Therefore, Spengler writes, it is ridiculous to classify the arts in accordance with the character of the sense-impression. For example, an outline drawing of Raphael is utterly disparate with a painting in light, shade and color characteristic of Titian. The former appeals to the eye while the latter is virtually music. Conversely, the Faustian musician need not hear his music with his ears as sense organs. It is significant that

> Beethoven wrote his last works when he was deaf — deafness merely released him from the last fetters. For this music, sight and hearing *equally* are bridges into the soul and nothing more. To the Greek this visionary kind of artistic enjoyment was utterly alien. He *felt* the marble with his eye, and the thick tones of an *aulos* moved him almost *corporally*. For him, eye and ear are the receivers of the *whole* of the impression that he wished to receive. But for us this had ceased to be true even at the stage of Gothic.[1]

Music (the most adequate expression of the infinite) in the Gothic era is "architectural and vocal" and expresses super-personal Form. Between 1500-1800 (which corresponds to the Classical 650-350) "it is instrumental music that develops into the ruling art" in the Faustian world. In this era counterpoint is developed, a natural outgrowth of the Faustian soul because "the symbolism of counterpoint belongs to extension and through polyphony signifies infinite space."[2] It was the great task of the Faustian soul "to extend the tone corpus into infinity, or rather to *resolve it into an infinite space of tone* . . . And thus was reached the great, immensely dynamic, form in which mu-

---

[1] *Ibid.*, p. 220.
[2] *Ibid.*, p. 229.

sic — now completely bodiless — was raised by Corelli and Handel and Bach to be the ruling art of the West. When Newton and Leibniz, about 1670, discovered the Infinitesimal Calculus, the fugal style was fulfilled." [3]

Music of the West reaches climactic greatness in string music, Spengler writes, especially in violin music. The violin is "the noblest of all instruments that the Faustian soul has imagined and trained for the expression of its last secrets, and certain it is too, that it is in string quartets and violin sonatas that it has experienced its most transcendent and most holy moments of full illumination. Here, *in chamber-music, Western art as a whole reaches its highest point.* Here our prime symbol of endless space is expressed as completely as the Spearman of Polycleitus expresses that of intense bodiliness." [1]

Painting in the West is dominated by musical feeling. Rembrandt's style parallels the organ works of Buxtehude, Pachelbel and Bach; the art of Poussin expresses the same symbolism as that of contemporary chamber-cantatas.[2] The eighteenth century painting of Watteau and Fragonard is music.

Architecture in the Baroque period also is music. Music, Spengler writes, "transmuted the architecture of Bernini's Baroque into accord with its own spirit" — ceilings, walls, ornaments become polyphonies and harmonies. The Dresden and Vienna fairylands are visible chamber-music of "curved furniture and mirror-halls, and shepherdesses in verse and porcelain. It is the final brilliant Autumn with which the Western soul completes the expression of its high style. And in the Vienna of the Congress-time it faded and died." [3]

The more traditionally educated reader (whose history is schematized into Ancient, Medieval, Modern) will won-

---

[3] *Ibid.*, pp. 230 f.
[1] *Ibid.*, p. 231.
[2] *Ibid.*, p. 220.
[3] *Ibid.*, p. 232.

der how Spengler fits into his portrait of the Faustian soul the apparent love of Western man for the Classical culture-ideal during the Renaissance era. Spengler shows rather brilliantly that Western man retained his Faustian soul during this era. He argues that the Renaissance must be understood as primarily an anti-Gothic movement, a "revolt against the spirit of the Faustian forest-music of counterpoint, which at that time was preparing to vassalize the whole form-language of the Western culture."[4] The attempted revival of the Classical style in its feeling of nearness and repose was a blissful interim rest period "free from the passionate movement of Gothic and Baroque." It was unsuccessful in its attempt to repeat the soul-form of the Classical style. It was essentially a "dream of Classical existence, the only dream of the Faustian soul in which it was able to forget itself."[5]

In painting the early "achievement of Giotto and Masaccio in creating a fresco art is only *apparently* a revival of the Apollinian way of feeling; but the depth-experience and idea of extension that underlies it is not Apollinian unspatial and self-contained body but the *Gothic field*."[1] Renaissance man was still Faustian in his interest in third dimensional space (depth) so important in painting from the time of Masaccio. Leonardo da Vinci, who epitomizes Renaissance Man more than any other individual, shows the Faustian soul in his chiaroscuro style of painting. This is really music for it denies corporal bounds to its painted subjects. Leonardo manifests the Faustian spirit in his approach to nature-knowledge. He discovered the inner secret of the circulation of blood which shows a Faustian interest in function versus interest in form and position of parts (Classical). He constructed a flying machine; the typical Faustian interest in conquest of space is conspicuous here.

---

[4] *Ibid.*
[5] *Ibid.*, p. 238.
[1] *Ibid.*, p. 237.

Michaelangelo, too, is obviously Faustian rather than Classical. For Phidias, the greatest Classical sculptor, "marble is the cosmic stuff that is crying for form"; for Michaelangelo "marble was the foe to be subdued."[2] The stone was his symbol of Death. "In it dwells the hostile principle that his daemonic nature is always striving to overpower . . ."[3] The Titanic energy of his great sculptures, the emphasis on the dynamic, the restless striving, prove him a Faustian giant far removed from the Classical spirit. Michaelangelo turned to architecture in his late years, "shattered the canon of Renaissance architecture and created the Roman Baroque,"[4] an architectural form which showed a contest of Force and Mass.

> He grouped the columns in sheaves or else pushed them away into niches. He broke up the storeys with huge pilasters and gave the facade a sort of surging and thrusting quality. Measure yielded to melody, the static to the dynamic . . .
> With Michaelangelo the history of Western sculpture is at an end. What of it there was after him was mere misunderstandings or reminiscences. His real heir was *Palestrina*.[1]

Baroque art and culture which succeeded Renaissance was a frank return to Faustian style after the abortive attempt at a Classical respite. The prime symbol, endless space, is manifested in many ways. Parks and gardens are planned for *distance* effects. There is the Faustian craving to climb high mountains "to be *alone* with endless space." Palestrina, Bach, Handel, Mozart, Beethoven, as we have already mentioned, express in the most adequate Faustian form—music—the *sehnsucht*, the longing for the Infinite

---
[2] *Ibid.*, p. 276.
[3] *Ibid.*
[4] *Ibid.*, p. 277.
[1] *Ibid.*, p. 277.

which gnaws at the heart of Faustian man. Oil painting shows the same preoccupation, not only in chiaroscuro and infinite space effects, but in the use of color. Colors, too, express the soul-form. The Classical colors are typically yellow, red, black, and white. Blue and blue-green were avoided, Spengler claims, because these are distance colors; they are "cold, they disembody, and they evoke impressions of expanse and distance and boundlessness." [2] They are "transcendent, spiritual, non-sensuous." Yellow and red are colors of the "crowd, of children, of women, and of savages," but blue and green, the "Faustian, monotheistic colors—are those of loneliness, of care, of a present that is related to a past and a future, of destiny . . ." [3] But the color which is the most adequate expression of the Faustian soul is brown. Brown is "the unrealest color that there is. It is the one major color that does not exist in the rainbow." The silvery, moist brown, greenish-brown, and deep gold tones used by painters from Giorgione through the Dutch painters show "almost a religious profession of faith." This color, brown, "possesses a mightier power over things than the greens of Leonardo's, Schöngauer's, and Grüenewald's backgrounds," and "carries the battle of Space against Matter to a decisive close." [4] Brown shows "an atmosphere of purest spatiality, which enveloped and rendered, no longer body—the human being as a shape— but the soul unconfined. And thus was attained the inwardness that in the deepest works of Rembrandt and of Beethoven is able to unlock the last secrets themselves — the inwardness which Apollinian man had sought with his strictly somatic art to keep at bay." [1]

With the end of Baroque the West ceases to be creative or profound in the expression of its soul-feeling, its prime symbol. This is shown in the browns of the romantic era

---

[2] *Ibid.*, p. 245.
[3] *Ibid.*, p. 246.
[4] *Ibid.*, p. 250.
[1] *Ibid.*, p. 250.

paintings of Constable. His browns are not Destiny, God, the meaning of life, but sentimentality, romance, a longing for a past forever gone.

Another important art form expressive of the prime symbol of a culture is drama. Western tragedy loves historical material, tragedies of the past [2] and of the future. Shakespeare's historical dramas illustrate interest in the past; Bernard Shaw's *Man and Superman* interest in the future. Goethe's *Faust* is another typical example of interest in the future; it represents men "yet to be born." Western tragedy shows its world-feeling also in being related to infinite space—Shakespearean tragedy, for example, has no unity of place or time. Greek tragedy, on the other hand, shows consciousness of its soul-form in its love for strict limitation of time, place and action. The Greek approach belongs to body, its myth-plots belong to the present. It is situation-drama versus Western action and biographical drama. In Apollinian drama man shows the grand gesture in the face of Fate (a static sculpture-like pose of the eternal present) whereas Faustian drama emphasizes nobility in *action*—dynamic, restless, never-ceasing movement into the infinite.

Apollinian art came to an end in Pergamum, the counterpart of Beyreuth (Wagnerian music-drama). The same discredited mythology, "the same ruthless bombardment of the nerves, and also (though the lack of inner power cannot altogether be concealed) the same fully self-conscious force and towering greatness." [1] In these last overripe stages of a culture size is an emphasis in all the arts (e.g. Wagnerian music-drama, the American sky-scraper in the West; in Apollinian culture the Colossus of Rhodes, Roman buildings). In all the arts there is artificiality;

---

[2] Related to this love for the past is the Faustian artists' love for painting old ruins, e.g., Claude Lorrain's landscapes. Western souls reverence great sculptural and architectural remains from the past because of their love for infinite time, as well as infinite space and infinite progressive action.

[1] *Ibid.*, p. 291.

there is no creation from inner necessity as in the creative days of the culture. In the Winter, in the "Last Act" of the culture-drama artists are mere copyists and craftsmen. For instance the Roman statue of *Augustus of Prima Porta* is a mere copy of Polycleitus' *Spearbearer;* Chinese painting has had stock forms for centuries which is true also for Persian-Arabian and Indian art.

In the Faustian world art today is:

> A faked music, filled with artificial noisiness of massed instruments; a faked painting, full of idiotic, exotic and showcard effects, that every ten years or so concocts out of the form-wealth of millennia some new 'style' which is in fact no style at all since everyone does as he pleases; a lying plastic that steals from Assyria, Egypt and Mexico indifferently . . .
>
> . . . Every modern age holds change to be development, and puts revivals and fusions of old styles in the place of real becoming. Alexandria also had its Pre-Raphaelite comedians with their vases, chairs, pictures and theories, its symbolists, naturalists and expressionists. The fashion at Rome was now Graeco-Asiatic, now Graeco-Egyptian, now (after Praxiteles) neo-Attic . . .[2]

To summarize, exoticism, eclecticism, and emphasis on size are characteristic of the last days of every great culture; we are in this stage today in the West.

The cycle applied to politico-economic organization in a culture. In the childhood of a culture patriarchal or feudal organization is characteristic. "Purely agrarian values" characterize the economic order, and the two prime classes, therefore, are Nobility and Priesthood. The peasantry is a third group but formless. History belongs to the classes or Estates, Nobility and Priesthood. In Spengler's words:

---

[2] *Ibid.,* p. 294.

In all high Cultures, therefore, there is a *peasantry* which is breed, stock, in the broad sense (and thus to a certain extent nature herself), and a *society* which is *assertively* and emphatically 'in form.' It is a set of classes or Estates, and no doubt artificial and transitory. But the history of these classes and estates is *world-history at highest potential*. It is only in relation to it that the peasant is seen as history-less . . . A Culture is Soul that has arrived at self-expression in sensible forms, but these forms are living and evolving. Their matrix is in the intensified Being of individuals or groups — that is, in that which I have just called Being "in form." And when, and not until, this Being is sufficiently formed to that high rightness, it becomes representative of a representable Culture.

This Culture is not only a grand thing, but wholly unlike any other thing in the organic world. It is the one point at which man lifts himself above the powers of Nature and becomes himself a Creator. Even as to race, breed, he is Nature's creature — he *is* bred. But, as Estate, he breeds himself just as he breeds the noble kinds of animal-plant with which he surrounds himself — and that process, too, is in the deepest and most final sense "Culture." Culture and class are interchangeable expressions; they arise together and they vanish together.[1]

The Nobility is a "higher peasantry" because it, too, is "the sum of blood and race." The architectural expression of the nobility, the castle, "was a development, by way of the country noble's house of Frankish times, from the peasant-dwelling."[2] The Nobility follows unconsciously the Destiny of the culture. "The noble is *man as history*." To him belongs intuitive shrewdness, action, sex, feeling, family life, "breed history, war history, diplomatic history."[4] Politics is his sphere for "politics in the highest

---

[1] *Ibid.*, Vol. II, p. 331.
[2] *Ibid.*, p. 336.
[3] *Ibid.*, p. 338.
[4] *Ibid.*, p. 339.

sense is life and life is politics!"[5]

The Priesthood is the class characterized by Intellect versus the intuitive life of the Nobility. The Priesthood is the Estate of Thinkers whose interest is in eternal truths. The true Priest stands outside Life, sex, family. He is the spectator interested in Causality (Space) rather than creative Time (Destiny).

> The 'priest in the man'—whether the man be noble or not— stands for a focus of sacred Causality in the world. The priestly power is itself of a causal nature, brought about by higher causes and itself in turn an efficient cause. The priest is the middle-man in the timeless extended that is stretched taut between the waking-consciousness and the ultimate secret; and, therefore, the importance of the clergy in each Culture is determined by its prime-symbol. The Classical soul denies Space and therefore needs no middle-man for dealings with it, and so the Classical priesthood disappears in its very beginnings. Faustian man stands face to face with the Infinite, nothing *a priori* shields him from the crushing force of this aspect, and so the Gothic priesthood elevated itself to the heights of the Papal idea.[1]

The scholar's life whether he is philosopher or scientist is like that of the Church in discipline and belief. Poverty, chastity and obedience are observed in the sense of self-sacrifice to knowledge or the School.

These two Estates, Nobility and Priesthood, dominate social life during the Gothic Period (900-1500) in the West; the Doric Period (1100-650) in the Classical world; the Old Kingdom (2900-2400) in Egypt; and the Early

---
[5] *Ibid.*
[1] *Ibid.*, p. 341.

Chou Period (1300-800) in Chinese culture.

In the Late Period of the culture there is the rise of towns and the "actualizing of the matured State-idea." A third class arises, the bourgeoisie, because of the trend towards city life and detachment from the soil. The bourgeoisie represents the "victory of money over landed property."[2] In the West this is the Baroque Period (1500-1800), the Middle Kingdom in Egypt, the Ionic Period in the Classical, and the Late Chou in Chinese culture.

The bourgeoisie, the Third Estate, in Western culture appears as the vanguard of democracy, as a protest against Estates.

> It rejects all differences not justified by reason or practically useful. And yet it does mean something itself, and means it very distinctly — the city-life as estate in contradistinction to that of the country, freedom as a condition in contrast to attachment. But looked at from within its own field it is by no means the unclassified residue that it appears in the eyes of the primary estates. The bourgeoisie has definite limits; it belongs to the Culture; it embraces, in the best sense, all who adhere to it, and under the name of people, populus, demos, rallies nobility and priesthood, money and mind, craftsman and wage-earner, as constituents of itself.[1]

The era ends with revolution and Napoleonism and gives rise necessarily to the Winter, the Civilization age of the culture. This is the period from Alexander the Great to the end of the Roman Empire in the Classical culture, from the Hyksos period to Rameses II in Egyptian, from the "Contending States" period to the end of the Eastern Han Dynasty in Chinese, and from 1800-2000 in the Faustian.

---
[2] *Ibid.*, end of Vol. I, chart of "Contemporary" Political Epochs.
[1] *Ibid.*, Vol. II, p. 358.

This epoch is characterized by the notion of the Fourth Estate, the "Masses" an inorganic, cosmopolitan phenomenon of the megalopolis. This fourth estate, the Mass:

> ... is the absolute of formlessness, persecuting with its hate every sort of form, every distinction of rank, the orderliness of property, the orderliness of knowledge. It is the new nomadism of the Cosmopolis, for which slaves and barbarians in the Classical world, Sudras in the Indian, and in general anything and everything that is merely human, provide an undifferentiated floating something that falls apart the moment it is born, that recognizes no past and possesses no future. Thus the Fourth Estate becomes the expression of the passing of a history over into the history-less. The mass is the end, the radical nullity.[2]

The materialistic skeptical philosophy typical of this era in the West is Socialism (Stoicism is the parallel in the Classical and Buddhism in the Indian). Socialism is the true Faustian form of skepticism since it emphasizes the ethic of deed, of action or Will. It is "scientific" another quality of the skeptical era — an era in which "brain rules, soul abdicates." Materialism, Darwinism and Socialism are interrelated and "only separable on the surface." The world-disillusion, the skepticism expressed in these thought-forms, presage the end of the culture as Vico also said, and each culture has its "own mode of spiritual extinction." Faustian man *shatters* his ideals; the Apollinian "watches them crumble before his eyes," while the Indian "withdraws from their presence into himself."[3]

Faustian man is now in the era of transition from the dictatorship of money and its "political weapon democracy" to the era of Caesarism which terminates the Culture. Faustian man in his resolve to be *master* of nature — a

---
[2] *Ibid.*
[3] *Ibid.*, Vol. I, p. 357.

necessary expression of his Destiny-Idea — has created the machine world of today. The Machine is devilish, says Spengler, because it signifies the deposition of God and the disintegration of the basic religious soul-form of the culture. The Machine has bred the entrepreneur, the engineer, and the laborer with the engineer as the crucial figure. Now is the time of the battle between Machine and Money: productive versus acquisitive economics; but the final conflict is between Money and Blood. The victory belongs to Blood (Caesarism). Spengler writes perhaps prophetically:

> The coming of Caesarism breaks the dictature of money and its political weapon democracy . . . The sword is victorious over money, the master-will subdues again the plunderer-will. If we call these money-powers 'Capitalism,' then we may designate as Socialism the will to call into life a mighty politico-economic order that transcends all class interests . . . *A power can be overthrown only by another power,* not by a principle, and no power that can confront money is left but this one. Money is overthrown and abolished only by blood. *Life* is alpha and omega, the cosmic onflow in microcosmic form. It is *the* fact of facts within the world as history . . . *World-history is the world court,* and it has ever decided in favor of the stronger, fuller, and more self-assured life — . . . Always it has sacrificed truth and justice to might and race, and passed doom of death upon men and peoples in whom truth was more than deeds, and justice than power. And so the drama of a high Culture — that wondrous world of deities. arts, thoughts, battles, cities — closes with the return of the pristine facts of the blood eternal that is one and the same as the ever-circling cosmic flow. The bright imaginative Waking-Being submerges itself into the silent service of Being, as the Chinese and Roman empires tell us. Time triumphs over Space . . .
> For us, however, whom a Destiny has placed in this Culture and at this moment of its development — the

moment when money is celebrating its last victories, and the Caesarism that is to succeed approaches with quiet, firm step — our direction, willed and obligatory at once, is set for us within narrow limits, and on any other terms life is not worth the living. We have not the freedom to reach to this or to that. but the freedom to do the necessary or to do nothing. And a task that historic necessity has set *will* be accomplished with the individual or against him.[1]

The Nazi nationalistic Socialistic Caesarism of "blood and soil" seems like an abortive attempt to fulfill Spengler's idea of historic necessity; but the year 2000 has not yet arrived. World-state Caesarism may appear.

Relativity of science, logic, and mathematics to the culture-form. Every culture-organism has a life-cycle from birth to death of about one thousand years. Each stage in the cycle is necessary in a definite chronological order. The content of each stage is the essential expression of the prime symbol of the culture. This is as true in science, logic and mathematics as in philosophy, the arts and social forms, Spengler maintains. This makes him a complete relativist. There is no progress, not even in science, for humanity as a whole; instead there are individually distinct great culture-organisms or macrocosmic personalities of equal interest and status. The "science" or philosophy of history is the comprehension of the life-cycle pattern of such a culture-organism.

This makes the logic of history and the mode of its comprehension entirely different from the logic of science. Both logics are a morphology, that is, both treat of general patterns. Science concerns itself with discovery of causal laws and relations and has to do with the mechanical, the extended, the Become, the Dead.[1] This type of morphology

---

[1] *Ibid.*, Vol. II, p. 507, the ending of Spengler's great work.

[1] This distinction between science and intellect, which deal with "dead" materials, versus intuition which treats of the "living" is central to Bergson's methodology also.

Spengler calls *Systematic*. The organic logic of history has to do with Direction, Destiny, Becoming, the Living. This type of morphology Spengler calls Physiognomic.[2] While the morphological element of the Causal is a Principle,

> the morphological element of Destiny is an *Idea,* an idea that is incapable of being 'cognized,' described or defined and can only be felt and inwardly lived. This idea is something of which one is either entirely ignorant or else —like the man of the spring and every truly significant man of the late seasons, believer, lover, artist, poet — entirely certain.[3]

In the same vein, Spengler claims that any man can be educated to comprehend Systematic, but "the man who knows history [physiognomic] is born."[4] The systematic spirit "is an autumnal and passing phenomenon belonging to the ripest conditions of a culture. Linked with the city, into which its life is more and more herded, it comes and goes with the city."[1] Art, on the other hand, which physiognomic comprehends, exists as long as the culture.

Science and scientific method even though treating of the dead and mechanical side of things have no universal validity. There are no universally valid scientific laws or universally valid systems of mathematics, nor is there even any universally valid system of logic. Spengler writes that "a mathematical, and generally a scientific way of thinking is right, convincing, a 'necessity of thought,' when it completely expresses the life-feeling proper to it."[2] The world of nature and science are creations of the culture organism.

---

[2] Spengler, *op. cit.*, Vol. I, p. 100.
[3] *Ibid.*, p. 121.
[4] *Ibid.*, p. 102.
[1] *Ibid.*
[2] *Ibid.*, p. 67.

> Every idea that is possible at all is a mirror of the being of its author. The statement that 'man has created God in his own image,' valid for every historical religion, is not less valid for every physical theory, however firm its basis of fact.[3]

Faustian mathematics takes the forms of *analytic* geometry, the infinitesimal calculus, multi-dimensional mathematical systems; in physics quanta of energy (not material particles) are the ultimate constituents of the universe; and in logic *functional* relations are important. Science and mathematical theories are symbols (myths) which express Faustian man's Prime Symbol — Infinite Space. The Infinite in dynamics and becoming, power and will are mythologized into "objective", scientific symbolic forms. (In this context it is interesting to note that Ernst Cassirer in his *Philosophy of Symbolic Forms* comes close to this same view.)

The Classical soul emphasizes the Finite, static, eternally present and non-temporal in its logic, science and mathematics. Euclidean mathematics is statically spatial and a closed system versus Western dynamic Leibnizian unlimited and functional forms. In Classical physics the atom is a shape or limited form, not the dematerialized quantum-energy phenomenon of the West. Spengler comments, "Every atomic theory, therefore, is a myth and not an experience. In it the Culture, through the contemplative-creative power of its great physicists, reveals its inmost essence and very self."[1]

Magian mathematics and science also are described as culture expressions.[2] The prime symbol of the Magian Macrocosmos is the Cavern (the Dome is the architectural ex-

---

[3] *Ibid.*, p. 381.
[1] *Ibid,.* p. 387.
[2] The Magian culture includes the near-Eastern peoples: Hebrews, Early Christians, Arabs, Persians, Armenians from the years 1 A.D.-1000 AD.

pression of its Idea). It expresses a static, but fairy-tale-like world of "secret forces." Therefore, this culture developed algebra in mathematics and chemistry in science.

Spengler thinks that he has demonstrated that there are no universal truths in mathematics or science,[3] and since these most objective aspects of knowledge are merely functions of a particular Culture-Soul, how much *more* relative are human ideas of the good or the beautiful. The ethical values, aesthetic values, and truth values (science included) which are given concrete form-expression in a culture are to be understood in relation to the feeling-core represented in the "prime-symbol" of the macrocosmic organism. This is their true significance. "Everything whatsoever that has *become*," Spengler says "is a symbol, and the expression of a soul." All research into the meaning of the past "reaches up to a final or superlative truth — *Alles Vergangliche ist nur ein Gleichnis.*" [4]

Summary statement of Spengler's theory of history. History is the study of the morphology of culture-organisms."*Cultures are organisms*, and world-history is their collective biography." [1] Cultures like men, animals and plants are "inward forms that constantly and everywhere repeat themselves," [2] and this repetition is the cyclical recurrence that makes the science of a morphology of history possible. The macrocosmic psycho-biological cycle of a culture is like that of the human individual, the microcosm, and governed by the same kind of inward necessity. In this way Spengler applies the organic macrocosm-microcosm philosophy so typical of Oriental thought, but gives

---
[3] From one point of view this is true and from another false. There has been progress in the attainment of more adequate and comprehensive theories in science from the time of the Greeks to our epoch. Scientific truths however, are not *absolute* truths; to this extent Spengler's relativism is justified.
[4] From Goethe's *Faust*. The translator renders it:
"All we see before us passing
Sign and symbol is alone." Vol. I, p. 102.
[1] *Ibid.*, p. 104.

377

it a much narrower application and range. *The Orientals extend the aesthetic continuum of the culture soul to the macrocosmic soul of the total universe of reality; and in this way man overcomes the transiency, the relativity of all of his works and knowledge.* Spengler's relativity would perhaps have been resolved in a similar way if he had developed a systematic metaphysics; but such a universal metaphysics would have refuted his theory of the relativity of all metaphysics, all creative works of the human spirit, to the culture-organisms of which they are simply the essential aspects.

---
[2] *Ibid.*

Chapter III

The Cyclical Pattern of Sorokin's Cultural Dynamics

Sorokin in his four-volume work *Social and Cultural Dynamics* (1937), the argument of which is telescoped into the one-volume *The Crisis of Our Age* (1941), marshalls much evidence to demonstrate, like Vico and Spengler, a definite and identical causal cyclical pattern in the dynamics (or significant movements) in every great culture. The cyclic pattern has three movements each of which follows necessarily from the previous one. The three movements are: (1) the Ideational, (2) the Idealistic, and (3) the Sensate. As in Spengler's work, the purpose of the morphological study of great cultures is to demonstrate the stage in the time scale of our Western culture at present and the prognosis for its future. He discovers by the application of his morphology as does Spengler that we are in the senile last stages of a culture cycle.

Every culture,[1] Sorokin says, begins with an *Ideational* stage. In Western society the Ideational stage was the medieval era. This era was a unified epoch integrated around

---

[1] Sorokin like all the previous thinkers we have studied conceives a culture as an integrated thing. Sorokin says: "Any great culture instead of being a mere dumping place of a multitude of diverse cultural phenomena, existing side by side and unrelated to one another, represents a unity or individuality whose parts are permeated by the same fundamental principle and articulate the same basic value." Pitirim A. Sorokin, *The Crisis of Our Age* (New York: E. P. Dutton, 1941), p. 17.

the same supreme principle of true reality and value: an infinite, supersensory, and superrational God, omnipresent, omnipotent, omniscient, absolutely just, good, and beautiful, creator of the world and of man. Such a unified system of culture based upon the principle of a supersensory and superrational God as the only true reality and value may be called ideational.[2]

In Greek culture the same religious premise grounds the culture from the eighth to the sixth centuries B.C.; Brahmanic Indian culture, Buddhist and Taoist cultures show the same integration idea in their beginnings.[3]

The decline of the Ideational stage is caused by the emergence of a new idea, "namely, that *the true reality and value is sensory.*"[1] This is the scientific, materialistic approach to reality — it affirms that the real is only what can be perceived by the sense organs of sight, sound, touch, smell, taste. The new sensory or empirical approach is the opposite of the Ideational, but the culture does not swing at once to this, its opposite. Instead it combines the sensory or empirical with the supersensory, superrational *ideational forms.* This combination Sorokin calls the *Idealistic* phase of the culture cycle. This Idealistic phase in Western culture occurred in the thirteenth and fourteenth centuries. For example, St. Thomas Aquinas combined the supernatural (ideational) Biblical views of reality with the empiricism of Aristotelian philosophy. In Greek culture this ideational synthesis was accomplished in the fifth and fourth centuries B.C. It is the time of great and definite system building in all culture fields.

Then the dynamics of the culture proceeds very definitely towards greater and greater decline of the ideational elements (the fundamental integrating religious idea) and

---

[2] Pitirim A. Sorokin, *The Crisis of Our Age* (New York: E. P. Dutton, 1941), p. 19.
[3] *Ibid.*
[1] *Ibid.*

towards the greater and greater increase of the sensate elements until at last the sensate becomes dominant. This *Sensate* epoch is characterized by the predominance of the empirical sensuous secular elements in every area of the society. This era began in the West around the sixteenth century, and with the Hellenistic phase in the Classical world.

To summarize:
>Thus the major principle of medieval culture made it predominately otherworldly and religious, oriented toward the supersensuous and permeated by this value. The major principle of the idealistic culture was partly supersensory and religious and partly 'this-worldly" and secular. Finally, the major principle of our modern sensate culture is predominantly 'this-worldly,' secular, and utilitarian. All these types — ideational, idealistic, and sensate — are exemplified in the history of Egyptian and Babylonian, Graeco-Roman, Hindu, Chinese, and other great cultures.

Sorokin supports his thesis by an examination of all the aspects of a great culture: the fine arts, science, philosophy and religion, ethics and law, social organization and relations.

The cycle in the fine arts. Ideational art in the West has for its intention the expression of "the supersensory kingdom of God. Its 'heroes' are God and other deities, angels, saints and sinner, and the soul, as well as the mysteries of Creation, Incarnation, Redemption, Crucifixion, and Salvation, and other transcendental events. It is religious through and through." [2] The emotional tone of this art is "pious, ethereal, and ascetic," [3] and *"its style is and must*

---
[1] *Ibid.,* p. 21.
[2] *Ibid.,* p. 31.
[3] *Ibid.*

be symbolic."[4] Art works are symbols of a spiritual world which cannot be revealed in its essential nature in any sensuous form; sensuous forms are merely signs, symbols of a transcendental realm. In Christian art the dove, olive branch, fish, vine and branches did not signify their sensuous counterparts but "values of the invisible kingdom of God."[5] This early art is archaic in its external crudity; it is not executed by professionals for aesthetic enjoyment, but is done anonymously for the purpose of aiding believers to commune with the spiritual or God-world.

In support of Sorokin's thesis that the ideational, symbolic approach is characteristic of the dawn of a new culture, we can point to examples of this in Oriental cultures such as the Buddhist. In early Buddhist art there is no representation of Buddha himself; instead there is a symbol, the Bodhi Tree, which signifies the spiritual idea of Enlightenment.

The next phase of the cycle, idealistic art, begins with the advent of sensate ideas. *Sensate art* is therefore delineated next by Sorokin. Realism is the keynote. The subject matter is the ordinary everyday world of the senses:

> Empirical *paysage,* empirical man, empirical events and adventures, empirical portraiture — such are its topics. Farmers, workers, housewives, girls, stenographers, teachers, and other human beings are its personages. At its overripe stage, prostitutes, criminals, street urchins, the insane, hypocrites, rogues, and other subsocial types are its favorite 'heroes.' Its aim is to afford a refined sensual enjoyment: relaxation, excitation of tired nerves, amusement, pleasure, entertainment. For this reason it must be sensational, passionate, pathetic, sensual, and incessantly new. It is marked by voluptuous nudity and concupiscence. It is divorced from religion, morals, and other values, and styles itself 'art for art's sake.' Since it must

---
[4] *Ibid.*
[5] *Ibid.,* pp. 81 f.

amuse and entertain, it makes wide use of caricature, satire, comedy, farce, debunking, ridiculing, and similar means.

It's style is naturalistic, visual, even illusionistic, free from any supersensory symbolism.[1]

Idealistic art, the second movement in the dynamics of a culture as manifested in art-forms, combines sensate and ideational elements. The sensate elements are used only in their "sublimest and noblest aspects."[2] The heroes of its subject-matter are "partly gods and other transcendental creatures; partly the empirical man, but in his noblest aspects."[3] It consciously refuses to treat the ugly, debasing and vulgar as fit subjects for art. Its emotional mood is one of serenity. (Here Sorokin differs from Spengler who applies serenity only to Classical art.) The style is "partly symbolic and allegoric, partly realistic and naturalistic."[4] This is true of the great Gothic cathedral art, especially that of the thirteenth century, and of Greek art of the Golden Age, i.e., Greek art of the fifth century B.C.

A fourth kind of art is *eclectic art.* This has no real style but is a conglomeration of "anything and everything." It is a phenomenon of the disintegration stage of a culture, the last stages of the sensate.

Sorokin illustrates his cycle-pattern with many examples from the cultures of the world. For brevity we shall emphasize the cycle as applied to the Western world, first the Graeco-Roman culture and secondly our more recent Western culture which began with the medieval.

In Greek culture the archaic period of the eighth to the end of the sixth century B.C. is the ideational period. In this era objects are not represented realistically, but geometrical forms and similar symbols are employed to rep-

---

[1] *Ibid.,* p. 32.
[2] *Ibid.,* p. 33.
[3] *Ibid.*
[4] *Ibid.,* p. 34.

resent the spiritual world of religious values. Then the idealistic phase emerges with its climax in the Golden Age (fifth century B.C.). The great creators in this era are Phidias, Aeschylus, Sophocles and Pindar. Idealized naturalism is the keynote, a half religious, half-empirical style. Nobility, serenity, lofty idealism are the feeling tones of the Parthenon, of the sculptures by Phidias, Polycleitus and Myron, of the great tragedies and the great poetry of this epoch. It is the best exemplification in any culture, Sorokin rightly says, of the idealistic phase. The sensate phase begins with the Hellenistic era, approximately the third century B.C. and continues to the fourth century A.D. when the ideational phase of the subsequent culture begins. The sensate era is marked by genre art, illusionistic relief sculpture, literal realism in sculpture in the round, overripe sensualistic ornamentation, eclecticism, sensationalism.

Christian culture begins its ideational phase as the successor to the deceased Classical. The medieval sculpture, mosaic decorations, and architecture are all devoted to God. The churches and the later cathedrals are the Bible in stone. Painting, too, is symbolic and other-worldly. The emphasis in literature is religious—Biblical. There is no really secular literature until the twelfth century.[1] Drama consists of the church service, religious processions, and miracle and mystery plays. Music is Gregorian chant for the purpose of singing the Mass, the church liturgy. Professional artists did not exist. Art was a form of devotion to God among the creators of the illuminated manuscripts, or the workers on churches or cathedrals, or those who sang in the choirs.

With the beginning of the thirteenth century the Ideational phase dawns. As in the Greek idealistic era, there is interest in the noblest aspects of the empirical world of sense. Again as in the Greek world, the artist does not

---

[1] *Ibid.*, p. 40.

duplicate reality but represents idealized types and great events. Its style is "serene, calm, free from any frivolity, comedy or satire, violent passions or emotions, anything debasing, *pathetique*, or macabre. It is the art of a pure nun who for the first time notes the beauty of the empirical world — the spring morning, the flowers and trees, the dew, the sunshine, the caressing wind and blue sky."[2] St. Francis of Assisi's *Hymn to the Sun* is one of the most eloquent expressions of the soul of this era, for St. Francis in his spirit embodies the pure saintly soul who notices the beauty of the empirical world. In music the idealistic phase begins a century later.

Secular trends increase until finally the sensate epoch dawns at the close of the fifteenth century. It is the era of secular emphasis, "divorced from religious, moral, and civic values." It reaches its climax "and possible limit in the nineteenth century."[1] As we have said above, sensate art chooses for subject matter ordinary everyday individuals, then degenerates into depicting subsocial, voluptuous, pathological characters; in literature and drama as well there is sensationalism, caricature, satire, comedy, vaudeville, operetta — all in Hollywood style. Professional artists cater to a public for the most part uneducated in art values. Art works are now "made for a market, as a commodity to be bought and sold like any other commodity."[2] In music there is ever greater increase in complexity and ornamental flourishes. It is significant that orchestras increased conspicuously in size alone from Monteverdi's time (about 1600) when there were about thirty instruments, to the eighteenth century when there were as many as sixty instruments, to the nineteenth and twentieth centuries with orchestras of a hundred or more instruments.

Although Sorokin seems to think of the thirteenth century when Thomistic idealistic culture was dominant as

[2] *Ibid.*, p. 42.
[1] *Ibid.*, p. 43.
[2] *Ibid.*

the zenith of achievement in Western culture and the sensate era as a decline from this grand peak, he praises some of the great creative products of this epoch. He writes:

> Finally, respecting the inner value of its foremost creations, Western sensate art requires no apologia. Bach, Mozart, and Beethoven; Wagner, Brahms, and Tschaikowsky, need not apologize to any composer of any previous period. A similar generalization holds good for Shakespeare, Goethe and Schiller; Chateaubriand, Hugo, and Balzac; Dickens, Tolstoi, and Dostoevski; for the builders of the mightiest skyscrapers; for the most eminent actors; or for the most distinguished painters and sculptors from the Renaissance to the present time. Any master of our sensate art is as competent in his own field as almost any master of earlier periods and cultures.[3]

In this, the twentieth century, Sŏrŏkin finds that our arts are for the most part decadent; only architecture gives signs of hope of a new integration.[1] Spengler and Toynbee, also, are convinced that this is a decadent era in all culture areas; we are ripe for a new ideational age.

The cycle in the system of truth: science, philosophy, and religion. In the ideational era truth is that which is revealed supernaturally and may be called "truth of faith. It is regarded as infallible, yielding adequate knowledge about the true-reality values."[2] Sensate truth is "truth of the senses, obtained through our organs of sense perception."[3] Idealistic truth is a synthesis of ideational and sensate "made by our reason,"[4] *e.g.* the Thomistic approach to truth. The radical clash is between ideational and sensate truth. As an example Sorokin mentions the fact

---
[3] *Ibid.*, p. 55.
[1] *Ibid.*, p. 50.
[2] *Ibid.*, p. 81.
[3] *Ibid.*
[4] *Ibid.*

that Christianity (then in its early or ideational stage) was called an abominable superstition by Roman intellectuals of the sensate stage of the Classical culture — such men as Tacitus, Pliny, Suetonius and Marcus Aurelius. On the other hand, Christians like St. Paul called the sensate or empirical wisdom of this world foolishness with God; Tertullian makes the non-sensate, non-rational character of ideational truth very clear in the famous statement quoted by Sorokin:

> The son of God is crucified; that is not shameful because it is shameful [that is from the sensate standpoint]. And the Son of God died; that is credible because it is absurd. And he rose from the dead; that is quite certain because it is impossible.[5]

Sorokin comments that "what is impossible or untrue from the sensate standpoint may be possible and quite true from the standpoint of the Christian truth of faith, and vice versa."[1] Christian ideational truth had as did Augustine only two interests, God and the soul.

Sensate truth favors "the study of the sensory world, with its physical, chemical, and biological properties and relationships."[2] Therefore "natural science replaces religion, theology, and even speculative philosophy."[3] The sensate trend began to gain momentum during the Renaissance, was dominant in the eighteenth century and reached a peak in the nineteenth and twentieth centuries. The sensate system of truth is skeptical towards any supersensory reality or value, especially the world of revealed religion. In philosophy empirical, pragmatic, utilitarian systems are preferred versus those based upon ideational

---
[5] *Ibid.*, pp. 84 f.
[1] *Ibid.*, p. 85.
[2] *Ibid.*, p. 87.
[3] *Ibid.*

or idealistic truths; materialism becomes a dominant worldview with man himself de-spiritualized and treated in terms of causal mechanisms such as conditioned response, psychoanalytical "complexes," socio-economic determinants, etc. All knowledge, even sensate empirical scientific knowledge, is "relative"; there are no absolute truths or values. The relativity, Sorokin comments, gives rise eventually to "skepticism, cynicism, and nihilism. The very boundary line between the true and the false, between right and wrong, disappears, and society finds itself in a state of veritable mental, moral, and cultural anarchy." [4]

Ideational truth as a system is the dialectical opposite of the sensate. Truth in this system is intuitional based upon "revelation, divine inspiration, and mystic experience." [1] Revealed religion and theology "become the queen of genuine wisdom and science, empirical knowledge serving as a mere handmaid." [2] Ideational truth emphasizes "eternal verities, in contradistinction to the temporal of the senses . . . It is absolutistic, non-utilitarian, non-pragmatic." [3]

The idealistic system of truth synthesizes the other two opposing systems. It incorporates "the three distinct elements of sensory, religious, and rationalistic truth. The systems of Plato and Aristotle, of Albertus Magnus and Saint Thomas Aquinas, are supreme examples, attempting to embrace in one organic whole divine as well as sensory and dialectic truth." [4]

Sorokin concludes from these three approaches to truth that there is no one absolute system. The rhythmic cycle of truth in every culture: ideational, idealistic, sensate; then repetition again and again as a new culture arises out of the old — this rhythm proves that there cannot be

---

[4] *Ibid.*, p. 98.
[1] *Ibid.*, p. 102.
[2] *Ibid.*
[3] *Ibid.*
[4] *Ibid.*

"only one valid system of truth."[5] Scientific truth (Sorokin considers this as sensate for the most part) is not the only valid kind of truth; the 'crisis" in this truth-system of contemporary culture lies in taking it thus. It is an error to believe that this kind of truth is destined to progress indefinitely. The rhythmic cycle of truth in history proves this notion of linear progress false; secondly, genuine truth even the great scientific truths belong actually in the ideational category. The pioneer theoreticians in science such as Galileo, Newton, and Einstein used intuition and deductive reasoning more than sense organs in the great hypotheses they invented. Sense organ verification entered the picture only at the end as confirmation from certain theoretically deduced observation areas. Such sense organ verification might be a mere flash of light on a screen—unintelligible except from the point of view of elaborate mathematical constructions. The conclusion is that sense organ observation contributed very little to the development of the greatest and most fruitful theories of science.[6]

Sorokin concludes that the right approach to truth in all fields is the "three-dimensional" or "integral" one which combines the three aspects of faith (intuition), reason, and sensation.[1] Culture-eras exaggerate each one and this is the dynamic cause of the cyclic rhythms.

Western culture today exaggerates the sensate phase in philosophy, science, and religion (social gospel is emphasized versus spiritual truths of faith) and this is similar to the sensate situation in the fine arts. This exaggeration has led to the "decadent state — the phase of transition."[2]

>Other forms of culture are now looming on the horizon, destined to carry on, in their own peculiar manner, the task of creative evolution. When these forms, in turn, have exhausted their inner vitality, a new

[5] *Ibid.*, p. 103.
[6] *Ibid.*, pp. 106-109.
[1] *Ibid.*, p. 112.
[2] *Ibid.*, p. 132.

sensate culture will again doubtless emerge; and thus *the creative 'eternal cycle'* will persist, as long as human history endures.[1]

The cycle in ethics and law. Ideational ethics is related to a supernatural realm. "The norms of such ethics are regarded as revealed by, or emanating from the Absolute; therefore as absolute, unconditional, unchangeable, and eternal."[2] Sensory pleasure is irrelevant to this approach to ethics; the sense world, in fact, is looked upon as a false, illusory realm and an obstacle to spiritual fulfilment.

Sensate ethics takes the opposite point of view. It is thoroughly hedonistic and regards "sensory happiness, pleasure, utility, and comfort, in their refined or unrefined form, as the supreme value."[3]

Idealistic ethics is "an intermediary synthesis of ideational and sensate values."[4] This system recognizes God, the "supersensory Absolute," as the chief value, but differs from the ideational view in recognition of "those sensory values that are the noblest and that do not militate against the Absolute."[5]

In Western culture ideational ethics (Christian) began to become dominant after the fourth century and reigned supreme until the thirteenth. The central principle is "the all-embracing, all bestowing, and all-forgiving love of God for man, of man for God, and of man for man."[6] Christian ideational ethics "raises man to the highest level of sanctification, and protects him unconditionally against any use as a mere means to an end."[7]

Idealistic ethics reached dominance in the thirteenth to the fifteenth century. But sensate ethics gains strength in the fourteenth and fifteenth centuries until it becomes dominant in the sixteenth the era of the Reformation and the

---
[1] *Ibid.*, p. 132.
[2] *Ibid.*, p. 135.
[3] *Ibid.*
[4] *Ibid.*, p. 137.
[5] *Ibid.*

High Renaissance. "The hedonism, sensuality, and paganism of the ethics of the Renaissance are well known."[1] The Protestant movement "was largely utilitarian and sensate . . . money-making was declared the sign of God's grace . . ."[2] Utilitarianism, capitalism, paganism, Protestantism are parallel growths of sensate ethics, the system which has dominated our culture for the last four centuries.

The cycle in philosophy of law has been the same as in ethics. Ideational law is absolute in all cultures; it is law given by the divine power or powers. In Western culture this is Biblical law, the Ten Commandments and the Sermon on the Mount are examples. Punishment of violation of the law is not only in the sensory world but in the supersensory because violation is considered sin against God not merely man. "Almost every law action . . . is prescribed to the last detail through the pronouncement of certain sacred formulae, through definite sacred actions . . ."[3] Judges of violations of law are directly or indirectly "of the sacerdotal order, assisted by oracles, prophets, seers, saints, and the like."[4]

Sensate law is the direct opposite in its system. Law is taken as completely man-made for the utilitarian purpose of protection of the life, property, security and happiness of either certain classes of society or in democratic states (theoretically) of all men. Punishments are sensory and for the pragmatic purpose of revenge, or example, or re-education of the violator, or the security of society. The judges are secular. The government "that enacts and enforces such a code is a secular — not a theocratic — government, based either upon military and physical power, upon riches and abilities, or upon the mandate of the electorate."[1]

---
[6] *Ibid.*, p. 139.
[7] *Ibid.*
[1] *Ibid.*, p. 140.
[2] *Ibid.*
[3] *Ibid.*, p. 149.
[4] *Ibid.*, p. 150.

Idealistic law is intermediate between ideational and sensate. It was dominant in the Thomism of the thirteenth century.

Western culture is now in the disintegration stage of sensate ethics and law as in every other aspect of culture. Ethical values and the idea of law have become so utterly debased and so "relative" and therefore meaningless that the door has been opened to the "might is right" idea. The immense power of the "underworld" gangs, the growing juvenile delinquency are results of our devaluation of ethical values and our utilitarian approach to law. Instead of liberating man from religious superstitions it has made him "a mere electron-proton complex or reflex mechanism devoid of any sanctity or end value ... If he is useful for this or that, he may be treated decently and cared for as we care for a useful animal. If he is harmful, he can be 'liquidated,' as we exterminate harmful snakes." [2]

Sensate ethics and law will liquidate man, Sorokin says, (it has already caused two world wars) unless there is a return to another ideational form of ethics and law to reintegrate man again.

The cycle in the pattern of social relationships. Sorokin thinks that there are only three basic patterns of social relationships of man to man and group to group. These are: *Familistic* in which the bond is mutual love; free *contractual* relationships in which the bond is an agreement or contract entered upon for the mutual benefit of the contracting parties, but not based on love or hate; and *compulsory* relationships "imposed by one party upon the others, contrary to their wishes and interests." [3]

In the ideational era of a culture familistic relations prevail as in the feudal era of Western culture (eighth to the twelfth centuries).

Contractual relationships grow as cities are founded— in Western culture between the thirteenth and sixteenth

---
[1] *Ibid.*, p. 154.
[2] *Ibid.*, p. 164.
[3] *Ibid.*, p. 167.

centuries. From the sixteenth to the eighteenth centuries compulsory relationships increased. However the nineteenth and twentieth centuries, the era of capitalism, has been the Golden Age of Contractualism. Contractualism is the primary note in all business fields, and in many professional services. In politics Contractualism is characteristic of democratic governments. In religion church membership is contractual (in Protestant churches one is free to become or not to become a member). In marriage the bond has tended to become more and more contractual, a civil contract can bind a marriage. Divorce is also contractual as a result of the contractual nature of marriage. Contractualism emphasizes individual liberty of entering into contracts of many sorts direct and indirect for one's advantage. The basis is therefore in the Original Sin of egoism to use the language of the Great Religions. Individualism in the contemporary Western sense (which has degenerated into selfish egoism) is a concomitant of capitalism. It means, Sorokin says, *sensate liberty* versus *ideational liberty*. Sensate liberty means the freedom to satisfy one's desires; thus if one's means of satisfying his desires are insufficient one is not free, but if one's means are sufficient or more than sufficient to satisfy his desires he is free. The man of the ideational era limited his sense desires and concentrated on inner freedom, unlike contemporary sensate man whose materialistic, sensate desires continually outrun his means of satisfying them. Idealistic man has a place for both material satisfactions but in restrained moderation, and cultivation of inner spirituality and freedom. Western culture today, however, has chosen sensate liberty and this has contributed to the crisis in contractual relationships, the dominant form in social relations. The crisis is evident among the governments of this twentieth century: Nazism, Fascism, Communism as totalitarian regimes abandoning contractual relationships in favor of *compulsory*. Even in democratic countries government-controlled social relationships (compulsory) are increasing rapidly.

This is true especially in the economic field, *e.g.* the large taxes collected from private individuals for government spending in many areas. This is part of the "weakening, disintegration, and elimination of the institution of private property"[1] which has been part of the contractual system. Corporations and trusts are other encroachments upon the individualism associated with private property. Sorokin maintains that "corporate economy is a decentralized totalitarianism, while the totalitarianism, of the Communist, or Fascist, or Nazi type is the economy of a centralized corporation."[2]

The contractual system is disintegrating in the family; too many homes are mere places to sleep overnight with the parents and children at various different places. The contractual system has disintegrated in international relations to a large extent; threat of force and not agreements is the significant factor. The only remedy, Sorokin believes, is:

> A preliminary reconstruction of absolute moral values and norms, with their *'dura lex sed lex,'* obligagatory for all, universally binding, not to be brushed aside in the interest of relative, expedient pseudovalues . . . It means the replacement of sensate mentality by an ideational or idealistic *Weltanschauung*.[3]

The rhythmic pattern and its recurrence in other cultures such as the Graeco-Roman suggest a return to the ideational family relationship founded upon mutual love (the Christian ethic which followed the Graeco-Roman). Liberty must again be understood in its ideational form: inner spiritual freedom from which all true freedom follows. The spirit must again conquer the flesh and revivify

---

[1] *Ibid.*, p. 184.
[2] *Ibid.*, p. 186.
[3] *Ibid.*, p. 203.

mankind. Life must be lived in awareness of the unity at the spiritual level of all men. We have noticed in Parts I and II of this study the universal agreement that this is a necessary goal if spiritual freedom and bliss, the only genuine freedom and bliss, are to be attained for mankind.

Sorokin, especially in his more recent works, shows that this goal must be the foundation for a new ideational or idealistic era about to dawn — an era which will be integrated around the idea of Creative Altruism.

Dawn of a new Culture Epoch: Era of Creative Altruism and the Supraconscious level of human life. The new era about to supercede the dying sensate epoch will be one of a new intense spirituality as we said above. Like Sri Aurobindo Sorokin believes that the global politico-economic and general cultural situation is such that man will be compelled to revolutionize his entire nature or perish. In the *Reconstruction of Humanity* Sorokin examines what he calls sardonically "quack cures for war and impotent plans for peace."[1] These are the "political cures," *viz.*, democracy, the United Nations, and World Government; "economic cures and plans," *viz.*, capitalism, and the communist, fascist, and socialist economies; and "scientific, educational, religious, and other cures and plans." All are found sadly lacking in curative power including the religious cure because, Sorokin points out, the world's religious bodies

> have failed to mitigate war and other forms of conflict because they have not practiced what they have preached. In proselytizing they have tended to use the gospel of love to mask the sword of destruction and degradation ... As long as the chasm between preaching and practice remains, there is no reason to believe that the religions of the present time or of the future can eliminate war and ensure a lasting peace.[2]

---

[1] Pitirim A. Sorokin, *The Reconstruction of Humanity* (Boston: The Beacon Press, 1948), Part I, pp. 7-57.
[2] *Ibid.*, p. 44.

The only cure which will be able to create a new culture era for the human race — the cure we must apply or perish — is Creative Altruism. Man must reintegrate himself and the dawning new culture cycle around this idea. Humanity must be "transfigured" into a new altruistic level of consciousness which Sorokin calls the supraconscious level, the egoless, ineffable state of organic integration with society, the cosmos of nature and the Infinite emphasized as man's goal in all the yogic or mystical philosophies (see the chapter on yogic or mystical philosophies above, Part I, and relevant passages elsewhere in this part; and Part II the chapters on Aurobindo and Radhakrishnan). This supraconscious level as man's necessary immediate destiny and goal parallels Sri Aurobindo's evolutionary goal of Supermind. Sorokin expresses his admiration of and agreement with Sri Aurobindo and Hindu yogic philosophies in general as well as the similar Taoist, Buddhist, Moslem and Christian mystical philosophies all of which emphasize the supraconscious level of a creative altruism. It is this which must be the foundation of a new vital spiritual life which in turn will create a new world order.

In *The Ways and Power of Love: Types, Factors, and Techniques of Moral Transformation,* Sorokin gives much evidence to show that human nature can attain the level of Creative Altruism, the supraconscious mind-state. Early in the book he describes what he means by this mind-state and distinguishes it from the lower levels of the Unconscious, the Bioconscious, and the Socioconscious. These latter three plus the supraconscious make up the "fourfold mental structure and energies of man." The Unconscious is the level of "undifferentiated total life energy."[1] It comprises the "reflexological, instinctive, and unconscious excitations and inhibitions, drives and activities of the human organism necessary for animal life, growth, and sur-

---
[1] Pitirim A. Sorokin, *The Ways and Power of Love* (Boston: The Beacon Press, 1954), p. 85.

vival."[2] The Bioconscious in the person appears when biological tensions become conscious. For example, if one becomes hungry, his "nutritional ego" occupies his conscious attention; if sex tensions become conscious, the "sex ego" is in the forefront of consciousness. In addition to this kind of biological ego-consciousness, Sorokin adds the biological "age egos of the individual." These are "the egos of baby, adolescent, mature man, old man."[3] (cf. Aurobindo's similar pattern of levels.)

The Socioconscious in man consists of "the conscious sociocultural energies, activities, egos, and roles."[1] Each "person possesses as many sociocultural egos, roles, and activities as there are sociocultural groups with which, voluntarily or not, he is connected . . ."[2] Most individuals have a family ego, a state-citizenship ego, a nationality ego, a religious-affiliation ego, an occupational ego and lesser ego roles such as club membership. These various egos of the same person are for the most part very different; for example the religious going-to-church ego is usually in our culture very different in its value-system and attitudes from the occupational ego. It is the "totality of these egos," Sorokin explains, which occupies "almost the whole field of our conscious mentality . . ."[3]

A constructive reintegration of these egos is badly needed; the present chaotic schizophrenic condition of man can only bring disaster. Such an era of constructive reintegration of the human being around the supraconscious level of Creative Altruism is about to dawn unless mankind annihilates itself. The Supraconscious in man is the highest level of personality, often called the Divine. It is the "fountainhead of the greatest achievements and discoveries in all fields of human creative activity: science,

---

[2] *Ibid.*, p. 84.
[3] *Ibid.*, p. 89.
[1] *Ibid.*, p. 89.
[2] *Ibid.*, p. 89.
[3] *Ibid.*, p. 91.

religion, philosophy, technology, ethics, law, the fine arts, economics, and politics."[4] It "creates and discovers through supraconscious intuition,"[5] not discursive reason or other conscious processes. It is utterly different from the Unconscious which is the infra-conscious (cf. Aurobindo). Sorokin states emphatically that the *"supraconscious is egoless:* it transcends ego entirely and unconditionally."[1] (This was made clear in our study of the Oriental yogic philosophies.) "The field of any ego or its constellations is strictly limited to the *bioconscious and sociocultural conscious levels of personality."*[2] The supraconscious, Sorokin explains, is the Atman-Brahman or the Purusha of the Upanishads, Bhagavad Gita, or the Yoga of Patanjali; it is the Enlightenment experience (satori) of Zen and other forms of Buddhism; it is the experience of the Tao in Taoism; it is the experience of God in Occidental religions as *mystics* experience God.

Sorokin proceeds next to a study of the "ways of altruistic growth" and the "techniques of altruistic transformation of persons and groups." In this latter section of his book he shows how this transformation of human nature to the supraconscious level has already been brought about on a small scale by means of attitudes of love in a group; by "inner integration and reintegration of one's egos, values, and norms of conduct"; by confession, purgation, and reformation; by yoga methods and techniques, e.g. the yoga of Patanjali (discussed above) or the "integral yoga" of Aurobindo (discussed above); by monastic methods of "supraconscious meditation and creativity," and monastic methods of "competition in humility," and universal love.

Altogether Sorokin thinks that he has marshalled enough evidence to show that it is possible for human beings, or at least their leaders, to attain the supraconscious level es-

---
[4] *Ibid.,* p. 98.
[5] *Ibid.,* p. 99.
[1] *Ibid.,* p. 99. Sorokin's italics.
[2] *Ibid.* Sorokin's italics.

sential to the continuation of human life on this planet.

The final chapter of *The Ways and Power of Love* is entitled "From Tribal Egoism to Universal Altruism." This is a sublime chapter, full of the profound wisdom of the saints of all the ages in all the cultures of the world. It shows plainly how impractical, if not absolutely impossible, are attitudes of petty selfish egoism in the present crisis of the world's history. The petty local, limited altruism within an in-group — the family, the religious group, the politico-economic group (Capitalism, Socialism, Communism), the national-patriotic group — creates tensions, hatred, and war between the in-group and the outsiders. This "tribal altruism" is no longer workable in the age of the atom-bomb and interglobal economic and cultural interdependence. Our sensate culture, unfortunately, has in the name of science led man to identify himself with the animals: this has been a large factor in the beastliness, the wars, the moral corruption of our dying sensate era. "If this tragic self-degradation of man and its terrible consequences are to be ended, all animalistic self-identification of man must be replaced by the conception of the total man as the unconscious, conscious, and especially the supraconscious being." [1]

The individual attempting to live at this highest level— the supraconscious level of the saints—must reorganize his social affiliations. He must belong only to groups whose activities emphasize or are harmonious with ideals of a *practising* universal love. The greatest leaders of the human race, guides for the new ideational era, are "the greatest heroes of the sublimest love." [2] These men "inspire vast multitudes to imitate their magnificent examples," (cf. Toynbee's "mimesis" concept below) and "for moral ennoblement of humanity the emergence of one hero of love, like St. Francis or Gandhi, is more important than the publication of thousands of utilitarian, hedonistic, and

---
[1] *Ibid.*, p. 481.
[2] *Ibid.*, p. 484.

'rational' books on ethics."[3]

Altruistic love is the central value at the supraconscious level. It is "universal, perennial, and infinitely creative,"[1] and is "acceptable for all human beings." It is the only value that "can integrate into one unified system the multitude of diverse moral values of different individuals and groups and can place each value at its proper place and rank in its vast system."[2] Such a system is valid for all humanity.

Egoism, from narrow self-centeredness to the larger tribal egoisms, is the enemy of this sublime altruistic love. Egoism manifests itself dangerously in the social structure in hatred and in competition for superiority and domination. This hatred and competitiveness are, Sorokin says, "deeply ingrained in man." Nevertheless these ugly vices can be sublimated. Hatred can be directed against humanity's enemies such as poverty, disease and war; competitiveness can become constructive in competition in creative works for human benefit or in competition in *humility* and universal love instead of in dominance.

Sorokin believes that the time is ripe for the initiation of the new idealistic epoch which will usher in a new and better culture-era for the human race. He thinks that "the existing unconscious, conscious, and supraconscious powers of man are sufficient for elimination of most of the interhuman wars, as well as for a splendid renaissance of man himself, of his culture and social universe."[3] History is, in fact, forcing us to choose either the predatory policies of individual and tribal selfishness that lead . . . to inevitable doom, or to embark upon the policies of that universal solidarity that brings humanity to the aspired for heaven on the earth,"[1] the Golden Age we have described in many of the

---
[3] *Ibid.*
[1] *Ibid.*, p. 485.
[2] *Ibid.*, p. 485.
[3] *Ibid.*, p. 488.
[1] Sorokin, *Ibid.*, p. 489.

foregoing chapters as the longed for goal of history for so many of the world's peoples.

Summary of Sorokin's culture-cycle pattern of history. Sorokin calls his rhythmic pattern of human history a "creative 'eternal cycle' " that "will persist, as long as human history endures." [1] It is the mode of creative evolution at the human cultural level. Each phase of the pattern creates great works in the ideational, the idealistic, the sensate styles. The spectator with the "bird's eye" can appreciate all three styles whereas the frog-eyed man understands and appreciates only the one phase of which he is a part. The form-pattern ideational-idealistic-sensate is the eternal cyclic pattern which enables the observer to determine the "age" of a culture. Sorokin, like Vico, Ibn Khaldun, and Spengler, thinks there is a pattern in the history of cultures, i.e., that history can be made a sociological science as Vico affirmed in his work *The New Science*. Although Sorokin defines a culture as an integrated entity, he does not use the term "organism" in his definition. Here he is closer to Vico. All four — Vico, Ibn Khaldun, Spengler and Sorokin — agree that a culture begins with a religious world-view which becomes more and more secular with the advent of city life and finally degenerates into skepticism, cynicism, even nihilism, until the culture disintegrates completely. Spengler differs most from Sorokin and the others in his (Spengler's) extreme relativism. Spengler argues that each culture is to be appreciated as a great unique personality. There is no general spiral progress with one culture building upon the knowledge of the preceding. Sorokin (and probably Vico) admits spiral progress — one culture, such as the Christian, does especially in its idealistic and sensate stages, build upon another even though all is done in a new style. The new style for our dawning new culture-cycle must have for its integration idea "creative altruism." Sorokin

---

[1] Sorokin, *The Crisis of Our Age, op. cit.*, p. 132.

in his emphasis upon a spiritual regeneration of man around this great idea has much in common with Oriental thinkers of the past, represented in the twentieth century by such giants as Aurobindo and Radhakrishnan. Toynbee, whose philosophy of history is the subject matter of our next and final chapter in this section, believes the goal of history is much the same. After an analysis of the culture-cycles of the world's great civilizations, he too thinks that the transfiguration of man—or at least of man's leaders—is essential if human civilization is to continue upon this earth.

Chapter IV

Cyclical Patterns in Toynbee's Historical Thought: The Cyclical Pattern in the Rise and Fall of the Great Civilizations

Toynbee's philosophy of history is not, from the point of view of total human history, cyclical; yet there is a definite cyclic pattern described by Toynbee in the rise and fall of the great cultures of mankind. However one culture is parent to another which results in the overall progress of the human race towards a religious goal. The total pattern of human history is, therefore a spiral one; but of most interest to our theme is the cyclical pattern Toynbee applies to all the significant civilizations of the world.

The cyclical pattern of every great culture. A culture begins in a response to some significant challenge from either the natural or the social environment; the subsequent creative growth of the culture in "self-determination" is due to creative individuals or minority groups; the breakdown of the civilization is caused by "failure of self-determination" owing to loss of creativity on the part of the creative minority; the disintegration stage follows in which definite social groups express the decay of the culture: the creative minority becomes the dominant minority, there is an internal proletariat and an external proletariat; the arts show vulgarity and barbarism. The disintegration of the culture necessitates some mode of salvation. The only mode which can appeal to the immense majority is religious. A saving religion is born; the internal proletariat rallies around it as do many of the other classes. Then a new culture arises centered upon this integrating religious idea; it has to meet new challenges from the natural and social environment, growth is due again to a creative minority which eventually becomes sterile and the culture breaks down. This is the cyclic pattern followed by all great cultures of the past, Toynbee believes. He attempts to demonstrate this thesis empirically by an examination of all the great cultures of human history. From Toynbee's wealth of material we shall give but one or two examples of each stage in the cycle to illustrate its significance.

First stage of the cycle: challenge and response. Toynbee is primarily a religious thinker. He expresses the significance of his idea of the cause of the genesis of a civilization in religious symbolism. The symbol is the famous myth related both in the *Book of Job* and in Goethe's *Faust*. Toynbee says that Goethe's *Faust* expresses the symbol most adequately. Mephistopheles makes a wager with the Lord that Faust can be made to succumb to evil forces and lose his soul. The Lord gives Mephistopheles permission to tempt Faust in order that Faust may be aroused by his challenge to creative activity. Toynbee believes that God though perfect permits man to be challenged in order that further creation might be accomplished. In logic this is a contradiction, since a perfect Being cannot create anything more, but in myth and poetry both ideas may be affirmed; and since man does seem to create, the myth seems more adequate than logic. (Toynbee's difficulty is overcome in Oriental thought, as we have seen above in Parts I and II, in the view that Spirit or supraconscious mind or Supermind transcends the level of intellect or logic.) God, then, in the symbolism of Goethe's *Faust* permits adverse circumstances (symbolized by Satan) to challenge man out of a Yin state of sloth (Toynbee borrows the term *Yin* from Chinese philosophy) into a state of creative activity

(Yang). The dynamic creative movement begun flowers into a great civilization.

Only six civilizations, Toynbee thinks, have emerged directly from primitive life: the Sumerian, the Egyptian, the Minoan, the Sinic, the Mayan, and the Andean. The Sumerian and Egyptian were stimulated into creativity first by the challenge of the physical environment, the desiccation of Afrasia; the Sinic similarly met the challenge of life in the Yellow River Valley, a difficult spot; the Mayan civilization began with the challenge of the tropical forest; and the Minoan with the challenge of the sea.

Other civilizations emerged from the ruins of previous cultures; these are called *affiliated* civilizations *apparented* by prior ones. These affiliated civilizations emerged initially out of the dynamic act of secession of the proletariat from a decadent culture. More will be said about this below.

The proletariat rallies around a new religious idea and a new civilization is born. Then in a growing civilization further challenge from the physical and social environment is offered and met creatively. The civilization in its nascent and growing stages may move to "new ground" which provides the stimulus of a challenge. For example, Scotland, England, New England provided challenges of a difficult physical environment that stimulated further growth of Western culture. There is the type of stimulus called "blows," *e.g.*, the blows dealt Athens by Persia which stimulated Athens to tremendous achievements: not only was she victorious over Persia, but she showed her greatness in the priceless culture of the fifth and fourth centuries B.C. bequeathed to the affiliated Western Christian culture.

Then there is the stimulus of "pressures." London became the capital of England, Toynbee writes, because this city "had borne the heat and burden of the day" and was able in 895 A.D. to win a decisive battle against the Danes who were pressing the English led by Alfred-the-Great.

405

This pressure from the Scandinavians felt also by the European mainland across the English Channel "gave birth to the new kingdoms of England and France." [1]

"Penalizations" are another means of stimulating creative activity in civilizations. Traditions of many peoples speak of "lame smiths" and "blind poets." The creativity of the Jews (penalized because of their religion) has been outstanding. Forbidden in the Middle Ages and Renaissance to enter other occupations, they excelled in economic activities very often; they cultivated the intellect in professional fields, also, (great musicians, and many great scientists and philosophers have been Jews). Other religious minority groups such as the Puritans, penalized in England, helped create another nation as a branch of Western civilization.

To summarize, the challenge of Hard Countries (such as the Yellow River Valley), New Ground, Blows, Pressures and Penalizations provide the dynamic for continued creative growth in a civilization. These challenges, however, must be 'enough and not too much." As in the case of the individual, too difficult a challenge is destructive and too easy a challenge does not bring forth the creative potentiality of which he is capable. The Golden Mean of "enough and not too much" is the most efficient kind of challenge in evoking the greatest creative response in individuals and in civilizations.

Second stage of the cycle: the growth of civilizations. Toynbee first makes clear that growth is not to be identified with geographical expansion since the militarism which makes this possible leads to fraticidal conflicts and is a sign of the decline of a culture. The period of the Crusades in Western history is an exception, however. In the contemporary world such expansion is a sign of decadence. Another phenomenon often identified with growth is pro-

---

[1] Arnold J. Toynbee, *A Study of History*, abridgement of Vols. I-VI by D. C. Somervell (New York and London: Oxford University Press, 1947), p. 123.

gress in techniques; this, Toynbee says, is not a sign of growth. Growth means that the field of action is shifting all the time from the external environment into the interior of the civilization. For example the social and economic problems of feudalism, an internal challenge, were met by the response of capitalism. In contemporary society the challenge of industrialism and democracy is not receiving a creative response and this is a sign of decadence. Toynbee summarizes his view of growth thus:

> We conclude that a given series of successful responses to successive challenges is to be interpreted as a manifestation of growth if, as the series proceeds, the action tends to shift from the field of an external environment, physical or human, to the *for interieur* of the growing personality or civilization. In so far as this grows and continues to grow, it has to reckon less and less with challenges delivered by external forces and demanding responses on an outer battlefield, and more and more with challenges that are presented by itself to itself in an inner arena. Growth means that the growing personality or civilization tends to become its own environment and its own challenger and its own field of action. In other words, the criterion of growth is progress towards self-determination; and progress toward self-determination is a prosaic formula for describing the miracle by which Life enters into its Kingdom.[1]

This notion of growth resembles that of Hegel and Marx. Hegel and Marx both think of the goal of society as Freedom which is the stage in which there are no *external* determinants for man; it is the stage when man himself self-consciously determines his world from the powers in his own nature (the Absolute acts in man in Hegel's view — naturalistic evolutionary man in the Marxian).

---
[1] *Ibid.*, p. 208.

Spengler emphasizes still more the self-determination of the growth of every high culture.

Toynbee next turns to an analysis of growth. He thinks that growth is the work of creative individual geniuses or at most of creative minorities. This has been true in religion (e.g. Moses and the Hebrew prophets, Jesus, Buddha, Mohammed, Zoroaster, Lao Tse), in the growth of political ideals (e.g. democracy), industrialism and capitalism, science, art and philosophy. The creative minority in social fields such as religion, education, economics and politics gains the adherence of the vast majority of the society by means of *mimesis* or mechanical imitation. It is unfortunately true, Toynbee comments, that the masses of mankind are incapable of realizing the insights of the great geniuses and must perform acts which show their adherence to the ideas of these great men in a merely mechanical way. This is true in religion, for "if we glance at the great religious organizations extant in the world today, Christian, Islamic and Hindu, we shall find that the great bulk of their nominal adherents, however exalted the creeds to which they profess lip-service, still live in a mental atmosphere which, so far as religion is concerned, is not far removed from a simple paganism." [2]

These creative individuals or minorities follow a characteristic pattern of "withdrawal and return." Toynbee gives many illustrations. Moses withdrew to the top of Mt. Sinai alone and returned with the Law which provided a basis for Hebrew ethics and social life; in Plato's Myth of the Cave, the philosopher withdraws to behold the Vision of the Idea of the Good, then returns to lead others to the goal and to reorganize human society around the vision; Jesus withdraws in the Temptation episode and returns to found a Kingdom of God, finally Jesus withdraws to Heaven in the Ascension and is to return as the Messiah of the Second Coming; Buddha withdraws to discover the secret of life and the universe and returns to enlighten all

---

[2] *Ibid.*, p. 214.

mankind; Machiavelli the practical politician was forced to remain during the last years of his life in perpetual exile on a farm on the Florentine countryside, but he "returned" on a more ethereal plane in the great treatises on politics which he left to Western culture; Dante too, was exiled from Florence and returned on the ethereal plane with his great literary and philosophical work *The Divine Comedy*. Creative growth of the inner (ethereal) kind is brought to great cultures in this way.

Creative minorities exemplify the pattern also. In Classical culture Athens withdrew from Greek affairs in the eighth, seventh and sixth centuries but returned in the fifth century B.C. to challenge Persia and become the "education of Hellas." Italy in the thirteenth, fourteenth and fifteenth centuries stayed out of Europe's quarrels and 'returned" on the ethereal plane to contribute to Western culture with great creations in the arts. England in the Elizabethan Age and seventeenth century in her "splendid isolation" developed parliamentary government (democracy) and Industrialism as gifts to the Western world. Russia has withdrawn from European affairs and isolated herself from the West. Toynbee once believed she would "return" with a solution for the problem unsolved in Western culture — industrialism and democracy — but he has since changed his mind.

Significance of growth in the physiognomy of a culture. The growth brought about by the creative individuals, creative minorities, or both, gives rise to a definite culture-pattern for the civilization. Greece developed an aesthetic culture — beauty was the central value; the good was proportion, harmony in the soul and state; truth was discovery of the proportions and harmonious forms (such as law-patterns) in nature, for example the notion that the astronomical bodies must make the most harmonious music because of the perfect proportions and symmetries of their motions. India developed a religion-centered culture as we have noted in our chapter on cyclical views of the cosmos

409

in Indian thought. The West has developed a machine-centered culture. Industrialism and democracy are its characteristic end-developments.

Third stage of the cycle: the breakdown of civilizations. Toynbee rejects what he calls the "deterministic solutions" of the Orient and Greeks (described above in Part I) to the problem of the breakdown of a civilization. These theories, he claims, have no empirical support. What he objects to in these theories is their omission of the "empirical' fact of the overall progress of the human race since the first civilizations, especially in religion as we shall see below. He appeals to science, also, as having "knocked the bottom out of this theory, at any rate so far as any civilization now extant is concerned." He quotes Sir James Jeans, the great astronomer-physicist, in refutation of a cyclical view of human history:

> Taking a very gloomy view of the future of the human race, let us suppose that it can only expect to survive for two thousand million years longer, a period about equal to the past age of the Earth. Then regarded as a being destined to live for three-score years and ten, Humanity, although it has been born in a house only seventy years old, is itself only three days old ... Utterly inexperienced beings, we are standing at the first flush of the dawn of civilization ... In time the glory of the morning must fade into the light of common day, and this, in some far distant age, will give place to evening twilight, presaging the final eternal night. But we children of the dawn need give but little thought to the far-off sunset.[1]

In part I of this book, however, we noted that the time-span of Oriental cosmic cycles are of immense length, a fact which Toynbee apparently seems to neglect. It is true,

---

[1] *Ibid.*, pp. 247 f. Toynbee quotes this from Jeans, *Eos: or the Wider Aspects of Astronomy* (no date given), pp. 12-13, 83-84.

nevertheless, that the primitivistic [1] approach to cosmic and human culture cycles (versus the progress-idea) is the one generally held, and here probably Toynbee may be right in affirming empirical support for his view in opposition to the primitivism of the ancients.

Toynbee's criticisms of the modern organismic cyclical view of Spengler are (1) societies or cultures are not organisms. Human organisms are the components of societies or cultures, but the societies are "the intelligible fields of historical study," and "the common ground between the respective fields of activity of a number of individual human beings, who are themselves living organisms . . . . cannot conjure up a giant in their own image out of the intersection of their own shadows and then breathe into this unsubstantial body the breath of their own life." [2] Therefore, Toynbee argues — and this is objection (2) which follows from (1)—no civilization is biologically predetermined to follow a life-span pattern. Breakdowns of a culture are not caused by the biological age of a macrocosmic social organism.

Toynbee concludes that the empirical evidence of science and history favors a *non-deterministic spiral theory philosophy of human history*. This theory reconciles cyclic patterns with progress. The analogy of the Wheel, Toynbee says, is the best symbol of the spiral cycle-pattern:

> The movement of the wheel is admittedly repetitive in relation to the wheel's own axle, but the wheel has only been made and fitted to its axle in order to give mobility to a vehicle of which the wheel is merely a part, and the fact that the vehicle, which is the wheel's *raison d'etre,* can only move in virtue of the wheel's

[1] The "primitivistic" approach affirms that the Golden Age of the world and human history is the primeval era, the First Age of the past. See discussions of this in the Oriental and Greek views in Part I above and the Christian-Moslem-Zoroastrian-Marxian One-Cycle views of Part II.
[2] Toynbee, *op. cit.,* p. 248.

circular movement round its axle does not compel the vehicle itself to travel like a merry-go-round in a circular track.

This harmony of two diverse movements — a major irreversible movement which is born on the wings of a minor repetitive movement — is perhaps the essence of what we mean by rhythm; and we can discern this play of forces not only in vehicular traction and in modern machinery but likewise in the organic rhythm of life. The annual procession of the seasons, which brings with it the annual withdrawal and return of vegetation, has made possible the secular evolution of the Vegetable Kingdom. The sombre cycle of birth, reproduction and death has made possible the evolution of all the higher animals up to Man . . .

Thus the detection of periodic repetitive movements in our analysis of the process of civilization does not imply that the process itself is of the same cyclic order as they are. On the contrary, if any inference can legitimately be drawn from the periodicity of these minor movements, we may rather infer that the major movement which they bear along is not recurrent but progressive . . .

The dead civilizations are not dead by fate, or 'in the course of nature,' and therefore our living civilization is not doomed inexorably in advance to 'join the majority' of its species. Though sixteen civilizations may have perished already to our knowledge, and nine others may be now at the point of death, we — the twenty-sixth — are not compelled to submit the riddle of our fate to the blind arbitrament of statistics. The divine spark of creative power is still alive in us, and, if we have the grace to kindle it into flame, then the stars in their courses cannot defeat our efforts to attain the goal of human endeavour.[1]

Toynbee concludes that since breakdowns of civilizations have no cosmic causes outside of human control the true causes lie elsewhere. First he considers "loss of command over the environment" as a cause. He concludes that this

---

[1] *Ibid.*, pp. 253-254.

is actually a result and not the cause of the breakdown of the culture. He considers first the loss of command over the physical environment which amounts to decline in techniques, but he has demonstrated already under the "growth of civilizations" that there is no significant correlation between either growth or decline of techniques and the growth or decline of a civilization. For example the abandonment of the irrigation technique used in Ceylon in the days of its high Indic culture was not a cause of the decline of the culture but a result of wars. The irrigation works were destroyed so often by invaders that attempts to rebuild them were discouraged. Wars caused by breakdowns in the body-social caused this case of the abandonment of a technique. In Greece the Peloponnesian War is the parallel sign of a parallel phenomenon. Greece was depopulated as Italy later, not by a failure in engineering technique but by wars caused basically by spiritual breakdown. This is true today also, Toynbee claims, with reference to techniques in the arts. For example, in Western culture there has been no loss of technique in sculpture, painting, and literature. The abandonment of the traditional techniques is caused by abandonment of our traditional spiritual heritage and this is a symptom of the spiritual breakdown of our culture. Loss or abandonment of techniques, then, is not the cause of the breakdown of a culture but *may* be a result.

Is loss of control over the *human* environment the cause of a breakdown? The classic defense of this theory, Toynbee reminds us, is found in Gibbon's *The History of the Decline and Fall of the Roman Empire*. It is Gibbon's thesis that the Roman Empire fell because control over the human environment was insufficient to prevent the "triumph of Barbarism and Religion." Gibbon's error, Toynbee comments, was "that the 'triumph of Barbarism and Religion' was not the plot of the piece, but only an epilogue to it— not the cause of the breakdown but only an inevitable accompaniment of a dissolution in which the long process of disintegration was bound to end."[1] Actually, Toynbee points out—and here he agrees with Spengler—the Roman Empire as a Universal State represents the last phase of a civilization; the "triumph of Barbarism and Religion" signifies only that the body-social had disintegrated so badly that it alienated vast numbers the secession of which caused the decease of this Classical culture.

Many other examples from human history are given by the immensely learned Toynbee to show that loss of command over the physical and/or human environment cannot be a sufficient cause for a breakdown. Just as Growth in a culture is an inner spiritual development, so a Breakdown has an inner spiritual source and cause. A breakdown is caused by "loss of self-determination."

Loss of self-determination, then, is the cause of a breakdown. Toynbee's main idea, here, is that this loss of self-determination results in the schism and disintegration of the body-social: the creative minority becomes a dominant minority; the proletariat secedes; the total result is loss of harmony between the parts of the society and with this the loss of self-determination.

Toynbee gives us what he believes to be the major reasons for the disharmony which parallels loss of self-determination. The first class of causes comes under the category of "social enormities." This means the attempt to force "new wine into old bottles" as the proverb puts it; applied to society it means "introduction of new social forces—aptitudes or emotions or ideas—which the existing set of institutions was not originally designed to carry."[2] When this occurs either there is (a) Adjustment: new institutions are created or the old suitably reorganized; or (b) Revolution: these are "violent because they are the belated triumphs of powerful new social forces over tenacious old institutions"[3] (the growth of society is hazardous if this occurs);

---

[1] *Ibid.*, p. 261.
[2] *Ibid.*, p. 279.
[3] *Ibid.*, p. 281.

or (c) *Social enormities. A breakdown is the diagnosis when this occurs.* These enormities are "the penalties which the society has to pay when the act of mimesis, which ought to have brought an old institution into harmony with a new social force, is not simply retarded but is frustrated altogether."[1]

Mimesis is, however, in itself a cause of breakdown. Since mimesis is necessary in the growth of a society and is accomplished by mechanical means either of social pressure or actual force, there is always the danger that these mechanical devices will result in disruption of the body-social. Until all men can really acquire some glimmering of the mystic saintliness which has illuminated the great souls the inner dynamics of the society based upon the "mechanicalness of mimesis" must almost of necessity lead to a breakdown.

The great social enormity of our time is the abortive attempt to force the new wine of democracy and industrialism into the old bottles of the national state. The spirit of democracy and the economic interdependence of all peoples calls for world-wide fraternity and cooperation without the parochialism of national states. War today is a weapon of "nationalist fanaticism" and even the Church has become too often a tool of narrow nationalist interests. Within industrialized countries democracy means the necessity for the state to control key industries "to curb the excessive power over other people's lives which is conferred by the private ownership of such industries"[2]; and the state can "mitigate the ill effects of poverty by providing social services financed by high taxation of wealth. This method has the incidental social advantage that it tends to transform the state from a war-making machine—which has been its most conspicuous function in the past—into an agency for social welfare."[3] Toynbee believes our culture must lose its "rugged individualism" not only as applied to individuals but to nations. Only a world-wide cooperative society—

---

[1] *Ibid.*

cooperative on both a cultural and economic basis—can bring mankind into harmony today; the alternative is destruction (at least for Western civilization).

A second group of causes for the breakdown of a civilization is classified under the general category of "the nemesis of creativity." This manifests itself as (1) Idolization of an ephemeral Self, (2) Idolization of an ephemeral institution, or (3) Idolization of an ephemeral technique. The first, idolization of an ephemeral self, is well illustrated with an example taken from the Classical society (called the Hellenic by Toynbee). The greatest city-state of this culture, Athens, the "education of Hellas" had enormous pride in her spiritual superiority, yet she could not devise a plan for the political unification of Greece; this was beyond her moral stature. The tragic result was the Peloponnesian War. This war was the event which directly ushered in the breakdown of the Hellenic culture.

Idolization of an ephemeral institution, the second major cause under the "nemesis of creativity," is apparent as a cause of the breakdown of the Hellenic culture. The institution of the city-state was idolized. This was the major spiritual cause of the Peloponnesian War which in its turn led to the rapid decline of the Hellenic culture. There is a close parallel in our world today in the idolization of the nationalistic state. States must give up worship of the ephemeral institution of the national state with its supreme sovereignty or our civilization will be destroyed. Parliaments based on locality representation are for the most part another idolized institution which is outmoded and a cause of disharmony in the social order.

Idolization of an ephemeral technique is the third cause under the classification "nemesis of creativity." This, too, exemplifies the truth that "pride comes before a fall." The dinosaurs and other enormous reptiles who excelled in a definite technique of survival were not plastic enough to

---

[2] *Ibid.*, p. 291.
[3] *Ibid.*, p. 291.

evolve a new technique when conditions changed. The more adaptable life forms superceded them. This is true also in warfare. For example the Spartan phalanx had been a very successful technique in warfare but it "rested on its oars"; and in the fourth century B.C. "it saw itself ignominiously worsted: first by an Athenian swarm of peltasts—a host of Davids with which the phalanx of Spartan Goliaths found itself quite unable to cope—and then by the tactical innovation of the Theban column."[1] Then the Athenian and Theban techniques were superceded by the Macedonian formation.

All of the above forms of "succumbing to the nemesis of creativity" are passive, due to the pride in one's own accomplishments that causes "resting on one's oars."[2] "Pride cometh before a fall." The *active* form of succumbing to the nemesis of creativity takes the pattern expressed in the Greek formula: *koros, hybris, ate*. The objective meaning of these Greek words are respectively: surfeit, outrageous behavior, and disaster. The subjective meaning is: "*koros* means the psychological condition of being spoilt by success; *hybris* means the consequent loss of mental and moral balance; and *ate* means the blind headstrong ungovernable impulse which sweeps an unbalanced soul into attempting the impossible."[3] This pattern is illustrated very clearly in the Biblical story of David and Goliath. Goliath, although unprepared for the new military technique of David, is so spoilt by his military victories that he takes the initiative and challenges David to battle. This results in disaster—death to him. This pattern, Toynbee says, is typical of all militarism. The militarists believe in the invincibility of their forces; they win a victory; but ultimately opposing militarists will win the victory over them. The saying, "Those who take the sword will perish by the sword," sums up the truth of "the *sui-*

---

[1] *Ibid.*, p. 332.
[2] *Ibid.*, p. 336.
[3] *Ibid.*, pp. 336-337.

cidalness of militarism." Toynbee gives many historical examples of the disastrous fall of militaristic powers to other conquerors.

Another active form of "succumbing to the nemesis of creativity" is the ruin caused by "the intoxication of victory." For example Pope Gregory VII (Hildebrand) used armed might to strengthen the Papacy spiritually and free it from secular control and interests; but this technique boomeranged and armed might was used in turn against the Papacy. War costs money and this need led to questionable ways of collecting it. Both Holy Roman Empire and the Papacy weakened themselves; France became strong and kidnapped the Pope (1305-78), and the Schism (1379-1415) followed. Toynbee summarizes the situation thus:

> Intoxicated by the successes which their hazardous maneuver obtained for them in the earlier stages of their struggle with the Holy Roman Empire, Gregory VII (Hildebrand) and his successors persisted in the use of force until victory on this non-spiritual plane became an end in itself. Thus, while Gregory VII fought the Empire with the object of removing an Imperial obstacle to a reform of the Church, Innocent IV fought the Empire in order to destroy the Empire's own secular authority.[1]

The causes of a breakdown are basically spiritual and foremost is *hybris* (pride)—pride in institutions, techniques, one's "self" as a personality or a culture—which causes the resting on one's oars rather than response to new challenges. Or, pride in one's successes "intoxication of victory" either on the spiritual or military plane, the active form of the pride that comes before a fall, causes a breakdown. Toynbee sums up what the Bible (interpreted by St. Augustine) and Greek tragedy tell us: The proud man is riding for a fall. Pride and sloth lead to the lack of

---
[1] *Ibid.*, p. 355.

necessary creativity to keep the culture as a whole in the growing stage. Social enormities then develop that signal the breakdown of the culture.

Fourth stage of the cycle: the Disintegration of Civilizations. The pattern of disintegration, Toynbee writes, is a standard one in all civilizations. This pattern is the following: (1) a time of troubles, (2) a universal state, and (3) an interregnum. (This pattern is similar to Vico's, Ibn Khaldun's, and Spengler's.) However, instead of stage (3) petrifaction may set in at stage (2). The Egyptiac civilization showed such a petrifaction, when instead of dissolution being completed by running out into an interregnum when the Hyksos invaded (sixteenth century B.C.), it remained in a static (petrified) culture-state for two thousand years, *i.e.*, until the fifth century A.D. The Sinic (Chinese) civilization showed petrifaction after the revolt by the founder of the Ming dynasty against the universal state established by the Mongols. In addition there are fossilized fragments of great cultures, *e.g.*, of the Indic and of the Syriac. [2]

Whether there is petrifaction or dissolution the time of troubles and universal state are characteristic of the disintegration stage. In the time of troubles the body-social is invariably split into three classes: a dominant minority, the internal proletariat, and the external proletariat. Each of these classes creates its characteristic institution: the dominant minority creates the universal state; the internal proletariat a universal church, and the external proletariat the barbarian war bands. Toynbee arrives at this analysis primarily through his careful study of the fall of the Hellenic civilization. For example, in this society the creative minority (represented at its best by the leaders of the Athenian culture) failed repeatedly to meet the challenge of political unification of the Greek city-states; Macedonia and then Rome under the Augustan principate and subse-

---

[2] *Ibid.*, p. 361. The fossilized fragments of the Indic are listed as the Jains in India, Buddhists of Ceylon, Burma, Siam, Cambodia, Tibet, Mongolia; of the Syriac: Jews, Parsees, Nestorians, and Monophysites.

quent Empire also failed. During this time of troubles from the Peloponnesian Wars through the Principate and Empire, society became split into the three classes mentioned. The dominant minority developed the universal state in grand form in the Roman Empire; the internal proletariat developed the Christian religion as the universal church; the Gaulic and other border "barbarians" who respected Roman culture in the early days of the Empire became militant enemies, "barbarian war-bands," in the latter days of Rome.

Each of these classes needs further explanation. It is almost inevitable that a creative minority degenerate into a dominant minority. The small creative group leads the society mainly through mimesis, a mechanical "social drill" method rather than by "conversion" *i.e.* through imparting to the majority the same kind of inspired illumination they (the creative minority) originally received. The general population respect the creative minority while it is creative and are willing to follow its leadership. When this leadership ceases to be creative and war and other forms of chaos result, the creative minority enforces its leadership upon the general population and becomes then a *dominant* dictatorial minority. This "Caesarism" (Spengler's name for this phenomenon) is accepted by the masses of the people as the alternative to chaos. They are accustomed to the mechanical "follow the leader" social drill pattern (mimesis) from the very beginnings of the society so there is nothing new in accepting the dictates of a leader-group, now a master-group.

The dominant minority, now a tyrannous group ruling for the most part in its own selfish interests, squeezing all the tax money possible out of the masses of the people for war and satisfaction of luxurious tastes, alienates its own populace and its neighboring barbarian peoples. These become a proletarian group. Toynbee defines the proletarian class as those who are *in* but not *of* the society. They are the "disinherited classes" inside the society and the border barbarians outside the society exploited wherever possible for the selfish interests of the dominant minority. (This description fits Ibn Khaldun's and Vico's picture of a declining civilization.)

This schism of the body social (split into the aforementioned three groups) is the conflict of opposing forces which results in new creations: a universal state (*cf.* Vico's "monarchy" as the remedy for these conditions), a universal church and the barbarian war-bands. The schism as secession of the proletarian groups represents the *withdrawal* pattern explained above; the new creations represent the *return*. Withdrawal-and-return or schism-and-palingenesia are the phrases Toynbee uses to characterize these disintegration phenomena standard for every culture.

The most significant creation during the disintegration period is that of the internal proletariat: the universal church. In his later series of volumes Toynbee sets forth the thesis that the progress of mankind lies in the development of higher religions; civilizations are subsidiary to this development. The disintegration of civilizations performs the function of challenge to greater creativity in religion. This creativity comes out of the internal proletariat, but not the group collectively; such creativity is the work of great geniuses. For example, "the appearance of Moses is synchronized with the decadence of the 'New Empire' in Egypt and the appearance of Abraham with the last days of the Sumeric universal state, after its short-lived reconstruction by Hammurabi,"[1] the Eighth Century Prophets with the Assyrian decline, the Prophets of the Exile (Ezekiel, Second Isaiah, Jeremiah) with the Babylonian, and finally Jesus with the decline of the Hellenic.

The internal proletariat of the contemporary Western world has several origins. One is out of the intelligentsia, "a class of liaison officers who have learnt the tricks of the intrusive civilization's trade so far as may be necessary to enable their own community, through their agency, just

---

[1] *Ibid.*, p. 386.

to hold its own in a social environment in which life is ceasing to be lived in accordance with the local tradition and is coming more and more to be lived in the style imposed by the intrusive civilization upon the aliens who fall under its dominion." [2] The man of the intelligentsia is an outcaste socially from the alien culture by whom he is employed and an outcast, too, among his own countrymen. Still worse eventually there are too many candidates for the jobs to be filled and many in this educated group then suffer from unemployment. (This happened to the Hindu intelligentsia during the British Raj.) Another source of the proletarian class is from the ranks of lower middle class groups who have received a secondary or even university education and then are unable to find suitable employment. This group, Toynbee is aware, was the backbone of the Fascist Party in Italy and the National-Socialist Party in Germany. Impoverished and unemployed groups among the peasant and laboring classes are still another source of the proletariat.

The proletarian groups may make either a gentle or a **violent response to their oppression. In the era of the Roman Empire** (the disintegration stage of the Hellenic society) the gentle proletarian response was embracement of the Christian religion. The Sinic (Chinese) internal proletariat "found a religion in the Mahayana which was a transformation, out of all recognition, of the preceding Buddhist philosophy." [1] Similarly, Toynbee adds, "In Marxian Communism we have a notorious example in our midst of a modern Western philosophy which has changed, in a lifetime, quite out of recognition into a pro**letarian religion, taking the path of violence and carving out its New Jerusalem with the sword on the plains of Russia."** [2] This new "proletarian religion" has already deteriorated in Russia, Toynbee thinks, into traditional Western type nationalism whereas the Western nations have

---

[2] *Ibid.,* p. 394.
[1] *Ibid.,* p. 399.
[2] *Ibid.*

been becoming more Marxist, i.e. they have been socializing (income tax, socialized medicine, government ownership of communications). Moreover Marx derived all that is constructive, his concern for the exploited classes and his ideal of the classless cooperative community, from his Hebrew-Christian background and not from the logic of the Hegelian dialectic.[3] Marx has performed the function of reminding Christianity of its secular validity, since the only constructive response to the unmet challenge of industrialism and democracy *is* a cooperative community on a world-wide basis. The Christian Church, Toynbee believes, has still the most adequate answer to the unmet challenge; but a spiritual rebirth of the Church is essential. The Church needs to revive its deep spiritual philosophy among at least a significant vanguard creative minority group or some other religion will take the leadership of the proletarian groups.

The *external* proletariat as a class is "charmed" Toynbee says by the dominant creative society while it is in a state of economic, political and cultural growth, but withdraws its support when Mammon, Mars, and Moloch begin to rule.

The *limen* or buffer zone between the civilization and the "barbarians" is then replaced by a *limes* or military frontier and the barbarian warbands or external proletariat appear. The most recent illustration of this phenomenon in the Western world has been in the Near East. Nassar is attempting to lead the Arab nations (whose internal proletariat is at the "barbarian" level in many ways) in war against the Western nations who have "interests" in the Near East. These are among our "barbarian warbands." Toynbee mentions another far more sinister group of barbarians—real barbarians. He notices that we breed our own barbarians such as the gangsters in the big cities in the United States and other Western countries; the Nazis were the organized barbarian war-bands inbred in Germany, the Fascists in Italy. "We are betrayed by what is false with-

---

[3] *Ibid.*

in," [1] Toynbee concludes.

Toynbee ends his discussion of the three groups into which the body social splits in the disintegration stage with some important comments upon the significance to these three groups of the "taint" of an alien culture. For example the dominant minority that provided the second universal state for the Indic culture was British. This British dominance was greatly resented by the Indian Hindu culture. On the other hand an indigenous dominant minority, the Romans, provided the universal state for the Hellenic civilization. Rome was accepted and even praised in her latter days when her efficiency was at low ebb. Alien cultural inspiration is a handicap also to an external proletariat. For instance the proletarian Mongols were hated by the Chinese because their "barbarism was mitigated, however slightly, by a tincture of Syriac culture derived from Nestorian Christian pioneers"; the Manchus, however, were accepted because uncontaminated by an alien culture; the Hyksos were violently disliked by the Egyptians because of their alien culture, whereas the Libyans, complete barbarians, were not resented when they were the invaders.

An alien inspiration, on the other hand, is a great asset to a religion in winning the allegiance of the internal proletariat—and the creation of a Universal Church is the work of this class. The reason for this is plain. The internal proletariat is estranged from "the broken-down society from which it is in process of secession, is seeking a new revelation, and this is what the alien spark supplies; it is its newness that makes it attractive."[2] Toynbee adds that the new revelation must be adapted to the society to which it is offered. Christianity of non-Hellenic inspiration borrowed its church organization from the Roman civil service, its philosophy from the Hellenic culture, its ritual from the Mysteries, converted many pagan festivals into Christian ones, and replaced the cult of heroes with that of the saints.

---

[1] *Ibid.*, p. 419.
[2] *Ibid.*, p. 426.

It is very significant, however, Toynbee emphasizes, that most religions have an alien origin. Islam and Hinduism which are indigenous are exceptions. Since most do have this alien origin the single civilization cannot be the intelligible unit of study. Yet Toynbee has set up his work with the single civilization as such a unit and continues thus in the first half of his work. In his last volumes he has given up this approach since he thinks of religion as the key to history. Civilizations are merely handmaids to its growth from glory to glory.

Toynbee next attacks the phenomena of disintegration in the society from the point of view of its inward spirit, its soul, and describes the "schism in the soul" which occurs in this stage of every culture. It is this schism in the soul which is of fundamental significance; the schism in the body social is merely the "outward and visible sign of an inward and spiritual rift." [2] This spiritual rift shows itself in many ways in the behaviour, feeling, and life of the members of the culture. Toynbee classifies the responses, no longer creative, into two general types: passive and active. There are passive and active personal-behaviour and social-behaviour responses, passive and active feeling responses and passive and active responses on "the plane of life." [3]

On the plane of personal behaviour the passive response is *abandon*. The soul "lets itself go" and attempts in spontaneous behaviour to live according to nature and receive from nature again the gift of creativity. The active response is *self-control*. The notion here is that living according to nature is inimical to creativity, therefore the "natural passions" must be disciplined if creativity is again to be stimulated. Toynbee gives many examples of both responses in the disintegration stages of many cultures. The most familiar to Western readers is taken from the Hellenic "time of troubles." In Plato's *Symposium* we have the *abandon-response* illustrated in Alcibiades; the *self-control-response*

---
[2] *Ibid.*, p. 429.
[3] *Ibid.*, p. 431.

in Socrates. Later in Hellenic culture schools of thought, both claiming to advocate "life according to nature" advocated these responses as "natural." Diogenes the Cynic and his school are exemplars of the attitude of *self-control;* Epicureans (of the type reprimanded by Lucretius for taking Epicurus' name in vain) typify *abandon.*

On the plane of social behavior the phenomena are *truancy* and *martyrdom* as respectively the passive and the active responses. The truant makes the passive response. He is the man who believes that the social order has so lost its morale that he no longer owes it any allegiance; motivated by self-interest, he steps out of the ranks. In our Western society, a case in point Toynbee says, is the *"trahison des clercs"* the tragic truancy of our intellectuals to Christian ideals. This truancy began "when the 'clerks' repudiated their clerical origin by trying to shift the rising edifice of our Western Christian Civilization from a religious to a secular basis."[1] The leading example in England was Thomas Wolsey, Toynbee writes, who was responsible for the martyrdom of his two noble contemporaries, Thomas Moore and John Fisher, both exponents of Christian ideals.

Martyrdom, the active response, is illustrated in the Roman world by "Roman archaist converts to the philosophy of detachment," (the Stoic point of view). Marcus Aurelius is typical, "a prince whose title to the martyr's crown is not invalidated, but is on the contrary confirmed, by Death's refusal to cut this martyr's ordeal short by any *coup de grace* . . ."[2] A more constructive kind of martyrdom, in Toynbee's opinion, was that of the Early Christians since their indomitable spirit was the core around which the coming new civilization was able to develop. The Early Christians showed truancy too; many renegades weakened under persecution and denied their Christian faith.

On the plane of feeling the passive response is the "sense of drift"; the active the "sense of sin." The sense of drift

---

[1] *Ibid.*, pp. 443-444.
[2] *Ibid.*, p. 442.

is manifested in the popularity of the idea of Chance as dominant in cosmic and human processes during the disintegration stage of great civilizations. Plato in his *Politics* [1] describes the disintegration state in mythical form (as we noted in Part I, chapter VIII below in this book). Plato says that when God abandons the helm of the ship of Cosmic Order, Chance takes over and sheer chaos results. *Fortune* was a great and favorite goddess of the days of the Roman Empire. In our own culture Toynbee calls attention to the popularity of the idea of Chance during the nineteenth and continuing into the twentieth century especially in relation to economic theory. This idea of Chance appears in economics in the notion of *laissez-faire,* a "philosophy of practical life which was founded on a faith in the miraculous enlightenment of self-interest. In the light of a transitorily gratifying experience our nineteenth-century grandfathers claimed to 'know that all things work together for good for them that love' the Goddess Chance." [2] In the Sinic society in the second century B. C. this notion was popular in its Taoist form. Toynbee quotes the appropriate passage from the *Tao Teh Ching,* chapter 34 (Arthur Waley's translation called *The Way and Its Power*):

Great Tao is like a boat that drifts;
It can go this way; it can go that.

However, the dialectic of Chance drives one to its opposite, Necessity. The boat drifts, for example, because of definite "necessary" movements of the wind and waves, a physical kind of determinism. Democritus emphasizes this kind of determinism, but Toynbee thinks that it was Chaldean astrological deterministic theories rather than the materialism of Democritus which influenced Zeno, founder of Stoicism, in his doctrine of fatalism. In our discussion

---
[1] Toynbee refers to *Politicus,* 272 D 6-273 E 4.
[2] Toynbee, *op. cit.,* p. 445.

of Chaldean astrology (*supra* Part I, chap. II) we noted that Neugebauer disagrees with this view and thinks that astrology as a "science" was developed by the Greeks. Regardless of how it originated it is true as Toynbee says, that such fatalistic notions were popular in the declining years of the Graeco-Roman world.

In the Western civilization, Toynbee points to Marxism as the most significant example of the idea of Necessity developing out of the laissez-faire idea of Chance. In our chapter on Marxism we observed the Marxian idea of historical necessity in the bourgeois laissez-faire stage of economic development. In psychology determinism is the dominant notion in psychoanalysis. In the Western Christian religion sin has deterministic roots in the "original sin" of Adam inherited by every member of the human race; in Hinduism and Buddhism the law of Karma determines the outward and inward status of the individual soul. In these religions, nevertheless, the individual can improve and even overcome his "original sin" or his karmic predispositions and taints, so the idea of necessity is not at all absolute. Absolute determinism is found in Christianity especially in Calvinism and among the Moslems in their idea of Qismet (Fate). (We have discussed al-Ghazzali's extreme determinism above in Part II.) Toynbee quotes from Tawney's *Religion and the Rise of Capitalism* to show the parallel between Calvinistic notions that the world belongs to the elect and the Marxian idea that the world of the future belongs to the Proletariat. The confidence in such historical necessity does not really help to achieve the victory sought and believed in although it is a supposed aid in morale. The certainty of victory, Toynbee says, is an "act of hybris — and a supreme one — which invites its eventual refutation by the inexorable logic of events." [1] For example, Goliath's confidence in the necessity of his victory over David proved his undoing; the Muslims although successful in grand conquests fell upon evil days—the world has not been given

---
[1] *Ibid.*, p. 450

to them. The Calvinists and Marxians have not yet had a similar disillusionment, but Toynbee thinks it is forthcoming. These ideas are all forms of the "sense of drift" a *passive* feeling since nature, spiritual and social forces operate at a level beyond the control of the individual human creature.

The active response on the plane of feeling is the "sense of sin." For example in the Syriac society in the "time of troubles" when the brutal power of Assyria was the threat the great eighth century prophets of Israel and Judah preached that destruction by Assyria was imminent unless the Hebrews repented of sin and reorganized their decadent society in accordance with the laws of God. In the Hellenic society the Orphic movement after the breakdown of 431 B.C. (Peloponnesian War) shows that some members of this culture had a "sense of sin." In our Western world since the revival of Hellenism in the Renaissance we have tried to repudiate our Christian religion by treating sin as simply error or mistake rather than an offense against God and our souls. "It is no accident," Toynbee comments, "that the more up-to-date varieties of Protestantism, while retaining the concept of Heaven, have quietly discarded the concept of Hell and have surrendered the concept of the Devil to our satirists and comedians." [1] The cult of science successor to the cult of Hellenism speaks of psychic "complexes" or neuroses instead of sin, or of the determination of the man's physical and social environment as causes of his behaviour. Toynbee humorously quotes an incident from Samuel Butler's *Erehwon* to express our modern view of sin. One of the characters, Mr. Nosnibor has to send for the family 'straightener' (doctor) because he is having an attack of *embezzlement*.[2] Toynbee believes that we of the West must revive our sense of sin before our *hybris* leads us headlong into *ate*.

At the social level at the plane of feeling the passive re-

---
[1] *Ibid.*, p. 454.
[2] *Ibid.*, p. 455.

sponse is the "sense of promiscuity." This results from the loss of the sense of *style* in the civilization. Various and sundry styles are adopted at various times or chaotic combinations of styles; syncretism and promiscuity hold the day. This shows itself in *manners and customs*, in *art*, in *language* and in *religion*.

In *manners and customs* vulgarity and barbarism appear which show the sense of promiscuity. The dominant minority adopts the clothing style, the "democratic" manners and many customs of both the external and the internal proletariat. Although this is a result of the loss of style in the culture it has the advantage of bridging the gap between social classes. The dominant minority is now merging again from the class point of view into the great society from which it detached itself in the "time of troubles" when it became the dominant minority. In the present "time of troubles" of our Western World vulgarism and barbarism of manners among the dominant minority is obvious. Toynbee mentions the vulgar level of our motion-pictures which offer entertainment for all classes based upon what will please the masses (the proletariat); the radio and television have the same standard of entertainment; the public schools are more and more even at higher levels adapting themselves to the "mass man." Democracy and proletarian manners, dress, and behavior dominate all spheres of society. It is very significant that "the apache scarf, with its convincing air of negligence, had really been carefully arranged to conceal the obligatory white collar" among "aristocrats" of the dominant minority, "proof positive that the proletarian style was *a la mode*."[1] The external proletariat or "barbarians" in the late days of the Hellenic society were emulated. Whereas in the fourth century Roman names were adopted by barbarians, in the fifth century in Gaul some Romans began to adopt German names; the Emperor Gratian in the late fourth century

---

[1] *Ibid.,* p. 460.

adopted barbarian dress styles and barbarian sports. In Western culture the dominant minority adopted barbarous customs from the American Indians such as smoking tobacco, the log cabin of the Cherokee and Iroquois, cultivation of corn, and the birch canoe.

Promiscuity in art is apparent in its vulgarization and barbarism. Vulgarization appears in the Hellenic disintegration stage in the extravagant ornamentation popular in the Roman period; in Western culture in the decadent over-ripe ornamentation of Rococo and Baroque which reaches the maximum of vulgarization in the "chocolate-box" style of our Victorian commercial art, which "bids far to conquer the whole face of the planet in the service of a peculiarly Western technique of visually advertising the tradesman's wares." [1] The reaction to this travesty of art has been radical and has taken two principal directions. The pre-Raphaelite Byzantinism has inspired one group; the other has found inspiration in the barbarism of African sculpture (primitivism). This has been the recent inspiration in music (Jazz) and in dancing as well. Toynbee believes that these are promiscuous reactions to the non-creativity in the arts typical of every disintegrating culture, and here Spengler is in agreement.

The vulgarization of language is another form that the sense of promiscuity takes in declining civilizations. A well known example is the *koine*, the *lingua franca* vulgarization of the Greek language that developed in the time of troubles of the Hellenic culture. The *koine* of the New Testament and the Graeco-Roman world spoken by many diverse groups has nothing like the *style* and subtleties of the Attic Greek of Sophocles and Plato. A similar *lingua franca* of the Western civilization is the "Dog Latin" which was the international official language of Western Christian nations until the eighteenth century. This was the vulgarization of the classical Latin of Cicero and Virgil. When

---
[1] *Ibid.*, p. 466.

the Western nations developed their own languages, Italian, French, and English were adopted by peoples of other languages. Italian (Tuscan) became in its vulgarized *lingua franca form*, the language of the Levant at various times; French the *lingua franca* of much of Europe, Latin America, Syria, Egypt and North Africa; English in its *lingua franca* form is the language of India, is spoken widely in China and Japan and, of course, in much of Europe. An Arabic *lingua franca* is spoken widely in Africa.

Promiscuity in religion is manifested in disintegrating societies by syncretism. Toynbee sees examples of this in the Han Empire of the second century B.C. in Taoist eclecticism and in the eclectic Confucianism which succeeded it. In the Syriac society syncretistic tendencies began, Toynbee claims, after the death of Solomon. However the great prophets combatted this successfully. Nevertheless Judaism after the exile borrowed Zoroastrian ideas especially in the areas of angelology, demonology and eschatology. Eclecticism in religion and in philosophy was prominent in the Hellenic culture from the second century B.C. Christianity itself was a synthesis of Hebrew religion and Greek philosophy, and the New Testament written in the Greek koine with its sophisticated philosophical word overtones rather than the Aramaic *koine*. Toynbee notices that of the many rivals of Christianity in the Graeco-Roman world none went as far as Christianity in the process of Hellenization. Christianity he says, Hellenized itself "inwardly as well as outwardly. It was Christianity alone that went the length of expressing its creed in the language of Hellenic philosophy." [1]

Promiscuity in philosophy as in religion is shown in syncretisms. In the Hellenic society, for example, Neoplatonism borrowed elements from Oriental religious philosophies, from Pythagoreanism, from Plato and from Aristotle.

---
[1] *Ibid.*, p. 476.

The *active* response on the plane of feeling is the *sense of unity*. The universal state which inevitably develops at the disintegration stage leads man to project this unity on the political level to unity at the cosmic level and finally to conceive the unity of God. This development begins as we said with the political unification of the world into a universal state. In the Roman Empire (as a great example) this State is unified by Impersonal Law and by the personal Monarch. The unity of Impersonal Law impressed the educated dominant minority — these adopted the Stoic pantheistic philosophy in which God is the unified rational system, Logos, in nature, and this *is* Nature. The personal Monarch idea appealed to the proletariat, especially in Christian dress. The Monarch or personal God of the entire Cosmos is superior to Law, and as revealed in his Incarnation, he is Love beyond all legalism. This spiritual unification of the universe around a personal God of Love, Incarnate in Jesus and in man as the Holy Ghost is the religion that provided Unity in the physical and spiritual world for the proletariat; the Stoic notion of God as primarily rational law left the proletariat cold and unconvinced. Their simple minds and hearts rallied immediately, however, around the Christian God of Love. Toynbee concludes that the two major reasons why the "One True God" of the Hebrews, Christians, and Moslems has won the "supreme role" in the "mystery play which has for its plot the revelation of God to man," are (1) because he is a Personal God; and (2) because he is a jealous God, a God who brooks no rivals and thus eliminated competing deities completely. In cultures of the Orient, also, Toynbee shows us there have been active responses of a sense of unity in the "time of troubles" because the human problem and answer are the same, namely, the problem of the chaos of the social order and the solution of the universal state. In China Taoist and Confucian philosophies emphasized the organic unity of the cosmos during the Han dynasty. We have given these views which have become characteristic of

Chinese thought in Part I of this book in our chapter on Chinese cyclical views of history. In both East and West in philosophy and in religion the important thing to notice is the belief that there is a fundamental unity underlying the phenomenal world which is in itself rather illusory.

The passive and active responses on the planes of behaviour and feeling have now been reviewed. The responses on the plane of life remain for elucidation. The passive response on this plane is *archaism;* the active response *futurism.*

Archaism is the "conscious attempt to swim against the stream of life," the attempt to go back to an earlier happier time in the past. In Part I of this book we found that most ancient cultures believed in a Golden Age of the past from which subsequent eras show a progressive degeneracy. This is the psychology of archaism. In Western culture Rousseau's "return to nature" philosophy manifests this archaistic idea; the Fascist "corporate state" is another instance for it purports to be a revival of the political and economic regime of medieval Italian states; the Nazis show the same point of view since they attempted to revive the "cult of imaginary virtues of primitive Teutons," a reversion to Barbarism. In the arts, in language and literature and in religion archaism has been prominent in the disintegration stage of many great cultures. For example in the Hellenic world Hadrian filled his villa with archaic Hellenic sculpture of the seventh and sixth centuries B.C. in his reversion to past ideals; in our Western culture the Gothic Revival of the nineteenth century shows a similar nostalgia for a lost past and its attempted resurrection. In language and literature archaism is conspicuous in an Irish attempt to revive the ancient Gaelic, in Turkish attempts to eliminate Persian and Arabic words from the Ottoman Turkish vocabulary; in Zionist zeal for the revival of Hebrew (a dead language for twenty-three centuries) as the vernacular of the Palestinian state; and in Greek attempts to revive classical Greek as the modern spoken and written language.

In religion the British Anglo-Catholic movement has revived "medieval ideas and ceremonies which were abandoned and abolished" at the time of the Reformation about four hundred years ago. In Hellenic history Augustus when he came to power tried to revive the ancient Roman religion. In Japan Shinto was revived as a State religion for much the same purpose and reason as the Nazi attempt to revive Teutonic paganism. Both were "blood and soil" inspired and viewed their prevailing religions (Christianity in Germany, and in Japan Mahayana Buddhism) as foreign importations alien in inspiration.

Toynbee observes that archaism as a way of life is condemned to failure. It attempts to reconcile the past and the present without taking into account the trends of the present which are leading into the future. Archaism by attempting artificially "to perpetuate an anachronism" actually, by its failure, opens the door to its opposite, futurism.

Futurism is the active response on the plane of life. Like archaism it is a form of escape from the present disintegrating social order, but instead of escaping into the past, it escapes into an unknown future. Futurism has much appeal, Toynbee says, to souls disappointed with archaist remedies. These persons fly to the opposite extreme and wish to strike out into untried paths. Although there is disappointment in store for futurists also, futurism is "sometimes rewarded with a very different outcome; futurism sometimes transcends itself and rises into transfiguration." [1] Toynbee proceeds to give examples of the futuristic attempt at a new way of life. In dress and manners, he notes, Westernization of Russia by Peter the Great involved shaving of beards and the banning of Kaftans in Muscovy; in the Orient abandonment of customary manners and dress in favor of Western styles and customs has been

---

[1] *Ibid.*, p. 516.

true in many countries; but the attempt to have Jewish priests adopt the hat worn by the Hellenized dominant minority of the Seleucid states caused rebellion on the part of the Maccabees. Toynbee comments that the "ethos of futurism is essentially totalitarian ... The Jew who wears the petasus will soon frequent the Greek palaestra and will come to regard an observance of the rules of his religion as contemptibly old-fashioned and unenlightened." [2]

In politics futurism is expressed in the forcible eradication of geographical boundaries, or in the liquidation of corporations, parties or sects, or of entire classes of society. For instance geographical boundaries were abolished in the unification of France by the implementers of the French Revolution. The Feudal provinces with their customs barriers were abolished and France made into one fiscal area divided into eighty-three administrative departments. In our own day Stalin unified Russian states of diverse cultures and languages, but wisely permitted each state to retain its own culture and language. Liquidation of the bourgeoisie and nobility was, however, drastically performed.

In all the cultures of the world the most pronounced case of futurism is the book-burning done by Chinese Emperor Shih-Huang-ti. An act of this kind symbolizes the attempt to rid oneself completely of any ideas that might interfere with plans for a radically new social order. Shih-Huang-ti desired to establish a totalitarian military despotism and imagined that by burning literature (the *Classics* with the exception of the *Yi Ching*) which opposed this kind of government he could rid himself of subversive criticism. He was unsuccessful; as soon as he died there was a rebellion led by the peasant, Kao Tzu, who founded the Han Dynasty (third century B.C.). During the Han period the great Han emperor, Wu Ti, established the Classics as the basis of education for government officials.

---

[2] *Ibid.*, p. 517.

Kemal Ataturk used a similar device to divert the people of Turkey from their traditional culture into the Western pattern. Although he did not burn the traditional literature, he changed the alphabet. He saw to it that from 1929 all books, newspapers, and legal documents were printed in the Latin alphabet. The rising generation, educated in this Latin alphabet would be unable to read Persian, Arabic or Turkish literature which would require knowledge of a different alphabet as the key to these languages.

In the visual arts there is a style of painting called "futurism" but the best example is one that belongs to religious art. Like the secular-style futurist artist, the iconoclast wishes to abandon traditional art styles. The reasons, however, in the case of the iconoclast are theological, not aesthetic; e.g. the Orthodox Christian Church abandoned three-dimensional representations, but permitted two-dimensional "icons."

It is soon discovered that futurism is not the remedy for the basically spiritual ills of society in its declining era. Toynbee shows the inevitable "bankruptcy of futurism" in a well known example, the post-exilic history of the Jews. Futurism took the form of the Messianic hope — the Messiah, the "anointed of the Lord," was to usher in a new era of "peace on earth, good-will to men." [1] Only for a short period under the Maccabees did the little Jewish kingdom achieve autonomy; even then the notion of a universal kingdom on earth under the Messiah was from the mundane point of view ridiculous; the Jewish state was too small. Rome soon brought an end to Jewish independence. Nevertheless futurism continued and Zealots led revolutions. In 70 A.D. Jerusalem and the Temple were destroyed, but even then futuristic Zealots continued revolutionary activities until in 135 A.D. in the rebellion led by Bar Kokaba the Jews were utterly annihilated. But earlier than this and especially from the time of Roman domination in the

---

[1] See Part II, chapter II of this book, *supra*.

first century B.C. the Jews were discovering the Kingdom of God as a spiritual realm not of this world with a Messiah also not of this world — a Messiah who was God Himself as Saviour. This is the self-transcendence of futurism. Toynbee denies that this flight to a transcendent sphere of operations is "escapism." This is not escapism, he claims, because here men "have put their treasure in a purpose which is not Man's but God's, and which therefore can only be pursued in a spiritual field in which God is not an ally but the director of operations."[2]

This transference to the spiritual plane is the very reverse of escapism because, Toynbee says, it is able to transfigure our earthly life. The transference from earth to the idea of a "Kingdom of God which is not in Time at all but is in a different spiritual dimension, and which, just by virtue of this difference of dimension, is able to penetrate our mundane life and to transfigure it,"[1] has nothing in common with infantile escapism. On the contrary this shows spiritual maturity and high vision.

The transfiguration of earthly life is brought about by the spiritual movement called "withdrawal and return." Withdrawal taken alone may be sheer detachment. Detachment is intellectual, and is represented by philosophy in general and by the Stoic philosophy especially. The appeal of philosophy is to the head, not to the heart — even the intellectual is not satisfied by it as an answer to the total meaning of life — how much less can the philosopher's abstractions appeal or even be understood by the masses of humanity. The aloof philosopher's approach of detachment must be "eclipsed by the mystery of transfiguration." Only highbrows and economic materialists deny this, and "whoever may be right, they at any rate are wrong."[2] Because the philosopher's aim is an objective detachment from life and the universe, he cannot understand God's

---
[2] Toynbee, *op. cit.*, p. 524.
[1] *Ibid.*, p. 525.
[2] *Ibid.*, p. 528.

"withdrawal" to return. Toynbee here is referring to the Christian religious idea of Christ crucified (God's withdrawal) to return. Toynbee reminds us that St. Paul said that the idea of Christ crucified was foolishness to the Greeks; it is foolishness to the futurists also since the Kingdom is not of this world; the Kingdom of God is a spiritual reality (Compare the mandala symbolism and transformation idea of Part I above.) interpenetrating the present, and this is the idea of transfiguration.

Since the "withdrawal and return" movement which is transfiguration exemplifies (versus archaism and futurism) " 'transference of the field of action' from the macrocosm to the microcosm which manifests itself in the spiritual phenomenon of 'etherialization,' "[1] this is a growth phenomenon. Yet this growth is taking place in a disintegrating culture. Toynbee decides that this kind of growth belongs to some other species than that called a civilization. This kind of growth belongs to the progress of the spiritual Kingdom of God to which the rise and fall of civilizations minister. The creative movement of transfiguration at the end of the disintegration period is a spiritual rebirth, *Palingenesia:*

> In the first beat of the rhythm a destructive Yang-movement (the disintegration) passes over into a Yin-state (detachment) which is also a peace of exhaustion; but the rhythm is not arrested at the dead point; it passes over into a creative Yang-movement (transfiguration). This double beat of the movement of Yin and Yang is that particular form of the general movement of withdrawal-and-return on which we stumbled near the beginning of our study of disintegration and which we then called Schism-and-Palingenesia.[2]

---

[1] *Ibid.*, p. 530.
[2] *Ibid.*, p. 531.

This rebirth, comments Toynbee, is not the recurrence of a similar species of civilization, nor does it mean escape into a Nirvana. It does mean the kind of rebirth of which Jesus spoke to Nicodemus, "the attainment of another supra-mundane state to which the image of birth can be illuminatingly applied because this other state is a positive state of life — though one in a higher spiritual dimension than the life of This World." [3] In history the symbol of this Palingenesia was "the birth in the flesh of the King of the Kingdom of God." [4]

Toynbee proceeds to show the prime significance of the coming of this Saviour. First he discusses other types of saviours: (1) the "saviour with a sword." This is the Zealot type who would, as Peter, take the Kingdom of Heaven by storm; but the answer to this saviour is the famous one: "he who takes the sword will perish by the sword." History tells us that violent persecution failed to eradicate the Christian movement in the Roman world. (2) The second type of saviour is "the saviour with the time machine." He is the man who is either an archaist or futurist. We have already seen the futility of both of these approaches in renewing a decadent society. (3) The third type of saviour Toynbee mentions is the philosopher-king. This type of person, if he became a ruler, would rule by the power of mimesis, in itself a not too strong means of integrating society. Further, Toynbee says, even in Plato's ideal *Republic* the use of force when necessary is implied. Therefore "like the saviour with the 'time machine,' who in his pure form is likewise a political idealist, the philosopher-king is driven into proclaiming his own failure by drawing a weapon which convicts him too of being a 'saviour with the sword' in disguise." [1] (4) The fourth type is the only adequate type. This is the "god incarnate in a man." Jesus differs from the other types of saviours which

---
[3] *Ibid.*, p. 532.
[4] *Ibid.*, p. 532.
[1] *Ibid.*, p. 543.

turn out to be swordsmen in that he believed himself to be the Son of God. Other saviours, too, in human history and in many cultures have also claimed to be gods or the sons of gods. The dying and rising god cult was prevalent in all the ancient civilizations (Osiris, Tammuz, Attis, Persephone, etc.) There is, then, Toynbee says, a "god of many epiphanies" but of only one Passion. The other gods died out of despair, unwillingly, whereas Christ died out of love for men. Toynbee then quotes the passage from the Gospel of John "For God so loved the World that he gave his only begotten Son, that whosoever believeth in Him should not perish but have everlasting life." [2] There is but one Saviour, Jesus Christ, Toynbee concludes, who is the only true "God incarnate in a man."

The climax and goal of human history for Toynbee as for St. Augustine is the appearance of God in the world as Jesus to redeem mankind through the death on the cross.

The rhythmic pattern of disintegration. In the growth stages of a civilization there is the rhythmic pattern of challenge — response. A challenge is offered the society which is met by a successful response; this response generates a different challenge which in its turn is met with a successful response. There is no absolute reason why this should not go on indefinitely. However past civilizations have broken down and disintegrated because challenges were not met creatively. When this happens there is a breakdown and disintegration ensues. The rhythmic pattern which describes the period following a breakdown in a civilization is in most cases the following: rout-rally-rout-rally-rout-rally-rout or three-and-a-half beats. This rhythm, Toynbee thinks, applies to the Hellenic civilization. The date 431 B.C. (the Peloponnesian War) is the first rout; the "social gospel of Homonoia or Concord preached by Timoleon at Syracuse and in a far wider sphere by Alexander the Great," [1] in the fourth century B.C. is the

---

[2] *Ibid.,* p. 547.

first rally (an attempt to answer the challenge of unification of city-states—further attempts were the Stoic ideas of a world commonwealth) this is followed again by a rout with the beginning of the Hannibalic War in 218 B.C.; another rally follows with the universal state founded by Augustus in 31 B.C.; but then there is another rout upon the death of Marcus Aurelius in 180 A.D.; then follows the last rally in 284 under Diocletian; and finally the last rout with the interregnum which follows upon the break-up of the universal state.

Toynbee finds this three and a half beat rhythm of disintegration in the Sinic society, in the Sumerian, and in Orthodox Christendom. In the Hindu civilization there are but three beats thus far; the final half-beat in the universal state provided by the British Raj is not yet complete, Toynbee writes, in the middle of the nineteen forties. This halfbeat has been completed however, now, and India is perhaps in an interregnum—in the travail of giving birth to a new society.

In our own civilization Toynbee discovers the same ominous rhythm. He dates our first rout in the sixteenth century with the "wars of religion." The troubles in the Church and in the rising national states were not met creatively; the century of wars of religion was the result. A rally occurred in the Eighteenth Century but this was a temporary respite since the peace of this era was not founded upon Christian faith, hope and love, but upon "the Mephistophelian maladies of disillusionment, apprehension and cynicism."[2] This rally therefore led shortly to another rout the French Revolution and the numerous subsequent wars resulting from our unsuccessful efforts to answer the major challenges of our time—Industrialism and Democracy. The national sovereignty idea is incompatible with Industrialism and Democracy. The next rally, Toynbee thinks, will be a universal state, the only adequate answer

---

[1] *Ibid.*, p. 549.
[2] *Ibid.*, p. 553.

to the challenge. The Nazis tried to give us such a state by force, but the sword cannot save our culture and the world for reasons already given. What is needed is a family of free nations dwelling together harmoniously and cooperatively. Toynbee sees no "absolute law of historical determinism" which compels us to believe that our civilization is doomed even though the probabilities are high that our society like those of the past will conform to the "rhythm of disintegration" and end with a universal state followed by destruction and an interregnum.

Toynbee ends his first series of volumes with further comments upon "standardization through distintegration." In all cultures there are the same "standard" three classes in the disintegration era: the dominant minority who establish the universal state, the internal proletariat who rally around a redeeming religion—a Universal Church—and the external proletariat who father the coming Heroic Age of a subsequent civilization. It is the redeeming religion which is the most significant and the real purpose of the rise and fall of secular civilizations, of the entire historical process, Toynbee concludes, in his second series of volumes.

The significance of Religion in a philosophy of history: the churches "a higher species of society." The historical unit of study, a particular civilization, heretofore taken to be the "intelligible" unit has turned out, Toynbee concludes in his second series of volumes, to be in a limited sense only an intelligible unit. This is because Toynbee has decided definitely in the latter half of his work that the progress of religion is the measuring rod for progress in history. He emphasizes the idea expressed earlier in *Civilization on Trial* (1948) that the function of civilizations is the "continuous upward movement of religion." [1] The relationship between civilizations and the progress of religion are mainly three: (1) the very failure of secular

---

[1] Arnold J. Toynbee, *Civilization on Trial* (New York: Oxford University Press, 1948), p. 236.

civilizations causes man to rise to ever higher spiritual planes. For instance Christianity was a response to the failure of Hellenic civilization. This is "revelation through tribulation." [2] Civilizations perform the function of showing man that salvation is not of this world but lies on the spiritual plane symbolized by the "church" (the higher religions) versus the secular life emphasized by "civilization" at its height. Civilization as such breeds *hybris* which leads inevitably to *ate*. But the suffering and disaster caused by the failure, the breakdown and disintegration, of almost all of the great civilizations of human history (and imminently our own) contributes immensely to spiritual progress—redemption through suffering. "If religion is a chariot, it looks as if the wheels on which it mounts towards Heaven may be the periodic downfalls of civilization on Earth." [3] (2) Contemporaneous civilizations provide stimuli for the development of the higher religions. It is very significant that the great creative religious developments have occurred at places that were crossroads of the world. For example, Palestine was such a place. The stimuli given by interchange of ideas provided by the location of the country itself, the frequent threats of national disaster (also caused by the geographical location of the country), as well as the actual disasters such as the "Babylonian captivity"—another result of the political importance of Palestine as a crossroads of the world—all these stimuli caused by geographical location aided in the development of spiritual creativity on the part of great prophets such as Amos, Hosea, the first and the Second Isaiah (stimulated by the chastisement of the Exile experience). Islam developed at Mecca, another crossroads—a crossroads of the Arab world; Mahayana Buddhism developed at another crossroads. Toynbee in general holds that the great religions are born in "meetingplaces of civilizations." [1]

---

[2] Arnold J. Toynbee, *A Study of History*, 12 vols. (London: Oxford University Press, 1934-61), Vol. VII, p. 420.

[2] Toynbee, *op. cit.*, *Civilization on Trial*, p. 235.

[1] *Op. cit.*, *A Study of History*, Vol. VIII, pp. 90 ff.

(3) The third major relationship between civilizations and the progress of religion is another case of contact between contemporary civilizations. The internal proletariat of a disintegrating civilization usually adopts an "alien" religion because its own indigenous religion and culture has proved a failure. This alien religion is, of course, one developed by a contemporary society. In the case of the Hellenic disintegrating world, the proletariat adopted the "alien" religion of the contemporary Syriac (or Palestinian) culture, Christianity.

Civilizations perform the function of the advancement of religion, the "universal churches" of mankind. In the progress of religion lies the highest kind of progress for the human spirit, Toynbee thinks. This is because Religion unites the truths of the heart and the head into one whole. The truths of the Heart belong to the realm of intuition and the subconscious; the truths of the Head to Intellect. Intuition and the subconscious give us music, poetry and the visual arts; the intellect gives us science. Reason (or intellect) criticizes the subconscious for its simple-mindedness in belief in God; "conversely in the sight of the Subconscious, the Reason is a heartless pedant who has purchased a miraculous but superfluous command over Nature at the sinful price of betraying the Soul by allowing her primordial vision of God to fade into the light of common day." [2] Head and heart can be reconciled and harmonized when it it is understood that each expresses in its own characteristic language "different aspects, planes, and dimensions of Reality." [3]

The myths of religion have been badly misused by theology which attempts to place them on the literal truth-plane of intellect and science. The religious myth such as the Virgin Birth expresses symbolically the truth of intuition and the Heart that men encountered "a man through whose personality God's light streamed into his fellow

---

[2] *Ibid.*, Vol. VII, p. 501.
[3] *Ibid.*, p. 512.

men's souls, not darkly, as through a glass, but undimmed, as through an open window." [1] Or, take the doctrine of the presence of Christ in the Eucharist:

> Which is the more significant truth about bread and wine? The spiritual truth that, in the Eucharist, they bring the Soul into communion with God? Or the scientific truth that they keep a physical organism alive in virtue of such-and-such tissue-repairing and such-and-such energy-giving ingredients? And which is the more significant truth about the birth of a new man into the World? The spiritual truth that, through the tender mercy of our God, the dayspring from on high hath visited us? Or the scientific truth that an embryo has been conceived in such-and-such a way by sexual intercourse, and has passed through such-and-such physical metamorphoses between conception and birth? In the realm of spiritual values, bread and wine exist for the sake of the Eucharist, not of the food-supply and conception and birth take place for the sake of the Incarnation, not of man-power. And, if Science, using the same words in a different sense of her own, declares that the spiritual usage of them is, if taken literally intended, untrue, and, if symbolically intended, unscientific, Religion can have the last word if she is content to retort that, for her, the scientific meaning is trivial and irrelevant. She does not expose her mythological expression of spiritual truth to any damaging scientific attack unless she stakes the perverse theological claim that her truths are true in the scientific sense as well as in the spiritual.[2]

Like St. Augustine and St. Thomas Toynbee believes that Truth is, however, ultimately one. He says:

> The buried pinnacle of rock on which rational truth is founded may be situated not very far below the sur-

---
[1] *Ibid.*, p. 503.
[2] *Ibid.*

face, while spiritual truth may be based on the rockbottom of an abyss; but, however great the difference in the level may be, the foundations of both kinds of truth alike go down to the rock, and at either level it is the same rock, living yet invisible, that bears the weight on its atlantean shoulders.[3]

The source of this Truth of both intuition and intellect, Heart and Head is the One True God discovered by the higher religions, and this is why religion is the chief business of the human race and religious progress the criterion of human progress in general. The higher religions are distinguished by having "as a member the One True God" whether he be conceived as the Jews, Christians and Moslems represent Him or as the Mahayana Buddhists and Hindus represent Him.

Worship of the One True God especially as avatar (Hinduism), bodhisattva (Mahayana Buddhism) or as Jesus (the sole avatar of the Christian religion), in other words God as Love is the universal significance and business of the churches as a higher species of society. Thus conceived these churches have had the following functions: (1) They have given "power to overcome the discord which was one of the inveterate evils of Human Society,"[1] (2) They have "offered a solution of the problem of the meaning of History,"[2] (3) They have "inspired an ideal of conduct which could be an effectively potent spiritual stimulus for the superhuman effort of making Human Life possible in This World."[3] (4) They have prevented the idolatry "inherent in mimesis when this was oriented ... towards one of Man's fellow human creatures"[4] instead of towards the One True God. Toynbee elaborates on these four functions to show that the churches have kept alive the spiritual life

---
[3] *Ibid.*, p. 505.
[1] *Ibid.*, p. 507.
[2] *Ibid.*
[3] *Ibid.*
[4] *Ibid.*

of man while civilizations have degenerated into gross materialism. Progress therefore belongs to the churches rather than to the civilizations as such.

The future progress of humanity lies in the hands of the Churches particularly the churches to which the great majority of the human race belongs: Christianity, Islam, Mahayana Buddhism and Hinduism. Toynbee writes that "in the next chapter of a henceforth oecumenical human history, the four higher religions sprung from the ruins of civilizations of the second generation" [5] will have close contacts with one another. The outcome is "evidently likely to inaugurate a new era in human life in this world." [6]

The immediate issue, however, is the conflict between the Communist and the non-Communist worlds. The United States and the West must practice effectively and in a revolutionary way the true social gospel of Christianity to win the respect and support of the three-fourths of the world's population who are oppressed. [1] If the West could do this its civilization may be rejuvenated and prolonged indefinitely. Toynbee says that

> if the grace of God were to bring about this miracle in ex-Christian Western hearts genuinely smitten with contrition, and not merely with a self-interested alarm, by the hammer strokes of a Communist challenge, then an encounter between the Modern Western World and Russia, which has already changed the course of Russian history by prolonging the life-span of a time-expired Russian universal state, might also change the course of Modern Western history by rejuvenating a body social in which the familiar symptoms of disintegration had already made their appearance. If this encounter were to have this outcome, this might prove to be the opening of a wholly new chapter in the history of Mankind.[2]

---
[5] *Ibid.*, Vol. VIII, p. 628.
[6] *Ibid.*
[1] *Ibid.*, pp. 147-149.
[2] *Ibid.*, p. 149.

Western man has the freedom to do just this if he will. In a section in Volume IX entitled "Law and Freedom in History," Toynbee argues that the "laws of nature" and the "laws of God" are not incompatible. For example in psychology the exploration of the subconscious reveals *not* the laws of Logic but "laws" of poetry and mythology. Yet it is true that all "laws" are "natural" laws and laws of God therefore. Is man free to rise above some of the "natural" laws or is he subject to natural sociological laws of historical development as affirmed by Marxist-Leninist philosophers of history (discussed in chapter X, Part II of this book)? Toynbee's answer to this problem of man's freedom is affirmative. Man is free to the extent that he follows the highest Law of God which is Love. This is the Law that cancels out the other sociological-historical "laws" which show, Toynbee believes, the high probability that our civilization is doomed. Western man, Toynbee says in chorus with most of the alert observers is running the gauntlet between fraticidal conflict of parochial states and of a universal state to be established by a knockout blow. The totalitarian, materialistic Communist universal state, Toynbee thinks, would mean continuing rule by a dominant minority already corrupted by a decadent Western materialism. (Toynbee agrees with Ibn Khaldun, Vico, Spengler and Sorokin that materialist philosophies are characteristic of the decline period of any culture.) Communism's success, if won "would prove to be a Dead Sea fruit; for the Human Heart is the only realm on Earth in which a religion can reign, and nothing so surely alienates the Heart as an attempt to force an entry into it by breaking the will with the bludgeon of political coercion." [1] The Saviour with the Sword of the Futurist type is not the answer to our civilization's reintegration and creative progress.

The United States as leader of the opposition to Russia is far too much turning to archaism especially in the economic field. This demonstrates the Marxian predictions

---

[1] *Ibid.*, Vol. VII, p. 416.

and shows the "laws" operating in the sociological sphere. Americans think that laissez-faire economy, successful in the past in an open frontier economy,—"free enterprise" as it is called—is the solution to all economic and class conflicts throughout the world. Russia's solution which is the opposite is much more appealing to the three-fourths of the peoples of the world which belong to the underprivileged of humanity (this includes most Negroes in the United States). Russia has set for them the example of a poor peasant country which has made good. Nevertheless, the Russian solution if universally applied would prove abortive because of its materialistic philosophy and coercive methods. The Middle Way of the Scandinavian countries is best, Toynbee concludes. Here the economic, class and international problems are approached and solved with constructively active but non-coercive methods. This Middle Way represents the meeting-point of Communism and the "free-enterprise" world; perhaps a Universal Federation of States might form around this idea or develop out of the present veto-ridden East-West split United Nations. If the West could overcome its materialism and transfigure itself by a return to the Law of God, Love, it could "overcome the world." The vast majority of mankind which are the depressed peoples could look to it for guidance until they were themselves rehabilitated and able to take care of themselves. If there could be such a Universal Community of peoples the creativity in Thought and in Art might be boundless. Toynbee's frank opinion is that only a minority would prove to be interested in this kind of activity. The great majority in all likelihood would not be capable of creativity or even of interest in such areas. Nevertheless this majority must not be tempted into leading the life of a City of Swine when the immense leisure afforded them by man's humanitarian control over nature through machinery comes into being. Religion is the answer which Toynbee offers to this problem. Religion must be the "high calling" to which the vast majority can devote themselves to prevent misuse of leisure time. For that matter, Religion is the most important realm of the Spirit for all men, the "masses" or the great creators in the arts and sciences; since "the true end of man" is "glorifying God and enjoying Him . . ." [1] as St. Augustine and St. Thomas emphasize.

The "straits ahead" for the contemporary human world are very dangerous. A course must be steered between a Scylla of Christian orthodoxy [2] which supports an archaic traditionalist dead world and the Charybdis of Communism [3] which "offers a stone for bread." [4] Communism worships Leviathan and the traditionalists the Homunculus of the national state. Of the two choices Leviathan is better than homunculus. [5] The West will lose unless it follows true Christianity including its Social Gospel. But it is hard for rich men and rich nations to enter the Kingdom of God; only the Law of God, Love, is equal to the transfiguration of souls necessary for the task.

The bodhisattva who can guide us in this task is St. Francis of Assisi, the "most god-like soul" who has been "born into the Western World so far." [1] Toynbee adds, "A disciple of Saint Francis who followed faithfully enough in the saint's footsteps to participate in the saint's gift of receiving Christ's stigmata would know, with the knowledge that comes only through suffering, that this sacrifice had been accepted by the Lord." [2]

Summary of Toynbee's Spiral Cyclical View

Toynbee concludes from his immense and painstaking researches into human history that every civilization seems to follow the pattern of a period of development and growth by responding creatively to challenges which give rise to

---
[1] *Ibid.*, Vol. IX, p. 640.
[2] *Ibid.*, p. 643.
[3] *Ibid.*
[4] *Ibid.*
[5] *Ibid.*, p. 621.
[1] *Ibid.*, p. 644.
[2] *Ibid.*

further challenges until a state of surfeit or *hybris* is reached by the creative minority. This creative minority at this point fails to respond creatively to the significant challenge or challenges offered and there is a breakdown. The time of troubles ensues and the disintegration period sets in. This is characterized by a standard kind of Schism in the Body-Social. The heretofore creative minority becomes a dominant minority and alienates the masses of the people who had until this time followed their leaders out of respect for their creativity. The alienated masses of the people include not only the depressed classes but many others who also feel that they are *in* but not *of* the society and this group Toynbee calls the Internal Proletariat. There is an External Proletariat, also of Barbarian Warbands, who when the Society was creative emulated and respected it. Schism in the Soul reveals itself in the variety of ways of behavior, feeling, and life described above. The rhythmic pattern of disintegration is in three and a half beats: rout-rally, rout-rally, rout-rally rout. There is usually one rally followed by a rout during the time of troubles and one rout followed by one rally in the period of the universal state, then finally the rout which ends the civilization. "Civilizations," Toynbee says, "may be *cyclic* and *recurrent*, while the movement of religion may be served and promoted by the cyclic movement of civilizations round the cycle of birth, death, birth." [1]

The Churches Toynbee concludes, in his second series of volumes are the higher species of society in which there is continuous progress, a progress aided by the failures of secular civilizations—actually *caused* by these failures. The goal of history becomes for Toynbee that of St. Augustine, salvation of human souls for the Kingdom of God rather than any kind of overall secular progress. Toynbee says:

> In the Age of the Civilizations, progress, in so far

[1] *Toynbee, Civilization on Trial, op. cit.,* p. 236.

as human minds had entertained this idea at all, had often been identified with the progressive improvement of some terrestrial institution: a tribe, a city-state, an empire, a church, a system of knowledge or 'know-how,' a school of art, a code of morals. If this conception of the meaning of progress were credible to the pilgrim-citizens on Earth of the *Civitas Dei,* they would indeed be of all men the most miserable, since they are aware that, in a terrestrial life infected with Original Sin, neither souls nor institutions can carry progress to perfection, and are also aware that, whatever may be the ultimate destiny of souls, institutions are earth-bound creations of Man in an imperfect world whose limitations they can never transcend . . . *The touchstone of the value of an institution is whether it helps or hinders Man to find his way back to his Maker,* and an institution will become an obstacle to Man's true end of glorifying God and enjoying Him forever if it is taken as being an end in itself instead of being used as the mere means that is all that it truly is.[2]

In an Appendix to Volume VII of Toynbee's *Study of History,* Martin Wight as a "Christian Historian" points out that Toynbee's historical goal seems to be the rallying of the world around true Christianity. Wight writes that it will appear to the Christian Historian

> that, just as you have abandoned your original judgment that all civilizations are philosophically equivalent and have found that 'civilizations . . . have ceased to constitute intelligible fields of study for us and have forfeited their historical significance except in so far as they minister to the progress of Religion,' so the suppressed logic of your argument (rather than the weight of your evidence) drives on towards discarding your assumption that all higher religions are spiritually equivalent, and to the conclusion that the higher religions in their turn cease to be intelligible

---

[2] Toynbee, *A Study of History,* 12 vols., *op. cit.,* Vol. VII, p. 561. (my italics).

fields of study and forfeit their historical significance except in so far as they are related to Christianity.[1]

Man's goal is a supernatural one on a spiritual plane, an Other World beyond this one, a goal which man accepts by faith and intuition.

The Oriental philosophies we have studied above, both classical and twentieth century are even more emphatic about the spiritual plane as man's goal; they too agree that the plane of Spirit is higher than the plane of Intellect (buddhi). This idea has been so central in Oriental philosophies that they show a far more mature development of it than is ordinarily found in the Christian world—reintegration of man into one organic spiritual body (versus the schizophrenic finite and unreal ego) is their aim. The great twentieth century Hindu philosophers, Aurobindo and Radhakrishnan, also center their philosophies of history upon man's ultimate achievement of the level of spirit (called the supermind or superman level in evolutionary development by Aurobindo). Sorokin acknowledges our debt to the Oriental thinkers and utilizes the same concept of the historical goal with his notion of the supraconscious level of creative altruistic love as the essential basis for a new culture cycle.

This goal of harmony and unity in one eternal spiritual consciousness with egoism extinguished forever—an old and familiar goal in the Oriental philosophies—is foreign to the majority of the intellectual leaders of the West. It is an optimistic sign of the closer meeting of East and West, prophesied by Professor Northrop, when men with rich backgrounds in Western culture like Sorokin and Toynbee conclude with the great Oriental philosophers that man's historical goal is to reach the plane of Spirit, the plane of altruistic love. To attain this goal Toynbee wants to take definite action; man must make the world as Utopian as

---

[1] *Ibid.*, p. 748.

possible. Here again Radhakrishnan and Aurobindo agree. Toynbee says that to make this world more Utopian technology and science must be utilized to the utmost to enable man to live the life of Spirit—the life of creativity in the visual arts, in music, in literature, in philosophy and in theoretical knowledge of all kinds. But unless the Heart is right and Love rules, all of these glories of the human spirit will come to naught; destruction will overtake us. Progress lies first of all in the realm of religion intelligently comprehended. Seek ye first the Kingdom of God. i.e., the supraconscious level of altruistic love—the level of Spirit—, and all things will be added unto you.

Toynbee concludes that history through the cyclic pattern of the rise and decline of great civilizations shows an upward direction in the development and progress of the great religions of mankind, especially of Christianity which Toynbee implies is the greatest of all and the most potent of any to lead us forward in a continuous spiral progress. (The great Oriental thinkers will no doubt excuse Toynbee's bias in favor of his own religion.) [1]

It is true that Toynbee rejects the characteristic Eastern view of human and cosmic history as the repetition of never-ending cycles identical in form; nevertheless his own view turns out to be not very different. We have seen below in the relevant chapters that in the Eastern philosophical religions secular and cosmic history, both of which are on the material plane, are important only as the school for souls whose ultimate destiny is graduation to the spiritual plane of union with the Ultimate Being beyond this world of cyclical change. Toynbee is saying very much the same thing; but as a Faustian man, child of his Western cultural tradition, he lays more emphasis upon *action* than the East (until recently—e.g. the philosophies of Aurobindo and Radhakrishnan). Toynbee desires action to free all men—all must be as sons of God, equal in status with material needs so well satisfied that the life of the Spirit will be given the encouragement to blossom into full flower.

---

[1] In Vol. XII (published too late for my use) Toynbee asserts that no one religion has a monopoly on spiritual truth.

CONCLUSION: SIGNIFICANCE OF THIS STUDY

Section 1. Is the Cyclic Patterning of History Defensible?

It seems to be the view of most contemporary historians and historiographers that no one has given us the absolute pattern, cyclical or non-cyclical into which fall the important aspects of human history.* Unlike events in the physical world historical events, it is well known, cannot be repeated in laboratory experiments to confirm or refute pattern or non-pattern theories. [1] The historical past is an enormously complex concatenation of events and we cannot be sure that those selected as worthy of notice by historians are the significant ones. Since this seems to be the state of affairs in the attempt to approach history as a science, many historians hold the view expressed by Professor Gottschalk that it is difficult for historians "to explain the 'actual' historical universe by any generally acceptable principle." [2] Most therefore prefer a "pluralistic" approach to an understanding of causes operative in history [3] and organize events around social, cultural, political, and economic "causes" and developments. Even here the way in which the historian orders facts "according to an idea must in part at least, be conceived in one's own mind." [4] The "infinite complexity" of events in any year, decade, century, or epoch makes selection necessary and what the historian selects and how he orders his selected facts is to a certain extent imaginative. His pattern of organization of the events of history may be entirely rejected by later historians as negligent of the truly significant events, since by that time the historical world scene has proved other

---

* Notes for this chapter are on pp. 476 f.

events the really significant ones. This may continue to occur indefinitely during the course of human history on this earth.

This somewhat "relativist" view has been expressed most clearly by Carl Becker. Becker affirms that the personal background of the individual historian, the epoch in which he lives and the "climate of opinion" of his cultural environment determine in large measure his manner of writing history. Becker defends this relativism against attacks of philosophers of history (such as Mandelbaum) who attempt to refute it. Mandelbaum, however, concedes that history has needed revision; for example Karl Marx drew attention to the importance of economic causes heretofore neglected by historians.[5] It is true, none the less, Mandelbaum adds, that such revisions of history are accepted only because there is objective recognition that many new facts previously neglected have been uncovered. This uncovering of new facts will probably continue in history as in the physical sciences and other fields of knowledge, for perfect truth has not yet been reached in any single generation.

Such criticisms, which are typical, of the predicament of the professional historian should do two things: (1) It should make us skeptical of any particular philosophy of history which pretends to be an absolute one; (2) It should make us appreciative of, and open-minded towards, attempts of past cultures and of present Eastern and Western cultures to solve the problem of the meaning of human history. Cyclical patterning of history in its various forms described above has been and still remains man's most valiant effort to make history into sociological science, the "New Science," to use the words of Vico.

We have seen how this kind of patterning began very early in the history of human thought with the mythopoeic *pars pro toto* methodological approach common among ancient thinkers. The "part" the sun cycles of day and night, the annual cycle of the seasons, the moon cycle, and biological cycles of birth, maturity and death became applied to the "whole" and the cyclical idea of the Great Year of the Cosmos developed. Professor Northrop makes clear that the East retained this aesthetic, this concrete sensuous approach to time and causality. It became the "law of karma" which sees all the phenomena of the universe as a cyclical sequence of perpetually born and perishing particulars; and "this is the concept of causality in a non-technological society." (Northrop, "Man's Relation to the Earth," *op. cit;* p. 1058.) The Great Year cyclical idea of time reached its climax in Indian thought (Hindu, Buddhist and Jaina). In Indian thought the Great Year of the Cosmos with its subdivisions has a very precise pattern repeated *ad infinitum.* The function, meaning, and significance of the process is spiritual progress for the souls involved in it—such progress as will enable the enchained souls to escape out of it forever. Such a view is apt to be disparaged as "mythical" by Western minds ignorant of the deeper meaning of Oriental thought. We have tried to show the profound symbolism involved in Oriental cyclical ideas which have their counterpart, also in Western thought.

Section 2. Eastern and Western Cyclical Philosophies Compared: Similarity in Goal and Meaning of History

The mythopoeic formulations of some of the Eastern philosophies of history are not intended as literal truths. The foremost thinkers, Hindu, Buddhist, or Jaina, use such cosmic cyclical myths as SYMBOLS in their significance; literal truth is subordinated to symbolic spiritual meaning. The repetitious cycles of the material cosmos signify the fleeting transience, the ultimate meaninglessness of the matter world, *i.e.,* the world of egoistic secularism and materialism. The individual must escape from the bondage of such a bubble-world, ephemeral as the physical body which is its basis, into the spiritual world of eternal reality. He joins his spirit to the Center, the One Infinite spiritual being as we saw in our exploration of yogic methods and goals which are based upon a cyclical view of the cosmos.

For all Oriental cyclical philosophies—Hindu, Buddhist, Jaina, or Chinese Taoist yoga systems—spiritual freedom is the goal. This means escape from the bondage of the matter world of desires centered upon ego-consciousness— a world of fragmentation and disintegration—to the world of spiritual unity and integration with the One, the Center, who is at the same time the All. To be reintegrated with this one spiritual reality, source also of the maya-world of physical things, is freedom—freedom from all the limitations of bondage to the finitude of the life-death cycles of the *samsara* world. Such a metahistorical goal for the human race and the denizens of other universes (included also in Oriental thought) gives history a purpose, *viz.*, release (freedom) of souls.

Such an other-worldly goal does not mean a do-nothing policy with reference to social conditions in this world. On the contrary on the basis of the metaphysical knowledge that the separate ego is unreal, all men become parts of onself. The yogi who has achieved such knowledge through direct realization such as Ramakrishna in recent Hinduism, takes on what the Mahayana Buddhists call a bodhisattvic consciousness. As Evans-Wentz tells us the Mahayana Buddhist symbolic myth explains that the bodhic forces of the bodhisattvas "modify the harshness of the unenlightened Nature," and through the permeating influences of their all-embracing love, mankind is led "towards a perfected social order on Earth." [6] We have already cited Zen Buddhism, popular both in East and West today, as a philosophy which emphasizes the *mandala* idea of Centering— the spiritual unity of all men and things in the cosmos— again a metaphysical basis for human unity and mutual help. Cyclical philosophies of the Orient do not result, therefore, in a narrow other-worldliness; they do emphasize that spiritual freedom and maturity consist in the realization that the separate ego is the real myth and that the human goal is the Center, unity with the Infinite One, who is All.

The goals of the Moslem and Christian apocalyptic one-cycle ideas of cosmic and human history are in many ways similar to the Oriental views. History, cosmic and human, is much shorter—telescoped into one grand cycle with absolute beginning and end. Nevertheless, the goal is much the same—freedom from the matter world of birth and death through entering the world of the Center, God's spirit-world. (The *mandala* theme of reintegration with Ultimate Reality is repeated.) In God's Paradise the soul becomes an eternal angelic member. The soul's opportunity of saving itself is telescoped, also, into the fleeting period of one lifetime at the end of which it is saved or lost for all eternity.

The Indian one-cycle views we examined—Radhakrishnan's and Sri Aurobindo's—are much more tolerant and liberal. In their acceptance of the doctrine of transmigration common to Oriental thought in general countless opportunities are provided the soul for its salvation. At the same time, being born as a man is a rare opportunity and a serious responsibility, therefore, in relation to the expedition of salvation. Altogether, human life and history are very significant in both Indian one-cycle and multi-cycle views. The goal in these as in the Christian and Moslem apocalyptic one-cycle systems is an eternal spiritual life in unity with the Center, the One. Here the soul enjoys the highest freedom, knowledge and bliss.

Toynbee in his study of culture cycles arrives at the same conclusion as to the goal and meaning of human history. The cycles of the rise and fall of civilizations have for their goal the Kingdom of God which because of Original Sin (compare Oriental ego-consciousness) cannot be realized in its fullness on this earth. Toynbee repeatedly emphasizes the idea that "My kingdom is not of this world." Man's ultimate goal is in another plane, as in the Oriental philosophies, the purely spiritual Kingdom of Heaven, God's own Realm of Spirit. This again is union with the Center as the metahistorical final goal of man which is exactly the goal of the Oriental philosophies. All secular history, Toynbee argues, is for the purpose of the development of the spiritual life of mankind in the great religions. Secular history by its show of weakness due to Original Sin, the cause of the decline and fall in the cycles of the great cultures, drives man to the Other World, the eternal one of Spirit. In this way religion has evolved to higher and higher levels. Spiritual development is the meaning and goal of history for Toynbee as for the Oriental thinkers with its climax and goal in complete realization and maturity on the spiritual plane which makes possible eternal life in God. Toynbee, true to his Western tradition of emphasis upon technology and social activism, presses man to work hard to make this world the scene of the highest spiritual creativity; nevertheless the final goal is Heaven, the only realm in which true Freedom is attained—the freedom from egoity which makes freedom from sins of selfishness and pride (the basic "original sins") possible at last.

In Hegel's thought the significance and goal of history is much like that of the Oriental schools in so far as the goal of the individual human personality is concerned. Man's goal as a finite individual is realization of his identity with the Absolute, the Infinite. This again is the yogic return to the Center. Hegel's metaphysics differs, however, from the predominant Oriental schools in the affirmation that the individual or finite aspects of the worlds of nature and history are the necessary concrete manifestations of the Absolute Spirit which would be a No-thing, an unreality, without these concrete manifestations; whereas in most Oriental philosophies the Infinite is fully as real apart from any of its concrete appearances; this is true also in Zoroastrian Hebrew-Christian and Moslem thought. The history of the universe and man in Hegel's thought is of vital significance, therefore, since it is the necessary expression of God's being. This makes development and progress (in accordance with Hegel's dialectical cycle) essential in the cultural history of man, since greater and greater approximations to the nature of the Whole is the driving force.

Sorokin's culture cycle theory, too, belongs to the group of philosophies of history which attribute greatest importance to the life of the spirit. Following Ibn Khaldun, Vico and Spengler, Sorokin like Toynbee thinks of religious faith as the most potent factor in integrating a large civilization and in stimulating its creative growth. When the religious as the supersensory or supraconscious is integrated with the empirical-sensory and the rational we have a Golden Age in a culture such as Periclean Athens or the Thirteenth Century in Western Culture. The name "Idealistic" or "Integral" is significantly applied to such an epoch. The present Sensate Era of our culture is dying out, Sorokin shows, and there is evidence for believing that a new Integral culture-epoch is dawning. In science, for example, mechanistic materialistic approaches are losing ground; this is true in physics, biology, psychology and the social sciences. Sorokin writes that today the total reality is

> thought of as an infinite X of numberless qualities and quantities: spiritual and material, temporal and timeless, ever-changing and unchangeable, personal, spatial and spaceless, one and many. In this sense it is conceived as the veritable *coincidentia oppositorum, mysterium tremendum and fascinosum.*[8]

The egoless Superconscious breaks in upon creative individuals with its illuminating ideas: religious, philosophical, scientific, aesthetic. Reason and the empirical-sensory modes of knowledge must then test these illuminating ideas **(except in music and other art-forms)**. The Integral Era now dawning will be dominated by the Superconscious in

Teilhard de Chardin (see below) gives convincing scientific arguments for this view.

Section 3. Cosmic Cycles and Contemporary Science

The "scientific" school of thinkers already discussed above [9] made valiant attempts to ascertain the cyclical rhythms of this universe, this Macrocosm. The pantheistic naturalistic cosmology of Heraclitus elaborated by the Stoics was a beautifully symmetrically balanced cyclical system. Contemporary cosmologies are not too radically different, even though a rhythmic balance of cosmic cycles has not yet been verified. At present the two most favored cosmological theories, the "continuous creation" and the "explosion" (or similar hypotheses) do not posit macrocosmic cycles of a continuously repetitive kind. The expanding universe is thought by most astrophysicists to be an irreversible process. The school of explosionists led by such men as Lemaitre and Gamow posit a beginning from the explosion of a Primeval Atom (Lemaitre) or of *Ylem* (Gamow). The macrocosm goes through one cycle only from beginning to end. This corresponds on the microcosmic scale to the one-cycle apocalyptic theories of human history we have discussed.

The "continuous creation" theory of Hoyle, Bondi, Gold, Sciama and others "works" beautifully from the theoretical point of view. The only theoretical difficulty is the idea of creation *ex nihilo* of hydrogen atoms, but the Gamow theory tells nothing, either, about origins, i.e., about the nature of the world before *Ylem* appeared.[10] The continuous creation theory is close in spirit to the cosmological speculations of Hinduism and Buddhism and the pantheistic thinkers of the West such as Hegel and Spinoza. This is because the continuous creation view affirms an infinite "steady-state" universe. Cyclical evolution takes place in every star and in every galaxy of stars; here the law of entropy is true. The expanding universe is accepted; all galaxies will eventually recede beyond the possibility of our receiving their light and so will be nonexistent for us. However, hydrogen atoms are appearing in space to form new nebulae which will evolve into new galaxies; therefore a cross-section of any part of the "infinite" spatial world will always look the same. The matter and form of the universe have always been and always will be the same; the cross-section of the cosmos we see now is the type for all the infinitude of time.[11] Hoyle, one of the foremost proponents of this theory says:

> We arrive at a Universe in which the individuals — the clusters of galaxies — change and evolve with time but which itself does not change. The old queries about the beginning and end of the Universe are dealt with in a surprising manner — by saying that they are meaningless, for the reason that the Universe did not have a beginning and it will not have an end. Every cluster of galaxies, every star, every atom had a beginning, but not the Universe itself. The Universe is something more than its parts, a perhaps unexpected conclusion.[12]

Hoyle posits an infinite universe, infinite in time and in space. As in Spinoza's pantheistic philosophy, the macrocosmic physiognomy — the "face of the Whole Universe" — is eternally the same.

Western one-grand-cycle theories are not consistent with such a view but the Hindu, Jaina, Buddhist and Chinese philosophies of history (cosmic and human) cohere with it perfectly. World system after world system, each of the same fundamental pattern, appears out of the void and finally disappears. Hoyle is affirming much the same thing. Each galaxy evolves through the same pattern and then disappears into boundless space. Only the total Infinite Universe remains the same. In this Spinoza-like view man's its illuminative insights into truth, beauty, and the good, but reason and the empirical-sensory will implement, will bring into concrete actuality a new Global cultural era centered around the Integral idea.

The importance of the supraconscious (which is egoless) in Sorokin's thought shows a close affinity with the Oriental points of view, especially the philosophies of history of Śri Aurobindo and Radhakrishnan both of whom think that the dawning new epoch of history will be the epoch in which Spirit will be dominant over intellect; in other words it will be the epoch of Sorokin's Creative Altruistic Love. Aurobindo like Sorokin speaks also of a coming integral era — one in which matter, life, mind, and spirit will be harmoniously integrated by the Spirit, the Supraconscious evolutionary level about to appear and supercede the present level of Intellect. Sorokin differs somewhat in emphasis upon the rational and the empirical-sensory as equal partners in human creativity; nevertheless there is more than enough sympathy and agreement between the two approaches to found a new common Global *Weltanschauung*. As Northrop says, we need the intense supraconscious spirituality of the East (the aesthetic component) combined with the scientific knowledge and technology of the West (the theoretic component) to establish a new era for the human race.

Is it possible to reconcile these philosophies of the Spirit which are so much alike in both East and West with the Marxian ideas of the meaning of human life and history? The dialectical materialism of the Marxists is professedly atheistic and centered upon the material enjoyments of life in this world. The material productive forces of society are the "gods" which "create" the cultural edifices of man whether directly or indirectly. Man's goal is to enjoy the products of these productive forces in this world in this one and only life given him. The goal of history will be reached when the vast majority at last own collectively the means of production. Then poverty can be abolished and all men will be able to lead a secure comfortable life of real freedom. This goal is achieved in an apocalyptic one-grand-cycle of human history from primitive communism to a communism at the highest level (in which the means of production will be adequate to provide a good life for each member of the human race). The achievement of this goal is Freedom for the entire human race; no man will any longer be a slave to the insecurities of existence. Each man will be free to develop his potentialities for the benefit of all; and all will be concerned for the well-being of each. The central ethical principle at this level is "From each according to his ability; to each according to his need." Such a principle presupposes a return to the Center (the Mandala-of-the-Return), if only at the human level, in a **kind of collective or common consciousness of humanity** with the loss of individual or ego-consciousness. In this respect there is a fundamental bond linking the Marxian historical goal with the Eastern and Western philosophies just described. There is a basis here for a synthesis of both points of view metaphysically. The Marxians may come to the view, or at least permit the view in their circles, that the egoless state in which the individual identifies himself with the larger whole of all humanity is actually a spiritual state. The realm of spirit as Whitehead, Santayana, Shankara, Aurobindo, the Taoists, Avicenna, the Sufis, Spinoza, Western mystics and Radhakrishnan, and many other thinkers and schools have shown is not one of superstitious belief in ghosts and demons, or "pie in the sky"; but the realm of spirit is the Macrocosmos in which the individual human soul integrates itself as an organic member in the process known as "Centering" by the yogis or "individuation" by the Western psychologist, Jung. The religious philosophies of history at their highest levels are important in emphasizing this, man's membership in an eternal Macrocosm. There is no reason why Marxists should ban this idea since they eulogize Science, and Science sees man as an integral part of the total universe.

goal would be Spinzoa's: to realize the identification of one's body-atoms and of one's rational nature ("soul" or "mind") with that of the total Universe, the ultimately real and eternal Organism whose physiognomy we perceive in our minute cross-section of its matter-side (the galaxies) and its thought-side (physical "laws"). [13]

Such an organismic view of the universe, of cosmic and human history, was set forth most poetically in Chinese thought. The Chinese cyclical views grounded philosophically in the mystical Taoist intuitive realization of the oneness of man with the Macrocosm have attained a high degree of insight into the nature of the universe and man's place in it. Ch'an (Zen in Japanese) Buddhism has borrowed its fundamental idea, *viz.*, that man and all things in nature are integral parts of one spiritual reality, the Tao. All things come from the Tao, all things are immersed in it, and all return to it in the everlasting cycles of phenomenal existence. This is the Secret of the Golden Flower discussed above [14] and the key to the appreciation of Chinese and Japanese nature paintings which are the inimitable symbolic expressions of this organismic philosophy of the universe.

In recent Western philosophies of history Spengler is the great thinker who has applied a philosophy of organism to the culture cycles of human history. The history of a culture cycle — Apollinian, Magian, Faustian, Egyptian, Chinese or any other — is that of a macrocosmic organism that runs through a life cycle of birth, adolescence, maturity and old age. The astronomers of today carry this organismic idea through onto the cosmic plane — our galaxy and all others have a growth and decay cycle. Only astronomers of the Hoyle-Gold-Bondi school give infinite life to the "Face of the Whole Universe," the macrocosmic living organism. Everywhere else the cyclical idea applies in one way or another. The cyclical philosophies of history whether applied to cosmic or human history seem validated, therefore, if the observer takes a macrocosmic standpoint;

and since astronomers today think it extremely probable that there are great numbers of planets (at least one-hundred million [15]) suitable for the development of life in the vast universe, no doubt the history of life from one-celled forms to mind-forms — and whatever may lie beyond — has been repeated. This is probable, especially if Hoyle's viewpoint is accepted. The Oriental cyclical views may have by intuition hit upon a true idea about the ultimate nature of the phenomenal universe. Another Oriental idea, the idea of karma, though couched in the mythical language of the primitive culture in which it arose contains scientific truth. Our Western science accepts the idea of the "continuity of the germ plasm." The individual is as old as his germ plasm which is as old as the ancient epoch of the one-celled organisms and his future age is as old as whatever supra-human beings become his blood successors in the future evolution of the human race. This is real biological karma. On the psychological side the psychologist, Jung, is famous for his theory of the "racial unconscious." This might be carried back to the single-celled organism days or the days of the inorganic atoms, and forward to whatever sublime (we hope!) state into which we humans might evolve.

Section 4. Prognostications: The Next Epoch in History

If the idea of the blood unity of the human race defended both by science and the philosophico-religious systems we have surveyed is accepted, as eventually it must be, the next epoch of human history should develop upon two planes interacting the one with the other. The one plane, secular and this-worldly will strive to create a more godlike existence in this life on earth for all human brothers as men like Marx, Sorokin, Radhakrishnan, Toynbee and Aurobindo believe. But these thinkers (except Marx) argue that human unity cannot be attained on a lasting basis unless men look beyond this material world to the spiritual plane as their ultimate goal and "home." The great Oriental thinkers — Hindu, Buddhist, Jaina, Moslem — and the Western one-cycle thinkers aim at escape altogether from the bondage of the cyclical phenomenal world of material existence, the realm of appearance and relativity. The soul must make its escape through union with the Eternal, the Real behind the Appearances of this maya world. The great mystics of the East and of the West (*e.g.* Meister Eckhart and St. John of the Cross of the West whose experiences parallel those of the Eastern yogis) have already experienced this state of the Eternal Real. They have continued to live in this world, but without the Original Sin of ego-consciousness. Perhaps they prefigure the next stage of spiritual development in human evolution as great prophetic thinkers like Sorokin, Aurobindo and Radhakrishnan believe. Such a god-man of the future ideally might live in two worlds simultaneously as Sri Aurobindo predicts; for this god-man will understand himself as one of the many "centers of consciousness" of the Eternal. Such a man's actions will be entirely egoless since they will manifest this knowledge. One can scarcely imagine what a society of such god-men might be like. All the nightmare ills of humanity — greed, lust, war, poverty, crime and hate — will be gone forever; this is certain. Then adventures in the life of Spirit, the realms of cosmic knowledge, of creativity in art forms, will reach new and sublime heights. We can make only wild surmises about such a future. Such a wild surmise, beyond the imagination of a yogi or a Jules Verne, has been made by a Western physics professor, J.H. Rush who predicts:

> The apotheosis of *homo sapiens* may come in 1,000,000 years or so when man liberates his soul from his body — that fragile retort of flushing chemicals and psychic shocks. Then, an incorporeal spirit drawing energy from the stars, he can take off for a new realm, new challenges, and new secrets.[16]

If this should happen, man would indeed free himself from the cycle of births and deaths both on the microcosmic and macrocosmic levels; history would be swallowed up into "eternity" the consummation offered by both Eastern and Western philosophies.

Another dramatic and deeply inspirational view is given us by the geologist and anthropologist Teilhard de Chardin in his book *The Phenomenon of Man*.[17] Chardin's ideas are supported very ably, says Julian Huxley, by the scientific evidence of the directional changes in the evolution of life (the biosphere) out of matter and of the mind (the *noosphere*) out of life. Chardin argues that since Life has shown a directional trend towards greater complexity in which greater Centralism was always an essential aspect (for example organisms develop a head when complexity appears) man's further evolution will show a greater Centralism. Science and technology have made this somewhat of a reality already and the trend of World Culture will continue until it (world-culture) becomes an organic whole. Man has already evolved a new "layer" around the planet Earth beyond the life-layer or Biosphere; this is the *noosphere* or psychosocial layer which has changed the face of the planet earth outwardly, and inwardly the noosphere is our entire spiritual cultural heritage—or spiritual atmosphere—in which we have our being. Evolution is now driving us beyond the noosphere (the highest goal of which is the Centralism of an organic democratic global culture) towards Omega. (Omega is the opposite of Alpha or the lowest evolutionary level of physical particles.) Omega as a new evolutionary level should be unknowable; nevertheless Chardin believes that on the basis of knowledge of all the prior tendencies of evolutionary development, we can say that Omega will be an eternal irreversible state (*cf.* J. H. Rush quoted above) characterized by Personalization. By this he means that each Person will be a center of superconsciousness in a purely spiritual organic whole. In Christian phraseology God will be "all in everyone."[18] This corresponds with Sri Aurobindo's prediction of the next stage of evolution.

This organic spiritual society will be brought into being in the not too distant future because man, already at the level of the *noosphere,* can do much to speed up evolutionary process through his rapidly increasing knowledge of his own physical and mental and social sheaths of being. Man can change the face of the earth and of human social organization and institutional life through "eugenics applied to society," and through research in the theoretical sciences he can learn more and more of nature's secrets. Reason and science can do these things; but Religion is necessary also to give us faith that we can discover nature's secrets, faith that there will be progress in all aspects of life for the human race, and most of all faith in love "the special binder or cement which will associate our lives together, vitally, without diminishing or distorting them." [19] If this psychosocial Centralism should be attempted by brute force, so that science could be used for the enslavement and mechanization of human beings, Omega would never be reached. Evolution would remain static after the zenith of mechanization was reached (the status of the insects such as the bees and ants who have mechanized their social life demonstrates this.) Chardin thinks that "love alone is capable of uniting living beings in such a way as to complete and fulfill them, for it alone takes them and joins them by what is deepest in themselves." [20] Love is a cosmic phenomenon as the "affinity of being with being," [21] and it is "the more or less direct trace marked on the heart of the element by the psychical convergence of the universe upon itself." [22] Chardin reminds us that the great mystics have been filled with love which is a "resonance to the All — the keynote of pure poetry and pure religion."[23] Moreover Love and Thought grow together; and Love reveals "a deep accord between two realities which seek each other; the severed particle which trembles at the approach of the rest." [24] Love integrates man with man and man with the Cosmos. "A universal love is not only psychologically possible; it is the only complete and final way in which we are able to love." [25] Such love of cosmic proportions is vital in the yogic Eastern mystical philosophies where there is the emphasis, expressed so well in mandala symbolism, of Centralism: unity with the eternal spiritual reality as the Core of Being, and love for all persons and for all animate and inanimate objects as phenomenal aspects of that Core of Being.

All the philosophies of history we have examined emphasize Love as the constructive and cohesive bond through which human societies grow and flourish; a world Global Society can only grow and flourish on the basis of the same bond of love. We have, in Part I, chapter VII, described Jung's views as a psychologist of man's basic need for the kind of love which is actually a reintegration of the person with all humanity and with the cosmos. Jung's individuation process of realization of the "self" coincides with Chardin's notion of the further and more adequate "hominisation" of man. The coming organic Global Culture will in its development necessitate the flowering of persons who have achieved, who live in, the spiritual atmosphere of such self-realization. In this state of Peace and Freedom man can develop altruistically his reason and scientific knowledge to such an extent that the eternal Omega is already a "present reality" as the "mysterious centre of our centres." [26]

Altogether, Chardin, like so many of the philosophers we have already discussed, Eastern and Western, thinks that through the "conjunction of reason and mysticism (love), the human spirit is destined, by the very nature of its development,to find the uttermost degree of its penetration with the maximum of its vital force." [27] By these means, Reason, Science and Love, a democratic but organic Global culture will come into being; then finally the eternal Omega state will be attained.

From the more prosaic and short-range point of view,

the culture-cycle theorists we have reviewed have less palatable prognostications. From the evidence of significant analogies with the rise and fall processes of other prior civilizations, they argue that we are at the end of an epoch. (The Hindus, Buddhists, Jainas, and others who follow the theory of cosmic cycles also believe that we are living in the last era of the cycle because human society is in such a degenerate state.) The first great culture-cycle theorist of European thought, Vico, would without much doubt predict "monarchies" as the resolution for the social and economic chaos prevailing in some democratic states. France seems to have been in such a chaotic state and there is a monarchic idea in the rule by de Gaulle. Even in the United States chaos may result unless the criminal elements and egotistic groups can be curbed. The world is so much an economic and geographic whole today, that Vico might even predict a world monarchy to resolve the everlasting conflicts among individual nations, each selfishly motivated. He might see the "inevitable" advent of another Augustus ushering in an era of world monarchy. This is what Spengler calls the era of *Caesarism*.

Spengler thinks that Western culture is ripe for Caesarism for the reasons given above.[28] Caesarism will be the last epoch after which the culture will disintegrate completely and a new world culture will arise inaugurated and established by the "colored" peoples of the world (the yellow, brown, and black peoples, *i.e.*, the Asiatics and Africans).

Toynbee, too, thinks Western civilization is doomed unless it turns to real Christianity which would mean a civilization very different from what we have now. It would amount to establishment of a new culture, for all institutions would have to be Christianized, *i.e.*, reorganized around fundamental Christian ethics of a *practising* brotherly love and cooperation. If our culture falls, however, it will mean another kind of progress — the only real progress of the human race since primitive times. This is the progress of Religion; the failure of every secular civilization means another milestone in the progress of the higher religions, those that emphasize human unity and Love as the basic ethical principles.

Sorokin, too, offers sufficient evidence that we are at the end of the sensate era of the culture cycle. A new culture is in the air and it will be founded upon a new Integral idea. Man will be raised to the supraconscious spiritual level of unified spirituality. Motivated by Creative Altruistic Love the human race will inaugurate a "new heaven and a new earth," for both spiritual and material life will be completely renovated.

Radhakrishnan hopes for the dawn of a new era of high spirituality, an epoch in which Spirit will supercede Intellect which has hitherto been the dominant element in man. The coming era of Spirit will be an epoch of world-wide human unity based upon intelligent love, and in general a world of cooperating individuals and national cultures. Intelligence and Love are the values that will be dominant.

There is general agreement that to build a new civilization greater than the old, which is what is essential in the next epoch of human history, we must lay a strong spiritual foundation lest the amazing technological scientific progress surely to be made engulf us in the horrors of the Brave New World of Huxley's book by that name. Huxley's sequel to this book recently published — *Brave New World Revisited* — contains the recipe for the foundation of a new world order. The recipe again is the familiar one which pervades so many of the philosophies we have examined: Reason and Love. Huxley states it thus:

> The value, first of all, of individual freedom, based upon the facts of human diversity and genetic uniqueness; the value of charity and compassion, based upon the old familiar fact, lately rediscovered by modern psychiatry — the fact that, whatever their mental and physical diversity, love is as necessary to human beings as food and shelter; and finally the value of intelligence, without which love is impotent and freedom unattainable.[29]

The human spirit must make a supreme attempt to establish these values or the next epoch of human history may resemble the tragic spectacle of Orwell's *Nineteen-Eighty-Four;* or worse, the horrible reduction of man — in a third world war, those left — to the brute state again. This is Vico's "extreme remedy" for societies too rotten for other remedies. Reason and Love and Work to implement these values are essential to save the human race from this last disaster. But if the atom bombs should destroy all of us, it might console us in our last surviving moments to realize that in the immensities of the cosmos enormous progress must have been made by other living forms; or, it is possible that there are planes of being utterly beyond the range of our spiritual perceptions. It would be vanity on our part to think that further development of individual and group spiritual life is dependent upon people of this planet alone, or that this kind of being exhausts reality. Nevertheless, it is our sacred mission to strive for the higher level of spirituality to which we are being forced on pain of extinction. Also, there is at least a possibility that we are at the highest level achieved by living forms in the cosmos (this is Chardin's opinion) and this would make it still more imperative that we achieve the high spiritual level of superconscious beings.

In the astronomical immensities of time and space — the infinities of time and space if Hoyle's astrophysics is accepted — the highest spiritual goals may already have been achieved many times in many galaxies. These goals are probably inconceivable to us at our present evolutionary level, although Chardin thinks we can anticipate the final goal. The full cycle of spirit achieved or adumbrated in the mystical experiences of Eastern yogis and Western saints may have already been achieved in innumerable galaxies and will continue such repetition if Hoyle's theories are correct. The Oriental cyclical views of Hindus and Buddhists may thus turn out to be intuitions of historical truth at the macrocosmic level.

Meanwhile, whatever might turn out to be true at the macrocosmic level or from the long-range point of view, we must confine ourselves (without losing the long-range vision) to the more immediate task of realizing the values of Intelligence and Love, the theoretic and aesthetic values Northrop has made so clear, in our personal relations, our social institutions, and in our international relations. We must see to it that the next great culture-cycle, without doubt a Global culture-era, is at a much nobler spiritual level than any before. This includes wise arrangements first of all for taking care of the health and economic and educational needs of all men on this earth. The use of atomic, solar, and ocean energies will make this practical. But even if the "extreme remedy" befalls us and we should fail through self-destruction as a race on this planet, there is still the consolation that some members of our race, *homo sapiens*, have succeeded in realization of the highest values of Love and Intelligence. These are the great Saints and Sages of East and West. This holy vanguard-army has shown us that road to true Freedom which we must make the immediate goal of human history. Higher values and goals doubtless lie beyond in the further evolutionary development of Man as men like Chardin and Julian Huxley believe, but we must first of all aim to realize these values in the present and coming new era of history or perhaps we shall have no further history as a race.

Notes

[1] Morris R. Cohen, *The Meaning of Human History* (La Salle, Illinois: Open Court Publishing Company, 1947), chap. II, "Metaphysics and History," pp. 35-76.

[2] Louis R. Gottschalk, *Understanding History: A Primer of Historical Method* (New York: Knopf, 1950), p. 212.

[3] *Ibid.*, p. 222.

[4] Pieter Geyl, "Prophets of Woe," *Virginia Quarterly* (October, 1950), pp. 587-602.

[5] Maurice Mandelbaum, *The Problem of Historical Knowledge* (New York: Liveright Publishing Corporation, 1938), pp. 298-300. See also Charlotte Watkins Smith, *Carl Becker: On History and the Climate of Opinion* (Ithaca: Cornell University Press, 1956), pp. 90-100.

[6] W. Y. Evans-Wentz, *Tibetan Yoga and Secret Doctrines,* According to the late Lama Kazi Dawa-Samdup's English Rendering with Introductions and Commentary by Evans-Wentz (London, New York: Oxford University Press, 1958), p. 149, n. 1.

[7] *Ibid.*

[8] Pitirim A. Sorokin, "Three Basic Trends of our Times," *Main Currents in Modern Thought* (January, 1960) Vol. 16, No. 3, pp. 58-64.

[9] *Supra*, Part I, chap. X.

[10] Gamow posits a contraction process prior to the expansion, but the latter ends in a dead universe, not a return to another contraction state in a cyclical rhythm. See *supra*, Part I, chap. X for a fuller discussion.

[11] *Ibid., (Supra*, Part I, chap. X).

[12] Fred Hoyle, *Frontiers of Astronomy* (New York: Harper & Brothers, 1955), p. 321.

[13] Benedict de Spinoza, *The Chief Works of Spinoza,* trans. R. H. M. Elwes (New York: Dover Publications, 1951) *Ethics*, Part II, Prop. XIII, note to Lemma VII, p. 96.

[14] See above, Part I, chap. VII.

[15] Harlow Shapely, "Coming to Terms with the Cosmos: Man Must Grow to Reach the Stars," *Saturday Review*, September 6, 1958. Shapely says that this number is conservative. He would multiply it by perhaps a million.

[16] J. H. Rush, "The Next 10,000 Years," article adapted from the forthcoming book by Rush, *The Dawn of Life*, in *The Saturday Review*, January 25, 1958. This book has now been published. (New York: Doubleday & Co., 1958.)

[17] Pierre Teilhard de Chardin, *The Phenomenon of Man*, trans. Bernard Wall and Introduction by Julian Huxley (New York: Harper & Brothers, 1959).

[18] *Ibid.*, p. 308.

[19] *Ibid.*, p. 284.

[20] *Ibid.*, p. 265.

[21] *Ibid.*, p. 264.

[22] *Ibid.*, p. 265

[23] *Ibid.* p. 266.

[24] *Ibid.*, p. 266.

[25] *Ibid.*

[26] *Ibid.*, p. 267.

[27] *Ibid.*, p. 285.

[28] *Supra*, Part III, chap. II.

[29] Quoted from Huxley's book *Brave New World Revisited* in *Saturday Review*, November 15, 1958; book review by Granville Hicks, p. 12, (published by Harper & Brothers, 1958).

BIBLIOGRAPHY

Anesaki, Masaharu. *History of Japanese Religion*. London: Kegan Paul, 1930.
Arberry, A. J. *Revelation and Reason in Islam*. New York: The Macmillan Company, 1957.
Aristotle. *The Basic Works of Aristotle*. Ross translation. Single volume edition. Edited by Richard McKeon. New York: Random House, 1941.
Augustine. *The Works of Aurelius Augustine*. A new translation. Edited by the Rev. Marcus Dods, M. A. Vols. I and II, *The City of God*. Translated by the Rev. Marcus Dods, M. A. Edinburgh: T. and T. Clark, 1871-72.
Aurobindo. *The Ideal of Human Unity*. New York: E. P. Dutton, Inc., 1950.
Aurobindo. *The Life Divine*. Pondicherry: Sri Aurobindo Ashram, 1955.
Aurobindo. *On Yoga: The Synthesis of Yoga*. Pondicherry: Sri Aurobindo Ashram, 1955.
Aurobindo. *The Problem of Rebirth*. Pondicherry: Sri Aurobindo Ashram, 1952.
Avalon, Arthur (Sir John Woodroffe), editor. *Tantrik Texts*, Vol. VII, *Shrichakrasambhara Tantra*, edited by Kazi Dawa-Samdup. London: Luzac & Co.; Calcutta: Thacher, Spink & Co., 1919.
Barton, George A. *Archaeology and the Bible*. Philadelphia: American Sunday-School Union. Seventh revised edition, 1937.
Becker, Carl. *Everyman His Own Historian*. New York: Appleton-Century-Crofts, 1935.
Bradley, F. H. *Appearance and Reality*. New York: The Macmillan Co., 1908
Charles, R. H. *Religious Devolopment Between the Old and New Testaments*. London, New York: Home University Library of Modern Knowledge, 1914.
Chatley, H. "Ancient Chinese Astronomy," *Occasional Notes, No. 5, Royal Astronomical Society*, 1939, pp. 65-74.
Chaudhuri, Haridas. *The Philosophy of Integralism*. Calcutta: Sri Aurobindo Pathamandir, 1954.
Cheng, Te-k'un. "Yin-Yang Wu-Hsing and Han Art," *Harvard Journal of Asiatic Studies*, Vol. 20.
Cohen, Morris Raphael. *The Meaning of Human History*. La Salle, Illinois: Open Court Publishing Company, 1947.
Collingwood, R. G. *The Idea of History*. Oxford: Clarendon Press, 1946.

Condorcet, Antoine Nicolas. *Sketch for a Historical Picture of the Progress of the Human Mind.* Translated by June Barraclough. New York: The Noonday Press, 1955.

Coomeraswamy, Ananda. *The Dance of Shiva.* Bombay, Calcutta: The Asia Publishing House, 1948.

Cornforth, Maurice. *Historical Materialism.* London: Lawrence and Wishart, 1953.

Cumont, Franz. *The Mysteries of Mithra.* Translated by Thomas J. McCormack from second revised edition. New York: Dover Publications, 1956.

Dentan, Robert Claude, editor. *The Idea of History in the Ancient Near East.* New Haven: Yale University Press, 1955.

Duyvendak, J. J. L. "The Mythico-Ritual Pattern in Chinese Civilization," *Proceedings of the 7th Congress for the History of Religions,* Amsterdam, 4th-9th September 1950, edited by C. J. Bleeker, G.W.J. Drewes and K. A. H. Hidding. Amsterdam: North-Holland Publishing Company, 1951, pp. 137-8.

Evans-Wentz, W. Y. *Tibetan Yoga and Secret Doctrines.* Translated by Chen-Chi Chang. Edited by Evans-Wentz. Second edition. London, New York, Toronto: Oxford University Press, 1958.

Finegan, Jack. *Light from the Ancient Past.* Princeton: Princeton University Press, 1946.

Finegan, Jack. *The Archaeology of World Religions.* Princeton: Princeton University Press, 1952.

Fitzgerald, C. P. *China: A Short Cultural History.* Fourth revised edition. New York: Frederick A. Praeger, Inc., 1954.

Frankfort, H. and H. A. et al. *Intellectual Adventure of Ancient Man.* Chicago: University of Chicago Press, 1946.

Frankfort, Henri. *The Birth of Civilization in the Near East.* Doubleday Anchor Books edition. Garden City, New York: Doubleday & Co., 1956.

Frazer, Sir James George. *Folklore in the Old Testament.* Abridged edition. New York and London: The Macmillan Company, 1923.

Fung, Yu-lan. *A History of Chinese Philosophy.* 2 vols. Translated by Derk Bodde. Princeton: Princeton University Press, 1952-3.

Gamow, George. "Modern Cosmology," *The New Astronomy* edited by editors of the *Scientific American.* New York: Simon and Schuster, 1955.

Gaster, Theodore H. *Thespis.* New York: Schumann, 1950.

Geyl, Pieter. "Prophets of Woe, *"Virginia Quarterly,* October, 1950, pp. 587-602.

Gibb, H. A. R. *Mohammedanism.* Mentor edition. New York: New American Library, 1955.

Gomperz, Theodore. *Greek Thinkers.* 4 vols. Translated by C. G. Berry. New York: Humanities Press, 1955.

Govinda, Anagarika. "Principles of Tantric Buddhism," *2500 Years of Buddhism,* edited by P. V. Bapat. Delhi: Publications Division, Government of India, 1959.

Granet, Marcel. *Chinese Civilization.* London: Routledge & Kegan Paul, Ltd., 1930.

Guenther, H. V. "Mantrayana and Sahajayana," *2500 Years of Buddhism*, edited by B. V. Bapat. Delhi: Publications Division, Government of India, 1959.
Guillaume, Alfred. *Islam*. Penguin edition. Baltimore: Penguin Books, Ltd., 1954.
Hartshorne, Charles, and Reese, William L. *Philosophers Speak of God*. Chicago: The University of Chicago Press, 1953.
Havell, E. B. *The Ideals of Indian Art*. London: John Murray, 1920.
Heath, Sir Thomas. *Aristarchus of Samos, The Ancient Copernicus*. Oxford: The Clarendon Press, 1913.
Heath, Sir Thomas. *History of Greek Mathematics*. 2 vols. Oxford: The Clarendon Press, 1921.
Hegel, Georg Wilhelm Friedrich. *The Philosophy of History*. Translated by J. Sibree. Revised edition. New York: Willey Book Co., 1944.
Hooke, Samuel H. *New Year's Day*. London: Gerald Howe, Ltd., 1927.
Hoyle, Fred. *Frontiers of Astronomy*. New York: Harper & Brothers, 1955.
Jeffery, Arthur. *Islam*. Edited by Arthur Jeffery. Library of Religion series. New York: The Liberal Arts Press, 1958.
Jung, Carl Gustav. *Psychology and Religion: West and East*. Translated by R. F. C. Hull. Bollingen Series XX. New York: Pantheon Books, 1958.
Jung, Carl Gustav. *Modern Man in Search of a Soul*. Harvest Books edition. Translated by W. S. Dell and Cary F. Baynes. New York: Harcourt Brace, 1933.
Jung, Carl Gustav. "The Spirit of Psychology," *This is My Philosophy*, edited by Whit Burnett. New York: Harper & Bros., 1957.
Khaldun (Ibn Khaldun). *The Maqaddimah, An Introduction to History*. Edited by Franz Rosenthal. 3 vols. Bollingen Series XLIII. New York: Pantheon Books, 1958.
Khemo (Bhikku Khemo). *What is Buddhism?* Third revised edition. Bangkok, Thailand: Prachandra Press, 1954.
Kramrisch, Stella. *The Art of India*. London: Phaidon Press, 1954.
Kroeber, A. L. *Anthropology Today*. Edited by A. L. Kroeber. See essay "Style," by Meyer Schapiro, pp. 287-311. Chicago: University of Chicago Press, 1953.
Lewis, Sir George Cornewall. *An Historical Survey of the Astronomy of the Ancients*. London: Parker, Son, and Bourn, West Strand, 1862.
Lovejoy, Arthur, and Boas, George. *Primitivism and Related Ideas in Antiquity*. Baltimore: Johns Hopkins Press, 1935.
Mandelbaum, Maurice. *The Problem of Historical Knowledge*. New York: Liveright Publishing Corporation, 1938.
Marx, Karl. *Capital*. Modern Library edition. Edited by Frederick Engels. Revised and amplified according to the fourth German edition by Ernest Untermann. Translated from the third German edition by Samuel Moore and Edward Aveling. New York: The Modern Library, Random House, n. d., copyright 1906 Charles H. Kerr and Company.

Marx, Karl and Engels, Friedrich. *Selected Works.* 2 vols. London: Lawrence and Wishart, 1950.
Maspero, G. *History of Egypt.* 2 vols. Edited by A. H. Sayce. Translated by M. L. McClure. London: The Grolier Society, n. d.
Mendelsohn, Isaac. *Religions of the Ancient Near East.* Edited by Isaac Mendelsohn. Library of Religion series. New York: The Liberal Arts Press, 1955.
Morgan, Kenneth W., editor. *The Path of the Buddha.* New York: Ronald Press, 1956.
Mus, Paul. *Barabudur. Esquisse d'une histoire du bouddhisme fondée sur la critique archéologique des textes.* 4 vols. Hanoi: Imprimerie d'extreme-Orient, 1935.
Needham, Joseph. *Science and Civilization in China.* 7 vols., vols. 1 and 2. Cambridge: The Cambridge University Press, 1954-56.
Neugebauer, Otto. *The Exact Sciences in Antiquity.* Princeton: Princeton University Press, 1952.
Nicholson, Reynold A., editor. *Rumi: Poet and Mystic.* Translated with Introduction and notes by Reynold A. Nicholson. London: George Allen and Unwin, Ltd., 1950.
Nietzsche, Friedrich, *The Complete Works of Friedrich Nietzsche.* Edited by Oscar Levy. Vols. XI and XVI. New York: Macmillan, 1913.
Nilson, Martin P. *Primitive Time Reckoning.* Oxford: Oxford Press, 1920.
Northrop, Filmer S. C. "Man's Relation to the Earth in Its Bearing on His Aesthetic Ethical and Legal Values," *Man's Role in Changing the Face of the Earth.* Edited by William L. Thomas et al. Chicago: University of Chicago Press, 1956.
Plato. *The Dialogues of Plato.* 2 vols. Translated by Benjamin Jowett. New York: Random House, 1937.
Radhakrishnan, Sarvepalli. "The Religion of the Spirit and the World's Need (Fragments of a Confession)" *The Philosophy of Sarvepalli Radhakrishnan.* Edited by Paul Arthur Schilpp. New York: Tudor Publishing Company, 1952.
Radhakrishnan, S. and Moore, Charles A. *A Source Book in Indian Philosophy.* Princeton: Princeton University Press, 1957.
Radhakrishnan, S. and Muirhead, J. H., editors. *Contemporary Indian Philosophy.* Second revised and enlarged edition. Muirhead Library of Philosophy. London: George Allen & Unwin, Ltd., 1952.
Radhakrishnan *et al*, editors. *History of Philosophy: Eastern and Western.* 2 vols. London: George Allen & Unwin, Ltd., 1952.
Reichwein, Adolph. *China and Europe.* New York: Knopf, 1925.
Reps, Paul. *Zen Flesh and Zen Bones.* Rutland, Vermont: Charles E. Tuttle Company, 1957.
Rowland, Benjamin. *The Art and Architecture of India.* Baltimore: Penguin Books, 1953.
Sacred Books of the East. Edited by Max Muller. 50 vols. London: Oxford University Press. Vols. XII and XLIII *Satapatha Brahmana;* vol. V *Pahlavi Texts;* vol. XXXIV *The Vedanta-sutras with Commentary by Sankaracharya.*

Sangharakshita (Bhikshu). *A Survey of Buddhism*. Bangalore, India: The Indian Institute of World Culture, 1957.
Sankaracharya. *The Crest-Jewel of Discrimination*. Translated with Introduction by Swami Prabhavananda and Christopher Isherwood. Hollywood, California: Vedanta Press, 1947.
Sankaracharya. *A Thousand Teachings*. Translated with notes by Swami Jagadananda. Mylapore, Madras, India: Sri Ramakrishna Math, 1949.
Sarton, George. *A History of Science: Ancient Science Through the Golden Age of Greece*. Cambridge: Harvard University Press, 1952.
Smith, Charlotte Watkins. *Carl Becker: On History and the Climate of Opinion*. Ithaca, New York: Cornell University Press, 1956.
Snellgrove, David, "The Tantras," Third Part of *Buddhist Texts Through the Ages*. Edited by Edward Conze in collaboration with I. B. Horner, David Snellgrove and Arthur Waley. New York: Philosophical Library, 1954.
Snellgrove, David. *The Hevajra Tantra*, 2 vols. London, New York: Oxford University Press, 1959.
Soothill, William Edward. *The Hall of Light*. Edited by Lady Hosie and G. F. Hudson. London: Lutterworth Press, 1951.
Sorokin, Pitirim A. *The Crisis of Our Age*. New York: E. P. Dutton & Co., 1941.
Sorokin, Pitirim A. *Social and Cultural Dynamics*. 4 Vols. New York: American Book Company, 1937.
Sorokin, Pitirim A. *The Reconstruction of Humanity*. Boston: The Beacon Press, 1948.
Sorokin, Pitirim A. *The Ways and Power of Love*. Boston: The Beacon Press, 1954.
Spengler, Oswald. *The Decline of the West*. 2 vols. Translated by Charles Atkinson. New York: Alfred A. Knopf, 1932.
Spiegelberg, Frederic. *Living Religions of the World*. Englewood Cliffs, N. J.: Prentice Hall, Inc., 1956.
Stalin, Joseph. *Dialectical and Historical Materialism*. Moscow: Foreign Languages Publishing House, 1951.
Stevenson, Mrs. Sinclair. *The Heart of Jainism*. London, New York, Toronto, Melbourne, Bombay: Humphrey Milford, Oxford University Press, 1915.
Thomas, Edward J. *The History of Buddhist Thought*. Second edition. London: Routledge & Kegan Paul, Ltd., 1953.
Toynbee, Arnold J. *A Study of History*. 12 vols. London: Oxford University Press, 1934-1961.
Toynbee, Arnold J. *A Study of History*. 2 vols. Abridgement of vols. 1-10 by D. C. Somervell. New York and London: Oxford University Press, 1947-1957.
Toynbee, Arnold J. *Civilization on Trial*. New York: Oxford University Press, 1948.
Tritton, A. S. *Muslim Theology*. London: Luzac & Company, 1947.
Vaillant, George C. *The Aztecs of Mexico*. Penguin edition. Baltimore: Penguin Books, Inc., 1950.
Vico, Giambattista. *The New Science of Giambattista Vico*. Translated from the third edition (1744) by Thomas G. Bergin and Max H. Fisch. Ithaca: Cornell University Press, 1948.

Virgil. *Virgil's Works: The Aeneid, Eclogues, Georgics.* Translated by J. W. Mackail. Modern Library edition. New York: Random House, 1934.

Waddell, L. Austine. *The Buddhism of Tibet or Lamaism.* Second edition. Cambridge: W. Heffer & Sons, Ltd., 1934, reprinted 1959.

Warren, Henry Clarke. *Buddhism in Translations. Harvard Oriental Series,* Vol. 3. Cambridge: Harvard University Press, 1922.

Wilhelm, Richard. *The Secret of the Golden Flower.* Translated into German and explained by Richard Wilhelm; translated into English by Cary F. Baynes; with a European commentary by Carl G. Jung translated by Cary F. Baynes. New York: Wehman Bros., 1955.

Yogindra, Sadananda. *Vedantasara or the Essence of Vedanta.* Mayavati, Almora, Himalayas: Advaita Ashrama, 1949.

Zeller, Eduard. *A History of Greek Philosophy.* Translated by S. F. Alleyne and others. Vol. I, *The Pre-Socratic Philosophers.* London: Longmans Green, 1881-88.

Zeller, Eduard. *Plato and the Older Academy.* New edition. Translated by Alleyne and Goodwin. London: Longmans Green and Co., 1888.

Zeller, Eduard. *Stoics, Epicureans and Sceptics.* Translated by Oswald J. Reichel. London: Longmans, 1870.

Zimmer, Heinrich. *Philosophies of India.* Edited by Joseph Campbell. Meridian Books edition. New York: Meridian Books, 1957.

Zimmer, Heinrich. *Myths and Symbols in Indian Art and Civilizaton.* Edited by Joseph Campbell. New York: Pantheon Books, Bollingen Series, 1946.

Zimmer, Heinrich. *The Art of Indian Asia.* 2 vols. New York: Pantheon Books, published for Bollingen Foundation, 1955.

ACKNOWLEDGMENTS

I wish to express my appreciation to the following publishers for permission to use quotations from books or articles under their copyright:

Princeton University Press for passages quoted from:
FUNG YU-LAN, *A History of Chinese Philosophy*, translated by Derk Bodde, 2 vols., second edition, 1952.
FINEGAN, JACK, *The Archaelogy of World Religions*, 1952.
FINEGAN, JACK, *Light From the Ancient Past*, 1946. Permission granted by the author, Professor Finegan, also.
MENDELSOHN, ISAAC, editor, *Ancient Near Eastern Texts Relating to the Old Testament*, published by Liberal Arts Press of the Bobbs-Merrill Company, Inc., under the title *Religions of the Ancient Near East*.

Brown University Press for passages quoted from:
NEUGEBAUER, OTTO, *The Exact Sciences in Antiquity*, published also by Princeton University Press, 1952. Copyright owner is Brown University Press.

The Bobbs-Merrill Company, Inc., for passages quoted from:
JEFFERY, ARTHUR, editor, *Islam*, 1958, Library of Liberal Arts No. 137.

Penguin Books, Ltd., Harmondsworth, Middlesex, England, for passages quoted from:
GUILLAUME, ALFRED, *Islam*, 1954.
ROWLAND, BENJAMIN, *The Art and Architecture of India*, 1953.

Doubleday & Company, Inc., for passages quoted from:
VAILLANT, GEORGE C., *The Aztecs of Mexico*, 1941, reprinted by Doubleday's permission as Penguin paperback.

Prentice-Hall, Inc., Englewood Cliffs, New Jersey, for passages quoted from:
SPIEGELBERG, FREDERIC, *Living Religions of the World*, 1956.

Grolier Incorporated, New York, for passages from:
MASPERO, G., *History of Egypt*, 2 vols., edited by A. H. Sayce, translated by M. L. McClure, n. d.

The Johns Hopkins Press, Baltimore, Maryland, for passages quoted from:
LOVEJOY, ARTHUR, and BOAS, George, editors, *Primitivism and Related Ideas in Antiquity*, 1935.

E. P. Dutton & Company, New York, for passages quoted from:
SOROKIN, PITIRIM A., *The Crisis of our Age*, 1941, reprinted by permission of the publishers.

Lutterworth Press, London, England, for passages quoted from:
SOOTHILL, WILLIAM EDWARD, *The Hall of Light*, 1951.

Bollingen Foundation, New York, for passages quoted from:
IBN KHALDUN, *The Muqaddimah*, translated by Franz Rosenthal, 3 vols., Bollingen Series XLIII, published by Pantheon Books, 1958.
ZIMMER, HEINRICH, *Philosophies of India*, edited Joseph Campbell, published by Meridian Books, New York, 1957.

The University of Chicago Press for passages quoted from:
FRANKFORT, H. and H. A. et al, *The Intellectual Adventure of Ancient Man*, 1946; published also as Penguin paperback, *Before Philosophy*, 1949. Copyright owned by University of Chicago.
HARTSHORNE, CHARLES, and REESE, WILLIAM L., *Philosophers Speak of God*, 1953.

Cornell University Press for passages quoted from:
VICO, GIAMBATTISTA, *The New Science of Giambattista Vico*, translated by Thomas G. Bergin and Max H. Fisch, 1948.

University of Madras, Madras, India, for passages from:
Samkhya-Karika of Isvara Krsna, translated and edited by S. S. Suryanarayana Sastri, 1935.

Yale University Press for passages quoted from:
DENTAN, ROBERT CLAUDE, editor, *The Idea of History in the Ancient Near East*, 1955.

The Library of Living Philosophers, Paul Arthur Schilpp, editor, Northwestern University, Evanston, Illinois, for passages quoted from:
The Philosophy of Sarvepalli Radhakrishnan, Library of Living Philosophers, Paul Arthur Schilpp, editor, published by Tudor Publishing Company, New York; copyright owned by The Library of Living Philosophers, 1952.

Swami Yogeshwarananda, Advaita Ashrama, Mayavati, Almora, Himalayas, for permission to quote passages from:
Vedantasara, translated by Swami Nikhilananda, 1949.

Oxford University Press, London, for passages quoted from:
The Thirteen Principal Upanishads, trans. R. E. Hume, 1921.
STEVENSON, MRS. SINCLAIR, *The Heart of Jainism*, 1915.
SNELLGROVE, DAVID, *The Hevajra Tantra*, 2 vols., London Oriental Series, Vol. 6, 1959.
W. Y. EVANS-WENTZ, editor, *The Tibetan Book of the Dead*, 3rd edition, 1957.
TOYNBEE, ARNOLD J., *A Study of History*, 2 vols., abridgement by D. C. Somervell, 1947-1957.
TOYNBEE, ARNOLD J., *A Study of History*, 12 vols., 1934-1961.
TOYNBEE, ARNOLD J., *Civilization on Trial*, 1948.
HEATH, SIR THOMAS, *A Manual of Greek Mathematics*, 1931 (Oxford, the Clarendon Press).
MCKEON, RICHARD, editor, *The Basic Works of Aristotle*, 1941, published by Random House, Inc., New York. Copyright owned by Oxford University Press.

Random House, Incorporated, for permission to quote from:
VIRGIL, VIRGIL's Works: *The Aeneid, Eclogues, Georgics*, translated by J. W. Mackail, Modern Library edition, 1934.

The Times, London, England, for permission to quote from:

"Radhakrishnan's Idealism," *The Times Literary Supplement* of May 3, 1934.

The Macmillan Company, New York, for passages quoted from:
ARBERRY, A. J., *Revelation and Reason in Islam*, 1957.

George Allen & Unwin, Ltd., London, England, for passages quoted from:
The Complete Works of Friedrich Nietzsche, ed. Oscar Levy, vol. XI, *Thus Spake Zarathustra*, trans. Thomas Common, 1916, and vol. XV, *The Will to Power*, trans. Anthony M. Ludovici, 1910.
RADHAKRISHNAN, S. and MUIRHEAD, J. H., editors, *Contemporary Indian Philosophy*, second revised and enlarged edition, Muirhead Library of Philosophy, 1952.
NICHOLSON, REYNOLD A., editor, *Rumi: Poet and Mystic*, translated with introduction and notes by Reynold A. Nicholson, 1950.

Scientific American, Inc., New York, for passages quoted from: *The New Astronomy* by the Editors of *Scientific American*, published by Simon and Schuster, New York, 1955. Permission received also from Simon and Schuster. Copyright held by Scientific American.

Alfred A. Knopf, Incorporated, New York, for their special generosity in permitting me to quote extensively from:
SPENGLER, OSWALD, *The Decline of the West*, translated by Charles Atkinson, 2 vols., 1932.

Lawrence & Wishart, Ltd., London, England, for permission to quote from:
MARX, KARL, and ENGELS, FREDERICK, *Selected Works*, 2 vols., 1950.
CORNFORTH, MAURICE, *Dialectical Materialism*, 1952.

The Ronald Press Company, New York, for passages quoted from:
MORGAN, KENNETH W., editor, *The Path of the Buddha*, "Buddhism in Tibet" by Lobsang Phuntsok Lhalungpa, 1956.

Farrar, Straus & Cudahy, Inc. for permission to quote from:
COOMERASWAMY, ANANDA, *The Dance of Shiva*, published 1948 by the Asia Publishing House, Calcutta, India. The Asia Publishing House and Dr. Coomeraswamy's widow, Mrs. Coomeraswamy, have also approved of allowing me to quote materials from this book. Copyright is owned by Farrar, Straus & Cudahy, Inc., of which Noonday Press, Inc., is a subsidiary.

Theodore H. Gaster and Doubleday Anchor Books for passages quoted from:
GASTER, THEODORE, *Thespis*, published by Schumann, 1950, second revised edition, Anchor Books, Doubleday & Co., 1961.

Harvard Journal of Asiatic Studies, Cambridge, Massachusetts, for permission to quote from:
CHENG TE-KUN, "Yin-Yang Wu-Hsing and Han Art," *Harvard Journal of Asiatic Studies*, Vol. 20, nos. 1-2.

Harvard University Press, Cambridge, Massachusetts, for passages quoted from:
WARREN, HENRY CLARKE, *Buddhism in Translations*, Harvard Oriental Series, Vol. 3.

Vedanta Society of Southern California, Hollywood, California, for passages quoted from:
SANKARACHARYA, *The Crest-Jewel of Discrimination*, translated with introduction by Swami Prabhavananda and Christopher Isherwood, 1947.
The Upanishads, translated by Swami Prabhavananda and Frederick Manchester, published by The New American Library, 1948.

John Murray, London, England, for permission to quote passages from:
HAVELL, ERNEST, B., *The Ideals of Indian Art*, 1920.

Phaidon Press, London, England, for passages quoted from: Kramrisch, Stella, *The Art of India*, 1954.

Charles E. Tuttle Company, Rutland, Vermont, for passages quoted from:
REPS, PAUL, *Zen Flesh, Zen Bones*, 1957.

Luzac & Company, Ltd., London, England, for passages quoted from:
AVALON, ARTHUR (Sir John Woodroffe), *Tantrik Texts*, Vol. VII, *Shrichakrasambhara Tantra*, a Buddhist Tantra, edited Kazi Dawa-Samdup, 1919.
RUSH, J. H., *The Dawn of Life*, 1958.

Saturday Review for permission to quote passages from: "The Next 10,000 Years," adapted from the forthcoming book by J. H. Rush, *The Dawn of Life. Saturday Review*, January 25, 1958. Permission granted also by the publishers of this book, Doubleday & Company.
HICKS, GRANVILLE, book review of *Huxley's Brave New World Revisited, Saturday Review* November 15, 1958. Permission granted also by publishers of the book, Harper & Brothers.

Harper & Brothers for passages quoted from:
HUXLEY, ALDOUS, *Brave New World Revisited*, 1958.
TEILHARD DE CHARDIN, PIERRE, *The Phenomenon of Man*, translated by Bernard Wall, 1959.
HOYLE, FRED, *Frontiers of Astronomy*, 1955.
JUNG, CARL G., "A Philosopher Among Souls," *This Is My Philosophy*, edited by Whit Burnett, 1957.

The Beacon Press for passages quoted from:
SOROKIN, PITIRIM A., *The Reconstruction of Humanity*, 1948.
SOROKIN, PITIRIM A., *The Ways and Power of Love: Types, Factors, and Techniques of Moral Transformation*, 1954.

Indiana University Press for passages quoted from:
FRANKFORT, HENRI, *The Birth of Civilization in the Near East*, 1956. Doubleday publishes paperback edition but copyright owned by Indiana University.

Gaekwad's Oriental Series, Oriental Institute, Baroda, India, Dr. B. Bhattacharya, General Editor, for permission to quote passages paraphrased from:
Trisastisalakapurusacaritra, translated by Helen M. Johnson, 2 vols., 1931-7, Gaekwad's Oriental Series, 51, 57. I have quoted passages and

a table from Finegan's *Archaeology of World Religions* which he has paraphrased and rearranged from this source.

Sri Aurobindo Ashram, Pondicherry, India, passages quoted from:
SRI AUROBINDO, *On Yoga, The Synthesis of Yoga*, 1955.
SRI AUROBINDO, *The Problem of Rebirth*, 1952.

Routledge & Kegan Paul, Ltd., London, England, for passages quoted from:
GRANET, MARCEL, *Chinese Civilization*, translated by Kathleen E. Innes and Mabel R. Brailsford, The History of Civilization series edited by C. K. Ogden, 1930, reprinted 1950.
The Secret of the Golden Flower, translated and explained by Richard Wilhelm with a European Commentary by C. G. Jung, translated into English by Cary F. Baynes, published by Wehman Brothers, New York, 1955.

Harcourt Brace & Company, Inc., for a passage quoted from:
JUNG, C. G., *Modern Man in Search of a Soul*, translated W. S. Dell and Cary F. Baynes, 1933, Harvest Book edition.

INDEX

A

Abraham 257, 270, 274, 339, 421
Adam 252, 253, 254, 255, 256, 257, 267, 269, 270, 274, 280, 332, 428
Adi-Buddha 83, 85, 87, 106, 150
Advaita Vedanta School of Philosophy 111, 115, 117, 121-129, 130, 131, 132, 146, 147, 151, 154, 155, 268, 271, 288, 303-304, 356
Aeschylus 384
African sculpture 431
Aga Khan 274
Agni 51-61, 95
Ahriman 237, 239, 240, 241, 242
Ahura-Mazda 237, 239-241
Akshobhya 84, 85, 104-107
Albright, William F., 25, 26, 28, 33, 44
Al-Ghazzali 257-258, 265, 266, 267, 271, 276, 279, 428
Ali 272, 274
Allah 256-258, 266, 267, 270, 273, 335
Amitabha 86, 104, 106
Amoghasiddhi 86, 104, 106
Amos 444
Anaximander 204
Anaximenes 204
Andean civilization 405
Anglo-Catholic 435
anima 132, 134
animus 132-134
anti-Christ 260
apocalypse and apocalypticism 245-250, 251-255, 256-267, 280, 287-298, 465
Apollinian culture 353-358, 360-371, 467
Arabian culture (see Magian)
Aratus, *Phaenomena*, 199, 201
Arberry, A. J., 275
archaism 434f., 439, 440, 449
archetypes 140-142, 252, 268, 271

Aristotle 216-220, 228, 262, 264, 271, 281, 324, 354, 388, 432
Arupaloka 90, 103
Ashvamedha 60-61
Assassins 274
Assyria 429
Ataturk, Kemal 437
Athens 404, 409, 416, 462
Atrakhasis Epic 25f.
Augustine, Saint 155, 250, 251-255, 257, 263, 266, 276-279, 289, 298, 300, 304, 306, 312, 316, 318, 319, 349, 350, 387, 418, 441, 446, 451, 452
Augustus 343, 435, 442, 473
Aurobindo 47, 127, 146, 156, 157, 298, 299-306, 308, 309, 311f., 313, 318, 319, 395, 396f., 398, 402, 454, 455, 463, 464, 468, 469, 471
Avadhuti 93
Avalokiteshvara 156
Avasarpini 69-73
Avatamsaka Sutra 79-81
avatar 236, 447
Averroes 262
Avicenna 262-265, 335, 354
Aztec time cycles 405

B

Bach 363, 365, 386
Bar Kokaba 437
Barbarian war bands 419, 421, 423f., 452
Baroque 354, 360, 363-366, 371
Becker, Carl 457
Bedouin 324-326
Beethoven 362, 365f., 386
Berossus 27-30, 211
Bhagavad-Gita (or *Gita*) 116, 304n., 398
Bodde, Derk 185
Bodhi Tree 382
bodhicitta 93

bodhisattva 102, 108, 156, 447, 451, 459
Book of Salvation 264
Bossuet, *Discourse on Universal History*, 278
bourgeoisie 371, 428
Bradley, F. H., 148, 316, 317
Brahma 35f., 43f., 47, 66, 123, 152, 308
Brahmaloka 90, 312, 316, 318
Brahman 36, 47-49, 111f., 121f., 124-127, 129f., 139, 146, 148, 150, 154-156, 269, 271, 288, 307, 354, 356, 398
Buckle, Henry Thomas, 323
Buddhagosa 61
Bundahish 238-240
Bushel (constellation), see also Ursa Major 162, 165f.
Butler, Samuel, *Erewhon*, 429

C

Caesarism 343, 355, 372, 373f., 420, 473
chakras 127-129 (Sanskrit spelling *cakras*)
Calvin, John, and Calvinism 278, 354, 428f.
Candali 93
capitalism 395, 399, 407
Cassirer, Ernst 339, 376
Catholic Encyclopaedia 277-278
Ceylon 413
Ch'an (or Zen) Buddhism 136, 138, 157, 193, 194, 467
Charles, R. H., 247
Cheng Te-k'un
Ch'ien Han Shu 165
Chinese culture (see also Sinic culture) 355, 358, 368, 371, 434, 467
Ch in dynasty 169, 172, 191
Chou dynasty 161, 165, 180, 184f., 185, 191
Chou Tun-yi 186
Christ 254, 255, 274, 279, 439, 441, 446, 451
Chuang-tzu 138, 193
City of God (Civitas Dei) 251f, 254f., 305, 453

City of Swine 450
Civilization on Trial 443
Classical Culture (see also Apollinian and Hellenic) 383, 409, 414, 416
Collingwood, R. G., 246, 280, 288
Communism 393-395, 399, 448-451, 464
compulsory social relationships 393f.
Condorcet 280f., 296
Confucius and Confucianism 181n., 191, 432f.
Constable 367
contractual social relationships 392-394
Coomeraswamy, Ananda 8, 38, 42f., 43f.
Cornforth, Maurice, 290, 292-294
creative altruism 395-397, 454, 463, 474
creative minority 403f., 408f., 414, 420, 452
cultural relativism 356

D

Daniel, Book of, 198, 245, 246, 247
Dante 264f., 280, 348, 409
David and Goliath 417, 428
Dawa-Samdup, Lama Kazi 90
democracy 342, 344, 348, 355, 371, 395, 407, 409, 410, 415, 423, 442, 472f.
Democritus 222, 427
Descartes 354
Destiny-idea 355-358, 360, 369f., 372, 375
Dharmakaya 92, 103, 105, 107
Diagrams of the Truly First and Mysterious Classic of the Transcendent Great Cave 186
Digambara 74f.
Diogenes the Cynic 426
Disintegration, Rhythmic pattern of, 441-443
Divine Comedy 143, 264f., 280, 348, 409
dominant minority 403, 414, 419, 420, 424, 430, 433, 443, 449, 452
Dumont, P. E., 29
Durga 38

E

Eckhart, Meister, 130
eclectic art 383
eclecticism 384, 432
ecyprosis 205, 222
Eden 71, 197, 235, 239, 250, 267, 280, 295, 298, 306
Egyptian culture 354f., 358, 370, 371, 381, 419, 424, 467
Egyptian mythology 2, 4, 5, 6, 7, 10n.3, 20f., 28, 33, 51, 97, 233-235
Einstein, Albert, 227, 389
Empedocles 206, 229
Engels, Friedrich, 290, 294-297
Enoch, Book of, 247f.
Enuma Elish 11-16, 21, 23f., 31
Epicurus 222-223, 426
eschatology 245-250, 251-255, 256-257, 280, 287-298, 317
Estates (Fourth Estate, the "masses"), 372
Estates (Nobility and Priesthood) 368-371
etherialization 439
Eucharist 446
Eudemus 220
Eusebius 220
Evans-Wentz, W. Y., 77, 82, 108, 459

F

Fall of Man 251-257, 267, 315f.
familistic social relationships 292, 394
fana 268, 270
fascism 393-395, 423, 434
Fatima 272
Fatimids 274
Faustian culture 353-358, 360-368, 371, 455, 467
Finegan, Jack, 70, 238f.
Fisher, John, 426
Fitzgerald, C. P., 160
Francis of Assisi, Saint, 385, 399, 451
Frankfort, H. and H. A., 5, 7, 16 n.1, 17
Frazer, Sir James George, 6, 17
Fung Yu-lan 191, 194
futurism 434-440, 449

G

Gabriel 270
Gamow, George, 228-230
Gandhi 399
Gaster, Theodor H., 16-18, 50
Gathas 237
Gayomard 239-242
Genesis, Book of, 251, 253
German World 285-286
Ghanta 86, 90
Gibbon, *Decline and Fall of the Roman Empire* 413f.
Gilgamesh Epic 1
Gnostic Being 299, 301-306
Goethe 354, 367, 377, 386, 404
Gomperz, Theodore, 208
Gothic 360, 362, 364, 370, 383, 434
Gottschalk, Louis R., 456
Graeco-Roman 381, 383, 394, 428
Granet, Marcel 170
Greek culture and world (see also Apollinian and classical culture) 284, 380f., 383f., 409, 439
Gregory VII (Hildebrand), Pope, 418
Guenther, H. V., 75 n.1
gunas 113f., 121f., 125

H

Hadith 259, 272, 333
Hadrian 434
Han dynasty 165, 169, 171f., 179f., 186, 194, 432f., 436
Havell, E. B., 3, 35, 41, 49
Heath, Sir Thomas, 208f., 210
Heaven 21, 72f., 97f., 102f., 124, 133, 159f., 165-167, 170, 173, 176-178, 180, 192, 238, 249, 256, 260, 265, 270, 280f., 295, 306, 334, 350, 408, 429, 461, 474
Hegel and Hegelianism 143, 198, 246, 281-289, 299, 300, 310, 316-318, 344, 349, 354, 407, 461, 462, 465
Hell 72-74, 102f., 124, 133, 241, 253, 257, 264, 265, 266f., 276, 334, 350, 429
Hellenic culture (see also classical and Apollinian) 416, 419, 422, 424f., 426f., 431-435, 441f., 444f.

491

Hellenistic 381, 384
Heraclitus 204f., 465
Hesiod, *Works and Days*, 196f., 212, 221, 225, 233, 246, 339
Hevajra Tantra 89, 92-94, 105
Hiranyagarbha 123
Historical Memoirs (by Ssu-ma Ch'ien), 170
historiography 349, 455f.
Hobbes, *Leviathan*, 327
Homer 340, 348
Hooke, Samuel H., 19, 20, 21
Hosea 444
Houris 266
Hoyle, Fred, 229-230, 465, 467, 468, 475
Hoyle, Gold and Bondi (Sciama and others) cosmological theory 229f., 465, 467
Hsia dynasty 171, 180, 183, 184, 185
Huai-nan-tzu 167f.
Huang-ti, Yellow Emperor, 159, 191
hun 132
Huxley, Aldous 474
Huxley, Julian, 470, 476
hybris 417f., 429, 444, 452

I

Iblis (see Satan)
Idealistic art 383-385
Idealistic culture (see also integral culture) 380, 395, 400, 462
Idealistic ethic and law 390-392
Idealistic truth 388
Ideational art 381f.
Ideational culture 379f., 383f., 394f.
Ideational ethics and law 390-392
Ideational truth 386f., 388f.
Imam 272f., 274
Incarnation 279, 310, 316, 381, 433, 440f., 446
Indian culture, 354-356, 368, 372, 380f., 409, 458
Indic culture (see also Indian) 419, 424, 442
individuation process 141f., 464, 472
Indra 152f.
industrialism 407, 409, 410, 415, 423, 442

Integral culture (see also Idealistic) 389, 395, 462f., 474
integral yoga 304
Intelligentsia 421f.
interregnum 442f.
Irwin, William A., 21
Isaiah, Book of, 235f., 248
Isaiah, First, 444
Isaiah, Second, 421, 444
Ishmael 257
Ishvara 3, 115, 121f., 124f., 127-129, 269, 307f.
Ishvara Krishna 113, 116, 134, 149
Isma'il 273f.
Isma'ili (Shi'ite) sect 271-276
I-wen Chih 165
Iyer, V. Subrahmanya, 148f.

J

Jacobsen, Thorkild, 11f.
jazz 431
Jeans, Sir James 410
Jeffrey, Arthur 258f.
jen 176
Jeremiah 245, 421
Jesus 259f., 270, 273-275, 408, 421, 433, 440f, 447
Jews 436f., 438, 447
Jinas 83-88, 94, 102, 104,
jivan-mukta 119
Job, Book of, 404
John, Gospel of, 441
John, St., of the Cross, 141, 469
Jung, Carl Gustav, 144f., 464, 468, 472

K

Kailasa, Mt., 40
Ka Kuan 137
Kalachakra 69, 74
Kali 38, 46, 127, 129
kamaloka 90, 103, 105
Kao Tzu 436
karma 74, 90, 102, 103, 116, 119, 141, 145, 151, 154, 311, 313, 317, 428, 458, 468
Khaldun, Ibn, *Muqaddimah*, 322-336, 431f., 345, 349, 350, 353, 401, 419, 421, 449, 462
Kitab Jami' al-hikmatain 275f.

Koran 256f., 259f., 265f., 267, 273, 275f., 333, 335
Kramrisch, Stella, 96-98
kundalini 127, 155, 300

L

laissez-faire 427f., 450
Lalana 93
Leibniz 194, 354
Lemaitre 465
Lenin 293
Leonardo da Vinci 364
Lévy-Bruhl 5
Lhalungpa, Lobsang Phuntsok, 67
lila 151, 299
lingam 38, 40, 42, 78
lingua franca 431-432
Lovejoy, Arthur, and Boas, George, 198, 215
Lu Pu-wei 171
Lucifer 253
Lucretius 223-225, 226, 426
Lu-shih Ch'un Ch'iu 171
Luther, Martin, 353
Luxuriant Dew of the Spring and Autumn Annals 173

M

Maccabees 437
Machiavelli 409
Madhyamika School 79, 91, 95
Magian culture 354f., 356, 359, 368, 467
Mahabharata 45f.
Mahavairocana 104
Mahdi 260, 273, 333
Maitreya 102
mandala 76-110, 111-158, 270-274, 276, 439, 459, 460, 464, 472
Mandate of Heaven 180, 184
Mandelbaum, Maurice 457
Mandukya Upanishad 122, 149f.
Manetho 234f.
Marcus Aurelius 221, 387, 426, 442
Mark, Gospel of, 248f.
Marx and Marxism 143, 281, 289-298, 306, 310, 317-319, 332, 407, 422, 423, 428, 429, 449, 457, 463f., 468
Mashya and Mashyoi 240f.
Maspero, G., 233f.

maya 79, 83, 87, 110, 121-129, 135, 144f., 149, 150, 154-157, 270, 308, 310, 459, 469
Mayan civilization 405
Mayan time cycles 4, 5, 33
Megalopolitan civilization 354, 372f.
Meru, Mt., 88f., 97f.
Messiah 241, 247f., 260, 408, 437f.
Michaelangelo 360, 365
Middle Way (Scandinavian society) 450
Milarepa 77, 82, 88
mimesis 415, 420, 440, 447
Ming T'ang 161, 166, 168f., 181 n.
Minoan civilization 405
Mithraism 2
Mohammed 256, 258, 262, 265, 267, 269, 270, 272, 273, 274, 328, 334
monarchy 342f., 344, 345f., 347f., 350, 473
Montesquieu 323
More, Thomas, 326
Moses 408, 421
Myron 384

N

Nairatmya 105
Nandi 41
Narayana 3, 35f.
Nasir-i Khusrau 275f.
Nazis 434, 443
Nemesius 220
Neo-Confucianism 171, 186f.
Neoplatonism 143, 251, 262, 264, 267, 268, 273
Neugebauer, Otto, 28f., 31 n., 210f., 428
New Year 3, 6, 7, 8, 10, 11, 16, 18-22, 24, 31, 33 n.3, 52, 179, 225
Next Text School of Confucianism 180 n.1
Nicodemus 440
nidanas 90
Nietzsche 223, 226f.
Nilsson, Martin P., 10
Nirmanakaya 85, 92, 105
nirvana 40, 61, 68, 75, 81, 89, 95, 102, 104, 105, 107, 109, 138, 156f., 268, 356, 440
noosphere 470f.

493

Northrop, F. S. C., 144f., 195, 454, 458, 463, 476

O

Oedipus 358
Old Text School of Confucianism 180 n.1
OM 128, 149
Omega 470f., 472
Orwell, George, 475
Ovid, *Metamorphoses*, 198-201, 246

P

palengenesis 317, 439, 440
Palestine 444
Palestrina 365
Patanjali 116f., 398
Paul, St., 142, 248, 387, 439
Peloponnesian War 416, 420, 429, 441
Peter 440
Peter the Great 435
Phidias 365, 384
Physiognomic 375
Pindar 384
Plato 207-216, 354, 388, 408, 425, 427, 432, 440
Plotinus 130
p'o 132
Po Hu T'ung 182, 185
Pole Star 135f., 163, 165
Polycleitus 363, 368, 384
Prajapati 52, 53, 54-57, 59-61, 95, 97, 123
Prajna 81-83, 86, 91, 104f., 122
Prajnaparamita 87
prakrti 114-116, 118-121, 124, 310
pratibimba 99
Prime Symbol 374, 376f.
primitivism 431
proletariat, external, 328, 403, 419, 423, 430, 443, 452
proletariat, internal, 328, 403f., 414, 419-421, 424, 428, 430, 433, 443, 445, 452
Providence 252f., 257-258, 278f., 289, 346, 349, 350f.
Puranas 152
Purgatory 143, 280, 333, 334
Puritans 406

Purusha 113, 115-120, 310, 398
Pythagoreans 205f., 432

R

Radhakrishnan, 112f., 146, 156, 298, 304, 306, 307-319, 396, 402, 454, 455, 463, 468, 469, 474
Raleigh, Sir Walter *The History of the World*, 278
Ramakrishna 127, 129, 155f., 268, 459
Rasana 93
Ratnasambhava 86, 104, 106
Reconstruction of Humanity (Sorokin) 395
Rembrandt 363, 366
Renaissance 364f., 386f., 391, 429
resurrection 241f., 248-250, 255, 260, 262f., 265, 333f.
Resuscitation of the Sciences of Religion 257
Revelation, Book of 249f., 254, 262
Roman civilization 284f., 286, 339f., 347f., 368, 371, 387, 414, 419f., 422, 424, 430f., 432f., 437, 440
Rosenthal, Franz, 336
Rowland, Benjamin, 49, 97, 99, 104f., 107
Rumi 269f.
Rupaloka 103
Rush, J. H., 469f.
Russia 409, 422, 448f., 450
Ryonen 138

S

Sachchidananda 155, 303
samadhi 47, 119, 129, 134, 156, 301
Samantabhadra 102
Sambhogakaya 92, 103, 105, 108
samsara 51, 68, 74f., 78-81, 83, 87, 89f., 93, 95, 98, 104-109, 128, 138, 151, 153f., 156, 268, 459
Sangharakshita, Bhikshu, 74, 80-82
Sankhya 113-120, 309, 354f.
Saoshyant 241
saros 211
Sarton, George, 210
Satan 238, 249, 253f., 404
Saviour as Philosopher-King 440
Saviour with a Sword 440, 449
Saviour with a Time-Machine 440

Schweitzer, Albert, 75, 145
Seneca 221f.
Sensate art 382f.
Sensate culture 380f., 384-386, 390, 394, 399, 462, 474
Sensate ethics and law 390-392
Sensate truth 387-388, 389
serpent symbolism 2, 3, 4, 5, 40, 41, 69, 234f., 249, 253
Shakespeare 358, 367, 386
Shakti 42, 47, 78, 79, 83, 127-129, 134, 150f., 155f.
Shang dynasty 161, 172, 180, 183f., 185
Shankara 111, 121, 129, 146f., 154-156, 218, 304, 308, 316, 464
Shaw, Bernard, 367
sheaths of the Self 112, 118, 122-124, 125f., 128, 131, 132, 149f., 264, 276, 471
Shih Huang-ti 168, 172, 191, 436
Shi'ites 260, 271f., 333
Shingon Buddhism 81, 104, 105
Shinto 435
shirk 258
Shiva 3, 35-44, 78f., 128f., 150, 152, 308
Shri Yantra 77-79
Shun 159, 184, 191
shunyata 79, 82, 83, 87, 90-93, 102f., 106, 157
Simplicius 220
Sinic civilization (see also Chinese culture) 405, 419, 422, 427, 433f., 442
skandhas 85-87
Snellgrove, David, 82, 88, 89
Social enormities 414, 415, 416
Socialism 355, 372f., 395, 399
Socrates 285, 354, 426
Song of the Sky Pacer 163f.
Soothill, William E., 163
Sophocles 384
Sorokin, Pitirim A., 324, 336, 379-402, 449, 454, 462f., 468f., 474
Speiser, E. A., 30f.
Spengler, Oswald, 218, 322, 324, 336, 339, 343, 353-378, 379, 383, 386, 401, 408, 411, 419, 449, 462, 467, 473
Spiegelberg, Frederic, 50f.

Spinoza 193, 271, 464f., 466, 467
Ssu-ma Ch'ien 169, 170, 185
Ssu-ma Tan 170
Stalin, Joseph, 291, 294, 436
Stevenson, Mrs. Sinclair, 71, 74
Stoics 220-222, 289, 355, 372, 427, 433, 438, 442, 465
stupa 89, 95, 96-108
Style in a culture 359-368, 430-432
Sudhana 80, 102, 105
Sufis 130, 266-271, 354, 464
Sumerian civilization 405, 442
Sumerian King List 27-29
Sung dynasty 171, 186
Sunnis 271, 276, 333
supraconscious mind-state 396-400, 404, 454, 455, 462f., 470, 474
sushumna 127
swastika 3, 5, 6, 74, 78, 97, 98
Syriac culture 419, 424, 429, 445
Systematic 375

T

T'ai Chi 130f.
Taittiriya Upanishad 112, 309
Tan Hsuan Tzu 163
Tao and Taoism 130-133, 135f., 139, 187, 398, 432, 433, 459, 464, 467
Tao Teh Ching 130, 427
Tatianus 220
Tawney, *Religion and the Rise of Capitalism,* 428
Taylor, A. E., 208
Teilhard de Chardin, Pierre, 470-472, 464, 475f.
Tertullian 387
tetractys 208f.
Thessalonians, First, 248
Third eye 41, 47, 90, 135
Thomas Aquinas, Saint, 277f., 380, 388, 446, 451
tirthankaras 72, 73
Toynbee, Arnold, 278-279, 298, 324, 328, 336, 349, 350, 386, 402, 403-455, 461, 462, 468, 473
trahison des clercs 426
transfiguration 438, 439, 451
transformation process 141-143, 439
Tree of Life 20f., 235, 250
trigrams 188

495

Tsou Yen 171-173, 174, 179
turiya 149
Turkey 437
Twelvers 272f.

U

Uma 38, 42
Universal church 420f., 423, 443, 445
Universal state 414, 419f., 424, 432f., 442, 443, 448, 449
Upanishads 112, 122, 149f., 212, 309, 398
Upaya 81-83, 86, 104f.
Ursa Major 130, 162
Utsarpini 69-73

V

Vairocana 86, 104f., 106
Vaisvanara 124
vajra 86f., 90f.
Vajra-mandala 91
Vajrasattva 83-87, 106f., 150
Vajra-yogini 90f.
Vico, Giambattista, 218, 279, 322, 336, 337-352, 353, 372, 379, 401, 419, 421, 449, 457, 462, 473, 475
vihara 88f.
Virgil, 202
Vishnu 3, 35-37, 45f., 112, 150, 152f., 308

W

Wagner 386
Wagnerian music-drama 367
Wang Mang 181 n., 185

Ways and Power of Love (Sorokin) 396-401
Whitehead, Alfred North 6, 8, 464
Wight, Martin, 453
Wilhelm, Richard, 130, 132
Wolsey, Thomas, 426
Wu, emperor, 169, 170, 436

Y

yang 131f., 134f., 150, 159f., 169, 172-177, 181 n., 182, 183, 185, 187, 192, 405, 439
yantra 77-79, 83
Yao 59, 163, 191
yasti 97
Yellow Emperor (see Huang-ti)
Yi Ching 186f., 436
yin 131, 134f., 150, 159f., 169, 172-177, 181 n., 182, 183, 185, 187, 192, 404, 439
Yogacara School 79, 95
Yogindra, Sadananda 121-123
yoni 78
Yu 159, 171, 184, 191

Z

Zaidites 272
Zarathustra 226
Zealots 437
Zen Buddhism (see also Ch'an) 136-138, 157, 194, 398, 459, 467
Zeno (Stoic) 220, 427
ziggurat 33 n.3, 50f.
Zimmer, Heinrich 4, 69, 77, 78, 111, 155
Zoroaster 237-239, 241f., 243

Library and Learning
Resources Center
Bergen Community College
400 Paramus Road
Paramus, N.J. 07652-1595

Return Postage Guaranteed